PHENOMENAL—BUT TRUE!

Here is the real-life story of one of the most extraordinary human beings the world has ever known.

EDGAR CAYCE . . .

the man whose uncanny powers of clairvoyance provided him with miraculous insights that went far beyond the realm of reality— baffling doubters, astounding believers . . . and almost always being proved correct.

There is a river, the streams whereof shall make glad the city of God . . .

Psalms 46:4

THE STORY OF

EDGAR CAYCE

There Is a River

BY
THOMAS SUGRUE

REVISED EDITION

A.R.E. Press • Virginia Beach • Virginia

Preface

The story of Cayce properly belongs in the history of hypnosis, as a chapter in evidence for the theories of Armand Marc Jacques de Chastenet, Marquis de Puysegur. It was de Puysegur, not Mesmer, who in 1784 discovered hypnotism. De Puysegur's famous subject Victor went into a sleep instead of a convulsion while being magnetized, and in that state showed remarkable intelligence and apparent powers of clairvoyance. Further experiments brought the same results. Other patients, when put to sleep, showed like powers. Walter Bromberg, in *The Mind of Man,** says: "Dull peasants became mentally alert, and could even foretell events or understand things ordinarily obscure to them. Somnambulists made medical diagnoses in other patients brought before them, and foretold the future. The magnetizer of the 1820s merely brought his patient before a competent somnambulist, and waited for the diagnosis . . . If only modern science had such aids! The clairvoyance of somnambulists became a fascinating game."

But the fascinating game was not encouraged, either by the French Academy or by the medical profession, and it suffered the fate of other fads. A generation later Andrew Jackson Davis, the "Poughkeepsie Seer," was practicing medical diagnosis by clairvoyance in America, but he remained obscure and is not even mentioned in textbooks and histories of hypnotism. Hypnotism, in fact, will have nothing to do with clairvoyance; it has renounced its own mother.

Edgar Cayce practiced medical diagnosis by clairvoyance for forty-three years. He left stenographic reports of 9,000 of these diagnoses to the Association for Research and Enlightenment,

The Mind of Man, by Walter Bromberg, Harper and Brothers, New York, 1937.

Inc., along with hundreds of complete case reports, containing affidavits by the patients and reports by physicians. There are hundreds of people throughout the United States who will testify, at the drop of a hat, to the accuracy of his diagnoses and the efficacy of his suggestions for treatment.

He did not use his ability except to prescribe for the sick and to give spiritual advice and vocational guidance when these were specifically requested. He never made any public demonstrations of his powers; he was never on the stage; he never sought any publicity; he did not prophesy; he did not seek wealth. Often his economic status was quite precarious; at best it never rose above modest security. During the period of the Cayce Hospital he was paid only seventy-five dollars a week for his services.

His unquestioned personal integrity, plus the excellent and voluminous records of his work and the long period that they covered, made him an ideal subject for scientific study. But scientists shunned him. He and his friends regretted this; it might have been more evidential if they, not I, had made this report.

I first met Edgar Cayce in 1927. At that time I made most of the preliminary notes and sketches for this book. Since then I have continually added to the material, enjoying the complete cooperation of the members of the Cayce family, and being accorded access to the files at all times. From June, 1939, to October, 1941, I was a guest in the house on Arctic Crescent, seeing and interviewing Mr. Cayce every day, and examining material from the files. I spent many summers at Virginia Beach, particularly those of 1929, 1930, and 1931.

In addition to the members of the Cayce family I have had the good fortune to know intimately most of the other characters in the story. One of the first and most important contributors to my dossier was Mr. Cayce's father, the late Leslie B. Cayce. Another was Carrie Salter House, who with her husband, the late Dr. House, and her son, Tommy, were invaluable aids and stanch friends through the years. I was not privileged to know Mr. Cayce's mother—she died in 1926—but her children and her grandchildren have described her to me so often and so well that I feel her portrait, as I have drawn it, is an accurate one.

I knew Mrs. Cayce's mother, Mrs. Evans; and Gray Salter, like the Cayce boys and Tommy House, has long been a friend. I have known two of Mr. Cayce's sisters, Annie and Sara, for many years. Other members of the Cayce and Salter families I have met and talked with from time to time. All have aided me, and by comparing and paralleling the reports they gave me of incidents and conversations with those of other participants, in many cases I have been able to arrive at that rounded, objective viewpoint of events which is the biographer's goal. On the other hand, I have gradually acquired a knowledge of and a fondness for all these people which is comparable to a novelist's feeling for the characters he has created. That is why the biography, in many parts, reads like a family chronicle.

The Norfolk and Virginia Beach Study Groups of the Association for Research and Enlightenment have been of great help to me, as have been the staff members of the Association, particularly Miss Gladys Davis, Mr. Cayce's secretary for twenty-two years. In the end, however, it was Hugh Lynn Cayce who not only led the horse to water, but made him drink; and it was my wife who acted as typist, proofreader, editor, and nurse to my crotchets and doldrums. To them I am deeply grateful. If I have done a good job it is because of them and despite myself.

I last saw Edgar Cayce in August, 1944, when he visited me in Florida. He was weary then, tired to the depths of his being. He talked eagerly of the future of the Association; he spoke wistfully of the time when he might retire. He liked the warmth and brightness of Florida; he loved the Australian pines that grow near the water. "Pick out a place for me here," he said, "and I will come back and stay." He went home the next day. His last letter to me, written in longhand, on the stationery of the Hotel Patrick Henry in Roanoke, was dated September 11, 1944. It said, in part, "My hands won't let me use the machine. I doubt whether you can read this but I hope you can make some of it out. I am not doing too well; sort of a stroke I guess. They have come in a kind of series. I hope to get back to work for a while yet, and I want to hold out until the boys get home. I can't much more than put on and take off my clothes. I can't tie my shoe laces or knot my tie. But I am hoping to be better soon. There is so much to be done and so many who need help . . . "

Thomas Sugrue

May 11, 1945
Clearwater Beach, Fla.

Introduction

Edgar Cayce: Ordinary Man, Extraordinary Messenger
by Mitch Horowitz

The year 1910 marked a turning point in Western spirituality. It saw the deaths of some of the most luminous religious thinkers of the nineteenth century, including psychologist-seeker William James; popular medium Andrew Jackson Davis; and Christian Science founder Mary Baker Eddy. These three figures deeply impacted the movements in positive thinking, prayer healing, and psychical research.

Their death that year was accompanied by the rise to prominence of a new religious innovator—a figure who built upon the spiritual experiments of the nineteenth century to shape the New Age culture of the dawning era.*[1] In autumn of 1910 *The New York Times* brought the first major national attention to the name of Edgar Cayce, a young man who later became known as the "father of holistic medicine" and the founding voice of alternative spirituality.

The Sunday *Times* of October 9, 1910, profiled the Christian mystic and medical clairvoyant in an extensive article and photo spread: *Illiterate Man Becomes a Doctor When Hypnotized*. At the time Cayce (pronounced "Casey"), then 33, was struggling

---

*[1]The term "New Age" is often used to denote trendy or fickle spiritual tastes. I do not share in that usage. I use New Age to reference the eclectic culture of therapeutic and experimental spirituality that emerged in the late-twentieth century.

to make his way as a commercial photographer in his hometown of Hopkinsville, Kentucky, while delivering daily trance-based medical "readings" in which he would diagnose and prescribe natural cures for the illnesses of people he had never met.

Cayce's method was to recline on a sofa or day bed, loosen his tie, belt, cuffs, and shoelaces, and enter a sleep-like trance; then, given only the name and location of a subject, the "sleeping prophet" was said to gain insight into the person's body and psychology. By the time of his death in January 1945, Cayce had amassed a record of more than 14,300 clairvoyant readings for people across the nation, many of the sessions captured by stenographer Gladys Davis.

In the 1920s, Cayce's trance readings expanded beyond medicine (which nonetheless remained at the core of his work) to include "life readings," in which he explored a person's inner conflicts and needs. In these sessions Cayce employed references to astrology, karma, reincarnation, and number symbolism. Other times, he expounded on global prophecies, climate or geological changes, and the lost history of mythical cultures, such as Atlantis and Lemuria. Cayce had no recollection of any of this when he awoke, though as a devout Christian the esotericism of such material made him wince when he read the transcripts.

Contrary to news coverage, Cayce was not illiterate, but neither was he well educated. Although he taught Sunday school at his Disciples of Christ church—and read through the King James Bible at least once every year—he had never made it past the eighth grade of a rural schoolhouse. While his knowledge of Scripture was encyclopedic, Cayce's reading tastes were otherwise limited. Aside from spending a few on-and-off years in Texas unsuccessfully trying to use his psychical abilities to strike oil—he had hoped to raise money to open a hospital based on his clairvoyant cures—Cayce rarely ventured beyond the Bible Belt environs of his childhood.

Since the tale of Jonah fleeing from the word of God, prophets have been characterized as reluctant, ordinary folk plucked from reasonably satisfying lives to embark on missions that they never originally sought. In this sense, if the impending New

Age—the vast culture of Eastern, esoteric, and therapeutic spirituality that exploded on the national scene in the 1960s and 70s—was seeking a founding prophet, Cayce could hardly be viewed as an unusual choice, but, historically, as a perfect one.

A SEER IN SEASON

It was this Edgar Cayce—an everyday man, dedicated Christian, and uneasy mystic—whom New England college student and future biographer Thomas Sugrue encountered in 1927. When Sugrue met Cayce, the twenty-year-old journalism student was not someone who frequented psychics or séance parlors. Sugrue was a dedicated Catholic who had considered joining the priesthood. Deeply versed in world affairs and possessed of an iron determination to break into news reporting, Sugrue left his native Connecticut in 1926 for Washington and Lee University in Lexington, Virginia, which was then one of the only schools in the nation to offer a journalism degree to undergraduates. (Sugrue later switched his major to English literature, in which he earned both bachelor's and master's degrees in four years.)

As a student, Sugrue rolled his eyes at paranormal claims or talk of ESP. Yet Sugrue met a new friend at Washington and Lee who challenged his preconceptions: the psychic's eldest son, Hugh Lynn Cayce. Hugh Lynn had planned to attend Columbia but his father's clairvoyant readings directed him instead to the old-line Virginia school. (The institution counted George Washington as an early benefactor.) Sugrue grew intrigued by his new friend's stories about his father—in particular the elder Cayce's theory that one person's subconscious mind could communicate with another's. The two freshmen enjoyed sparring intellectually and soon became roommates. While still cautious, Sugrue wanted to meet the agrarian seer.

Edgar and his wife Gertrude, meanwhile, were laying new roots about 250 miles east of Lexington in Virginia Beach, a location the readings had also selected. The psychic spent the remainder of his life in the Atlantic coastal town, delivering twice-daily readings and developing the Association for Research and Enlightenment (A.R.E.), a spiritual learning center that remains active there today.

Accompanying Hugh Lynn home in June 1927, Sugrue received a "life reading" from Cayce. In these psychological readings, Cayce was said to peer into a subject's "past life" incarnations and influences, analyze his character through astrology and other esoteric methods, and view his personal struggles and aptitudes. Cayce correctly identified the young writer's interest in the Middle East, a region where Sugrue later issued news reports on the founding of the modern state of Israel. But it wasn't until Christmas of that year that Sugrue, upon receiving an intimate and uncannily accurate medical reading, became an all-out convert to Cayce's psychical abilities.

Sugrue went on to fulfill his aim of becoming a journalist, writing from different parts of the world for publications including the *New York Herald Tribune* and *The American Magazine*. But his life remained interwoven with Cayce's. Stricken by debilitating arthritis in the late 1930s, Sugrue sought help through Cayce's medical readings. From 1939 to 1941, the ailing Sugrue lived with the Cayce family in Virginia Beach, writing and convalescing. During these years of close access to Cayce—while struggling with painful joints and limited mobility—Sugrue completed *There Is a River*, the sole biography written of Cayce during his lifetime. When the book appeared in 1942 it brought Cayce national attention that surpassed even the earlier *Times* coverage.

DOCUMENTING THE PROPHET

Sugrue was not Cayce's only enthusiast within the world of American letters. *There Is a River* broke through the skeptical wall of New York publishing thanks to a reputable editor, William Sloane, of Holt, Rinehart & Winston, who experienced his own brush with the Cayce readings.

In 1940, Sloane agreed to consider the manuscript for *There Is a River*. He knew the biography was highly sympathetic, a fact that did not endear him to it. Sloane's wariness faded after Cayce's clairvoyant diagnosis helped one of the editor's children. Novelist and screenwriter Nora Ephron recounted the episode in a 1968 *New York Times* article.

"I read it," Sloane told Ephron. "Now there isn't any way to test a manuscript like this. So I did the only thing I could do."

He went on:

> A member of my family, one of my children, had been in great and continuing pain. We'd been to all the doctors and dentists in the area and all the tests were negative and the pain was still there. I wrote Cayce, told him my child was in pain and would be at a certain place at such-and-such a time, and enclosed a check for $25. He wrote back that there was an infection in the jaw behind a particular tooth. So I took the child to the dentist and told him to pull the tooth. The dentist refused—he said his professional ethics prevented him from pulling sound teeth. Finally, I told him he would have to pull it. One tooth more or less didn't matter, I said—I couldn't live with the child in such pain. So he pulled the tooth and the infection was there and the pain went away. I was a little shook. I'm the kind of man who believes in X-rays. About this time, a member of my staff who thought I was nuts to get involved with this took even more precautions in writing to Cayce than I did, and he sent her back facts about her own body only she could have known. So I published Sugrue's book.

Many literary journalists and historians since Sugrue have traced Cayce's life. Journalist and documentarian Sidney D. Kirkpatrick wrote the landmark record of Cayce in his 2000 biography *Edgar Cayce*. Historian K. Paul Johnson crafted a deeply balanced and meticulous scholarly analysis of Cayce with the 1998 *Edgar Cayce in Context*. And the intrepid scholar of religion Harmon Bro—who spent nine months in Cayce's company toward the end of the psychic's life—produced insightful studies of Cayce as a Christian mystic in his 1955 University of Chicago doctoral thesis (a groundbreaking work of modern scholarship on an occult subject) and later in the 1989 biography *Seer Out of Season*. While Harmon Bro died in 1997, his family has a long—and still active—literary involvement with Cayce. Bro's mother, Margueritte, was a pioneering female journalist in the first half of the twentieth century who brought Cayce national attention in her 1943 profile in *Coronet* magazine: "Miracle Man of Virginia Beach." Bro's wife June and daughter Pamela actively teach and interpret the Cayce ideas today.

There exist many other works on Cayce—it would take several paragraphs to appreciate the best of them. But it was Sugrue, an accomplished print journalist who worked and convalesced with Cayce for several years, who fully—and this word is chosen carefully—captured Cayce's *goodness.*

Sugrue's historical Edgar Cayce is the man who grew from being an awkward, soft-voiced adolescent to a national figure who never quite knew how to manage his fame—and less so how to manage money, often foregoing or deferring his usual $20 fee for readings, leaving himself and his family in a perpetual state of financial precariousness. In a typical letter from 1940, Cayce replied to a blind laborer who asked about paying in installments: "You may take care of the [fee] any way convenient to your self—please know one is not prohibited from having a reading . . . because they haven't money. If this information is of a divine source it can't be sold, if it isn't then it isn't worth any thing."

Sugrue also captured Cayce as a figure of deep Christian faith struggling to come to terms with the occult concepts that ran through his readings beginning in the early 1920s. This material extended to numerology, astrology, crystal gazing, modern prophecies, reincarnation, karma, and the story of mythical civilizations, including Atlantis and prehistoric Egypt. People who sought readings were intrigued and emotionally impacted by this material as much as by Cayce's medical diagnoses. What's more, in readings that dealt with spiritual and esoteric topics— along with the more familiar readings that focused on holistic remedies, massage, meditation, and natural foods—there began to emerge the range of subjects that formed the parameters of therapeutic New Age spirituality in the latter twentieth century.

ESOTERIC PHILOSOPHER

Cayce did more than assemble a catalogue of the dawning New Age. The spiritual ideas running through his readings, combined with his own intrepid study of Scripture, supplied the basis for a universal approach to religion, which, in various ways, also spread across American culture. Sugrue captures this especially well in chapter fifteen, which recounts Cayce's metaphysical explorations with an Ohio printer and Theosophist named Arthur Lammers. Cayce's collaboration with Lammers, which began in the autumn of 1923 in Selma, Alabama, marked a turn in Cayce's career from medical clairvoyant to esoteric philosopher.

Licking his wounds after his failed oil ventures, Cayce had resettled his family in Selma where he planned to resume his career as a commercial photographer. He and Gertrude, who had long suffered her husband's absences and unsteady finances, enrolled their son Hugh Lynn, then sixteen, in Selma High School. The family, now including five-year-old Edgar Evans, settled into a new home and appeared headed for some measure of domestic normalcy. All this got upturned in September, however, when the wealthy printer Lammers arrived from Dayton. Lammers had learned of Cayce during the psychic's oil-prospecting days. He showed up at Cayce's photo studio with an intriguing proposition.

Lammers was both a hard-driving businessman and an avid seeker in Theosophy, ancient religions, and the occult. He impressed upon Cayce that the seer could use his psychical powers for more than medical diagnoses. Lammers wanted Cayce to probe the secrets of the ages: What happens after death? Is there a soul? Why are we alive? Lammers yearned to understand the meaning of the pyramids, astrology, alchemy, the "Etheric World," reincarnation, and the mystery religions of ancient Egypt, Greece, and Rome. He felt certain that Cayce's readings could part the veil shrouding the ageless wisdom.

After years of stalled progress in his personal life, Cayce was enticed by this new sense of mission. Lammers urged Cayce to return with him to Dayton, where he promised to place the Cayce family in a new home and financially care for them. Cayce agreed, and uprooted Gertrude and their younger son, Edgar Evans. Hugh Lynn remained behind with friends in Selma to finish out the school term. Lammers's financial promises later proved elusive and Cayce's Dayton years, which preceded his move to Virginia Beach, turned into a period of financial despair. Nonetheless, for Cayce, if not his loved ones, Dayton also marked a stage of unprecedented discovery.

Cayce and Lammers began their explorations at a downtown hotel on October 11, 1923. In the presence of several onlookers, Lammers arranged for Cayce to enter a trance and to give the printer an astrological reading. Whatever hesitancies the waking Cayce evinced over arcane subjects vanished while he was in his trance state. Cayce expounded on the validity of astrology even as "the Source"—what Cayce called the ethereal intelligence behind his readings—alluded to misconceptions in the Western model. Toward the end of the reading, Cayce almost casually tossed off that it was Lammers's "third appearance on this [earthly] plane. He was once a monk." It was an unmistakable reference to reincarnation—just the type of insight Lammers had been seeking.

In the weeks ahead, the men continued their readings, probing into Hermetic and esoteric spirituality. From a trance state on October 18, Cayce laid out for Lammers a whole philosophy of life, dealing with karmic rebirth, man's role in the cosmic order, and the hidden meaning of existence:

In this we see the plan of development of those individuals set upon this plane, meaning the ability (as would be manifested from the physical) to enter again into the presence of the Creator and become a full part of that creation. Insofar as this entity is concerned, this is the third appearance on this plane, and before this one, as the monk. We see glimpses in the life of the entity now as were shown in the monk, in his mode of living. The body is only the vehicle ever of that spirit and soul that waft through all times and ever remain the same.

These phrases were, for Lammers, the golden key to the mysteries: a theory of eternal recurrence, or reincarnation, that identified man's destiny as inner refinement through karmic cycles of rebirth, then reintegration with the source of Creation. This, the printer believed, was the hidden truth behind the Scriptural injunction to be "born again" so as to "enter the kingdom of Heaven."

"It opens up the door," Lammers told Cayce. "It's like finding the secret chamber of the Great Pyramid." He insisted that the doctrine that came through the readings synchronized the great wisdom traditions: "It's Hermetic, it's Pythagorean, it's Jewish, it's Christian!" Cayce himself wasn't sure what to believe. "The important thing," Lammers reassured him, "is that the basic system which runs through all the mystery traditions, whether they come from Tibet or the pyramids of Egypt, is backed up by you. It's actually the right system. . . . It not only agrees with the best ethics of religion and society, it is the source of them."

Lammers's enthusiasms aside, the religious ideas that emerged from Cayce's readings did articulate a compelling theology. Cayce's teachings sought to marry a Christian moral outlook with the cycles of karma and reincarnation central to Hindu and Buddhist ways of thought, as well as the Hermetic concept of man as an extension of the Divine. Cayce's references elsewhere to the causative powers of the mind—"the spiritual is the LIFE; the mental is the BUILDER; the physical is the RESULT"— melded his cosmic philosophy with tenets of New Thought, Christian Science, and mental healing. If there was an inner philosophy unifying the world's religions, Cayce came as close as any modern person in defining it.

CAYCE'S "SOURCE"

Religious traditionalists could rightly object: Just where are Cayce's "insights" coming from? Are they the product of a Higher Power or merely the overactive imagination of a religious outlier? Or, worse, are his phrases the type of muddle-fuddle produced by haunts at Ouija board sessions?

Cayce himself wrestled with these questions. His response was that all of his ideas, whatever their source, had to square with Gospel ethics in order to be judged vital and right. Cayce addressed this in a talk that he delivered in his normal waking state in Norfolk, Virginia, in February of 1933, just before he turned fifty-six:

Many people ask me how I prevent undesirable influences entering into the work I do. In order to answer that question let me relate an experience I had as a child. When I was between eleven and twelve years of age I had read the Bible through three times. I have now read it fifty-six times. No doubt many people have read it more times than that, but I have tried to read it through once for each year of my life. Well, as a child I prayed that I might be able to do something for the other fellow, to aid others in understanding themselves, and especially to aid children in their ills. I had a vision one day which convinced me that my prayer had been heard and answered.

Cayce's "vision" has been described differently by different biographers. Sugrue recounts the episode occurring when Cayce was about twelve in the woods outside his home in western Kentucky. Cayce himself places it in his bedroom at age thirteen or fourteen. One night, this adolescent boy who had spoken of childhood conversations with "hidden friends," and who hungrily read through Scripture, knelt by his bed and prayed for the ability to help others.

Just before drifting to sleep, Cayce recalled, a glorious light filled the room and a feminine apparition appeared at the foot of his bed telling him: "Thy prayers are heard. You will have your wish. Remain faithful. Be true to yourself. Help the sick, the afflicted."

Cayce did not realize until years later what form his answered prayers would take—and even in his twenties it took him years to adjust to being a medical clairvoyant. As his new powers took shape he labored to use Scripture as his moral vetting mechanism. Yet he consistently attributed his information to the "Source"—another subject on which he expanded at Norfolk:

As a matter of fact, there would seem to be not only one, but several sources of information that I tap when in this sleep condition.

One source is, apparently, the recording that an individual or entity makes in all its experiences through what we call time. The sum-total of the experiences of that soul is "written," so to speak, in the subconscious of that individual as well as in what is known as the Akashic records. Anyone may read these records if he can attune himself properly.

Cayce's concept of the "Akashic records" is derived from ancient Vedic writings, in which *akasha* is a kind of universal ether. This idea of universal records was popularized to Westerners in the late nineteenth-century through the work of occult philosopher, world traveler, and Theosophy founder Madame H.P. Blavatsky.

A generation before Cayce, Blavatsky told of a hidden philosophy at the core of the historic faiths—and of a cosmic record bank that catalogs all human events. In Blavatsky's 1877 study of occult philosophy, *Isis Unveiled*, the Theosophist described an all-pervasive magnetic ether that "keeps an unmutilated record of all that was, that is, or ever will be." These astral records, wrote Blavatsky, preserve "a vivid picture for the eye of the seer and prophet to follow." Blavatsky equated this archival ether with the "Book of Life" from Revelation.

Returning to the topic in her massive 1888 study of occult history, *The Secret Doctrine*, Blavatsky depicted these etheric records in more explicitly Vedic terms (having spent several preceding years in India). In the first of her two-volume study, Blavatsky referred to "Akâsic or astral-photographs"—inching closer to the term "Akashic records" as used by Cayce.

Cayce was not the first channeler to credit the "Akashic records" as his source of data. In 1908, a retired Civil War chaplain and Church of Christ pastor named Levi H. Dowling said that he clairvoyantly channeled an alternative history of Christ in *The Aquarian Gospel of Jesus the Christ*. In Dowling's influential account, the Son of Man travels and studies throughout the religious cultures of the East before dispensing a message of universal faith that encompasses all the world's traditions. Dowling, too, attributed his insights to the "Akashic records," accessed while in a trance state in his Los Angeles living room.

Cayce, like Blavatsky, equated *akasha* with the Scriptural Book of Life. This was an example of how Cayce harmonized the exotic and unfamiliar themes of his readings with his Christian worldview. In a similar vein, he reinterpreted the ninth chapter of the Gospel of John, in which Christ heals a man who had been blind from birth, to validate ideas of karma and reincarnation. When the disciples ask Christ whether it was the man's sins or those of his parents that caused his affliction, the Master replies enigmatically: "Neither hath this man sinned, nor his parents: but that the works of God should be made manifest in him" (John 9:3). In Cayce's reasoning, since the blind man was born with his disorder, and Christ exonerates both the man and his parents, his disability must be karmic baggage from a previous incarnation. Cayce made comparable interpretations of passages from Matthew and Revelation.

In another effort to unite the poles of different traditions, Cayce elsewhere associated his esoteric search with Madame Blavatsky's. On four occasions he reported being visited by a mysterious, turbaned spiritual master from the East—one of the *mahatmas*, or great souls, whom Blavatsky said had guided her.

THE LEGACY

Neither Cayce nor Sugrue lived long enough to witness the full reach of Cayce's ideas. The psychic died at age sixty-seven in Virginia Beach on January 3, 1945, less than three years after *There Is a River* first appeared. Sugrue updated the book that year. After struggling with years of illness, the biographer died at age forty-five on January 6, 1953 at the Hospital for Joint Diseases in New York.

The first popularizations of Cayce's work began to appear in 1950 with the publication of *Many Mansions*, an enduring work on reincarnation by Gina Cerminara, a longtime Cayce devotee. But it wasn't until 1956 that Cayce's name took full flight across the culture with the appearance of the sensationally popular book *The Search for Bridey Murphy* by Morey Bernstein. Sugrue's editor Sloane, having since warmed to parapsychology, published both Cerminara and Bernstein.

Bernstein was an iconic figure. A Coloradan of Jewish descent and an Ivy League-educated dealer in heavy machinery and scrap metal, he grew inspired by Cayce's career—partly through the influence of Sugrue's book—and became an amateur hypnotist. In the early 1950s, Bernstein conducted a series of experiments with a Pueblo, Colorado, housewife who, while under a hypnotic trance, appeared to regress into a past-life persona: an early nineteenth-century Irish country girl named Bridey Murphy. The entranced homemaker spoke in an Irish brogue and recounted to Bernstein comprehensive details of her life more than a century earlier.

Suddenly, reincarnation—an ancient Vedic concept about which Americans had heard little before World War II—was the latest craze, ignited by Bernstein, an avowed admirer of Cayce, to whom the hypnotist devoted two chapters in his book.

In the following decade, California journalist Jess Stearn further ramped up interest in Cayce with his 1967 bestseller, *Edgar Cayce, The Sleeping Prophet*. With the mystic sixties in full swing, and the youth culture embracing all forms of alternative or Eastern spirituality—from Zen to yoga to psychedelics—Cayce, while not explicitly tied to any of this, rode the new vogue in alternative spirituality. During this time, Hugh Lynn Cayce emerged as a formidable custodian of his father's legacy, presiding over the expansion of the Virginia Beach-based Association for Research and Enlightenment, and shepherding to market a new wave of instructional guides based on the Cayce teachings, from dream interpretation to drug-free methods of relaxation to the spiritual uses of colors, crystals, and numbers. Cayce's name became a permanent fixture on the cultural landscape.

The 1960s and 70s also saw a new generation of channeled literature—Cayce himself originated the term *channel*—from higher intelligences such as Seth, Ramtha, and even the figure of Christ in *A Course in Miracles*. The last was a profound and enduring lesson series, channeled beginning in 1965 by Columbia University research psychiatrist Helen Schucman.

A concordance of tone and values existed between Cayce's readings and *A Course in Miracles*. Cayce's devotees and the *Course*'s wide array of readers discovered that they had a lot in common; members of both cultures blended seamlessly, attending many of the same seminars, growth centers, and metaphysical churches.

Likewise, a congruency emerged between Cayce's world and followers of the twelve steps of Alcoholics Anonymous. Starting in the 1970s, twelve-steppers of various stripes became a familiar presence at Cayce conferences and events in Virginia Beach.

Cayce's universalistic religious message dovetailed with the purposefully flexible references to a Higher Power in the "Big Book," *Alcoholics Anonymous*, written in 1939. AA cofounder Bill Wilson, his wife Lois, his confidant Bob Smith, and several other early AAs were deeply versed in mystical and mediumistic teachings. Whether they viewed Cayce as an influence is unclear. But all three works—the Cayce readings, *A Course in Miracles*, and *Alcoholics Anonymous*—demonstrated a shared sense of religious liberalism, an encouragement that all individuals seek their own conception of a Higher Power, and a permeability intended to accommodate the broadest expression of religious outlooks and backgrounds.

The free-flowing tone of the therapeutic spiritual movements of the twentieth and early twenty-first centuries had a shared antecedent, if not a direct ancestry, in the Cayce readings.

* * *

Sugrue's *There Is a River* remains an irreplaceable record of Cayce's development as a spiritual messenger and pioneer. The biography captured the seer as the person who Cayce himself said he was: An ordinary man who struggled with his apparent psychical abilities and the universal religious ideas that travelled through him.

But Sugrue's biography accomplished more than just that. *There Is a River*, in its own right, became a formative document of New Age spirituality. In exploring Cayce's career, Sugrue highlighted and popularized core themes from the Cayce readings—including past-life experiences, alternative medical treatments, the imperative of the individual spiritual search, and the idea of religion as a practical source of healing.

Sugrue demonstrated how Cayce—a committed Christian, a Sunday school teacher, and, by his own reckoning, an everyday man—developed into the founding prophet of Aquarian Age spirituality. In capturing the drama and events of Cayce's journey, Sugrue elevated the clarity and endurance of the seer's message.

September 2014
New York City

* * *

Mitch Horowitz is a PEN Award-winning historian and the author of *Occult America* and *One Simple Idea: How Positive Thinking Reshaped Modern Life*. He has written on alternative spirituality for *The New York Times, The Wall Street Journal,* and *The Washington Post*. Visit him @MitchHorowitz and www.MitchHorowitz.com

1

Uncle Billy Evans huddled in the rear seat of his cab and watched the afternoon train pull into the Louisville and Nashville Railroad station in Hopkinsville, Kentucky. It was a cold, still afternoon in January, 1912.

A stranger stepped off the Pullman. Uncle Billy left his warm seat and went to meet him.

He was a large, tall man, wrapped in a heavy overcoat, with its collar turned up to protect his ears. He let Uncle Billy take his two suitcases and followed him to the cab.

"I am looking for a man named Edgar Cayce," he said while the old black man stowed the bags away. "Can you take me to him?" He spoke quickly, with a thick, Germanic accent.

Uncle Billy straightened himself and shivered a little.

"Mr. Edgar's gone home for the day," he said. "And it's a mile and a half out there to the Hill. Miss Gertrude's mighty sick these days, and Mr. Edgar's there with her most o' the time."

The stranger settled himself in the cab and Uncle Billy tucked a blanket around his legs.

"They don't have many visitors, on account of Miss Gertrude," he went on. "Lord, I hope nothin' happens to that child!"

"She is his daughter?" the stranger asked.

Uncle Billy finished with the blanket.

"No, sir. Miss Gertrude is Mr. Edgar's wife," he explained. "Now, I can take you to the hotel and first thing tomorrow morning . . . "

"We will go now to the house," the stranger said. "And tell me, why is it so cold down here in the South?"

"Lord God, sir!" Uncle Billy said. "This ain't the South! The South's way down yonder!"

He pointed.

"This here's Kentucky, and the Lord ain't got a bit o' use for it!"

He paused before closing the door.

"You think you'll be warm enough ridin' way out there and back again?" he asked.

"I will be comfortable," the stranger said. "Let us go quickly."

Uncle Billy closed the door and climbed to his box, muttering. The two horses, eager for exercise, started briskly down East Ninth Street, turned left along the park, and headed out East Seventh Street. The town fell behind and the street became Russellville Road. Houses gave way to brown, rolling hills, and bare fields looted of their crops. A single bright spot loomed through the dusk. On a hill higher than the rest and covered with trees, a gray, rambling house stood with its face to the north, the four white columns of its porch glistening in the sidewise glance of the winter sun. Beyond it the road swerved to the right. Just before the cab reached the carriage entrance leading to the house on the hill, it stopped. A little off the road, almost hidden by a giant oak and some maple trees, was a small cottage, brightly painted in green and white. Uncle Billy got down from his box and opened the cab door.

"In here, sir," he said.

The stranger got out, stretched, and looked around him.

"He doesn't live in the big house?" he said, as if disappointed.

Uncle Billy pointed to the glistening columns.

"That's the Hill," he said. "It's the old Salter Place, where Miss Gertrude's folks live. This here"—he pointed to the cottage— "is Miss Lizzie's little place. Miss Lizzie is Miss Gertrude's mother. She lives up at the Hill with Miss Kate."

The stranger smiled a little.

"Do your southern ladies never marry?" he said.

"Oh, they's all married," Uncle Billy said, "but they ain't got no husbands, except Miss Gertrude. They's dead."

The stranger changed the subject.

"What does this land produce?" he asked, waving his arm toward Hopkinsville.

"Dark tobacco," Uncle Billy said.

"Dark?" The stranger looked thoughtful. He stared at Uncle Billy.

"Dark tobacco," Uncle Billy repeated. "Hopkinsville is famous fo' being the dark tobacco market of the whole world."

"It is also famous for another thing that is dark," the stranger said. Then he added, as if to himself, "Funny place to find it."

He started for the cottage. Uncle Billy crawled into the cab to wait.

The young man who opened the cottage door was slim and almost as tall as the stranger. Without saying anything the stranger stepped into the hallway. "You are Edgar Cayce?" he asked.

"I am," the young man answered.

"I am Dr. Hugo Münsterberg, of Harvard," the stranger said. "I have come here to expose you. There has been entirely too much written about you in the newspapers lately."

He looked quickly around the hallway and peered into the living room, which opened from the hallway to the right.

"What is your *modus operandi?*" he said. "Where is your cabinet?"

The young man had not moved. He looked dazed.

"I don't know what you mean," he said.

Dr. Münsterberg struck the air impatiently with an arm.

"The cabinet, the cabinet," he said brusquely.

The young man recovered himself suddenly. He smiled and led the way into the living room.

"Come in and sit down," he said. "I will take your coat. There is a fire in the fireplace. But I have no cabinet. I don't use any apparatus at all, if that's what you mean. I could lie down on the floor here and go to sleep, if I wanted to."

Dr. Münsterberg came into the room but did not sit down or remove his coat. From its inner pocket he took a sheaf of newspaper clippings.

"There's been too much publicity for this thing not to be a fake," he said, putting the clippings on a tea table.

Idly the young man leafed through the clippings. Apparently he had seen them before. One was a full-page display from the Sunday magazine section of the New York *Times* for October 9, 1910. The headline said, ILLITERATE MAN BECOMES A DOCTOR WHEN

The first paragraph read:

> The medical fraternity of the country is taking a lively in-
> terest in the strange power said to be possessed by Edgar Cayce
> of Hopkinsville, Ky., to diagnose difficult diseases while in
> a semi-conscious state, though he has not the slightest knowl-
> edge of medicine when not in this condition.

There was a photograph of the young man, another of his
father, a mustached gentleman named Leslie B. Cayce, who was
described as the "conductor" of the hypnotic sleeps; and a third
picture showing a young physician named Dr. Wesley H. Ketchum,
who had reported the phenomena to the American Society of
Clinical Research, of Boston. There was a drawing which showed
the young man lying on a table, asleep, while a weird demon
of the other world hovered over him.

"All this was done without my knowledge or permission,"
the young man explained to Dr. Münsterberg. "I was in Alabama at the time. I didn't know anything about it."

Dr. Münsterberg stood with his back to the fireplace, warm-
ing himself.

"You say you do not have a cabinet," he said. "Do you allow
yourself to be seen? Are the lights on?"

"Oh, it's always very light," the young man said. "I give the
readings in the morning and afternoon, two each day. If there
isn't enough light we have to turn on the lamps, so the stenographer can see to take down what I say."

"And the patient? Where is the patient?"

"Most of them are at home, wherever that is. They just read
me the address, and I seem to find the place all right."

"You do not examine the patients beforehand?"

"Oh, no. I don't know anything about medicine when I'm
awake. I prefer not to know even the name of the person before
I go to sleep. The names wouldn't mean much to me, anyhow.
Most of the people are from out of the state somewhere."

"They tell their symptoms in letters to this . . . Dr. Ketchum?"

"Oh, no. We only want to be sure that they really need help.
That's all."

Dr. Münsterberg watched the young man's face while he talked. It was a frank, open countenance. The cheeks were round, the nose straight, the chin receding but not weak, the eyes gray-blue and friendly. His hair was straight and brown. He spoke with a soft drawl. He looked about twenty-five.

"You are how old?" the doctor asked.

"Thirty-four. I'll be thirty-five in March."

"You look younger. What is your name? You are Irish?"

"No, it was originally Cuaci. Norman-French, I reckon. Our records don't go back to the country from which we came originally. Our direct ancestor is Shadrach Cayce. He lived in Powhatan County, Virginia, and his sons fought in the Revolution. They received land grants in Tennessee and Kentucky from the government, and that's why we're here."

He went to a square-topped walnut table in the corner of the room. His stride was quick and sure, his step soft, like a man used to hunting and life in the open.

"This table came from Virginia more than a hundred years ago," he said.

"You were born on a farm?" Dr. Münsterberg asked.

The young man came back to the tea table and sat down.

"Yes, sir. I was born here in Christian County. The Cayces used to own nearly all the land between Hopkinsville and the Tennessee line. That's about fifteen miles. But my great-grandfather had four sons and my grandfather had seven sons, so by the time all the land was split up there wasn't a great deal left for my generation. So I'm a photographer."

"But you do not work at that now, of course."

"Oh, yes. That's in the contract I have with my partners. They have to furnish me with a studio and equipment. That's where I make my living. I can only give two readings a day, you see, and some of them are for people who have no money."

Dr. Münsterberg laughed a little and shook his head.

"Either you are a very simple fellow," he said, "or you are very clever. I cannot penetrate your ruse."

The young man shook his head mournfully.

"I'm the dumbest man in Christian County," he said, "when I'm awake."

"But when you are asleep you know everything. Is that it?"

"That's what they tell me. I don't know. The people say I tell them how they feel better than they know how to tell it themselves. They take the medicines and the treatment I prescribe, and they get better. The stenographer takes it down and gives the patient a copy. Dr. Ketchum adds whatever comment is needed. That's all I know."

"You have no explanation for this? There is no tradition of psychic power in your family?"

"They say my grandfather was a water witch. He would walk around with a forked hazel twig in his hand and tell the farmers where to dig their wells. They always found water there, so they said.

"He was supposed to be able to do other things, too, such as make a broom dance, but that was probably just talk. There's nothing funny about my father except that snakes love him, and he hates them."

"Snakes are fond of your father?"

"They used to follow him home from the fields. They would wrap themselves around his hat brim if he laid his hat down in the field. It got on his nerves so much that he gave up farming. The family has lived in town for about fifteen years now."

"And you have been doing this business how long?"

"The readings? Oh, just regularly since all the publicity started a year ago. I didn't pay much attention to it until then. I just did it for friends, and people round about who asked me now and then."

"What have been your studies? Not medicine, you say?"

"No. I never got further than what would be first year in high school. I was graduated down in the country, where they have nine grades."

"But since then you have read a lot, naturally."

"Well, I like to read, and I used to work in a bookstore, but I reckon my taste isn't very high. You can look through the bookcase there in the hall if you like."

Dr. Münsterberg went immediately into the hallway.

"We will see what you read. It should be interesting," he said.

He began taking books from the cases, stacking them on the

floor. Some he flipped open, running through the pages quickly;
these he dropped carelessly, so that some of them fell face open
on the floor.

"There seems to be nothing worthwhile here," he said. "*The
Harvester, The Common Law, The Rosary, Girl of the Limberlost,
The Trail of the Lonesome Pine* . . . Let me see what are these
large volumes . . . *Judge* magazine and *Red Book* magazine."

"I have them bound each year," the young man explained.
"We like to keep them."

"*The Circular Staircase, The Awakening of Helena Richie*
. . . who is this E. P. Roe? Ah, you have a complete set of his
works!"

"Those are my wife's. I gave them to her years ago. E. P. Roe
is her favorite novelist."

"Hmmmm. Yes, I see now. Love stories . . . what trash! Here
is *The Doctor.* No, it is a novel. *The Jungle, Coniston, The Clans-
man, Rebecca of Sunnybrook Farm, The Cardinal's Snuffbox*
. . . some poetry here . . . hmmm . . . it is Ella Wheeler Wilcox."

He straightened himself and turned back to the living room.

"Well, there is nothing here," he said. "I shall have to look
further."

"Perhaps you would like to see a reading?" the young man
said. "The copies are kept at the office, downtown, but I have
my wife's readings here. We had a check reading for her the
other day. The doctors all said she would die. She has tuberculosis. But she is getting better by following the readings."

He was eager now; his face shone.

"I'll get it!"

He went into a room across the hall, returning almost immediately with two sheets of typewritten manuscript. Each sheet
carried his picture at the top, with the legend, "Edgar Cayce,
Jr., Psychic Diagnostician."

"The printer made a mistake," he said, handing the sheets to
the doctor and pointing to the legend. "He got me mixed up
with my Uncle Edgar and put me down as junior. I'm not."

Dr. Münsterberg began to read the sheets. The young man
stepped away politely and sat down by the tea table.

"I cannot learn much from this; I am not a medical doctor,"

Dr. Münsterberg said. He looked quickly at the young man to see how this was taken.

The young man offered another suggestion.

"There are some people you might go to see, who have had experience with the readings. They could tell you whether they work or not. You could see Mrs. Dietrich, and some of the others . . . Mrs. Dabney, Miss Perry . . . Mrs. Bowles, maybe."

"Good," the doctor said. "You will write down their names and addresses?" He continued to read.

The young man went to a desk against the wall and wrote on a pad. Dr. Münsterberg watched him, returning to his perusal of the manuscript sheets when the young man finished and looked up.

"Here are the names and addresses. Uncle Billy can take you to all of them. They are too far apart to walk. Are you planning to stay here tonight? We're going to have a reading in the morning. Perhaps you'd like to watch it."

"I intend to stay," the doctor said, putting the manuscript sheets on the tea table. "I will take a room at the hotel. Tonight I will visit these people and question them."

"The owner of the hotel, Mr. Noe, is one of my partners. You'll probably find Dr. Ketchum and my father there, too, later on."

"Good. I shall endeavor to see them."

He tucked the sheet with the names and addresses into an inside pocket.

"Well, we meet again, tomorrow, eh?"

"Yes, sir."

"Oh, there is one more thing. To what power or force do you and your associates attribute this phenomenon?"

"We don't know, sir, except for what the readings have said themselves."

"You mean what you have said while asleep."

"Yes, sir. It's here, in this New York *Times* story."

He picked up the clipping and read from it.

"This is what I said when they asked me to explain the thing: 'Edgar Cayce's mind is amenable to suggestion, the same as all other subconscious minds, but in addition thereto it has the power to interpret to the objective mind of others what it acquired from the subconscious state of other individuals of the same kind. The subconscious mind forgets nothing. The conscious mind receives the impression from without and transfers all thought to the subconscious, where it remains even though the conscious be destroyed.'"

He folded the clipping and returned it, with the others, to Dr. Münsterberg. The doctor looked him squarely in the eye.

"The story of the subconscious mind can be told in three words," he said. "There is none! . . . Well, I shall continue my investigations."

He went out without shaking hands or saying good-bye. The young man watched through the living-room window until the cab drove away. Then he went into the room across the hall, taking the manuscript sheets with him.

On the far side of the room, on a massive oak bed, lay a frail, dark-haired girl, almost lost in the great expanse of sheets and counterpane. In the twilight only her outline was visible; she was a shadow on the bed. The young man lit one of the lamps on the dresser and brought it to the sick table. Her face leaped up at him like a flame. Her eyes were dark, but a fierce light shone from them. Her cheeks were bright red. Her oval face was like a miniature portrait come to life. Her face was worried, quick, yet the words came softly.

"Who was that man, Edgar? What did he want? You're not going off with him somewhere, are you?"

The young man leaned down and kissed her forehead.

"Just a professor from Harvard," he said. "He came all the way down here to expose me."

She seemed relieved.

"No wonder his voice sounded so officious. What did he say?"

"Nothing much. He dumped all the books on the floor and called me a simpleton."

The girl sighed.

"I declare I don't know where people learn such bad manners," she said. "What time is it? Mother ought to be bringing Hugh Lynn down soon."

"They're coming now. I hear Hugh Lynn banging that gate again. It's five o'clock."

He went to the front door and opened it. A little boy with fat cheeks grabbed him around the legs.

"Hey, Dad, the bears are after me again!" he cried.

The young man smiled at the lady who had come with the boy and waved a hand against the cold air that was blowing in on him.

"Go 'way, bears!" he said.

The little boy released his legs and walked into the hallway.

"Almost got me that time," he said.

"What about your grandmother?" the young man said. "Aren't you afraid the bears will get her?"

"No," the boy said. "They don't eat ladies. Only little boys."

He struggled out of his coat and ran into the bedroom, shouting, "Muddie, the bears didn't get me again!"

The lady who had come with him took off her black coat and black hat, revealing a black dress, high at the throat, and black hair brushed straight away from her forehead.

"How is Gertrude?" she said to the young man.

"About the same," he answered.

They went into the bedroom together. The girl turned her head and smiled at her mother.

"Hugh Lynn says Aunt Kate made him some ginger cookies," she said.

"Kate's a fool," her mother said. "Hugh Lynn's like a ball of butter now and she keeps feeding him sweets. How do you feel?"

"All right, I reckon."

"I'll get you freshened up for dinner. Edgar, who was that who just drove away from here? Anyone I know?"

"No. Some professor from Harvard, down here to investigate me and show me up as a fake, same as they all try to do."

"He spilled our books all over the floor and called Edgar a simpleton," the girl said. Her voice was resentful.

"I noticed the mess as I came in. Well, you've got to expect that sort of thing from Yankees. They don't know any better, poor souls."

"I think they know what's right as well as anyone else," the girl said. "They just think they're better than we are, that's all."

"Don't excite yourself, child," her mother said. "That white trash isn't worth it. Edgar, why don't you get some decent school to investigate you, like Washington and Lee? Harvard is just a pesthole of Republicans. You know that."

"This man is a foreigner," the young man said. "A German, I would say, from his accent."

"Oh, well, that explains everything. Here, take Hugh Lynn out of here while I fuss around with Gertrude some."

The young man and the boy went into the living room.

"Was that a bad man who was here, Dad?" he asked.

The young man lifted him high in the air and set him down by the fireplace.

"No, he wasn't bad. Nobody is really bad. People just make mistakes. They don't understand about God."

"Do you understand about God, Dad?"

"Nobody really does. But I try to remember that God is the only One who really knows anything, and that He told me what He wants me to do in the Bible. So I try to do that."

The little boy nodded.

"Let's play bears," he said. "You be the big bear who's chasing me."

*   *   *

Uncle Billy huddled in his cab outside the large house on South Walnut Street. In the living room of the house his fare sat, overcoat removed, listening to a mild, lovely woman, whose face became radiant as she told her story.

"When our daughter, Aime, was two," Mrs. Dietrich began, "she caught grippe. After apparently recovering, she became afflicted with convulsions. She would fall down suddenly and her body would stiffen until it was rigid. Her mind stopped developing.

"We had all sorts and kinds of doctors. They did her no good, and after two years of futile experimentation we took her to Evansville, Indiana, to see Dr. Linthicum and Dr. Walker. They said it was a type of nervousness, and they treated her for months, but she didn't improve.

"We brought her home. We had treatments here, but she got

worse—twenty convulsions a day, sometimes. Her mind became a blank.

"We took her to Dr. Hoppe, in Cincinnati. He said she had a rare brain affliction that was invariably fatal.

"We brought her home to die. Then one of our local friends, Mr. Wilgus, told us about Edgar Cayce."

Dr. Münsterberg interrupted. "This Mr. Wilgus . . . was he connected with the young man Cayce in any way?"

"Oh, no, except that he had always been interested in him. Mr. Wilgus is one of our most influential citizens. He used to hunt a good deal down on the Cayce property, and when Edgar was a boy Mr. Wilgus used to hire him as guide. One day a piece of shot glanced from a bird which Mr. Wilgus had brought down and struck the boy in the cheek. Mr. Wilgus felt so conscience-stricken that he always kept an eye on Edgar and tried to help him out.

"At any rate, Mr. Wilgus had readings, and on the advice of one of them went to Cincinnati for a minor operation, which he said vastly improved his health.

"He urged us to give the young man a chance—you understand, of course, that he was not in the business of giving readings at the time. This was in the summer of 1902, nearly ten years ago. Edgar was then working in Bowling Green, in a bookstore."

Dr. Münsterberg nodded. "I understand," he said. "We will proceed."

"My husband asked him to come here, and he did. He wanted no other remuneration than the railroad ticket. He said the trip gave him a chance to see his girl. They were married the following year, I believe.

"He came with Mr. Al C. Layne, the local man who was at the time conducting the readings and giving some of the treatments."

Dr. Münsterberg interrupted again. "He was a doctor, this Layne?"

"He was studying osteopathy at the time. Later he was graduated in the profession. His wife had a millinery shop in Hopkinsville and Edgar Cayce's sister was employed there."

"Mr. Layne put Cayce into a trance," Dr. Münsterberg said. "Did either of the men examine the child?"

"No. They saw her, but I remember Edgar saying how he did not see how it could help her. I remember how young and boyish he looked. I thought to myself, 'How can this boy be of any help to us when the best doctors in the country have failed?' You see, we knew his family and we knew Edgar. He had very little schooling."

"You were skeptical, then?" Dr. Münsterberg asked.

"I hoped for a miracle, as any mother would."

The doctor nodded.

"He removed his coat and loosened his tie and shoelaces. Then he lay on that sofa there"—she pointed and the doctor looked—"and apparently went to sleep. After a few minutes Mr. Layne spoke to him, telling him to have before him the body of our child, who was in the house, and to examine her and tell what was wrong with her body.

"I could not believe my ears when the sleeping man began to talk and said, 'Yes, we have the body.' His voice seemed different. It seemed—well, authoritative."

Dr. Münsterberg nodded. "Exactly," he said.

"He told us that on the day before she caught grippe she suffered an injury to her spine, and the grippe germs had settled in the spine, causing the attacks. He then told exactly where the lesion was and gave instructions for correcting it osteopathically.

"He could not possibly have known of the injury to her spine beforehand. I alone knew of it, and had not considered it serious—or even an injury."

"But you are sure it happened?"

"The day before Aime caught grippe she was getting out of the carriage with me. She slipped and struck the end of her spine on the carriage step. She jumped up as if unhurt, and I thought no more of it."

"The lesion was discovered where he described it?"

"Yes. Mr. Layne gave Aime a treatment that night. Next day we took another reading. He said the adjustment had not been properly made."

"Very interesting," Dr. Münsterberg said. "He told the man, Layne, his own conductor, that he had not carried out instructions?"

"Yes. Then he told what had been done that was wrong, and explained how to do it the right way. Layne tried again that morning. In the afternoon another reading was taken. Still the correction had not been made. Layne tried again. The next morning a reading was taken and the treatment was approved.

"Edgar returned to Bowling Green, and Mr. Layne, who lived in Hopkinsville, continued the treatments. He came every day for three weeks.

"At the end of the first week Aime's mind began to clear up. She suddenly called the name of a doll of which she had been fond before the attacks occurred. A few days later she called me by name; then she called her father. Her mind picked up just where it had left off three years before, when she was only two."

"She advanced rapidly then?"

"Quite rapidly. Soon she had the mind of a normal five-year-old. After the three weeks of treatment we had a check reading. At that time he said the condition had been removed. There was never any more trouble. Aime today is a normal girl of fifteen. She'll be finished with her lessons in a few minutes and I will bring her in."

"Yes, yes. I would like to see her."

"I don't know what this strange ability is," Mrs. Dietrich went on. "We have only our own experience and the experiences of our friends by which to judge. But so far as we know it always works. Edgar Cayce is certainly no charlatan. He's one of the pillars of the Christian Church, and so far as anyone knows he has never taken advantage of anyone. It's just the other way around. People are always taking advantage of his good nature and his generosity."

"Of course," the doctor said, "of course."

He answered automatically, as if he had not quite heard what she was saying but was aware that she had stopped.

He was staring past her, dreamily, at the sofa on which, ten years before, the young man he had visited that afternoon had gone to sleep.

* * *

The man with the mustache paused to measure the distance between himself and the cuspidor. Accurately he spat into it. His listeners, grouped around him in the foyer of the Latham Hotel, waited respectfully.

Leslie Cayce went on with his story.

"Well, you can see for yourself that he was a normal boy, except in school. There, he was dull. No doubt about it. He dreamed too much; all his teachers told me that. When he was twelve years old he was still in the third reader.

"That was in the spring of 1889. My brother Lucian was teaching the school. One afternoon Lucian met me and told me he had asked Edgar to spell 'cabin' and the boy couldn't do it. 'I hope I did right, Leslie,' Lucian said. 'I made him stay after school and write the word five hundred times on the blackboard.' 'Do as you like, Lucian,' I said. 'You're the teacher.'

"Well, I felt mighty badly, mighty badly. Maybe it's my own fault, I thought. Maybe I don't spend enough time with the boy. Maybe he just needs somebody to bring him out properly, you know?

"So that night I sat down with him and we took hold of the spelling lesson. Well, there didn't seem to be anything I could do to get the lesson into his head. I'd think he had it; then when I'd close the book and ask him to spell the words, he couldn't do it.

"First thing I knew it was nearly eleven o'clock. The boy was tired, I knew, so I told him he might better go to bed. 'Just let me rest for five minutes,' he said to me, 'and I'll know the lesson.' 'All right,' I said, just to humor him, you know.

"Well, I went into the kitchen to get a glass of water. I puttered around with a few things, then went back to the living room. There he was, asleep in the chair, with the spelling book for a pillow. I laughed and gave him a shake. 'Wake up, Old Man,' I said, 'time for bed.'

"Well, he woke up right off, and said, 'Ask me the lesson. I know it now.' I was sure he didn't, but to humor him I asked him a few words.

"Well, dogged if he couldn't spell them. I asked him some more and he knew them. 'Ask me anything in the book,' he said. He seemed all excited. So I skipped through the book, and no matter what I asked, he knew it.

"Then he began telling me what other words were on the page with the words I asked him, and what the pictures were on the pages, and the numbers of the pages. He knew that book as if he had it in his hands looking at it."

Dr. Münsterberg leaned forward. "What was his explanation?" he asked. "What did he say had caused this?"

"All I could ever get out of him was that he suddenly felt that night that if he slept a little on the book he would know the lesson. And he did.

"After that he slept on all his lessons, and he knew them all perfectly. He began to hop grades like he was skipping rope."

"His memory of these lessons, did it persist?" Dr. Münsterberg asked.

"Never forgot any of them. Even to this day he remembers them."

"Very interesting. And you recall no peculiar circumstances or accidents at his birth, or in his youth, before this?"

"Not a thing, except milk on the breasts."

"Milk on the breasts?"

"Cried for a month after he was born. Nobody knew what the trouble was. Then old Patsy Cayce—black woman at my father's house, used to be a slave—she came over and asked my wife for a needle. 'Boil it up first,' she said. Then she took it and pricked a little hole in the nipple of each breast, and dogged if milk didn't come from them. After that the baby never cried much at all."

"I have heard of that," Dr. Münsterberg said, "in my medical studies."

"Are you a medical doctor as well as a Ph.D.?" Dr. Ketchum asked. He was a smiling, quick-moving, bright-eyed man, in his middle thirties.

"Oh, yes," Dr. Münsterberg said, "I have a medical degree. I studied both at Leipzig and Heidelberg."

"Then I may tell you of some of my cases?" Dr. Ketchum said.

"I am most interested to know what school of medicine he endorses," Dr. Münsterberg said. "For the Dietrich child he prescribed osteopathy."

"He uses all schools," Dr. Ketchum said, "and often for the same case. He sometimes gives osteopathy along with electrical treatments, massage, diet, and compounds to be taken internally.

"He sometimes calls for herbs that are hard to get or for a medicine we haven't heard about. Sometimes it's just come on the market, sometimes it's been off the market for a while."

"Always he seems to know everything," Dr. Münsterberg said. "You would say that he was . . . quoting from a universal mind, perhaps?"

Dr. Ketchum nodded sagely. "I have often thought so," he said. "In one of the earliest readings I conducted a preparation was given called 'Oil of Smoke.' I had never heard of it, nor had any of our local druggists. It was not listed in the pharmaceutical catalogues. We took another reading and asked where it could be found. The name of a drugstore in Louisville was given. I wired there, asking for the preparation. The manager wired back saying he did not have it and had never heard of it."

"This was given for what?" Dr. Münsterberg asked.

"For a boy with a very obstinate leg sore," Dr. Ketchum said.

"We took a third reading. This time a shelf in the back of the Louisville drugstore was named. There, behind another preparation—which was named—would be found a bottle of 'Oil of Smoke,' so the reading said. I wired the information to the manager of the Louisville store. He wired me back, 'Found it.' The bottle arrived in a few days. It was old. The label was faded. The company which put it up had gone out of business. But it was just what he said it was, 'Oil of Smoke.'"

"Very interesting," Dr. Münsterberg said. "Very interesting."

Leslie Cayce cleared his throat and spat again into the cuspidor.

"I remember a case," he said, "when the boy was in Bowling Green . . . "

*   *   *

The young man sat at the kitchen table of the Cayce home on West Seventh Street, looking miserable, staring into the cup of coffee set before him. His mother, a gray-haired woman with a tired, pretty face, sat opposite him, looking at his downcast head and bent shoulders.

"I don't know what happens to all the pairs of rubbers you get," she said. "You'll be lucky if you don't catch cold, walking two miles to get here and two miles back again in a snowstorm with nothing on your feet but those light shoes."

"It wasn't snowing when I started," he said.

"You should wear rubbers anyhow. The ground is cold and damp even when there isn't snow."

She smiled.

"Well, I'm glad you came, anyhow. It's nice to see you. I know you're working too hard, staying at the studio all day and being up with Gertrude at night. You shouldn't bother even to talk with these people who come here to do their so-called 'investigations.' If you ask me I think most of them are bigger fakes than the poor soul they try to bedevil. They go and get a little learning and then run around being superior to everybody else."

"He didn't bother me, mother, except to start me bothering myself again. I could see his viewpoint: standing there, asking me questions, and comparing the answers with what he knows to be true in science. I kept realizing more and more that the only answer that to me would answer the whole thing satisfactorily would just make him certain that I'm crazy."

His mother nodded.

"Everybody takes it for granted—even the best Christians, the ministers and missionaries—that the things that happened in the days of the Bible and the days of the saints can't happen now," she said.

He shook his head gloomily, agreeing with her.

"Suppose I had said to him, 'Dr. Münsterberg, when I was quite young I became attached to the Bible. I resolved to read it once for every year of my life. When I was twelve years old I finished it for the twelfth time . . . reckon I whizzed through it most of those times, reading the parts I liked best.

"'I had built a little playhouse for myself in the woods on a creek that ran through the old Cayce place, by a bend at the willows. Every afternoon I went there to read my favorite book. One spring day when I was reading the story of Manoah for the thirteenth time, I looked up and saw a woman standing before me.

"'I thought it was my mother, come to fetch me home for the chores. Then I saw that she was not my mother, and that she had wings on her back. She said to me, "Your prayers have been answered, little boy. Tell me what it is you want most of all, so that I may give it to you." I was very frightened, but after a minute I managed to say, "Most of all I would like to be helpful to other people, especially children." Then she disappeared.'

"Suppose I told him that, and then, how the next day in school I couldn't spell a word, and was kept after school, and how that night I slept on my spelling book and knew everything in the book when I woke up. What would he say to that?"

Wistfully his mother looked at him.

"I reckon they'd have the wagon after you and send you up the road to the asylum," she said. "But to me it's the most beautiful story I've ever heard. I remember the first day you told it to me . . . the day it happened, before you even knew it meant anything. And we never told it to anyone else . . . You were so solemn, and so worried about what it meant. And you looked so angelic. I prayed then that you would always remain that way."

He was embarrassed and drank his coffee noisily.

"That's the trouble," he said. "If it had happened to an angel it would be all right. But I'm no angel. There are so many people who are better than I am. Why did it happen to me, unless it's the work of the devil?"

His mother got up and took her Bible from the kitchen shelf.

"Good men," she said, "always worry about that. You'll find it in here"—she tapped the Bible—"everywhere you look. You know that. It's the people who are actually the tools of the devil who never worry about whether they are wrong or right. They're sure they are right."

"But we're sure the readings are right . . . "

"So long as you are right, son, they will be right. The devil cannot speak through a righteous man. I saw the Dietrich girl on the street yesterday. She's a beautiful girl, and as bright as can be. There's proof on every street in this town that the readings are right."

She opened the Bible and turned to the Gospel of St. John.

"We read this together the day you had the vision. I found it for you, remember? It's in the sixteenth chapter.

"'Verily, verily, I say unto you, Whatsoever ye shall ask the Father in my name, he will give it you. Hitherto have ye asked nothing in my name: ask, and ye shall receive, that your joy may be full.'"

"Yes, I remember," he said. "St. John: 'Let not your heart be troubled . . . In my Father's house are many mansions: if it were not so, I would have told you. I go to prepare a place for you . . . that where I am, there ye may be also . . . love me . . . keep my commandments . . . '

"Read from the fifteenth, Mother."

She began: "I am the true vine, and my Father is the husbandman . . . "

When he left she kissed him and patted his shoulder.

"As long as I'm sure of you, I'm sure of the readings," she said, "and I'm still sure of you. Now put on your father's rubbers and don't fuss about it."

He stepped into a night that was quiet, windless. The snow fell straight down, noiselessly. Large, fuzzy flakes fell on his cheeks, his nose, his lips, his eyelashes. He turned east and started the long walk home.

Behind him, down the rolling hills and shallow vales of Christian County, snow fell on the scattered farms of the Cayces, and on the creek that runs through the old place, where it bends to pass the willows.

*   *   *

During the night the snow stopped. Only a light covering was on the ground next morning when Dr. Münsterberg left the hotel and walked to North Main Street. He turned right at the corner

and went halfway down the block, stopping at the red-brick building next to the bookstore. A sign pointed the way upstairs to the
"Cayce Studio." The doctor trudged up the steps and paused in
the hallway. One door led to the studio, another was labeled,
"Edgar Cayce, Psychic Diagnostician."

The doctor opened this door, entering a small reception room.
Beyond it was a large office room. From his place behind a
massive desk Leslie Cayce waved him in.

"Our patient ought to be here soon. Due on the ten o'clock
train from Cincinnati," he said. "Sit down."

The room was elaborately furnished. It held two large rocking chairs, two overstuffed easy chairs, a center table, a desk
and typewriter for a stenographer, and Leslie's desk. All these
were bedded in the pile of an enormous, deep rug.

Dr. Münsterberg sat down but did not remove his coat. He
complained of the cold.

"Edgar's in the studio, developing some plates," Leslie explained. "He'll be here shortly. The reading is set for ten-thirty.
I have ten-twenty now."

"Where will the reading take place?" the doctor asked.

There was a small room opening off the large one. In it was
a high, bare couch, like a doctor's examination table. Near it
was a small table and chair. Straight chairs sat against the wall.
Leslie pointed to the room.

"In there," he said. "Edgar lies on the couch. I stand by him
to give the suggestion and read the questions. The stenographer
sits at the table and takes notes."

"And on the couch he will put himself into this state of self-
hypnosis, only waking when you suggest it?"

"Yes."

"That will be very interesting. That is what I wish to see," the
doctor said.

The door opened and Dr. Ketchum came in. With him was a
sallow-faced man who identified himself as the patient. He was
escorted to the large desk, where he sat with Leslie Cayce, answering questions and filling out several blanks. Dr. Ketchum
chatted with Dr. Münsterberg. In a few minutes a young lady
entered, took a pad and some pencils from the stenographer's

desk, and went into the small room, seating herself at the table.

"And here is the young man himself," Dr. Münsterberg said as the door again opened.

The young man smiled and shook hands. Then he took off his coat and loosened his tie.

"You are going to lie on that couch and sleep?" Dr. Münsterberg asked, pointing into the small room.

"Yes," the young man said. "I'll bring a chair in and you can sit right beside me."

"That will be unnecessary. My seat here is very comfortable. I can see the couch and hear what you say. I will remain here."

The young man went into the small room. Sitting on the side of the couch he unfastened his cuff links and loosened his shoe-laces. Then he swung his legs up, lay flat on his back, closed his eyes, and folded his hands on his abdomen.

Leslie Cayce escorted the patient into the small room and gave him a straight chair. Dr. Ketchum remained in the large room, as a courtesy to the visitor. Leslie Cayce stood by the couch, at his son's right hand, and prepared to read from a small black notebook.

Dr. Münsterberg watched the young man keenly. His respiration deepened gradually, until there was a long, deep breath. After that he seemed to be asleep. Leslie Cayce began to read from the black notebook.

"Now the body is assuming its normal forces and will give the information which is required of it. You will have before you the body of"—he gave the patient's name—"who is present in this room. You will go over the body carefully, telling us the conditions you find there, and what may be done to correct anything which is wrong. You will speak distinctly, at a normal rate of speech, and you will answer the questions which I will put to you."

For several minutes there was silence. Then the young man began to mumble in a voice that sounded faraway and haunting, as if he were speaking from a dream. Over and over again he repeated the patient's name and the phrase, "present in this room."

Suddenly he cleared his throat and spoke distinctly and forcibly, in a tone stronger than that he used when awake.

"Yes, we have the body," he said. "There is a great deal of trouble in this system.

"Along the spine, through the nervous system, through the circulation (which is perverted), through the digestive organs, there is trouble . . . also inflammation in the pelvic organs, trouble with the kidneys and slight inflammation in the bladder. Seems that it starts from digestive disturbances in the stomach. The digestive organs fail to perform their function properly . . . there is lack of secretion along the digestive tract . . .

"The pancreas and liver are also involved . . . "

The voice went on, continuing the diagnosis. Dr. Münsterberg hunched forward in his chair, listening intently. His eyes went back and forth from the young man to the patient.

How did the patient feel?

"There is a dryness of the skin and disturbed lymphatic circulation, aching in the arms and legs, particularly noticeable under the knee, on the side of the leg . . . he feels stretchy when he gets up . . . pains in the arms, pains and a tired feeling between the shoulders and back of the head . . . "

How to cure all this?

Many things were to be done. First: "Get the stomach in better shape . . . we have some inflammation here. Cleanse the stomach: when this is done we will stimulate the liver and the kidneys . . . drink large quantities of water, pure water . . . hitherto we have not had enough liquids in the system to aid nature in throwing off the secretions of the kidneys . . .

"When the stomach is cleansed, not before, give small doses of sweet spirits of niter and oil of juniper . . . use vibrations along the spine . . . not manipulation but vibration . . . all the way up and down from the shoulders to the tip of the spine, but not too close to the brain . . . "

There were other things: exercises, a tonic, a diet. Then the voice said, "Ready for questions." Leslie Cayce read a few which he had written down in the notebook. They were promptly answered. Then the voice said, "We are through for the present."

From the notebook Leslie Cayce read the suggestion that, "Now the body will have its circulation restored for the waking state, and feeling refreshed and with no ill effects, you will wake up."

After about a minute the deep, long, sighing breath that had preceded the sleep was repeated. The young man's eyes opened. He stretched his arms over his head, yawned, rubbed his eyes, and sat up.

The stenographer got up from her seat and came into the large room, where she sat at her typewriter, preparing to transcribe her notes. Leslie Cayce stood by his son, waiting for him to get down off the couch. The patient stood up and stared at him, smiling awkwardly. Dr. Münsterberg suddenly surged up from his chair and walked into the small room.

"What do you think of this man?" he said to the patient.

"Well, he's described my condition and the way I feel better than I could possibly do it myself."

"Then, if I were you—" Dr. Münsterberg was measuring his words carefully—"if I were you I would do exactly as he says. From what I have heard and from the people I have talked with who claim his readings have helped them, I would say that some extraordinary benefits have come from these experiences. Where did you hear of this man?"

"I read about him in one of the Cincinnati papers. I wrote and asked for an appointment. Then I decided to come here for the reading."

"You told, in your letters, of your condition?"

"No, not a thing. I just said I wanted a reading."

"Remarkable, remarkable."

Dr. Münsterberg retreated within himself. His eyes glazed. He stood lost in thought.

The patient turned to the young man on the couch and offered his hand.

"Thank you very much," he said. "I don't know how to express my appreciation, but I'm going to follow all of your suggestions."

The young man shook hands and laughed.

"That's the best way to make me happy," he said. "If this thing works, we want to know about it. If it doesn't work, we want to know about it, even more so, because if it's a fake we want to stop doing it."

"Dr. Ketchum will explain how everything is to be done,"

Leslie Cayce said. He led the patient into the large room.

Dr. Münsterberg watched the young man tie his shoelaces. When the bows were knotted he said:

"Young man, I would like to know more about this. I have never encountered anything quite like it. I would hesitate to pass any opinion without a long and thorough examination. But if it is a trick, I am convinced you are not yourself aware of it."

"If it is a trick, doctor, I would like to know about it before I go too far and cause some harm," the young man said.

"I do not think it will cause harm," the doctor said. "But"— he glanced toward the large room—"I believe you are mixed up with the wrong crowd. This thing should not have a material aspect to it."

Quickly he thrust out his hand, seized the young man's hand and shook it.

"Well, I must be going," he said. "Keep your feet on the ground. Someday you may find yourself. However, if you never accomplish anything more than you did in the Dietrich case, you will not have lived in vain. I must go now."

The young man escorted him from the office. At the stairhead they parted. The doctor expressed a regret.

"It is too bad we could not know more about the so-called powers of your grandfather," he said. "It would be very interesting to know whether heredity is a possible source for this thing."

The young man watched him until he reached the street, then went into the photographic studio. In the great, bare room, with its prop chairs and backdrops stacked in a corner, Mrs. Doolittle was waiting for him with her small son.

"It's his fourth birthday," she explained. "I thought it would be nice if we had a picture taken together."

"Sure," the young man said. "Jim will be tickled. And this is Danny, I reckon."

"I'm Daniel Doolittle," the boy said solemnly.

His mother laughed. "He won't have the nickname," she said.

The young man posed them with Daniel standing beside his mother while she sat sidewise, looking over the back of a light, low parlor chair.

"You're too big to sit in your mother's lap, aren't you?" he said to the boy.

"A gentleman should always stand," Daniel said coldly.

The doctor's last words clung to the young man as he arranged the camera and inserted a plate.

"The so-called powers of your grandfather . . . "

Had his grandfather really possessed psychic powers? Had he inherited his abilty from old Thomas Jefferson Cayce, the tall, kindly man with a beard? His grandmother always told him there was nothing wrong with strange powers so long as they were used in God's work. She must have known about her husband's abilities, if he had them. Only once had she mentioned the subject. "Your grandfather could do certain things, but he always said they came from the Lord and were not his to be showing off and misusing." But what were they? Certainly his grandfather could not have given readings, or he would have done so. He always wanted to help people.

It was hard to remember him. There was the memory of going to the big house and sleeping with grandfather and grandmother, and waking up at night and feeling with his hands for their faces, to find which was which. If there was a beard, it was grandfather.

There was the memory of riding behind him on his horse, of listening to him call to the men in the tobacco fields, of hearing him ask the blessing at Sunday dinner.

There was that sunny, hot day in June, 1881 . . . the eighth of June.

The young man sighted through the camera. He saw Daniel's proud, unsmiling face, with its upturned nose and freckles.

He was just four himself on that June day.

"Quiet now. Watch my hand. Be still," he said.

He was just Daniel's age, and they were riding across the big field, heading for the barns . . .

He pressed the bulb. The shutter clicked.

2

They were riding across the big field, heading for the barns. The men were in the machinery house, repairing a binder, and Grandpa wanted to see how the work was coming. When they came to the pond that sat between the road and the barns the horse stopped.

"Better get down, Old Man," Grandpa said, "I'm going to give this fellow a drink."

He slid down and ran into the tall grass by the water, glad of the chance to get himself cooled off. It was hot up there on the horse, with Grandpa cutting off the breeze and the sun coming down on his bare head. His pants were wet from the lather of the horse and his hands were sweaty from holding Grandpa's belt. He squatted by the edge of the pond and stared into the water, looking for fish.

Grandpa walked the horse into the pond and waited while he drank, sitting in the saddle with his hands on his hips. Suddenly the horse threw up its head, reared, and plunged into deep water. Grandpa held his seat and grabbed the reins, pulling on them with all his strength.

The horse swam to the other side of the pond, galloped to the white rail fence surrounding the barns, tried to jump it, failed, and turned back to the pond. Somehow Grandpa retained his seat.

As the horse entered the water a second time he stumbled and went to his knees. Grandpa was thrown over his head, landing on his back. The horse got to his feet, reared again, and brought his forefeet down on Grandpa's chest. Then he turned and ran off through the field.

Grandpa's head was under the water. Old Man waited for him to get up. He called to him. There was no answer. Grandpa lay still. Old Man ran to get help as fast as he could.

Grandpa was dead. They carried him to the house, and Dr. Kenner came, but Old Man could hear his grandmother crying, and he knew it by the funny look on the faces of his uncles as they came out of the room. He sat in the kitchen and talked to Patsy Cayce about it.

"Grandpa's dead," he said. "The horse killed him. Now will they put him in the ground and bury him?"

"He'll go to the angels, Old Man," Patsy said. "Mistuh T. J. was a fine gentleman, and he'll go to the angels."

"Will I see him again?" Old Man asked.

Patsy bent down and peered at him.

"Sho' you'll see him again," she said. "Yo' has the second sight, ain't yo'?"

He didn't know what she meant by that. Suddenly he wanted his mother.

"I want to go home," he said.

"I'll take yo'," Patsy said.

She took his hand and went with him down to the road and across it, to the little farmhouse where they had been living since his father gave up keeping the store at the crossroads. He told his mother what had happened, and she sat for a long time and told him how death was just going back to heaven, and living down here was just being away from the angels for a while.

"But Grandfather was my friend," he said. "The angels should have known that. I needed him to take me riding; and he was going to teach me to fish and hunt."

"Perhaps he will, even if he is an angel," his mother said.

She took him back to the big house the next day, and he saw them come for the funeral, in their carriages. He saw all his uncles: Edgar, Clinton, Matthew, Robert E. Lee, Lucian, and Delbert Cayce. His granduncles were there, too: George Washington, James Madison, and Franklin Pierce Cayce. His Aunt Ella Cayce Jones was there, and his other uncles, the Majors. There were more aunts, too, from the other Major farms and the other Cayce farms. He couldn't remember all their names, and they all looked the same when they were dressed up anyhow.

He stayed at the house with Patsy when they took Grandpa and went away for the funeral. Standing by the window, watching the carriages disappear down the road, he could smell the apple blossoms and hear the bees rushing to their hives.

It was a lonesome day. He walked home by himself and went to play under the maple trees in front of the house, where his playmates came to meet him when it was too hot to play in the back yard.

They were nice little boys and girls, and he had wondered for a long time why other people didn't see them; but one day he found out that they didn't like other people to see them. His father came to ask to whom he was speaking, and when he turned around to point out his playmates, they were gone. They came back after his father left.

But his mother could see them sometimes, and it made him happy. One day she looked through the window and said, "Your playmates are waiting for you"; and when he went out, there they were, sliding down the hayrick.

*   *   *

It was a beautiful land in which to live. He loved the rolling red and black fields that turned green with crops in the summer, and the patches of forest that were haunted by shy animals and filled with pleasant sounds. He liked the big houses and the clusters of barns that dotted the landscape as far as his eyes could see. He could go to any one of the groups of barns and find some of his uncles or cousins working, and talk to them about fishing and hunting, about tobacco leaf, and about the weather.

There was always something doing in the barns, especially in autumn, when the tobacco was being fired. Great logs were rolled together and kept burning slowly, while the smoke rose to the eaves, where the tobacco hung. He liked to sit and become filled with the odor. He liked the smokehouse, too, where a smudge fire of hickory and sassafras chips sent incense drifting up to the bacon, the sausage, and the shoulders of ham.

In winter there were all sorts of chores to do among the long rows of stalls, in the harness room, among the nests of machinery, and in the room where seed was kept and prepared for spring.

By March the sun was lingering, and the earth turned wet and soft. The brooks became loud and filled their eddies with green scum. Walking along their edges he found crocuses lifting their heads. Shoots of jonquils pushed open the long rows of the gardens.

Soon there was planting, and in May and June the tobacco was put in. By then the woods were a fairyland, full of dogwood and redbud, hickory and red and white oak trees, hazelnut bushes, violets and jack-in-the-pulpits, skunk cabbage, pawpaws, and May apples—the little plant that is the mandrake of the Bible, with a blossom in May and a fruit that is ready to eat in late June and early July.

There were quail and rabbits, which he learned to hunt, as he grew older, with an ancient muzzle-loader. His equipment was a powder horn, a shot flask with caps, and a newspaper for wadding. Sometimes the newspaper was not tightly packed and would stream out when the gun went off, catching fire and making a wonderful sight.

There were plenty of fish, too, both in the brooks and in the ponds. In summer fishing was his greatest joy. Then the days were long and hot and the men worked in the fields. The women stayed indoors, canning fruits and vegetables, and he had no playmates but his sisters—a new one was being born all the time, it seemed to him, until there were four of them: Annie, Mary, Ola, and Sara. From them and their dolls he was glad to get away for long hours beside the water, dreaming as he waited for a fish to come and take the worm he offered. His little play folk came to him there, to be with him.

They were always his size; as he grew older, they grew older; what he wanted to do was always what they wanted to do. Sometimes there were only a few of them, sometimes there were many. One day they would be all boys, another day they would be all girls. They went away when another person came, unless it was little Anna Seay. She was a neighbor's daughter and just his age. The play folk seemed to like her, and she could see them and even talk with them.

She was inquisitive. One day when it rained and they all ran to the playhouse they had built in the top of one of the barns, she asked the play folk why they didn't get wet.

One of them said, "Oh, we can't get wet. We live in the flowers, and the music."

"What music?" Anna asked.

"The music of everything," the little fellow said.

Once he and Anna waded out to an island in the creek at the back of her father's farm, and there, at the water's edge, they found other little folk. But these would have nothing to do with them. They said they had never been girls or boys, and would rather play with the dragonflies.

He wondered if the play folk would ever come back after the cold winter during which Anna and her father both died of pneumonia. He thought that either they would go away with her, or she would come to him with them. When spring came and he went to the woods, they were there, but she was not with them. As he played with them he suddenly realized that they had stopped growing, that they were no longer keeping pace with him. He knew then that he was going to lose them.

He could barely remember the time when he had not known them. He had made a little house under the butter bean vines in the garden, and one day a boy came to play with him. He told his mother about him, but she had not seen him. The next day the boy came back and brought some others with him. It was after that, one day, that his mother saw them.

He dreaded the day when they would not come to meet him, but when it arrived he found that he didn't mind. He listened more intently to the calls of the birds and to the other sounds of the woods, until the living things around him took the place of his invisible friends. The loneliness he had been afraid of never came.

After a while his father began to run the store at the crossroads again. There he sat quiet among the barrels and boxes and listened to the men talk of politics and tobacco and the women discuss styles and the prices of things. He liked to listen to the grownups talk, while they bought yards of cloth, barrels of flour, sacks of rice, herbs, tea, medicine—everything they did not raise or make on their farms. With every dollar's worth of goods they were entitled to a drink from the whisky barrel, which stood in a corner with a dipper hanging above it. The men paid the bills and collected the premiums.

Next to his mother his grandmother was his best friend. His father was nice, but he didn't have time for a small boy; he was always smoking a cigar, pulling on his mustache, and talking to the men about politics; he was justice of the peace now, and everyone called him "squire." Grandmother was always alone, or just fussing around the kitchen with Patsy Cayce; she had lots of time to talk, and she liked him to tell her about seeing Grandpa. He saw Grandpa sometimes in the barns, usually when the tobacco was being fired. He never told anyone but Grandmother; it was a secret between them. Of course Grandpa wasn't really there; he was like the little playmates, you could see through him if you looked real hard.

He found that people meant things to talk about. Grandmother meant talking about Grandpa and about the farm, and about what he would do when he grew up. Patsy Cayce meant talking about good things to eat and about how fat he was getting, except that he wasn't, he was nearly skinny. His father meant talking about growing up and being a big fellow and going to school, and whether he had done his chores. Talking to his sisters meant listening to them tell about their dolls, and what they did that day, and what they were going to do tomorrow. His mother was the only one who didn't mean certain things. They just talked about everything and anything, and that was why he liked her best of all. She never laughed at him or teased him, so he never was afraid to tell her what he thought. She never needed to scold him, because he knew that she didn't like to, so he always did what she asked, and even more. It was nice to be with her and do things for her. She was a good friend.

He was seven before he went to school. That year his aunt, Mrs. Ella Cayce Jones, had a boarder named Mrs. Ellison, who had come from the West, where she had been a Mormon, and, so she said, one of the wives of Brigham Young. She had also been a schoolteacher, and the parents of the neighborhood asked her to conduct a class for the smaller children. Mrs. Jones provided a room in her house, and Squire Cayce brought his son and several daughters to the class.

Mrs. Ellison was a pretty, soft-spoken brunette. She was gentle with the children, and they loved her. The squire's son learned things quickly in her class, because he wanted to please her.

"I know my lesson," he would say, and she would bend down to question him. Then he could smell the sachet she wore, and sometimes her hair would brush against his cheek as she looked over his shoulder and listened to his answers.

But Mrs. Ellison went away when spring came, and in the fall they sent him to the subscription school, by the crossroads near Liberty Church. He was frightened the first day; the desk was too small for his long legs, he didn't know any of the lessons they talked about, and when the teacher spoke to him all the children watched him and he got his feet tangled under the desk and couldn't stand up.

He didn't like school. Every time the teacher called on him he was thinking about something else, and didn't know the answer to the question.

"Don't you ever stop dreaming?" Josie Turner, his first teacher, would say.

He tried to keep his mind on the lesson, but it was no use. While one of the other children was reciting he would look out the window, toward the woods, or his grandmother's, and away his thoughts would go.

Grandmother was building a new house. There had been a big fire the year before, and the old house had burned to the ground. Now the new one was nearly finished, and while the work was going on Squire Cayce decided to put up a place of his own.

He picked a spot just at the edge of the woods that stood between the barns of the big house and the road. It was a pretty place, and when the cottage that he and his brothers built was finished, everyone called it "the little house in the woods."

"Old Man, will you read the next sentence?" Josie Turner would say.

But he would be staring out the window, dreaming of his new home, and the brook that ran through the woods, and would not know the right place in the book.

When Dr. Doolin married Josie Turner and she left the school he had to do better, because his father took over the teaching job. His father was a stern man with a quick temper; he struck first and asked questions afterward. But still he dreamed and didn't know the lessons, until his knuckles had no skin on them for being rapped so often.

It was different when they took him to church. He was ten the first time he went to services at Old Liberty. He liked the story the preacher read from a book and wanted to know all about it. When they got home his mother gave him her Bible, and he read it all the afternoon, until she took it from him.

"You'll burn your eyes out," she said.

"I'll get you a Bible of your own, next time I go to town," his father said. He was proud of his son at last. "I'm glad you like the Bible. It's the greatest book in the world."

Next Sunday at services the preacher said the church needed a sexton.

"What is a sexton?" he asked his mother.

"He's the one who takes care of the building and cleans it up," she answered.

"I'll do it," he said. "I'll be the sexton."

It was a small building, and the work was not hard. He swept the floors, dusted the pews, and fixed the pulpit for the preacher. His father brought him a Bible from town. Mr. Hopper, the owner of the bookstore, had refused to take any money for it when he learned it was for a ten-year-old boy who had asked for it himself.

"Every boy should have a Bible," he told the squire, "and when a boy asks for it, it's a privilege to give it to him."

He wrote the date on the flyleaf—January 14, 1887—and began reading. By the end of June he had gone through the entire book.

That summer the Reverend John T. Hawkins held a series of meetings at Old Liberty, and stayed at the big Cayce house. Sitting by his grandmother's side, the new sexton heard his first theological discussions. He asked questions himself, and when Mr. Hawkins had gone he began to interrogate any preacher who came along. Whenever the officers of Old Liberty got together he was there, and it was he who usually started them discussing the Bible. He asked all of them questions: his granduncles George Washington and Franklin Pierce Cayce; his cousin Isaac H. Cayce; Daniel Owsley; his uncle by marriage, Ed Jones; and any others who would listen and give him answers. Once he had them started he withdrew and listened to the arguments and opinions.

Sometimes the men talked about things he did not understand at all. The congregation of Old Liberty belonged to the Christian Church, a sect of the Presbyterian Church. A branch of it had been founded in North Carolina by Barton W. Stone, and another branch had been founded in Pennsylvania by Alexander Campbell. It was in Old Liberty that these two men met for the first time.

The Christian Church practiced open communion and held the service every Sunday. It was when they talked about this, and about hymn singing and Stone's opinions and Campbell's opinions, that he was puzzled. Then he would quietly move away, open his Bible to a favorite passage, and live in the strength of Samson or David, or help heal the sick and the lame with Jesus.

One day he conceived a great ambition. Often one of the men would say, "Well, I've read the Bible through a dozen times, and it seems to me . . . " or another would say, "As often as I've read the Bible through it never seemed to me that . . . " He wanted to be able to read the Bible through many times. It would be nice if he could say that he had read the Bible, well, say, once for every year of his life. He had heard one of the men say, "I read the Bible through every year," and that gave him the idea. He would read as fast as he could until he had come even with his years, and after that he would have to read it only once a year to keep his record.

As soon as the idea entered his head he turned to Genesis and began the task. From then on he never went anyplace without his Bible, though he generally managed to conceal it so people didn't know he had it with him. He read at every possible moment, giving only the time that was absolutely necessary to his chores and paying almost no attention to his schoolwork, since his father was no longer the teacher.

When spring came he went to the woods behind his new home and built a retreat for himself. It was a lean-to, fashioned of saplings, fir branches, moss, bark, and reeds from the edge of the brook, and it stood by the willows, where the stream took a bend. The water always looked so inviting that he dug himself a well, to act as a filter. There, with the sun shining on him, he sprawled through the long spring and summer afternoons, reading as if possessed. When autumn faded and he had to go indoors, he huddled by the kitchen stove, undistorbed by his mother, who looked over his shoulder now and then to see what chapter he was reading and to whisper something about it that helped him to understand the words.

Again and again he went through the books and chapters, until the pages were as familiar to him as the pictures on the walls of the living room. Each time he waited from day to day with rising excitement for the great climax: the last chapter of Malachi, the end of the Old Testament, when the coming of the Lord was prophesied:

> "For, behold, the day cometh, that shall burn as an oven; and all the proud, yea, and all that do wickedly, shall be stubble: and the day that cometh shall burn them up, saith the Lord of hosts, that it shall leave them neither root nor branch.
>
> "But unto you that fear my name shall the Sun of righteousness arise with healing in his wings; and ye shall go forth, and grow up as calves of the stall."

Just four more verses, after that, and he could turn the page and find, "The New Testament of Our Lord and Saviour Jesus Christ." Then came the first chapter of Matthew:

"The book of the generation of Jesus Christ, the son of David, the son of Abraham . . . "

Then he was happy, because Jesus triumphed over evil, and healed the sick and the blind, and raised the dead. Even when they crucified Him, He rose from the dead and went to live with His Father in heaven. And in St. John He told His disciples how they could also go to heaven, and how all people could go there if they obeyed the law of loving God and each other.

When it was all over and the fiery Book of Revelation was finished he would rush back to the beginning, to be again with his heroes of the wilderness, Babylon, Egypt, and the Promised Land. Cain killed Abel, Noah built the Ark, Hannah bore Samuel, Lot's wife was turned to a pillar of salt . . . on and on marched the heroes and the villains, the wicked and the mighty.

So quickly did he read that, by his own count, he had been

from Adam to John a dozen times by the spring of his thirteenth year. As soon as the weather was good he went back to his retreat in the woods. There, one afternoon in May as he sat at the entrance of the lean-to, reading the story of Manoah, he became aware of the presence of someone else. He looked up.

A woman was standing before him. At first he thought she was his mother, come to bring him home for the chores—the sun was bright and his eyes did not see well after staring at the book. But when she spoke he knew it was someone he did not know. Her voice was soft and very clear; it reminded him of music.

"Your prayers have been heard," she said. "Tell me what you would like most of all, so that I may give it to you."

Then he saw that there was something on her back; something that made shadows behind her that were shaped like wings.

He was frightened. She smiled at him, waiting. He was afraid his voice would not make a sound, the way it did in dreams. He opened his mouth and heard himself saying:

"Most of all I would like to be helpful to others, and especially to children when they are sick."

He was thinking of Jesus and the disciples; he wanted to be like a disciple.

Suddenly she was no longer there. He looked at the place where she had stood, trying to see her in the beams of light, but she was gone.

He took his Bible and ran home, anxious to tell his mother about it. He found her in the kitchen, alone. She sat down at the table and listened to him.

When he finished he was suddenly ashamed.

"Do you think I've been reading the Bible too much?" he said. "It makes some people go crazy, doesn't it?"

She reached over and took the book from his hands. Turning its pages to the Gospel of St. John she read to him:

" . . . Verily, verily, I say unto you, Whatsoever ye shall ask the Father in my name, he will give it you.

"Hitherto have ye asked nothing in my name: ask, and ye shall receive, that your joy may be full."

She looked at him and smiled.

"You're a good boy, you want to help others, why shouldn't

your prayers be heard?" she said. "I don't think you need to stop reading the Bible. I'll know if something is going wrong with you. But we had better not tell anyone about this."

"No, I just wanted to tell you, so I'd know what to think. But what does it mean?" he asked.

She got up and went to where he was sitting and put her arms around him.

"It might mean that you're going to be a doctor, perhaps a very famous one, who will have great success with children," she said. "It might mean that you're going to be a preacher or a missionary. Sometimes, you know, men study medicine and then go out as missionaries, so they carry the word of God and help the sick in heathen lands at the same time."

"That's what I'd like to be, a missionary," he said.

"Well, let's get a start by cleaning the milk pails," she said. "Cleanliness is next to godliness."

That night he slept very little; the next day he was more than ordinarily dull and listless in school. The teacher, his uncle Lucian, asked him to spell "cabin." He couldn't do it. Uncle Lucian was irritated.

"Stay after school and write it five hundred times on the blackboard," he said.

It took a long time to write the word so many times. He was late getting home. There was no time to go to the woods; he had to hurry to get the afternoon chores finished before the supper chores were ready.

Squire Cayce was furious when he came in. The family was disgraced, he said. Uncle Lucian had told him what a stupid son he had. All during supper the squire talked about it. After supper he took the spelling book and the boy and went into the parlor.

"You're going to start learning your lessons or I'll know the reason why," he said. "Sit down here now and get to business."

It was a long evening. Time after time the squire would take the book and ask the lesson. The answers would be wrong. He would hand back the book and say grimly, "All right. I'll ask it again in another half hour."

The girls and the mother went to bed. At ten o'clock the answers were still wrong. The squire, exasperated, slapped the boy out of his chair, then hauled him up from the floor and set him down again.

"One more chance," he said.

At half past ten the answers were again wrong. Again the boy was knocked out of his chair, landing on the floor. Slowly he got to his feet. He was tired and sleepy.

As he sat in the chair he thought he heard something. His ears were ringing from the blow that had floored him, but he heard words, inside him. It was the voice of the lady he had seen the day before. She was saying, "If you can sleep a little, we can help you."

He begged his father for a rest; just for a few minutes. He would know the lesson then, he was sure.

"I'm going into the kitchen," the squire said. "When I come back I'm going to ask you that lesson once more. It's your last chance. You'd better know it."

He went out of the room. The boy closed his spelling book, put it back of his head, curled up in the chair, and almost immediately was asleep.

When the squire returned from the kitchen he snatched the book, waking him up.

"Ask me the lesson. I know it now," the boy said.

The squire began. The answers came quickly, certainly. They were correct.

"Ask me the next day's lesson. I'll bet I know that, too," he said.

The squire asked the next lesson. All the answers were correct.

"Ask me anything in the book," the boy said.

The squire skipped through the pages at random, asking the hardest words he saw. The answers were correct. The boy began to tell where the words occurred on the page and what the illustrations were.

"There's a picture of a silo on that page. The word 'synthesis' is just under it. S-y-n-t-h-e-s-i-s."

The squire closed the book and slammed it on the table. His patience was exhausted.

"What kind of nonsense is this?" he roared. "You knew that

lesson all the time. You knew the whole book. What's the idea? Do you want to stay where you are in school so you won't have any more studying to do? Are you as lazy as all that? Do you want to stay in the Third Reader all your life?"

"I didn't know it until I slept on it, honest," the boy said.

The squire knocked him out of the chair again.

"Go to bed," he said, "before I lose my temper!"

The boy ran upstairs, taking his book with him. Under the covers he prayed his thanks to the lady and hugged the speller.

Next morning after his father had gone he gave the book to his mother and asked her to listen to his recitation of the lesson. He still knew it. He told her what had happened and she kissed him and told him she was sure the lady was keeping her promise.

In school he was brilliant at spelling, but woeful as ever in his other subjects. He took the books home with him and put them under his pillow before going to sleep. Then he thought about the lady and prayed to her. Next day when Uncle Lucian asked him a question in geography the picture of a page in the textbook leaped to his mind, and he read the answer from it.

It was the same in other subjects. Each day he took his books home, and at night he slept on them. He had an idea that the first time was all that was necessary, but he wanted to take no chances. Besides, it would make everyone believe that he studied hard if he were seen with a lot of books.

He began to make progress as a scholar. Uncle Lucian advanced him a grade and spoke to the squire about it.

"He seems to know everything in the book, Leslie. No matter what I ask him, he has the right answer. It's almost as if he were reading it. But I know he doesn't cheat. He keeps his books in his desk and stands up and looks right at me when he recites."

The squire took his son aside when he got home and asked a few questions.

"What's going on? How do you do it?" he said. "Is there anything to that sleeping business you told me about?"

"That's all I do, just sleep on them. When I wake up I know everything in the book. I don't know how it happens, but it works."

The squire stroked his mustache.

"I hope you're not crazy," he said.

3

The presidential campaign of 1892 was exciting for Christian County. Cleveland was trying to regain the office he had lost to Harrison in 1888, and for a running mate he had Adlai E. Stevenson, a native of the county. Everyone turned out to support the local boy who had made good, and Squire Cayce, who loved politics in any form, made speeches, argued at the crossroads store, and promised to take his fifteen-year-old son to Hopkinsville, the county seat, for the celebration.

Cleveland won and plans wore made for a parade and a monster party. The day before it happened the new teacher at the school, Mr. B. F. Thomb, called the squire's son to his desk at recess time.

"Old Man," he said, "I've been talking to your father. I remarked to him that you were my best student; that you always knew your lessons. He told me that you go to sleep to learn them. Others have mentioned the same thing. What is it? How do you do it?"

"I don't know, really . . . I just seemed to know once that, if I put my head on a book and went to sleep, I'd know the lesson. Then I did it with other books, and it worked. I don't know what it is."

He was embarrassed, blushing.

"There's nothing odd about it," Mr. Thomb said. "Don't feel that you are different. There are many strange things in life that we know nothing about. How do you see your lessons, in pictures?"

"Yes, I see pictures of the pages."

"Well, I won't bother you any more about it. But I think it's something that should be studied. There are so many things we don't know about.

"Don't let it worry you, and don't stop doing it. There's no harm in it. Now run along and play with the rest of the boys."

He ran out and joined the game of Old Sow—a variation of Prisoner's Base—that the boys were playing. He ran faster than usual, and threw the ball harder, trying to forget the feeling that came over him when he thought about being different from others. People were always staring at him now, and the boys would holler, "Hey, Old Man, how about sleeping on our lessons for us?"

It was because his father told everybody about it. The squire was proud of his son, and wanted him to show folks how smart he was, and how quickly he could learn anything by sleeping on it.

He burned with shame every time he thought about it.

"Run, Old Man! Run!" the boys shouted.

He ran, and made it, but the ball hit him on the end of the spine just as he reached the base.

The bell rang then, and they ran into the classroom. All during the afternoon he acted queerly, laughing and giggling, making faces, throwing spitballs. Mr. Thomb was distressed, but did not keep him after school, thinking his questions had upset the boy.

Going home he rolled on the ground, jumped into ditches, and stood in the middle of the road, stopping buggies and teams with upraised hands. At home his mother had put some green coffee beans in a pan and was roasting them on the kitchen stove. He took the pan in his hands, unmindful of its heat, and went into the yard. There he sowed the coffee as if it were seed.

During supper he threw things at his sisters, laughed uproariously, and made faces at his father. The squire put him to bed.

When he was under the covers he became serious. He gave instructions for a poultice, to be put on the back of his head, near the base of the brain. He was suffering from shock, he said, and would be all right in the morning if the poultice were applied.

"What shall I do?" the squire said to his wife.

"Make it," his wife said. "There isn't anything in it that can hurt him: corn meal, onions, and some herbs. Come and help me. I'll fix it."

When it was ready they put it on the back of his head, and
when he was satisfied with its position he relaxed and went to
sleep. Several times during the night he shouted, "Hurrah for
Cleveland!" and pounded the wall with his fist, but did not wake
up. To keep him from harming himself the squire pulled the bed
away from the wall.

When he opened his eyes the next morning neighbors and
relatives were sitting around the bed, keeping vigil.

"What's the matter?" he said. "Did I get run over?"

He remembered nothing from the time he had left Mr. Thomb
at recess. The squire told him what had happened.

"You told us it was a shock, and to put the poultice on the
back of your neck. How do you feel now?"

"I'm fine!" He jumped out of bed. "Can I still go to the celebration in town tonight?"

The squire beamed at his relatives and friends.

"Cured himself," he said. "Ever see the beat of it? I tell you
he's the greatest fellow in the world when he's asleep.

"Sure, we're going to the celebration, Old Man! We've got
two things to celebrate: Adlai Stevenson getting elected vice-
president and you getting better!"

The relatives and friends said nothing. With thoughtful faces
they watched the boy get dressed, then filed out of the room and
went downstairs. They did not talk among themselves until they
were out of the house.

Hopkinsville had its gayest time in generations that night.
Torchlights illuminated the streets, banners and flags and bunting
turned the business section into a carnival lot, whisky flowed as
easily as talk. Crowds jammed the sidewalks, overflowed to the
roads, inundated the saloons. The squire and his son wandered
about; the squire talked, took an occasional drink, listened to
his friends, laughed at their jokes. The boy said nothing. He
was having a good time with his eyes and ears. He even liked
the fist fights that broke out periodically. But when one man
pulled a gun from his pocket and shot another man who was
only ten feet away from where he stood with his father, a wave
of sickness swept over him and he wanted to go home. While
men and policemen milled around he sat down on the curb.

When the excitement was over the squire found him and patted him fondly on the head.

"Well, it's been quite a day, Old Man," he said. "Let's go back to the wagon. These people are getting too drunk. Somebody's apt to get hurt."

* * *

This was to be his last year in school. He was sixteen in March and big enough to do a man's work. His Uncle Lee gave him a job. Uncle Lee was farming the old place for Grandmother.

All that remained of his boyhood was the closing exercises at school. He was to recite a piece; he began searching through his English books, trying to decide which selection he liked best. His father settled the matter for him.

On one of his trips to town the squire met Congressman Jim MacKenzie, who had won fame for himself in Washington by fighting to have the tax removed from quinine. He had made a fiery speech in the House of Representatives and had been nicknamed "Quinine Jim." President Cleveland was sending him to Peru as minister, and he was at home for a visit before sailing to take over his post. He and the squire had a drink to celebrate the honor to Christian County.

The squire, pressed for something to match his friend's distinction, bragged about his son. The boy could remember anything, he said, if only he were allowed to sleep on it. The congressman was skeptical. The squire insisted. The congressman demanded proof. The squire offered to produce it: his son was to make a declamation at the school exercises in a few days. He would let the congressman select the declaration; the boy would sleep on it; the congressman could witness the results.

That gave the congressman an idea. The declamation would have to be long enough, and difficult enough, so the boy could not ordinarily learn it in the short time remaining before the exercises. Suppose he chose his own quinine speech? Would that be satisfactory?

The squire expanded. Not only would it be satisfactory, he would go further. He would promise not even to show the boy the speech. He would not even let him sleep on it.

Then how, the congressman wanted to know, could the boy learn it?

"I," the squire said, "will read it to him while he is asleep."

Thus it was agreed. The next night the boy went to sleep in an easy chair in the living room, first thinking about the lady and asking her, in his mind, to help him. Then, while he slept, the squire read the speech. It took him more than an hour. When he finished and the boy awakened, the test was given. The boy began to recite the speech. He knew it perfectly.

To make certain, the squire repeated his reading of the text the next night, and again the next. On the following night the exercises took place, with the congressman present. It was a hot night. There were other speeches, other declamations; awards were given, diplomas passed out. Then the boy recited his piece. It took him an hour and a half. The congressman and the squire were delighted. Everyone else had the fidgets.

So the summer came, and manhood. He didn't feel grown up, but he worked all day with the men in the fields, and they treated him as an equal. He ate most of his meals at the big house, and talked to Grandmother a good deal. She was sick; she had taken to her bed the day the tobacco was put in, in May. His mother nursed her, and in the evenings, when his mother went home to look after the girls, he would sit by her bedside and tell her about the day's work on the farm. Then she would tell him the things she had found in her thoughts during the day.

They were old things, queer things, things about farming and weather, things about the family and its members, funny things that had happened to her when she was young. Fondly she took them out of her mind for him to see, caressing them with the gentle hands of memory.

She told him all about the Cayces. She herself was one of the family. Her mother had been a granddaughter of old Shadrach Cayce, who left Powhatan County to live in Franklin, Tennessee.

"One of Shadrach's brothers, Archibald, went to South Carolina," she said. "He founded the town of Cayce in that state. It's not much of a place now, but there's a famous Cayce house there, with a desk from Cornwallis's tent in it, and it was from that place that a young lady named Emily Geiger set out one day on a ride that was a lot more exciting than Paul Revere's."

And she told him, while twilight faded and the odor of wisteria came into the room on the night air, of how pretty, eighteen-year-old Emily Geiger in 1781 rode a hundred miles on horseback from Cayce to Camden, carrying a message from General Greene to General Sumter, advising that Lord Rawdon's forces were divided and could perhaps be defeated if both American armies moved quickly and joined each other for the attack.

General Greene could find no one to take the message, because that hundred miles was through the worst Tory country in the south. When she heard this, Emily Geiger volunteered, and insisted that she be allowed to go. She was familiar with the road, she said, and the British, who were in command of it all the way, would be less likely to stop her than a man.

"She started on a good, strong horse, and everything went well until the afternoon of the second day. Then she was stopped by the British, questioned, and detained for search. While the men were waiting for two Tory women to arrive and conduct the search, Emily, alone in a room, tore the message into bits and ate it. She had committed it to memory of course.

"They had to let her go after searching her and finding nothing, and Lord Rawdon—it was his men who stopped her—gave her an escort to the home of some of her relatives, a few miles away. She would not stay the night, though, fearing pursuit, so after dark she mounted a fresh horse, rode all night and all the next morning, and on the afternoon of the third day reached the territory held by General Sumter. She delivered her message, the Americans got together and won the battle, and if that isn't better than Paul Revere, you tell me."

"That's a grand story. The Cayces have been in history all right, haven't they?"

"Then there was Pleasant Cayce, my granduncle, one of Shadrach's sons," she went on. "He went into Fulton County, Kentucky, and founded the town of Cayce there.

"William came here, of course, but his brother George went out to Illinois."

She laughed a little, and the great feather mattress trembled on its springs.

"The only word your great-grandfather ever heard from his brother was a letter in which George complained that he was being cheated out of some fence rails and was going to put the law on a fellow named Abraham Lincoln.

"Old William used to laugh over that. He had a great sense of humor, in some ways. I think it was a joke with him to name all his sons after Presidents—George Washington, James Madison, Franklin Pierce, and your grandfather, Thomas Jefferson Cayce. Everyone said it was because he was such a great patriot, but I always had a sneaking suspicion that he wanted to make sure none of his boys would ever be president, so he named them after fellows who already had been elected."

She sighed and let her smile run back into the lines of her tired face.

"I reckon I shouldn't be talking that way, when I'm going to meet my Maker so soon. But somehow I can't be solemn about it. They must have some good laughs for themselves up there. How could they stand it? It won't be heaven to me or your grandfather, either, if we can't have a good laugh now and then."

"You'll be up and around for the harvest," he said. "Mother says you're getting better every day."

"No, she doesn't, and you needn't try to fool me. I'm not a bit afraid to go. Why should I be? I've lived a long time. Why, I was an old woman the day you were born.

"I remember the day—March 18, 1877. It was a lovely Sunday. We had all the boys at the dinner table except Edgar and Leslie. They were the only two who were married then. Ella was there. She told us Dr. Doolin had gone over to the house. My goodness, your father was only twenty-three and your mother was barely twenty-one when you were born! Do you realize that?

"We all went over after dinner. The boys stood around on the porch with your father, and I could hear them arguing about crops and politics. It was so warm and sunny we opened some of the windows.

"I heard the first squall you made. It was at three o'clock, exactly. And I gave you your first bath."

She sighed again. Then the smile came back.

"It's wonderful what grows from those little things—babies. They're so little and so ugly and so helpless! And now this one is working on the farm for me: a grown man!"

She reached out and patted his arm.

"It isn't too hard for you, is it?"

"No, I like it."

"Tomorrow is the anniversary of your grandfather's death, the eighth of June, twelve years ago. You know the peach tree he planted in the orchard? The last tree he put there? I've shown it to you."

"Yes, I know it."

"Bring me a peach from it tomorrow. It's the last one I'll ever eat from that tree, I know. Will you bring it?"

"Sure, but you'll be eating a lot of them yet."

"Bring me one tomorrow; we'll see."

He brought her a peach from the tree the next evening. She ate it slowly, while he sat watching. When it was finished she gave him the pit and told him to plant it.

"Just for my sake," she said, "and your grandfather's."

She settled into her memories again.

"Your grandfather was a very remarkable man, you know. Anything he touched would grow. He had more than a green thumb; it was like magic. All the wells in this neighborhood were dug where he told the men to dig them, and they always found water.

"Many's the day a neighbor would come and ask him to locate a well for him. Off he'd go, and somewhere along the way he'd cut a hazel twig, with a good fork. Then he'd walk around the ground on which the farmer wanted the well, until the twig told him where to stop. The little branches on the fork of the twig would twitch. 'Right here,' he'd say, and there they'd dig, and there they'd find water."

"I've tried that. I tried it out in the woods behind the little house, and when I dug down a ways I found water."

"Yes, I believe you can do it. You're a great deal like your grandfather. It may be that you have the same powers. It may be that you have different ones. Your grandfather could never sleep on a book and wake up knowing what was in it. He fell asleep over many a one, but when he woke up he didn't know any more than before.

"But he could see things, the way you tell me you can see him in the barns sometimes. 'Oh, they're there for everyone to see,' he would say to me. 'It just needs a sharp eye.' But it needs more than that. It takes second sight, whatever that is.

"He could do things, too. He could make tables and chairs move, and brooms dance, without touching them. But he never made a show of it. I don't believe anyone ever saw him do it but myself. He used to say to me, 'Everything comes from God. Some men are more intelligent than others, and can make more money. Some can sing divinely, some can write poetry. I can make things grow. The Lord said there is set before each of us good and evil, for us to choose. So if I spend all my time making brooms dance and doing tricks for people's entertainment, that would be choosing evil.' "

"I reckon Grandpa was right," he said. "I don't like to do tricks for people, like that speech I had to recite. I'd like to help people and be a minister."

"You will, perhaps. But your first duty is to your mother. You're her only son, and she's a lovely woman. Sons mean more to a mother than anything else—more than daughters or husbands. Your father is a good man, but he has a large family and his job is a hard one. Sons can do little things for their mothers that husbands don't know how to do, anyhow. You must always be good to your mother."

"It's easy to promise you that. It's what I like to do best!"

"I hope you always will. Perhaps you'll be going up to town to live soon. Your father wants to go. Perhaps he should. He can do anything with people—he likes them and they like him. He can't do a thing with land or animals. It's strange, when he comes from generations of farmers. But perhaps he should go; perhaps he would do well in business or politics.

"Anyhow, you look after your mother. And don't be afraid of that power you have, whatever it is. Just don't misuse it. If you hear voices, compare what they have to say with what Jesus says in the Bible. If you see things, compare them with what you know to be beautiful and good. Compare everything with what your mother does and says and is. Never do anything that will hurt another person. Don't be afraid. Don't be proud."

She talked on quietly, her hand resting lightly on his arm.

"You will be meeting girls, and wanting them. You'll think they are wonderful creatures, and some of them are. But remember that they'll be wanting you, too. A man wants to fall in love . . . a woman wants to get married. You shouldn't be possessed too much. You're the kind that must keep a certain part free . . . maybe it's because it belongs to God, and shouldn't be taken by a woman. She's only flesh and blood . . . but he never thinks so . . . he wants to give her everything he has . . . even the littlest thoughts he thinks . . . "

She died on the day in August when they began to harvest the tobacco. He was holding her hand when it stopped trembling and turned cold. They buried her next to Grandpa, in the cemetery with all the other Cayces.

That was also the summer he fell in love. He was different from other boys, he knew. He didn't play baseball, or wrestle; he had never run a race, or spun a top, or picked a fight. He had never cared for girls. But now there was one he worshiped, and whenever he could he went to see her; sometimes he took her for rides in Grandmother's best buggy; sometimes they went on picnics or hayrides. He tried to act very grown-up for her. He smoked—but he didn't tell her that it was necessity: the odor of the tobacco in the fields and barns nauseated him so that to protect himself he had taken up the use of a pipe, which somehow cured the trouble. He talked about crops. He told her about the Sunday-school class he was teaching at Old Liberty. But on parties and picnics when the other boys got together and discussed ball games, horse races, county politics, gambling, and cockfights, he had to be silent. He didn't belong to that world.

One Sunday there was a picnic in the woods behind the little house where he lived. He led her to the bend of the creek at the willows, where he had built his lean-to and read the Bible. He had not been there for many years. The lean-to had fallen in, the well was filled up.

They sat by the creek and talked. He told her of his ambition to become a minister, of his love for her, even of his vision. She was the first to share it besides his mother. He proposed to her.

"I know we're only youngsters," he said, "but I'm going to work hard and amount to something.

"Maybe I'll be the best preacher in the county. We can have a church like Old Liberty, and a farm, with tobacco and all kinds of crops. We'll have a flower garden, and horses to ride, too."

She tossed a stone into the water. Suddenly she laughed.

"I like you," she said, giving his arm a squeeze, "but you're so funny. Only the colored people talk about seeing things that aren't there.

"Besides"—she looked away from.him—"I don't want to be a preacher's wife. It isn't any fun. I like to go to parties, and dances, and things. What's the use of being stuffy? I want a man—a real man of the world; one who will do manly things instead of just sitting around dreaming all the time."

She went to the water's edge.

"Then he'll come back and take me in his arms and kiss me and force me to love him. You would never do that. You'd rather read the Bible!"

He was shocked. He tried to argue. He told her that he wanted to love her the way she wanted to be loved.

"I don't believe it," she said. "And anyway—Pa says you're not right in the head."

He stopped arguing when he heard that. Her father was one of the doctors in the neighborhood. He talked with all the farmers. They must think the same thing.

They walked back to the other picnickers. He took her home and said good-bye. Her mother didn't ask him to stay for Sunday supper. He realized now that she had never been cordial, had never asked him for dinner, or even into the kitchen for a glass of milk.

That night he lay awake, wondering if he were crazy. He thought about the vision of the lady, of sleeping on his lessons, and what they said he had done after being hit by the ball at school. He thought about his love for the Bible. No other boy in the neighborhood cared about it at all.

When he finally fell asleep he dreamed. The next morning he remembered everything about it, and told it to his mother.

He was walking through a grove of small, cone-shaped trees. The ground was blanketed with vines bearing white starflowers. A girl walked by his side, clinging to his arm. Her face was veiled. They were happy, content, in love.

The ground sloped downward to a stream of clear water running over white sand studded with pebbles. Small fish swam in the water. He and the girl crossed to the other side and met a male figure, bronze skinned, naked except for a loincloth, and winged at the feet and shoulders. He carried a cloth of gold. They stopped when they came to him.

"Clasp your right hands," he said.

Over the joined hands he laid the cloth of gold.

"United you may accomplish anything," he said. "Alone you will do very little."

He disappeared.

They walked on and came to a road. It was muddy. While they looked at it, wondering how to cross it without soiling their clothes, the figure appeared again.

"Use the cloth," he said. Then he disappeared again.

They waved the cloth. They were on the other side of the road.

They walked on until they came to a cliff. It was smooth, offering no foothold. He found a knife, sharp enough to cut niches in the soft rock. He cut steps, and mounted the face of the cliff by them, drawing his companion up after him. Higher and higher they went, but the top was still out of reach.

There the dream ended.

"What do you think it means?" he asked his mother.

She laughed and gave him a pat on the shoulder.

"That one is easy," she said, "even for me. It's about your wife-to-be. You see, she's veiled, because you haven't met her yet. But she is waiting for you somewhere, and already your souls are in love and happy together. As soon as you meet her you will both know that. It's what we call falling in love, but it's just two souls that were destined to be together, recognizing each other.

"You cross the stream of water easily. That's the proposal, or engagement. It's so easy, and everything seems clear. Then you are married. The marriage bond is the cloth of gold, and whenever you get into a hard place, the love you have for each other, and your faithfulness to that bond, will see you through When two people are truly in love and are good and faithful Christians, nothing can stop them.

"And the cliff, of course, is your job of making a living and providing for your wife and family. That's why you had to do the work of cutting the steps.

"Now, don't you think that's a good explanation?"

"Yes, that sounds like the right interpretation. That must be what it meant, all right."

"Well, drink your coffee, then, and stop dreaming. Lee will be wondering what happened to you."

He felt much better.

*   *   *

The year turned its face to the west and died. With his mother gone, the squire's last interest in farming faded. He decided to move to town, and his wife agreed with him. In Hopkinsville the girls could attend school regularly, and the terms would not be hampered by planting and harvesting. Moreover, it offered more opportunities for some sort of work when they were finished with school, and provided a better environment for meeting prospective husbands.

The squire decided to sell insurance, and also got a job with the building and loan association.

"Well, Old Man," he said to his son, "what are you going to do? Coming up to the big city to seek your fortune?"

He would have liked to go to town, if it meant more school, but it didn't. It just meant a job, probably in a tobacco warehouse.

"I think I'll stay on the farm," he said. "Uncle Clint wants me to go over with him. I'd like to learn farming before I try anything else. Then I can always come back to it."

"Excellent idea," the squire said. "Well, we'll miss you."

They left on a cold January day. All their belongings were piled in one wagon, with the girls holding it down. Behind, and dropping more and more in the rear as mile after mile went by, he drove their cow. They reached town at dusk, and he stayed with them that night in the house they had taken on West Seventh Street. There was a barn for the cow, and the back yard stretched, unfenced, to good grazing land.

Next morning he walked through the town, looking for a lift down to the country. The place was too busy; he didn't like it. He got a ride with one of his cousins and went back to his uncle Clint's farm.

He liked his work, especially when spring came and he could get out of the barns and into the fields. He was alone most of the day then, plowing, fallowing, planting. He had lots of time to think about being a preacher, and about the vision, and the dream of the veiled lady and the cloth of gold. Mostly he thought about being a preacher.

He knew he had to get more schooling, but he thought he could manage that. First he would save some money of his own. Then, if he had a start, so that no one could doubt his good intentions, perhaps some friend, like Mr. Wilgus for instance, would let him borrow some. He could work while he was going to school, and if the lady continued to help him he could sleep on his lessons and get through all the classes before the regular time.

Mr. Wilgus still came down to hunt with him, and always looked at the little mark on his face where a piece of shot from his gun was lodged. It wasn't anything; one day he had been too close when Mr. Wilgus fired at a bird, and a piece of lead bounced and hit him. But Mr. Wilgus always seemed to be sorry about it.

"I hate to take you out with me when I'm going to shoot," Mr. Wilgus would say, "but there's no use in going alone, because by myself I never find anything."

Yes, Mr. Wilgus would probably help him, and some of the preachers would do what they could, because they seemed to like him. In the meantime he could keep reading the Bible and teaching Sunday school. Someday his chance would come. His father might even make a lot of money in Hopkinsville.

One day in late August Uncle Clint sent him to plow a corn-field, giving him a mule that belonged to one of the men who had been hired for the tobacco harvesting. All day he followed behind the mule, guiding the plow. Once he stopped to mend it. Kneeling, he suddenly was aware of a presence. He knew who it was, though he saw nothing.

"Leave the farm," she said. "Go to your mother. She needs you. You are her best friend; she misses you. Everything will be all right."

He knew that she was gone, after that, but he hesitated to look up. When he got to his feet he grasped the plow handles and kept his eyes on the ground.

When evening came he mounted the mule and drove to the farmhouse. As he came up the men looked at him queerly. The owner of the mule ran to him.

"Get down!" he shouted. "That mule will kill yon!"

He got down, bewildered.

"She's never been ridden," the man said. "Won't let anybody get on her. What happened?"

"Nothing. I just got on and rode her home."

One of the men said, "She's too tired to fuss. Good time to break her in. Give her a try yourself."

The owner mounted the mule. The mule threw him off. The men looked at the boy. Sick at heart, he turned and walked away. After supper he packed his belongings and walked to town.

4

It was a lonely life in town. He had no friends, there was nothing to keep him up at night, and no one got up until seven o'clock in the morning. From long habit he rose at dawn, though his new job at the bookstore did not require that he be at work until eight. To fill in the time he did chores for his mother. He liked to bring in the cow and milk her: she was an old friend, and she seemed to sympathize with his distrust of the town. She didn't like it either. Frequently she wandered during the night from the back yard to the bottom land a few hundred yards from the house, where no habitations were visible and a creek like the one at home meandered along.

He went there to hunt her one spring morning and saw a man sitting by the creek, reading a book. He was a well-dressed man, apparently not from Hopkinsville. He looked as if he might have come from a big city, such as Louisville or Cincinnati. He looked up from his book and smiled.

"Looking for a cow?" he asked.

"Yes, sir." The book he was reading had a familiar look to it.

"On the other side of the creek, just beyond that patch of brush."

"Thank you." The book looked very much like a Bible.

When the cow had been led across the stream the man looked up again.

"Nice animal you have there," he said.

"Yes, sir. She's a fine cow." It was the Bible. "Excuse me, sir, but isn't that the Bible you're reading?"

"Why, yes. Do you know it?"

"I've read it"—he tried to make his voice sound casual—"eighteen times, once for each year of my life."

"Well!" It sounded as if he wanted to say, "What for?" but he smiled again and closed the book.

"Can you sit down here and tell me about yourself? I'm interested. My name is Moody. Dwight L. Moody. I've come to town to preach a few sermons."

"At the Sam Jones Tabernacle? Wait until I stake out this cow."

"Yes, I'm to be at the tabernacle."

The cow preferred to stay near him. She was lonely and wanted to be milked.

"I was going to the meeting tonight. I like to hear preachers!"

"Good. Now tell me how you've managed to read the Bible so often."

"Well, it was just an idea I had, so one day . . . "

The cow waited. Now and then she went up and nuzzled her master, trying to coax him away.

"So now it's easy. I just read three chapters a day and five on Sunday, and I'm finished in a year."

"Have you thought of being a preacher, perhaps a missionary?"

"Oh, yes. That's what I want to be most of all. But there's one question I'd like to ask you. You're a preacher. Has God ever talked to you? Have you ever had visions?"

Mr. Moody smiled.

"Can you come here tomorrow morning?" he asked.

"Oh, yes. I'd like to very much."

"Be here early, and we'll watch the sunrise together. Wherever I am I like to find a quiet spot such as this and come each morning to watch the day begin. Come tomorrow and I'll answer your question."

They parted; the cow led the way home, anxious to get to the barn.

His mother was waiting with the milking pails.

"I was talking to Mr. Moody, the man who is going to speak at the tabernacle. He was down by the creek, reading his Bible."

"Mr. Moody? Why, he's a famous evangelist. What in the world was he doing talking to you?"

"We were talking about the Bible. I asked him if God had ever talked to him and he's going to tell me all about it tomorrow morning. We're going to his meeting tonight, aren't we?"

"Yes, your father has the tickets. Come, now, let's get the milking done."

She laughed.

"If you don't get into the worst mix-ups with your Bible! Did you tell him that you're missing the first twenty chapters of Genesis because a sheep ate them?"

The tabernacle, a gigantic auditorium seating five thousand, built by and named for the great evangelist Sam Jones, was filled that night when Moody appeared on the platform. For two hours he held his audience spellbound. Next morning when he reached the creek at the edge of town the boy he had met there the day before was waiting.

"Good morning, sir," he said. "You made a very fine sermon last night. Everyone was talking about it."

"Well, I'm glad to hear that, Edgar. How did you like it?"

Edgar . . . it was strange to be called that name. He had always been just Old Man to the folks he knew. Edgar sounded nice, even dignified, coming from Mr. Moody. It didn't sound sissy, the way he had always thought of it as being. It would be a good name for a minister: The Reverend Edgar Cayce will now deliver his famous sermon on The Bible and Its Meaning to Me.

"Oh, I liked it, sir. It was the finest sermon I ever listened to."

"Then it was a great success for me, too. If I really make an impression on one person with each sermon, I'll be doing well, very well.

"Now, I've been thinking about the question you asked me yesterday. What made you ask it? Have you heard God talking?"

"I don't know. I heard something. I don't know what it was. You see, when I was reading the Bible one day . . . "

They sat on a log, facing east. As the red edge of the sun came up the story unfolded—the vision, the voice, the dream, the lessons conquered by sleeping on books, the mending of the plow, the riding of the mule.

Mr. Moody listened, staring at the whirling, pitching, eddying water of the creek. When the story was finished he said:

"You're not crazy or queer. Lots of people have told me of visions and voices and messages from the beyond. Some of them are fooling themselves. I am sure you are not doing that.

"The Bible tells us about spirits and about visions. It seems that there is a difference between these things. The Bible speaks of being possessed by evil spirits and says, 'A man or woman that hath a familiar spirit, or that is a wizard, shall surely be put to death; they shall stone him with stones: their blood be upon them.' Then it speaks of visions, which seem to be the voices or messages of good spirits. God tells Aaron and Miriam: 'Hear now my words: If there be a prophet among you, I the Lord will make myself known unto him in a vision, and will speak unto him in a dream.'

"So it seems that we must be careful to differentiate between one and the other.

"But let me tell you of my own experience. That will answer your question about God speaking to me, and perhaps it will help you to understand the things that have happened to you.

"Some years ago I was in Cleveland. I had never before preached in that city, but the meetings were well attended and I seemed to be building up a following.

"Then one night I had a dream. I heard a voice say, 'Close the meeting and go to London, England.' I had never been to London; I had never been abroad. My managers were astonished when I said I was going to close up and leave. They said I had an open field in Cleveland and could consolidate my position with the people. They were very exasperated when I insisted, especially as I would give no reason for my action.

"I went to London, wondering what was to happen to me. Not knowing where to go I roamed the streets. I chose the poor districts—I felt more at home there.

"The houses were shabby, but one day I saw a tenement window with a flower box, full of geraniums. They had such lovely colors that I stopped to admire them. Then I heard a voice—a child's voice—singing 'Sweet Hour of Prayer.'

"I was impelled by something to enter the tenement. I walked up the stairs. The door to one of the flats was open. From inside came the child's voice.

"I went in—at the window, by the box of geraniums, sat a little lame girl, singing.

"'May I join you?' I said.

"Then I got the surprise of my life.

"'Oh, Mr. Moody, it's you! I know it's you!' the little girl said. 'I read about you in one of our papers and I've been praying ever since for you to come to London. You are Mr. Moody, aren't you?'

"My meetings in London began in that tenement room. I knelt down and prayed for the little girl.

"That's the answer to your question—if it is an answer. Certainly some good force directed me to London.

"So, you see, I don't think your dreams and visions are foolish. They mean something. Perhaps you are meant to be an evangelist. This part of the country has produced some fine preachers."

"I don't know, sir. It's always been my ambition to be a preacher, and sometimes I've thought that I'd like to be a missionary rather than stay at home. There was a preacher who had been a missionary stationed at our church once, and he told me all about his experiences in Africa and taught me to say the Lord's Prayer in Yoruba.

"But I haven't enough education, and I don't know how I'm to get it. I've got to stay with my mother and help her, especially while my sisters are young. I haven't the money to go away to school anyhow, and even if I did I have high school between me and college. I never went further than ninth grade. Still, I know I could learn quickly once I started, and I'm planning to start just as soon as I can."

Moody smiled and nodded understandingly.

"You've got to stay with your mother," he said. "That's a son's first duty. But don't give up hope. You may have to begin late, but that doesn't mean you won't succeed. Your love for the Bible and your visions mean something. The first and only real qualification for the service of God is the desire to be of service.

"You can do that even if you never go to school again. You can be an example to your fellow men. You can live a Christian life. And you can do charitable work and teach Sunday school."

"How can I teach Sunday school in this town? I did it in the country, but all the boys and girls in my church have either a high school or a college education."

"They may know a lot about books," Mr. Moody said, "but

they don't know this one." He tapped his Bible. "You do. You can teach it. Remember, Edgar, Christ didn't pick His apostles from the university professors. In fact they would have nothing to do with him because He did not agree with their theories. He chose simple fishermen."

Edgar—the name somehow seemed to be his own, at last—didn't feel any better. The time of Jesus and the Bible was far away. Things were different at the Ninth Street Church, which he attended, and the well-dressed, well-educated boys and girls in the congregation were far beyond his reach. How could he dare to teach them?

"Anyhow, keep the faith," Mr. Moody said. "If God wants you to serve Him he will make it possible for you to do so. We cannot penetrate His wisdom. We must have faith. I will think about your problem. If a solution to it occurs to me, I will get in touch with you."

They shook hands and parted. Edgar followed the cow to the barn and milked her. When breakfast was over he left the house and walked to the center of town.

The residential streets of Hopkinsville were shaded by tall trees that made frames for white-fronted houses sitting back behind long, shrub-studded lawns. When West Seventh Street reached Main Street the trees disappeared, and in summer the sun beat down without opposition on the courthouse and the squat, red-brick buildings of the business section.

The town was not yet a hundred years old—it had been laid out in 1799—but it seemed as if it had been there forever. Everything had an air of security, and the church spires seemed genuine symbols of eternity. When Edgar turned the corner into Main Street he felt that the stores and buildings he passed were as permanent and unchangeable as the hills and fields of his grandmother's farm. They were even more unchangeable, for the hills and fields were different with each season and each crop, and such things as new trees, a field fire, or a freshly painted fence were constantly changing the lines of the picture. On Main Street it was always the courthouse on the west corner, the Hopkinsville Bank on the east corner. Then came Wall's clothing store, Hoosier's tailor shop, and Hopper Brothers bookstore, where he worked. Beyond it was Thompson's hardware store, and across the street, Hardwick's drugstore. Just below the drugstore were Latham's dry goods store and Burnett's shoe store.

He entered the bookstore with his passkey and raised the summer shades that covered the windows. Then he let the awning down. The sun was already warm, and books and pictures had to be protected or they would fade.

The front portion of the store was occupied by showcases displaying framed pictures and bookcases containing current literature. Beyond, along the walls, were bookcases filled with textbooks for the local high school, the schools of the county, South Kentucky College, Baptist Girls College, and Ferrell's School for Boys, the town's principal seats of learning. In the rear were stationery and miscellaneous school supplies, picture frames and samples of picture molding, and a large rack for unframed pictures. Along the back wall were Mr. Will Hopper's desk and a safe. In the corner was a stairway leading to the balcony portion of the store, where the work of making picture frames was done and uncut frames were stored. A partition guarded a space fixed up as a bedroom, where Mr. Will slept.

Mr. Will woke up when the door of the store opened: it was his signal to get up. He came downstairs, said hello to Edgar, who was dusting the stock, and wheeled his bicycle out to the street. Mounting it, he rode to the Hopper family residence, a little beyond the town. He would return, after breakfast, with his brother Harry, who was his partner.

Their father had left them the store, and it was their father to whom Edgar was indebted for his job. Mr. Hopper had sent him his Bible, by way of his father, and had refused payment for it. When Edgar asked Mr. Will for a job he told him this. Mr. Will looked worried. He was a tall, slender, dark-eyed man, with a pleasant voice and a quiet, shy manner.

"But we don't need anybody," he told Edgar. "We don't need anybody at all."

"I've been to all the stores in town," Edgar said, "but this is the one I like best, so I want to work here."

Mr. Will was embarrassed by the praise. He told the boy to

come back the next day. Then Edgar met Mr. Harry, who was shorter than Mr. Will, blond, with a handlebar mustache. He said the store didn't need a clerk.

"But I want to work here," Edgar said. "This is the nicest store in town."

Mr. Will was sympathetic, and sentimental about his father. Mr. Harry was susceptible to flattery. They told him he could come in and work, but they couldn't pay him.

"That's all right," Edgar said. "I'll make myself so useful that you'll want to pay me."

He went to work, and at the end of a month the brothers, a little awkwardly, said they would like to reward him by buying him a suit of clothes. Would he accept? He was delighted. So were they. His appearance was more a reflection on them than on him. At the end of the second month they gave him fifteen dollars. They would give him the same amount every month, they said.

He had worked hard to win such approval, even climbing to the tops of the wall bookcases, where the statuary was kept, in search of dust. He was up there, one morning, when the brothers returned from breakfast. Passing him on their way to the rear of the store, Mr. Harry said:

"Be careful. Don't break anything up there!"

Mr. Will said:

"That's been needing attention for a long time. Be careful. Don't fall and hurt yourself."

It was the difference between the two men, though each was kind to him and both were satisfied with his work.

He was standing behind the counter with Mr. Harry on one of the hot, blistering days of late summer when a carriage drove up to the door and stopped. The girl who was driving looked in at them and beckoned.

"Know her?" Mr. Harry said. "Don't know as I do, offhand."

"Yes, sir. It's Miss Ethel Duke. She teaches school down in the country. Reckon she wants me for something."

He went out to speak to her, squinting in the bright light. The carriage looked cool, with its fringed top and leather seat. Ethel Duke leaned forward to shake hands with him.

"Hello, Old Man," she said. "How are you? Haven't seen you since you recited Jim MacKenzie's speech and nearly killed us all. How are all the family?"

"Fine," he said, shaking her hand.

She straightened and sat back in the carriage. The face of the girl who was sitting beside her came into view.

"I want you to meet my cousin, Gertrude Evans," Ethel said.

She was a slip of a girl, barely fifteen, but pretty, with brown eyes and a pale, oval face, like a cameo.

"Gertrude, this is . . . Old Man, what's your first name?"

"Edgar." He said it proudly now, remembering how Mr. Moody had addressed him.

"Edgar Cayce. He's from down in the country, where they have nothing but Cayces. He's working in the bookstore now."

"How do you do," Edgar said.

Gertrude looked at him. Her eyes passed over him like a shower of rain, cooling and drenching him at the same time. She did not smile.

"How do you do," she said.

"Old Man, how do you find life in town?" Ethel asked. "How do you like the parties?"

"Oh, I haven't been to any parties yet. I've only been here a few months." He started to tell her that he didn't even know any young people, but he caught Gertrude watching him from the corner of her eye and stopped.

"Then you shall," Ethel said. "We're having a lawn party at Gertrude's home Friday night. Will you come? We'd love to have you, wouldn't we, Gertrude?"

Gertrude looked across the street. "Why, of course," she said.

"It's the Salter place," Ethel said. "Its east of town, about a mile and a half, right at the bend in the road before the Western State Hospital. You can't miss it. It's up on a hill to the right. Be there at eight o'clock and see the moon rise. It's going to be full."

She drove off, waving good-bye. In the store Mr. Harry was talking to Mary Greene, his girl, who had come in while Edgar was at the curb. Mary was one of the teachers at South Kentucky College.

"The little one's pretty, Edgar," Mr. Harry said. "Who is she?"

"Her name is Gertrude Evans," Edgar said. He turned to watch the carriage round the corner.

"Was that Gertrude Evans?" Mary Greene said. "I've seen her at school. She's Sam Evans's girl, Harry."

Harry nodded.

"Mother's Elizabeth Salter," he said. "Didn't know she was so grown up. Has a couple of brothers, I believe."

"Do you know where the Salter place is?" Edgar asked.

Harry leaned on the counter and explained.

"About a mile and a half outside of town, on the bend just before the hospital. Sam Salter came here to put in the staircase in the hospital—the circular one. He was an architect, from Cincinnati, I believe.

"That was during the war, or thereabouts. I believe they shelled the place while it was being built. Ball went through the main wing.

"Well, Salter stayed to build the college here, so he just settled. Nice place out there. About ten acres. Fine orchard.

"This girl's father's dead—the one you just met. She lives out there with the old folks, she and her two brothers."

"Hugh and Lynn are the boys," Mary Greene said.

"Believe you're right," Mr. Harry said. "Then there's Kate. She's the next Salter girl, after Elizabeth. She'd be this girl's aunt. She married Porter Smith and went to Alabama, but he died and she came back home with her children. Her two boys are Porter and Raymond, and she has a stepchild, her husband's daughter by his first wife. Her name's Estella . . . Stella, I believe she's called.

"Then come the boys. They'd be this girl's uncles. Will and Hiram are the boys' names. Will works at the hospital and Hiram's in the railroad game."

"But the prettiest one of the whole family is Carrie," Mary Greene said. "She's the youngest Salter girl. She's Gertrude's aunt, but I don't believe she's more than a few years older. She's learning to be a milliner, though I don't see why."

"Why not?" Mr. Harry said.

"She should get married," Mary said, staring straight at him.

"Well," Mr. Harry said to Edgar, "now that you know all about the family, what's up? Having a date with Gertrude?"

"I'm invited to a party at her house Friday night," Edgar said. "A lawn party."

"Nice people," Mr. Harry said. "You'll like them."

Mary Greene looked at Edgar with new interest.

"There'll be lots of pretty girls there for you," she said. "Or have you chosen the one you want already?"

"No," Edgar said. "Oh, no!"

He went off to dust some books, feeling uneasy. The Salters sounded like important people. Perhaps they were like the fashionable families in the novels the lady customers were always buying. But Ethel Duke wasn't like that, and she was going to be there. Perhaps they were just nice people who were well-to-do, like the families in the Alger books who always helped the hero. Perhaps he was going to be like one of the Alger boys. He would meet the girl, have some adventures, win out in the end, and then his benefactor, who might be old Mr. Salter, would allow him to be engaged to his granddaughter, and supply him with money with which to go to school and become a minister. He would pay back the money, of course, and in the end he would have a fine church and a house for his family, and drive a pair of horses. He would be one of the most respected men in the town.

But it might be the other way round. They might not have anything to do with him because he was a poor boy without any education.

Anyhow, he had a new suit, and he would look as well as any of the rich boys who might be there.

When Friday came he left home right after supper. Darkness overtook him on the road, but the moon was rising as he approached the Hill, and he saw its silhouette above the trees that ran toward it up the slope. Behind it the lights of Japanese lanterns bobbed and flickered. The twilight wind brought him sounds of laughter and talk.

It seemed to him like an enchanted castle, too far away ever to be reached, though he kept saying to himself over and over again—to give himself courage—that it was a house much smaller than his grandmother's, on a good deal less land. But he knew that there was a difference. Grandmother's was a farmhouse. This was a residence. To live in such a house and not farm; to own the land and just live on it; that was the way gentlemen did.

There was a wire fence at the road. Two lanes led to the house, one a carriage walk, the other a footpath. He opened the gate at the footpath and walked up it, under great oak trees, towering maples, and finally to some locusts that were nearly a hundred feet high and moved their tops in the breeze like giants moving in another world.

He walked around the house and to the place where the lanterns were shining. It was a lawn that stretched from the back of the house to the orchard. Tables had been set out; on them were cut-glass bowls filled with lemonade and platters of cookies, cakes, sandwiches, and fruit. There were benches and chairs, but most of the young people were just sitting on the ground, using handkerchiefs or jackets or shawls to protect their skirts and trousers from grass stain.

Ethel Duke spied him and took his arm. She introduced him to the old folks—nice-looking, gray-haired people—and then to the others in the family: Mrs. Evans, Gertrude's mother, a dark-haired, quick, smiling woman; Mrs. Smith, Gertrude's Aunt Kate, a fat-cheeked, amiable lady with small hands and a small, pretty mouth; Carrie Salter, also Gertrude's aunt, a beautiful girl with great, shining brown eyes that dazzled him. He didn't remember what the others looked like after Carrie; she carried him away from Ethel and introduced him to her nephews, Porter and Raymond, and her brothers, Will and Hiram. She got him some lemonade, plied him with cookies, sat down with him on one of the benches, and had him talking about himself before he knew what was happening.

Later she introduced him to Stella Smith, her niece by marriage, and then she somehow guided him to Gertrude and got them talking to each other. Then she disappeared.

Gertrude was lovelier than he had dared to allow himself to remember. She was dressed in a white gown that swept to her ankles and drifted out from the skirt like a snowpile. She had a red rose in her hair. It was just the touch needed to complete the picture. He found himself thinking of sample frame moldings.

While he was debating which frame best suited her she took his arm and said, "Let's go down near the gate, where we can see the moon better. I love to watch it from there when it goes over the house!"

She led him around front and down the footpath.

"Listen to the trees!" she said.

They were whispering, the locusts far above, the oaks down close.

"Do you know what they're saying?" she asked.

He said no, he didn't. Did she?

She said, "No, but they're supposed to be the souls of lovers who were cruelly parted on earth, and now they meet in the trees on nights when the moon is full, and tell each other of their love."

"Oh," he said.

When they got to the fence she had him boost her up to the post, where she could sit comfortably.

"I could get up here by myself," she said, "but not with this dress on."

He took his pipe from a pocket and asked her if she objected to smoking.

"No," she said. "I think a man ought to smoke, and I like a pipe better than cigars."

When the pipe was lighted they looked at the moon. It was drifting upward, leaving the house behind.

"Tell me about yourself," Gertrude said. "What are you going to be? I'll bet you'll be the owner of the bookstore someday. Then you can have all the books you want to read. Oh, I think that would be the grandest thing! I love books more than anything else in the whole world!"

He had opened his mouth to speak when she said, "Tell me about yourself." Had she stopped there he would have said, "Someday I want to be a minister." His mouth closed quickly, his teeth bit into the pipe when she talked about the store, and owning it.

When he didn't answer she laughed and said, "I reckon you

think I'm silly, talking like that. But I always wonder what people are going to do.

"I think it's so fascinating to see a lot of girls and boys when they're young, and then when they grow up and begin to take their places in the world. You never can figure out what even your best friend is going to become.

"And now all the boys and girls I know are beginning to think about jobs and what they want to be."

"I reckon it's just about whatever job a fellow can get, some of the time," he said. He felt calm enough to answer her now, although inside of him something had upset and splashed him with a feeling that acted as if he were going to be sick later on.

"Only I wanted to work in the bookstore," he went on, "and I kept after Mr. Will and Mr. Harry until they took me in."

He laughed and knocked his pipe out on the fence post. He was afraid to keep on smoking, the way he felt.

"They said they didn't need anyone in the store, but I promised them they'd agree I was useful if they'd let me try. So now they can't get rid of me because they're used to having me around."

She laughed, too. It was nice to be able to laugh. It made the job of getting to know people easy. You just laughed with them over a few things, and you were friends.

"I knew that's the way you were," Gertrude said. "I'll bet if I buy a book from you, you'll make it a habit with me, and take all my money away."

They both laughed then, and he told her about all the new books at the store. She exclaimed at the mention of each one and pretended it was just what she wanted. They talked like that until she held out her arms to be helped down.

"We've got to go back," she said. "It's almost time for the party to break up."

Hurrying up the path she said, "I'll have to be saying good-bye to everyone, so I'll say it to you now. I hope you'll come again. Don't be a stranger."

"I won't," he said. He was afraid to take her hand. Then he realized that she had taken his.

"It was nice meeting you," she said.

She left him when they got back to the party, and after he had thanked the members of her family he slipped away and hurried down the carriage drive, which opened on the road a few yards nearer town than the footpath.

He wanted to walk home alone. The sickness was breaking out all over him, and he knew what it was. It had been there all the time, but Gertrude had made him face it. She had said what it was natural for other people to think. He had been going along pretending that what he wanted to happen really could happen, though he had known within himself that every day that passed made it more faraway and improbable. Now the limit had been reached. It was impossible for him to become a minister. He knew it.

Probably it had been impossible all along; he alone had believed it could be done. His mother had pretended to believe: when he talked about it she kissed him and hugged him and said, "I hope all your dreams will come true." But he could see now that her prayers were for a miracle, not for something that could happen naturally, even if everyone concerned tried his best.

If his grandmother had lived, or his grandfather, it would have been accomplished. They would have mortgaged the farm to pay for the necessary schooling. His uncles were not that much interested, either in him or in preaching. They had families of their own, and his ambitions would have seemed to them—if he had approached them seriously—as a lot of foolishness. His father was extremely amiable about the idea, since he admired ministers and men of learning almost as much as he did businessmen and politicians. But this amiability produced nothing specific in the way of money. There were four daughters in the family, and although business was sometimes good, business was also sometimes bad.

He was eighteen and a half. Suppose the miracle happened and he was able to begin school in the fall? He might get through high school in three years. He could sleep on some of the books; others concerned matters which he had to conquer while conscious—mathematics and grammar, for instance. They had to do with problems that had to be solved, not answers that had to be given. He would be entering college at twenty-one-and-a-half. He would be almost twenty-six before he entered a semi-nary. That was too old. By that time he ought to be married and have a family. He remembered now how Mr. Moody had said, "You may have to begin late," and then had said, "Keep the faith," and told him about the apostles being humble fishermen. Mr. Moody had seen that it was impossible. Everyone had seen it but himself.

He had stopped growing up, in his own mind, when he determined to be a minister. Time from then on had ceased to affect him; he remained always a boy who wanted to go to school and study to be a preacher. Meanwhile his legs had stretched, his voice had changed, manhood had arrived and taken possession of his body. Now, suddenly, it had taken possession of the rest of him. He felt woefully old and discouraged.

Life had passed him by, and he had not known it was moving. Now he was doomed to be a businessman, working in a store, wrapping packages for other people, going to church only on Sundays and meeting nights.

Eventually he would own the store, probably, and teach Sunday school. When the girls were raised and married he would build a house for his mother and father to live in. He would live with them, because by then he would be old, too, and naturally he would never marry. He would just do good for people and be nice to everyone. When Gertrude came into the store with her children he would ask her about them and talk to them, until she would turn away with tears in her eyes at the thought of the great love she had lost by not waiting for him.

Suddenly, just as the lump in his throat seemed about either to choke him or burst, a voice in his head—a man's voice, like his own—said, very sarcastically, "Well, what better way is there for a man to serve God and his fellow man?"

He stopped in his tracks; he could feel himself blushing. What better way, indeed, could a Christian live, than by just such a life as he had outlined? And he had thought of it only because he was pitying himself: pitying himself for losing the life of a minister with a rich congregation, a fine house, and a beautiful wife and children. A true preacher would be a missionary and own nothing but his Bible.

He walked on rapidly, still blushing. When a carriage with some of the guests from the party overtook him he was glad to accept the offer of a ride.

Sitting backward, with his feet swinging out into the night and his eyes fixed on the sky, he puffed at his pipe and was no longer sorry for himself. He was going to give up the idea of being a minister. He had to. But he wasn't going to give up Gertrude. He was going to marry her.

5

Time found it easy to weave years into the fabric of Hopkinsville. There was never any change in the pattern. The same streets and buildings were to be covered with snow during winter, dusted with wind in March, cleansed with rain in April and May, and baked during the long, bright days of summer. The winters were cold, the springs wet, the summers hot, and the autumns glorious with soft air and leaves turned yellow, russet, and gold.

To Edgar, who was in love and happy, the calendar and the earth were all that turned. His heart stood still, afraid to beat lest it tick away into memory the wonder of her feeling for him.

That he loved her was not a source of happiness to him: it was a hunger which had constantly to be fed, and which could turn from ecstasy to torture if the supply of nourishment were cut off. It was her love for him that constantly thrilled him: that she did not tire of him, that she liked being with him, that of her own choice she chose his company above anyone else's was at times almost more than he could bear. All his life he had yearned for things that were beyond him. He had become used to dreams that never came true. He was like a boy who had idly wished for wings and suddenly found himself flying through the air.

He would be thinking about her as he worked in the store—wrapping a package or putting some new books on the shelves—when it would strike him that she was probably at the same moment thinking of him. He would see her, moving through the living room, picking up the book he had brought her to read. He would see her hand reach for the pages. He would follow the blood of her pulse up the slim arm to the clear, small face and the dark eyes, always so full of concern. He would look at the masses of hair, piled on her head like a basket, and look down into her head, trying to see what thoughts of him were moving through it. His hands would tremble, his face would flush, and he would move quickly to do something that would take his whole strength, and help him to still the wild beating that came up from his heart and flowed out through every part of him.

He would move his thoughts away from her then, for safety's sake. He would send them through the house in which she lived, pausing at each detail, taxing his memory to remember how it looked, and what he had been told about it. It steadied him to do this. It made his mind work, while his heart, in the background, slowed down to a normal beat.

Next to the parlor of the Hill was the great hall, fronting on the porch, and larger than an ordinary room. In it were two large secretaries, one against each side wall. They were massive pieces of oak that reached to the ceiling. The upper part of each was shelved, with glass doors; the middle portion was a desk; the lower portion was shelved, with solid doors. Each desk had a lamp, and there was a large lamp, with a white shade, for reading. The shelves of the secretaries were filled with books; there were easy chairs scattered around for the library customers.

He had not seen the bedrooms—there was one on the other side of the hall and two more between it and the rear of the house—but he had heard about the middle one, which Aunt Kate shared with Gertrude's mother. There were two beds, of oak, and these beds had feather mattresses. Aunt Kate had plucked the feathers for her mattress; Lizzie, as Aunt Kate called her older sister, had plucked the feathers for her mattress. Each had done her own stuffing, sewing, and shaping. Every day they made up their beds, neither accepting assistance from the other. Each had her particular technique, and no one was allowed to touch either bed, for any purpose, except the owner. Each sister had a rocking chair. They were made of oak, with strong cane bottoms. As they moved about the house during the day they took their chairs with them, carrying them out into the back yard in summer. The chairs were as sacred as the beds, but their sanctity was sometimes violated. The sisters were continually accusing each other of occupying the wrong rocker.

In the rear of the house was the dining room. It had an enormous oak table that dwarfed all the other furniture—sideboard, chairs, buffet. In one corner, fastened against the wall, was a large medicine chest, full of all sorts of patented drugs and home remedies. Aunt Kate constantly predicted that everyone in the house was going to be poisoned, because medicines for the cows, chickens, dogs, and human beings were all kept together in the chest, without even a differentiation of shelves to identify them.

"I'll go in there some dark night and get the wrong thing," Aunt Kate would say, "and that will be the end of me."

Then there was the back room, with its famous potbellied stove. Old Mrs. Salter was a strict Christian. She constantly lectured her sons on such evils as cards, dice, and liquor, and promised dire punishment if she ever discovered evidence that the boys were indulging in any of them. One winter day she found a pack of cards in Will's pocket. She called the family together, made a speech, and, opening the door of the stove, cast the cards into the flames.

They were celluloid. The stove exploded, blowing off its door, tossing its lid into the air, and scattering fire over the room. No one was hurt, and the wandering firebrands were collected and extinguished. Mrs. Salter said nothing, but she seemed rather pleased. The explosion had somehow proved her point.

The residents of the Hill lived at peace with the world and warred pleasantly among themselves. Sam Salter had established complete democracy in his home. If a controversial subject were brought up at the dinner table, he insisted that each person present, even the smallest child, express an opinion on it. He was contemptuous of anyone who agreed with anyone else. Each person was an individual, he thought, and ought to differ with every other individual, however slightly, in all things. As an architect he believed all bricks should be the same size; as a man he believed all human beings should differ.

Thus Kate and her sister Lizzie lived harmoniously together without agreeing on a single thing. Kate looked after the animals—the cows, chickens, horses, and dogs; Lizzie looked after the plant life—the flower gardens and the orchard. Lizzie read omnivorously, preferring biographies and political treatises; Kate read the local newspaper each day, specializing in the social notes, births, deaths, and marriages. Lizzie was interested in politics and knew every officeholder in the community and state, either personally or by correspondence; Kate was interested in the social movements of people: she knew the genealogy of every family in the county. Lizzie carried on a voluminous and controversial correspondence; Kate considered communication to be a verbal art.

Together they ruled the Hill, following the death of the old folks in the years just after Edgar's meeting with Gertrude. They had been devoted to their parents, and they were determined to carry out the wishes which Sam Salter had reiterated time and time again.

"The house is free of debt," he would say. "I want it kept that way, so it can always be a haven for any member of the family, and any of his family. Keep it so that whenever one of you gets into trouble, or is sick, or needs help, he'll come back here. That's what a home is for. Something to fall back on. You came back, Kate, and you came back, Lizzie, and some of your children may have to do the same thing. Keep the place for them. I don't want them ever to be without a home, or to be forced to accept charity from a stranger."

The other children were home infrequently. Hiram worked for the Louisville and Nashville Railroad, and finally settled in Nashville. Will was a carpenter at the Western State Hospital, and eventually built a home for himself across the road from the Hill. Carrie, the younger sister, worked in Henderson, a nearby town, as a buyer for one of the department stores. She was home more frequently than her brothers, and because her age was close to that of Gertrude, Lynn, Hugh, Porter, Raymond, and Stella, she was an intermediary and peacemaker between the children and their mothers.

The whole family took Edgar in as one of them, and this, like Gertrude's love for him, filled him with wonder and trembling when he thought about it. Listening to them argue about the weather, the menu for Sunday dinner, patterns for dresses, the sermon of the preacher at their Methodist church, he could not understand how they were in agreement on such a controversial subject as a suitor for Gertrude. But if they recognized faults in

him they accepted them as they accepted each other's faults.
They invited his opinions on the things which they discussed,
and they disagreed with him heartily. He was delighted. It was
the kind of family life he dreamed about, but which in his own
home was not the rule.

Between himself and his mother there existed an understanding which he shared with no other human being; it was a state
of peace and love which he hoped someday would come to himself
and Gertrude. But his father looked on the world with such an
entirely different viewpoint that it was impossible even to disagree with him. To the things he expressed at the dinner table
Edgar could not even find opposites. So, for the most part, he
said nothing. His sisters were sometimes very close to him, sometimes oceans away. By degrees he realized that the most difficult and delicate of human relationships is that of brother and
sister. Riding or walking out to see Gertrude he would be aware
of a state of mind with regard to Carrie and Stella—who ap-
proximated at the Hill the position of his sisters at home—which
was different from the state of mind with which he approached
his own home when his sisters were there to greet him. The
reason for the difference was easy to recognize; he was only
worried that such things should be. He wanted tranquillity and
peace with all the people he knew, but most of all he wanted to
be able to relax in the knowledge that nothing was being held
back, nothing was closed away. It made him lonely when this
happened.

Loneliness was his great problem, even though he now was
acquainted with everyone in town; even though he now was a
Sunday school teacher, thank to his brilliance in answering
questions in Bible class. These things were merely hills that
led him down, on the other side, into wider and deeper valleys.
It was so easy to become acquainted with a lot of people, so
difficult to know one of them well.

He had not thought about it until he fell in love. Until then
he had been so absorbed in his own thoughts that it never occurred to him to be curious about what other people were thinking. Sitting beside Gertrude on their second date he had found
himself watching her as she stared off into space, wondering

what thoughts were passing through her head. He was jealous of them; he felt shut out, put away, as if he did not exist. Suddenly the enormity of the gulf that existed between himself and all other human beings was brought to his consciousness. No matter how close he might come to this girl, she could turn her head aside and be a million miles away. It was that way with everyone in the world.

People talked with each other about things that were common to them, and about other people and what was commonly known about them. But when they ceased speaking they looked away: upward toward the sky, downward toward the ground, or off to the horizon, and a dazed, dreamy look came into their eyes, as if they had been put under a spell. Then they were in their own world, away from everyone else. He became painfully aware of these worlds. He would be laughing or smiling or nodding at something one of his friends had said, and thinking of a reply, when that look would come into the friend's eyes, his head would turn aside, and Edgar would be alone.

Everybody had two worlds, one for himself, one for his fellow man. Even his mother, moving about the kitchen in the solitude of her work, showed changes in the expression of her face as thoughts drifted, raced, or piled one upon the other in her mind. As soon as she noticed his presence her eyes lighted up, she smiled, and the world which they shared enveloped her. The other world, in which she had been living by herself, disappeared.

He was no different himself; with everyone he knew, a separate situation existed. There were regular customers in the store; with each he shared different jokes, different subjects of conversation, different shoptalk. As a customer entered the store, Edgar's mind dropped into the correct slot, and the existence they had created took up where it had left off the last time they were together.

The better you knew a person the more things there were to talk about, and if you had a real good friend you didn't hold anything back. That was the way he felt about it, but now it seemed to him that other people, no matter how much they took you into their confidence, always held something back. Probably he did, too. He didn't tell his real, deep secrets to anyone but God. Other people must be the same. The privacy of thought was the dignity of man: that was why God made man with everything visible but the things that passed through his mind.

That was the secret of love, too. When you loved people you wanted to rush right into the middle of their thoughts and share all their joys and sorrows, helping them wherever it was possible. But if they didn't want you there, you were just a nuisance. It wasn't enough for you to love them; they had to love you. If they didn't, you couldn't get into their thoughts, and then you suffered.

He suffered with Gertrude. When they were together and she stopped to talk with someone else, or pat a dog, or pick a flower, he was envious of the person, the dog, or the flower. They wrenched her from him, and when she returned she stored something else in her mind that was apart from him—a little thing, but an addition to the long train that stretched back to the day she was born.

She had grown up without him: it bruised him constantly. When the family at the Hill was gathered he heard of past joys and sorrows in which he had not shared. Gertrude and her brothers and cousins would talk of their childhood escapades, and he would sit in silence, aching, while she was transported from the world she shared with him to the world she shared with them.

To marry her, to shut out from both their lives all but the existence they had begun to build together, was his only hope. Then slowly, bit by bit, they would grow together in their thoughts, so that when she went among other people he would not feel lonely, or be envious, because she would be carrying him with her, in her mind; she would think of them with his mind as well as her own, see them with his eyes as well as her own, talk to them with his opinions as well as her own. And he would do likewise. They would not be two persons then, but one.

After that, when he dreamed of walking through the forest and meeting the figure with the cloth of gold, the veil over the face of the girl by his side would be lifted, and he would see that she was Gertrude.

The dream had returned to him many times, and after he had

met Gertrude, and fallen in love with her, he had wondered why the veil was not lifted. Now he was sure that it was because the dream was a spiritual message, and to be truly married in the spiritual sense he and Gertrude would have to become one in their minds and hearts as well as in their souls.

For their love now was a veiled thing, hidden from their thoughts by the things they could not say, hidden from their hearts by the feelings they could not express. They only knew of it because of the yearning they had to be together, and the willingness they shared to sit quiet by themselves whenever they had the chance.

She was more pale and beautiful than ever. The death of her grandfather, followed by that of her grandmother, shook her frail health. She withdrew from South Kentucky College and remained at home, resting as much as her restless spirit would allow, taking the medicines and remedies Aunt Kate fixed for her, and reading the books Edgar brought her. Each month he brought her one of the new novels, and for a Christmas present he contrived to give her a complete set of the works of her favorite author, E. P. Roe.

He wanted to propose, but he wondered if he should. Perhaps he should wait until her health was restored; perhaps he should wait until he was financially able to set a date for the wedding. But the yearning to have her for his own, to hear from her lips the words which would mean that she cared for him above all others, was too much of a temptation. On a clear, cold night in March, 1897—the 7th—he asked her if she would marry him.

She looked squarely at him, and through him. Her brown eyes seemed to be considering his soul, reading the record of his iniquities and sins. His thoughts felt their nakedness. He fumbled for his pipe and tobacco.

Gertrude looked away. She stared at the hand-painted shade of the parlor lamp, dreaming.

Finally she said: "Getting married is so different from being in love. When you're in love and not married there are no responsibilities; everything is wonderful. But when a girl gets married she has so many things to think about. She has to think of her family, because she has duties and responsibilities to share with them. Then she has to think of herself, and whether she is fit to take over the burden of being a wife. She has to be a home-maker, and a cook and a mother. I'll think about it, Edgar. I'm not of age yet, and neither are you."

Hastily he crammed the tobacco into the pipe and lighted it. He felt foolish and irresponsible. He was confused, too. He had been thinking about the dream, and his mother's interpretation of it. She had said that the engagement was the easy part, and all was happiness during that period. But Gertrude was think-ing of the engagement in terms of the marriage. Her idea of happiness was the courting time before the engagement.

"You're right," he said. "We'd better not think about it now. We're too young. I'm sorry I mentioned it. Just don't think about it!"

"Of course I will!" Gertrude said. She looked at him in sur-prise. "We have to face these responsibilities sometime. I'm a grown woman, and I'm able to take my place in life. I just need a little time to consider everything before making a decision."

She sat up, straightening her back and tilting her head proudly. He blew a cloud of smoke to hide his smile; she looked so small, so pale, and so sure of herself.

"I'll give you your answer next Sunday night," she said.

"That's the fourteenth. I'll be here early," he answered.

She stood up.

"Then let's not talk about it any more. Let's find Carrie and Stella and play some whist."

She was nervous; she didn't want to be alone with him. He felt better; he was even confident, at least of Gertrude. During the whist he was particularly nice to Carrie and Stella. Gertrude would consult them, as she would all the family. He hoped they were for him.

It rained all day Sunday. When he went to the livery stable at five o'clock all the covered carriages were gone. He chose a saddle horse in preference to an open carriage. When he got to the Hill his outer clothing and the lower parts of his trousers were wet. Sitting before the fire in the living room, drying them, he said nothing until she put a hand on his arm.

"The answer is yes, Edgar," she said.

She hadn't looked at him. He didn't look at her. They sat,

staring at the flames, listening to the rain.

It seemed a long time before either spoke. Then Gertrude said:
"What are you thinking about?"

He turned his head toward her slowly, swallowed dryly, and
said:

"I was thinking that I'm going to have a hard time keeping
my pipe lit on the way home if this rain keeps up."

They laughed together, and he kissed her.

"I intended saying yes all the time," she said, "but I wanted
to make certain that everyone in the family agreed with me."

She laughed again.

"I thought some of them might object, but before I got through
asking each one I was jealous. They all seem to love you as
much as I do."

He kissed her again. Then he sneezed. Gertrude jumped up.

"I'd better put your feet in a mustard bath," she said. "You're
catching cold!"

*   *   *

The days of that spring were long and sweet. From the time
he got up in the morning until he fell asleep at night he followed the same general plan. When it was absolutely necessary
he thought about other things. When it wasn't, he thought about
Gertrude.

The week after she accepted him he purchased a diamond.
Then, in a burst of magnificence, he sent it to Rumania to be
cut. Gertrude traced the journey on a map.

"Imagine a diamond going all the way across the ocean, and
through most all of Europe, just to be cut for my ring!" she
said. "It makes my finger itch just to think about it!"

When the stone came back, and was set in the ring, and the
ring was on her finger, she carried her left hand as if it were a
chalice.

They went everywhere together now: to parties, picnics, dances,
baseball games—Gertrude's brother Lynn was one of the town's
best players—hay rides, and shows at Holland's Opera House.
Edgar bought a derby. Gertrude wore the most fashionable clothes,

brought to her by Carrie, who was now working for a department store in Springfield, Tennessee.

Long ago Edgar had lost his shyness and fear of people. Everyone in Hopkinsville, he had gradually discovered, was related to everyone else; whole gobs of them were his cousins. Behind the counter at Hopper's he acquired the ease necessary for surface acquaintanceship, which passed among most people, it appeared, for friendship. He met and became familiar with the boys and girls of his own age, and they turned out to be not the paragons of manners and education he had at first supposed, but ordinary youngsters trying to learn a little and enjoy themselves a lot. He sold them school supplies, listened to them complain about the difficulty of their lessons, and went with Gertrude to their parties and dances.

Some of them attended his Sunday school class. He had not forgotten Mr. Moody or the missions, and little by little his group had transformed itself into a special class for the study of mission work. Boys and girls from other churches joined it, and meetings were held in various of the churches. Edgar was unquestionably accorded an intellectual status above that of his students, although many of them had gone far beyond him in schooling. As Mr. Moody had said, they knew many books, Edgar knew one, but they were agreed that the one he knew was of more importance than the others.

The enrollment of members from other churches was what pleased him most.

"Someday," he told Gertrude, "all the churches will get together and be one again, the way Jesus intended. There were different sects in the Jewish faith when He lived, and He didn't approve of them. There are more Christian sects now than there were believers in the Lord when He was crucified. I don't think He'd like that."

"I don't think He'd like what has happened to Christianity at all," Gertrude said. "Nobody practices it."

"Some people try," he said. "They do the best they can."

"Most of them have a funny idea of what their best is," she answered.

For a moment she looked stubborn; her greatest hate was hypocrisy. Then she squeezed his arm.

"The leaves will be turning color in a few weeks," she said. "Can you smell autumn in the air?"

The seasons rolled on. His father complained all winter, as he had the winter before, and the winter before that, of pneumonia and an early grave, the only results he could foresee of constant trips to the Hill in rain, sleet, cold, and snow.

"Don't worry," his mother would say. "He already has a fatal disease. It will keep all the others away."

She watched him without his knowing it, nursing him with hope when the slow increase of his bank balance filled him with despair about getting married, soothing him with nonsense or tales of miracles when he worried about Gertrude's health, listening to his Bible lesson every Saturday night so that he would have the confidence of her approval when he went to teach it Sunday morning.

He watched her, too, without her knowing it, seeing the lines in her face loosen and relax as the girls grew up and became a help instead of a problem; watching the light in her eyes brighten as the squire's business became more solid, more dependable as a source of livelihood. She was getting older, but she was becoming happier.

Annie, the eldest of the girls, who was called "sister" by the family, was working in Mrs. Ada Layne's millinery shop. Annie was a pretty girl, shorter than her younger sisters, and more heavy-set, with dark-gray eyes and light-brown hair. She was chief adorer of her big brother. Ola was next; she was the student of the family—a tall, slender, dark-haired girl who was leading her class in high school, specializing in bookkeeping and business training. Mary was the next daughter, ready now for high school, and Sara was the baby, still in pigtails.

They were all upstairs with Ola, dressing her up for a date, on the Saturday night in June when Edgar, polishing his Sunday shoes in the kitchen, found it impossible to concentrate on his job. He threw the brush into the shoebox and turned to his mother. "I've lost my job," he said.

His mother stopped what she was doing and waited, not looking at him.

He explained. "Mr. D. W. Kitchen has bought a half interest in the store. Mr. Harry is married and living down in Tennessee, and he doesn't want to keep his part of the business. So I'm out. Mr. Kitchen will take my place himself."

His mother went on with what she was doing.

"What are your plans?" she said. "Have you thought of anything?"

"I've thought of everything, but it's not just a matter of another job. The bookstore was the place I liked to work in. I could get a job next door in the hardware store. Mr. Thompson would give me a job. But that wouldn't be the bookstore. That would be just a job. I know I wouldn't be happy."

"Why don't you leave Hopkinsville?" she said. "Why don't you go to some big city, like Louisville, and get a job in a bookstore there? You'd soon be getting more money, and be able to marry. There isn't much for an ambitious boy in Hopkinsville."

"You want me to go away?" He was surprised.

"I've kept you long enough . . . too long," she said. "But I needed you. Things are better now. The girls are more help than bother, and your father's doing well.

"You're the sort of boy who can do better for himself away from home, because at home you spend your time thinking of others and doing things for them. You've got to think of yourself and your future. You have a responsibility to Gertrude, and the children you'll have someday."

They were both silent. She bent over her sewing basket. He took the brush from the shoebox and shined the toes of his boots. After a while he looked up. She was trying to thread a needle, without success. He went over to help her. She gave him the needle and thread and reached for her handkerchief.

"After all," she said, "you're twenty-one. A mother has to give up her boy sometime. She can't expect to keep him forever."

He stabbed at the eye of the needle in vain.

*   *   *

"Edgar, why in the world don't you get out of this town?" Carrie said. "You're just wasting your time here, and you know it. The hardware store is bad enough, but a dry goods store is worse. In the shoe department!

"I know these stores, Edgar. I've worked in them. I work in one now. They'll just take everything out of you, and you get nothing for it in the end. You get back in the business you know, where you like your work and can get some place. Get a job in a bookstore."

"Where?" he asked.

"Anywhere," she said, "except in Hopkinsville. In Louisville, or Bowling Green, or Cincinnati. Goodness, you and Gertrude sitting around mooning over each other just give me fits. That child only weighs eighty pounds now, and there's nothing in the world the matter with her except she's so much in love with you she doesn't know what to do with herself, and she's worried sick about your job, and when you two can get married.

"You go away for a while and get a job that suits you, and believe me you'll both be better. Gertrude will get well if she knows you're happy; and as soon as you both have something to look forward to again you'll be better off."

It was a July day in Hopkinsville. They stood in the back of Richard's Dry Goods Store, in the shoe department, where Edgar worked.

He finished wrapping the shoes she had bought and handed her the package.

"You think about that, Edgar, and do something about it," she said.

When she had gone he went to the clerk's office and borrowed stationery and a pen. A plan had been growing in his mind for weeks. He decided to act on it.

In Louisville there was a large bookstore, J. P. Morton and Company. He wrote them, asking for a copy of their complete catalogue.

A week later it arrived. That night he slept on it. Meanwhile he had solicited letters of recommendation from every political officer, judge, doctor, lawyer, and businessman of his acquaintance in Hopkinsville and Christian County.

When he was sure that he knew the catalogue from cover to cover, he wrote a letter to the company, applying for a position as clerk. He received a polite reply, stating that no jobs were open at present, but that his application would be placed on file. By return mail he started the stream of letters of recommendation on its way. A batch went in every mail.

Three days later a telegram came from Louisville, signed by the manager of the bookstore. It read:

"Quit sending recommendations. Report for work August 1."

It was the twenty-ninth of July. Edgar withdrew his money from the bank, bought a linen suit, packed his belongings, spent the evening with Gertrude, and took a train early the next morning. Louisville bewildered him, until he discovered that he had bewildered J. P. Morton and Company. The clerks came to look at him. They shook his hand and told him that he had "sure put one over on the boss!"

"Nobody ever came to us with such recommendations," the manager admitted. "They must think you're the greatest man in the world over in Hopkinsville. But there really isn't a job here. You'll have to make one for yourself."

Edgar did his best, as he had with the Hopper brothers. He used his knowledge of the catalogue whenever possible. When a customer bought a book on a certain subject he would say, "We also have . . . " and recite the appropriate list of parallel works. One lady was so fascinated by this that she asked about books on all the subjects in which she had any interest. Edgar recited the names of the books dealing with them. Finally the lady accused him of learning the catalogue by heart. He admitted it. She told his employer, complimenting him on having such a bright clerk.

When she had gone the manager hugged Edgar.

"You've made a hit with the richest woman in town!" he said. "I've been trying to get her trade for years, and you've done it! From now on your salary is raised from seven-fifty a week to ten dollars!"

6

Gertrude ran into the yard, waving the letter. "He's coming home for Christmas!" she cried, landing in a heap on the grass in front of her mother, Aunt Kate, and Stella.

Her mother marked the place in her book and looked up, smiling.

"That's lovely," she said. "His mother will be glad to see him."

Aunt Kate finished a stroke of needle-point. Then she said, laughing:

"Heavenly day, Gertrude, Christmas is four months off. Why all the excitement?"

Gertrude jumped to her feet and grabbed Stella.

"Come on," she said. "Let's go for a walk."

They went around the house and down the path, in the cooling shade of the oaks and maples.

"It's just a year that he's been gone," Gertrude said, "and I thought he was never going to have a chance to come home. Now it seems that he hasn't been gone at all!"

They hung on the gate, looking down the road toward Hopkinsville. By stretching as far as she could, Gertrude was able to see the front of the little house where she had spent her childhood. It stood in a grove of trees just beyond the carriage gate. There she and Hugh and Lynn had played together, until the house was rented and they all moved to the Hill.

Her childhood seemed a long way off, as if she had lived it in another life, when she was someone else. The things that concerned her now had all begun at the gate on which she was perched.

"I remember the first night he came out here," she said to Stella. "He was so shy and bashful that I took him by the arm and led him down here, so he could get away from the crowd.

I was trying to put him at his ease and make him feel at home, but when I remember it now, it's a wonder he didn't think I was being bold."

Stella laughed.

"No one but yourself would accuse you of being flirtatious," she said. "You're not the type."

Gertrude looked at her seriously.

"Do you think I'm the type for marriage?" she asked. "Do you think I'll make a good wife?"

"Oh, yes," Stella said. "You'll spoil your husband, and spoil your children, and work yourself to death. That's the definition of a good wife—according to the men."

"I think two people have to learn gradually to forget what each one wants, when they get married, and find out what they want together," Gertrude said. "And the best way to do that is to have children and let the parents train themselves not to be selfish by sharing the child and all the things that parents want to do for a child."

Stella was suspicious.

"Did you read that in a book?" she asked.

Gertrude shook her head.

"I've been thinking all those things out for myself." She laughed. "I haven't had much else to do for a year."

"It's made you healthy," Stella said. "I didn't know that thinking was so good for muscles. Tell me, what do you expect of marriage, Gertrude?"

They talked on and on, while the day fought off its heat and waited for evening.

To Gertrude it was but a roll of the seasons and he was there, telling her about Louisville and admiring the new color in her cheeks and the new health that glowed from her. She was radiant.

She found him taller, heavier, but as young as ever in his admiration of her. He said nothing about the subject that was uppermost in both their minds until a few days before he was to leave. Then he explained his reticence.

"I've had all the raises I wrote you about," he said, "but I found that living expenses in Louisville just have a way of keeping up with your income, no matter what it is. By the time I got my first raise I was tired of the way in which I had been forced to live, so I expanded a little. With the next raise I expanded a little more.

"And they are still not paying me enough for two to live on comfortably.

"So I've decided to quit."

She looked frightened.

"I have another job, with my father. He has an excellent chance to sell fraternal insurance, going from town to town under the auspices of a society, and writing up the policies which they offer to all new members. The members always take the insurance, because it is very reasonable, and all that is necessary is to go to the places, meet the new members, and sign them up.

"But my father has his own business here in town, and he can't leave it. So he wants me to go into partnership with him and take the fraternal end. I'll go to the towns near here and be back home every weekend. It's a sure thing, and I'm certain to make more money than I did in Louisville. I can live at home, be with my mother, see you, and save enough money in a short time for us to get married."

Gertrude threw her arms around him in relief.

"I'm so happy!" she said. "I knew I couldn't let you go away from me again. I just knew it."

Back in Louisville the manager of J. P. Morton and Company accepted his resignation, but offered to keep him on the payroll if he would take with him, in his travels, a line of specialty books—ledgers, checkbooks, etc.—and introduce them in the towns he visited. He accepted gratefully. On February 1, 1900, Edgar Cayce, salesman and insurance agent, went on the road, touring the towns of western Kentucky.

Early in March he arrived in Elkton, a small town about forty miles from Hopkinsville. For several weeks, off and on, he had been suffering from severe headaches. One morning while in Elkton the pain was particularly bad. He stopped at a doctor's office and asked for a sedative. The doctor gave him a powder and told him to take it with a glass of water. He went back to his hotel and swallowed the dose.

When next he was conscious he was at home in Hopkinsville, in bed. Two doctors were in the room: the family physician, J. B. Jackson, and Dr. A. C. Hill. They were looking at him anxiously. He heard them talking to the squire, who told them that a friend of the family, a man named Ross Rogers, "come on Edgar in the railroad station over in Elkton, wandering around in a daze. Didn't seem to know Ross or anything. Had his overcoat on, but it was open, and his hat was gone. Ross brought him home. Ross was coming anyhow."

Edgar tried to speak, to ask questions, but his voice had dwindled to a faint, painful whisper. They gave him a gargle, but it didn't help. Finally he managed to tell his story, with whispers and gestures. The doctors examined him and said that except for his hoarseness he was all right. The sedative had apparently been too strong and had shocked his nervous system. Probably his sore throat came from wandering around the streets on a cold day with his coat open and no hat on.

They advised him to rest.

Next day he was up and about, ready to get back to work. But the hoarseness had not improved. Nor was it better the next day, nor the next. Dr. Manning Brown, the local throat specialist, was called in. He said something about aphonia and asked for permission to call in other specialists. They came in droves, each with a different theory. There was even a European specialist, who was visiting in a nearby town and came to Hopkinsville to see the "interesting case." Weeks slipped into months. Spring came, and summer. The hoarseness remained.

Edgar became suddenly aware, one day, that his condition was incurable. The doctors weren't visiting him with any idea of being helpful; they regarded him as a curiosity. Something one of them said as he came into Dr. Brown's office, and something in the way Dr. Brown introduced the newcomer, tore the veil away one morning. Edgar saw himself as others saw him: a man who had lost his voice and would never again be able to speak above a whisper.

For a while he found it impossible to give up hope. He was in the habit of expecting to get well; it was hard to break himself of the thought. For the faith he held in the doctors he found himself substituting a belief in miracles. It was only gradually, through acquiring the habit, that he was able to face the truth.

He had to have a job. That was the main force in conditioning him to his new environment. Salesmanship was impossible for a man without a voice; so was clerking; so, it seemed, was everything he had ever done. He could go back to the farm, but he recoiled from the thought. He needed the town; he was lonely, depressed, frightened. He wanted to be near lots of people, even though he couldn't speak with them or join with them in the things they did. He needed them. Left alone, there were problems he had to face, and he was not yet prepared to meet them.

The local photographer, W. R. Bowles, solved the problem of work. He offered a job as apprentice. Edgar accepted; it seemed to be just what he wanted. He would be with lots of people, but without the necessity of speaking with them—Mr. Bowles would do that. He would learn a trade which, whether his voice ever came back or not, would be a means of livelihood.

Another of the problems he had to face disappeared as soon as he took the job. Gertrude was delighted when she heard what he was doing. She had always been interested in photography and painting; she took photographs herself and tinted them.

"We can have our own studios!" she said excitedly. "I'll receive the people and tend to all the business of talking with them and showing them samples and prices, and you can take the pictures and do the developing. I can do tinting, too!"

He nodded, surprised. He had known that the loss of his voice made no difference in her feeling for him, but he had not been able to shake off the conviction that she was justified in breaking the engagement and therefore ought to do it. Somehow it had seemed to him that it was right that he be an outcast. That she not only did not think so, but was identifying herself with his misfortune and turning it into a blessing for them both, was a mystery of compassion and grace that numbed him. It had never occurred to him that she should do something for him. He had been solely concerned with doing everything for her.

But though she drew him closer to her, the sense of ostracism remained. There was a third problem. In the quiet of the studio darkroom, in the solitude of his walks to and from the Hill, in the time of prayer before going to sleep, he was haunted by God.

Had his voice been taken from him because it was meant to be the voice of a preacher? Was he being punished for not heeding the call to serve God? The angel who had appeared to him when he was a child, who had directed him from the farm to Hopkinsville: had she sent him on a mission he had failed to fulfill?

She had said to him: "Your prayers have been heard. Tell me what you would like most of all, so that I may give it to you." He had answered: "Most of all I would like to be helpful to others, and especially to children when they are sick." Then she had disappeared and the next day she had helped him with his lessons.

Why had she helped him with his lessons, if she had not meant him to study and be a preacher—or, as his mother had thought, a doctor? But these things had been impossible. He had done the best he knew how: he had taught Sunday school, formed a mission group, and tried to live like a true Christian. Was there something else he should have done?

Always there had been the feeling within him that he should spend all his time helping other people. But it was impossible to do that and make a living at the same time, unless you were a preacher or a doctor. The disciples of Jesus just left their work and followed Him. But if he did that, after whom would he follow?

When he asked his mother about it she tried to reassure him.

"I've never thought that your voice was meant to be that of a preacher," she said. "Preachers are all right, but they are the sort of people who expect virtue of other people. You're the sort who expects virtue of yourself. There's a difference. Not that preachers aren't all right. Most of them are fine people. But I never could really think of you as a preacher. You seem more like a good Christian. A good Christian is too busy being virtuous himself to worry about whether his neighbor is keeping the law."

She talked some more; she talked quite a bit, in fact, going on and on about things and people and duty and service, until suddenly he realized that she was not answering his question.

She was just talking, and she was worried—worried and puzzled and frightened, as he was.

*   *   *

Everyone in Hopkinsville went to Holland's Opera House when Hart the Laugh King came to town. Hart was a hypnotist; he got his laughs by putting people "under" and telling them to do ridiculous things, such as play hopscotch, imitate fish, climb nonexistent ladders, crochet imaginary doilies, etc. People loved to watch their cousins, friends, and enemies go through these routines, and when volunteers failed, Hart would sit on the stage and hypnotize the audience, swaying back and forth in his chair while he monotonously droned, "Sleep, sleep, sleep." Afterward he would go through the audience, looking for those who had succumbed. He would speak quickly to them, make passes with his hands before their faces, and they would awaken.

Usually he asked for a group to go up on the stage—a "class," he called it. Those who failed to react to his passes and words were dismissed, the others amused the audience. Once Edgar went up with a group of his friends, but he was dismissed.

Hart had a professional troupe, including a man who, when hypnotized, was instructed to remain rigid. Then a large rock was placed on his chest, and another member of the troupe, using a blacksmith's hammer, pounded on the rock until it broke. There were other acts, equally spectacular, and a special demonstration which did for Hart what the parade did for the circus. A local volunteer was given an object and told to hide it anywhere in town. Then Hart, in a carriage drawn by two horses, with a blindfold over his eyes and a man on either side of him, each holding a wrist, would retrace the man's route, telling the driver what turns to take and eventually finding the object. He never failed in these searches, nor did he ever succeed in convincing the skeptical that it wasn't a fake.

Hart usually stayed in town from ten days to two weeks, leaving when the crowds began to dwindle. He was a medium-sized man, with light-brown, wavy hair and hazel-green eyes that seemed uncommonly bright and alert. He wore no robes, used no lights or other paraphernalia, and credited his powers to the "new science" of hypnotism and clairvoyance.

Hypnotism at the time was enjoying a fad throughout the country. The French Academicians had spurned Mesmer and his theories, and although many reputable scientists had worked with hypnotism thereafter, under such titles as somnambulism and magnetic therapy, it had failed to win a clean reputation with science and medicine. In the United States it had both enthusiasts and exploiters. A New York physician, Dr. John P. Quackenboss, said that hypnotism was the medicine of the future, which would cure every illness by directing the unconscious mind of the sufferer to remove the cause and heal the wound. In Nevada, Missouri, a school of "Suggestive Therapeutics" was established by S. A. Weltmer with correspondence courses for those who could not attend in person. Every theater in the country, from time to time, featured a "professor," who offered to put anyone in the audience under his power.

Hart was not a therapist by trade, but he was a thoroughgoing showman. When he heard from some of the townspeople about Edgar's trouble, he accepted it as a challenge. For $200, he said, he would cure the hoarseness. If he did not succeed he would accept nothing for his efforts. Edgar's friends urged him to accept. Dr. Manning Brown smiled and said, "Why not?" The squire thought it was a good idea. He had never forgotten how Edgar had once cured himself by prescribing a poultice.

"Let him put you to sleep and see what happens," he said. "It can't do any harm."

The experiment was conducted in Dr. Brown's office. Edgar sat in an easy chair and did his best to cooperate. Hart began talking, waved his hands a little, then selected a shiny object from Dr. Brown's instrument tray.

"Look at this," he said. "Watch it closely. You are going to sleep now, to sleep . . . to sleep . . . sleep . . . "

When next Edgar was aware of what was going on, they were all smiling at him: Dr. Brown, the squire, and Hart.

"Say something," Hart said.

Edgar spoke. "Did I go under all right?" he asked.

His voice was a hoarse whisper. It had not changed.

The smiles faded.

"You talked quite normally under the spell," Dr. Brown said.

"Good as I've ever heard you," the squire said.

"You were fine," Hart said, "but you didn't take the post-suggestion. We'll try it again, after you've had a rest. I'm sure it can be done. You talked; that's the important thing."

He smiled again. The others nodded and also smiled. Next time the post-suggestion would probably take effect.

But it didn't. They tried that afternoon, and when Edgar awoke he was still hoarse, though he had talked again while "under." They asked him how his throat felt; Dr. Brown examined it. There was no change in its condition. It still seemed normal, as it had seemed to be during all the time of the affliction.

"He gets to the second stage of hypnosis," Hart said, "and then something happens. He won't go beyond it to the third stage, where he would take post-suggestion. But I'm sure he will eventually. We'll keep trying."

Hart was on his mettle now. Everyone in town knew about the experiments, and the local newspaper printed accounts of them. Professor William Girao, who taught psychology at South Kentucky College, asked permission to attend the meetings. He was a small man, an Italian with large, deep-set eyes and a mustache. He was quiet while the hypnotizing proceeded, making notes and occasionally asking a question of Hart.

In the end Hart had to give up. Theatrical bookings took him away from Hopkinsville, and although he returned for another try whenever he was in the vicinity, he admitted that he had failed.

"He won't take post-suggestion," he told Girao. "He won't go beyond the second stage."

Girao wrote an account of the experiments and sent it, with some clippings from the Hopkinsville *New Era,* to Dr. Quackenboss in New York. Dr. Quackenboss expressed interest in the case, entered into correspondence with Girao, and one day in the autumn turned up in Hopkinsville, ready to try his skill on Edgar.

He was a quick-moving, sharp-featured man, with a kindly, thoughtful attitude toward his patient. He asked a lot of questions, listened to the squire's account of Edgar's childhood experiences, took copious notes, and then began his experiments. He had no more success than Hart. Edgar would not go beyond the second stage; he would not take post-suggestion. In a final effort Dr. Quackenboss set about inducing a "deep sleep . . . a very deep sleep . . . a very, very deep sleep."

Edgar slept for twenty-four hours, impervious to all efforts to waken him. Everyone was frightened, and most of the doctors in town gathered for consultation. When the patient awoke it was naturally, as if it were morning. He said he felt fine, though his voice was no better. For days thereafter he could not sleep at all, except in cat naps. Then he got over it, and Dr. Quackenboss, relieved but still puzzled, left.

From New York he wrote to Girao that in thinking over his experiences in Hopkinsville he was convinced that there was a solution to the case. At the point where Edgar refused to take further suggestion he seemed to take charge of things himself, Quackenboss said. If the hypnotist were to suggest, at that point, that the patient talk about his own case, something interesting might result. Such things had been reported in France, many years before: patients under hypnosis showed powers of clairvoyance. Whether or not there was anything to it was problematical, but the chance was worth the effort.

The only hypnotist in Hopkinsville was Al C. Layne, a thin, frail man whose wife ran the millinery shop where Annie Cayce, Edgar's sister, worked. Layne was not in good health; he kept books for his wife and, to pass the time, studied suggestive therapeutics and osteopathy by means of correspondence courses. He had followed the accounts of the experiments in Dr. Brown's office with the greatest interest. When he learned from Annie that her brother and Girao were looking for a hypnotist, he begged for a chance to try his skill.

Edgar was willing, but his parents objected. He had been losing weight ever since the first experiment; he was nervous, fretful, high strung. The squire, at first hopeful of a cure, had become convinced that hypnotism was no more beneficial than medicine.

"First we had the doctors coming, one after another, poking

at him as if he was a sick sow," he said to his wife. "Now these
hypnotists are doing the same thing. They'll drive the boy crazy."

"He's not well," the mother said. "He's not eating or sleeping."

Edgar asked for a compromise. Let Layne try one experiment,
following the suggestion made by Dr. Quackenboss. If this did
not bring results, he would submit to no more hypnotizing.

Reluctantly they agreed. Annie brought Layne to the house
and introduced him. He was a wisp of a man, weighing hardly
a hundred and twenty pounds, with graying hair and a small
mustache. He was somewhere between thirty-five and forty,
though his apparent ill-health made it hard to judge. He was
anxious to make the test as soon as possible. The date was set
for the following Sunday afternoon, March 31, 1901.

Girao could not attend. Layne arrived about 2:30. The girls
had finished the dinner dishes and gone out. Edgar and his father
and mother were in the parlor. Edgar suggested that he put himself
to sleep—as he did when sleeping on his books—and that when
he was apparently "under," Layne make the attempt to talk to
him. He had discovered, he told Layne, that no matter what the
hypnotist did, it was his own thought that made him go to sleep.
Layne said that the more Edgar could do of his own volition,
the more they might accomplish. He agreed with the idea of
self-hypnosis, or, as he called it, "autohypnosis."

Edgar lay down on the family couch, a horsehair sofa that
had been part of his grandmother Cayce's wedding suite. He
put himself to sleep.

Layne, watching, saw the breathing deepen. There was a long
sigh, then the body seemed to sleep. The squire sat in a chair
near by. His wife, nervous, stood up. Layne began to talk in a
low, soothing voice, suggesting that Edgar see his body and
describe the trouble in the throat. He suggested that Edgar speak
in a normal tone of voice.

In a few minutes Edgar began to mumble. Then he cleared
his throat and began to speak in a clear, unafflicted voice.

"Yes," he said, "we can see the body."

"Take it down!" Layne said to the squire.

The squire looked at him helplessly. The nearest pencil was

in the kitchen, tied to the grocery list.

"In the normal state," Edgar went on, "this body is unable to speak, due to a partial paralysis of the inferior muscles of the vocal cords, produced by nerve strain. This is a psychological condition producing a physical effect. This may be removed by increasing the circulation to the affected parts by suggestion while in this unconscious condition."

"The circulation to the affected parts will now increase," Layne said, "and the condition will be removed."

Edgar was silent. They watched his throat. The squire leaned over and further loosened his son's shirt. Gradually the upper part of the chest, then the throat, turned pink. The pink deepened to rose, the rose became a violent red. Ten, fifteen, twenty minutes passed.

Edgar cleared his throat again.

"It is all right now," he said. "The condition is removed. Make the suggestion that the circulation return to normal, and that after that the body awaken."

"The circulation will return to normal," Layne said. "The body will then awaken."

They watched while the red faded back through rose to pink. The skin resumed its normal color. Edgar wakened, sat up, and reached for his handkerchief. He coughed and spat blood.

"Hello," he said tentatively.

Then he grinned.

"Hey!" he said. "I can talk! I'm all right!"

His mother wept. His father seized his hand and shook it again and again.

"Good boy! Good boy! Good boy!" he said.

7

They went into the kitchen to write down what had been said. The squire gave his version, Layne gave his. Edgar kept trying his voice. His mother busied herself with the coffee pot, smiling and drying her eyes as she bustled back and forth between the pantry and the stove.

"This is the greatest thing that ever happened to you, Edgar," Layne said, "but it may be the greatest thing that's happened to the rest of us, too.

"If you can do this for yourself, why can't you do it for others? It shouldn't be any more difficult for you to see another man while you're asleep than it was to see yourself."

"Maybe I was just reading my own mind," Edgar said. "Don't they say that there is a record in the mind of everything that goes on in the body?"

"He did it before," the squire said. "He saw himself when he was hit with a ball and prescribed a poultice."

Layne nodded. He had heard the tale.

"But he also saw books that were placed under his head," he said, "and afterward he could see the pages of the books in his mind. Why couldn't he see other people's bodies if they were before him and tell what was wrong with them?"

"I'm willing to try," Edgar said. He felt grateful to Layne and so happy that he could not have refused him anything within his power.

"Tomorrow," Layne said. "We'll try it tomorrow, on me. I've been ailing with stomach trouble for years. I've had all sorts of doctors look at me. I know their diagnosis. I'll be able to tell whether you are describing the right symptoms and how close you come to the right kind of treatment."

"Sounds crazy to me," Edgar said, "but I'll try it."

He laughed. He was so happy and relieved that he was ready to attempt anything, believe anything, do anything.

When Layne left, his mother said, "You may lose your voice again if you try what Mr. Layne suggests."

Edgar shook his head.

"I don't think so," he said. "If I have the power to help myself, then it can't be wrong to try and use it to aid someone else."

His mother was pleased. He had answered her in the language of morals, though she had not brought up such a question.

"I just wanted to hear you say it," she said. "I feel that way, too. Remember, I've often thought about you as a doctor, and we've always believed there was a reason for your experiences. This may be the answer."

The squire finished lighting a cigar and arranging the fire at its end.

"He'll cure anybody," he said. "I'll bet on it!"

Edgar looked at his mother.

"Don't forget to thank God for this miracle," she said. "It was He who performed it."

Next afternoon Layne arrived with a series of questions he had written concerning his condition. Edgar declined to read them.

"They wouldn't mean anything to me anyhow," he said.

As on the previous day, he put himself to sleep. Layne sat by, holding a pad and pencil. When Edgar woke up, Layne waved the pad at him gleefully.

"You went all over me!" he said. "Gave me a perfect diagnosis, told me how I feel, and what to do—medicines, a diet, and a set of exercises. If it works, our fortunes are made!"

Edgar looked at what Layne had written down. There were names of parts of the body, names of medicines and foods, and instructions for exercises.

"How could I tell you these things . . . ?"

He stopped, realizing suddenly that his voice was still with him, still normal.

"I've never heard of most of the names you have here," he went on. "I've never studied physiology, or biology, or chemistry, or anatomy. I've never even worked in a drugstore. Are these patent medicines?"

"Some of them are," Layne said. "Some are simple mixtures that don't require a prescription. I'm going to get them all and start the schedule. We'll see how it works. If I get well, we'll try this on others."

In a week Layne was so improved that he wanted to begin experiments with other people. Edgar was worried.

"How do I do it?" he asked.

"Clairvoyance," Layne said.

The word meant nothing to Edgar. He went to his mother and asked her the same question.

"In our dreams," she said, "we sometimes can do things that we can't do when we're awake. I have that happen to me often. Perhaps we have powers like that. Maybe everything is in us, as some people say—I've heard preachers talk about it—and it takes work and study to bring it out. You couldn't study, but you worked hard, and wanted to help others, and perhaps this is what the lady in the vision meant when she said, 'Your prayers have been heard.'"

He was not inclined to agree; he was afraid to. Sleeping on books and reciting lessons from them was one thing; telling a man what was wrong with him and prescribing medicines was quite another. He might kill somebody.

"There's no chance of that," Layne said. "I know enough about medicine to tell whether a thing is dangerous. Besides, medicines that might be poisonous or have narcotics in them require a doctor's prescription; we couldn't get them filled even if you prescribed them. So you'll have to give me simple remedies. I'll suggest that. If you name a medicine that I can't get, I'll ask you to name a substitute that is obtainable."

In three weeks from the time he began the treatments Layne felt so well that he rented two rooms over his wife's millinery store and fitted them as his office. He intended to practice suggestive therapeutics and osteopathy, he announced. Edgar knew that he was expected to help.

Meanwhile his voice was dwindling. Day by day it became weaker.

"We'll try again," Layne said. "Come over to the office and we'll break in the new couch. It just arrived."

Edgar went, doubting and worried.

When he woke from the self-imposed sleep his voice was normal again. There was no alternative now. He had to help Layne.

"I'm willing to try someone else," he said, "if you like. The only condition I set is that you don't tell me who the person is, either before or after. I don't want to know."

In a few days the attempt was made. When Edgar awoke Layne patted him on the shoulder.

"A perfect diagnosis," he said.

"How do you know?" Edgar asked.

"The doctor said the same thing, last week, only he didn't know a cure. You gave me one."

"Is it safe?"

"Perfectly safe. And simple. This thing is wonderful. It can't miss."

Months passed. Layne officially opened his office, with Edgar, as silent partner, doing the diagnosing and refusing to take any money.

"It's bad enough," he told Layne mournfully, "but to take money for it—that would be the end."

His father frequently came to the experiments, and it was a comfort to Edgar to know that someone was there to watch what went on while he was asleep and be sure that what Layne told him afterward was actually what had happened. It wasn't that he mistrusted Layne; he mistrusted himself, while he was asleep.

Layne found that he had to tell Edgar where the people were at the time. Some were in the outer office when, unknown to them, the experiments went on; others came for examination and were told to return in a few days for a diagnosis and outline of treatment. Meanwhile they were checked on by Edgar. Layne called the experiments "readings" and described Edgar's sleep state as "a self-imposed hypnotic trance which induces clairvoyance."

The patients, according to Layne, improved under the treatments, and many were cured. He himself was immensely better; at least there was no doubt about that. But Edgar remained uncomforted. One dead patient was all that was needed to make him a murderer.

He wanted to quit, yet he couldn't. About once a month his

voice dwindled and faded, and he needed Layne to give the suggestion necessary to its return. After a while the periods of its strength began to lengthen. He didn't know whether this was because he was gradually overcoming the condition or whether it was because he was allowing himself to be used for the help of others. Sometimes he hoped one way, sometimes the other.

Few people knew what he was up to. He told Gertrude, of course, and she was inclined to worry about it. There was a common belief at the time that subjects of hypnosis eventually went insane and that, at the very least, their health suffered from habitual immersion in trance.

"I'm glad you have your voice back, and I don't believe Layne is any Svengali," Gertrude said, "but I can't help feeling that it is not good for your health. I wish you'd stop."

"I wish I could," he answered.

Carrie Salter thought that Gertrude's fears and Edgar's doubts were nonsense. She went to Layne's office to witness the experiments, asked questions on the progress of the patients, and flatly said that God had given Edgar a gift intended to be used to help people.

"I don't care what the rest of you think," she said, "but believe me if I'm ever sick I'm going to get a reading from Edgar and I'm going to do just what it says. I don't believe the doctors know what they're talking about anyhow, at least half the time."

Such faith frightened Edgar. He prayed that either it be justified or the strange power be taken away from him.

* * *

He was a full-fledged photographer now, and with the return of his voice Mr. Bowles sent him on trips to the surrounding towns. In each place he set up shop for a few days, photographed the school children, newlyweds, and babies and made postcard pictures of the town hall and other public buildings.

On a night in May, 1902, he arrived in Lafayette. The hotel clerk had a message for him.

"You're to call the Bowling Green operator," he said. "There's a long-distance call for you."

The voice at the other end of the wire was familiar. It belonged to Frank Bassett, one of Hopkinsville's younger physicians.

"Got a job for you over here in Bowling Green, if you want it," Bassett said. "Friend of mine named L. D. Potter runs a bookstore. His right-hand man is leaving him to start in business for himself and he needs an experienced hand right away. I told him you were the fellow. It's a nice spot and the salary's good."

Edgar made up his mind while he was listening. He wanted to get away from Hopkinsville, from Layne, from the readings. It might be all right to give them, but he wasn't sure; he wanted time to think things over. What worried him most was that Layne was not a physician. With a doctor's approval, under a doctor's supervision, he would not have been afraid to try any kind of experiment; with a correspondence school healer it was different.

"I'll take the job," he told Bassett. "I'll go to Hopkinsville tomorrow and leave for Bowling Green tomorrow night."

When he entered the Potter store two days later he felt that he had come back home. There were the books he knew so well; there were the pictures, the frames, the stationery, the notebooks, and the fresh-smelling boxes of pencils. The customers even appeared to be the same—bookstore devotees, he had discovered, were a type. He slipped into the job as easily as into an old pair of shoes.

He found Bowling Green to be a pretty little city of 10,000, on the Barren River, at the junction of the Memphis division of the Louisville and Nashville Railroad. It bustled with students from three colleges: a business university, a Bible school, and Ogden College, an institution founded by a rich Bowling Green citizen to provide free higher education for the students of Warren County, of which the city was the seat.

The business life of the city clustered around Fountain Square, a lovely island of lawn and shade trees in the center of a sea of red-brick buildings and showy store fronts. State and College streets were its east and west boundaries; Main Street and Frozen Row enclosed it on the north and south. On State Street, a few doors past the end of the square, was the Potter store.

At the end of the first day Mr. Potter took him down State Street, past the square, to a large frame house, painted cream with white shutters and standing about as far north of the square as the store was south of it.

"This is Mrs. Hollins's place," Mr. Potter said. "It's a boardinghouse where a lot of the young professional folk stay. The meals are good, and it's only a short walk to the store. I think you'll like it."

They entered a large reception room. To the left was the dining room. Ahead was a stairway, leading to the second floor. Mrs. Hollins, a short, stout, smiling lady, came to greet them. She took Edgar upstairs to show him a room.

"The young men have the upper floor," she explained. "The ladies stay on the ground floor. I'm a widow, you know, with two daughters. They stay here with me. We've some real nice young men; I'm sure you'll like them. How would you like a roommate? I have a big room here, made for two. Just one boy in there now. Let's see if he's in. He's a doctor—eye, ear, nose and throat specialist. Here . . . "

She knocked at a door. It opened and a short, wiry young man stood looking at them and smiling.

"This is Dr. Hugh Beazley," Mrs. Hollins said. "Hugh, this is the new clerk at Potter's—Edgar Cayce's his name. He's thinking of putting up with us, if we can put up with him, eh?"

Edgar shook hands with the young man.

"You're from Hopkinsville, aren't you?" he asked. "I know about you, but I've never met you."

"You're one of the Cayces," Dr. Beazley said. "I've never met all of them. Has anyone?"

Mrs. Hollins stood, nodding and smiling.

"I'll go down and tell Mr. Potter you're going to stay," she said to Edgar. "If you two want to bunk together, all right. If not, I'll find another room."

"I'd love to have you move in," Dr. Beazley said. "I'd like some company."

"So would I," Edgar said. "I was afraid I was going to be lonesome."

They went down to dinner together, and at table Edgar met his dormitory mates. Two of them were brothers: Dr. John Blackburn, a medical practitioner who wore a full vandyke beard to disguise his youth; and Dr. James Blackburn, a dentist. The others were Joe Darter, secretary of the Y.M.C.A., and Bob Holland, who worked in a department store. They were all about Edgar's age. He liked them at once. They were friendly, helpful, and full of the joy of life. They were doing things that mattered, too; things that Edgar had always dreamed of doing. That night he wrote to Gertrude:

> This is the place for us. It's full of young people, and they are all busy doing something. The town is beautiful. At night it is quiet and the coolness from the trees in the square comes right in my window. The streets are so clean and the houses all look as if they had just been washed. You will love it, I know . . .

He joined the Christian Church and the Christian Endeavour Group. Joe Darter took him to lectures and parties at the Y.M.C.A. He opened a bank account. Life was beginning all over again.

The dream lasted two weeks. Then his voice began to fade. After closing time on Saturday he called Layne by long distance and whispered his predicament over the telephone. Layne told him to come to Hopkinsville. He took the night train, went to Layne's office the next morning, and put himself to sleep. When he awakened his voice was normal.

"This is liable to hit you at any time, Edgar," Layne said. "Why don ' t you let me come over to Bowling Green on Sunday once in a while? We can keep your voice in good shape, and I can ask about my patients."

Edgar was stuck.

"All right," he said.

At first Layne came twice a month. Soon the visits became weekly. It was a chore to ease Beazley out of the room every Sunday afternoon so the readings could be given. Edgar dared not tell any of his young doctor friends about it, or anyone in Bowling Green, for that matter. He was afraid. When he was with Beazley, the Blackburns, and his other new friends, or when he was with Gertrude, he knew exactly what he wanted. He wanted to live a normal, simple, ordinary Christian life, married to the girl he loved, living in the town he liked, with the friends he had chosen. He didn't want to be "queer" or "different." He didn't want to be a psychic medium, or a somnambulist, or a "mystic healer."

But when Layne talked about having increasing success with his patients, he was disquieted. Suppose he had a real power, and the use of that power for sick people was his mission? It seemed so simple: the vision, the ability to sleep on books and know their contents, the loss of his voice, its recovery through the discovery of his real power.

If only he could be sure. If only the doctors believed it, instead of Layne, with his correspondence school knowledge and his magnetic treatments.

Late in the summer, on a sticky August day, he received a telephone call from Hopkinsville. It was from Mr. C. H. Dietrich, former superintendent of the Hopkinsville public schools.

"Mr. Layne has told me of the things you have done for some of his patients," Mr. Dietrich said. "I have a little girl who's been ill for a long time. No one seems to be able to help her. There'll be a ticket waiting for you at the railroad station if you'll come over here Sunday and see what you can do for her. My wife wants you to come, too. I'll meet you at the station."

Edgar said he would go. Mr. Dietrich was one of the most eminent and respected men in Hopkinsville. He must know what he was doing. Still, it might be that he was at the end of his hope, ready to try anything. In that case, if all the doctors had given the child up, there was nothing to be lost by trying a reading.

At the station Edgar fingered the ticket curiously. It was the first material thing he had ever received for the use of his power. Could the thing really be worth something?

In Hopkinsville Mr. Dietrich, a small, quiet, reserved man, met him at the station with a carriage. On the way to the house he explained that his daughter, Aime, had been ill for three years. She was now five, and since the age of two, after an attack of grippe, her mind had not developed. She had been taken to many specialists; none had been able to cure her or even stop the convulsions which attacked her in increasing numbers. Her mind was a blank.

"She is at home now," Mr. Dietrich said. "We have had some treatments here, but she just gets worse—twenty convulsions a day, sometimes."

When they got to the house, Mr. Dietrich took him in to see the child. She was in her playroom, sitting on the floor with her building blocks. She looked like any normal, healthy girl of her age. A nurse sat in a chair nearby, watching her.

"Do you want to examine her?" Mr. Dietrich asked.

"No," Edgar said. She looked healthier than he felt.

In the living room Mrs. Dietrich was talking to Layne. Edgar, anxious to get it over with, lay down on the sofa and put himself to sleep. When he awakened, Mrs. Dietrich was weeping.

"Mr. Cayce," she said, "you've given us the first hope we've had for a normal baby. You'll just have to stay and see whether Mr. Layne makes the adjustments properly."

Edgar stared at her. "What did I say?" he asked.

"You told us that she slipped and struck the end of her spine while getting out of the carriage, a few days before catching grippe. The grippe germs settled in her spine and caused the attacks. Mr. Layne is to make some osteopathic adjustments, and she will recover."

Edgar looked at Layne and thought about jail. "Mail Order Osteopath and Somnambulist Partner Jailed For Medical Fraud," the papers would say.

"I'll telephone your employer and ask him to let you off," Mr. Dietrich said.

Edgar looked at Mrs. Dietrich. She was watching him, waiting for his answer.

"I'll stay," he said, in a voice that was barely audible.

He went to his home for dinner and spent the evening with Gertrude. Next morning he went to Dietrich's and gave a reading. When he awakened, Mrs. Dietrich smiled at him. "You'll have to stay a little longer," she said. "The adjustments have not been made quite correctly."

When he was able to get Layne alone, Edgar asked him if he knew what he was doing.

"Of course," Layne said, "but it's a difficult thing to get right the first time, and I'm being particularly careful and gentle, so the spine won't be bruised or hurt."

Layne tried again, and in the afternoon another reading was taken. The treatment was more nearly as it was desired, but still imperfect. Layne tried again, and next morning another "check reading," as Layne called it, was taken. This time the adjustments had been properly made.

Edgar left that afternoon for Bowling Green. Layne was to continue the treatments every day for three weeks.

"But I'll be over next week to see you," he told Edgar at the station.

When Layne arrived the following Sunday he had good news. The Dietrich child was responding. She had suddenly called the name of a doll of which she had been fond before her attacks began. A day after that she had called her mother by name, then her father.

"She's picking up where she left off," Layne said. "Mrs. Dietrich says her mind is in the state of development it had attained just before it went blank."

At the end of three weeks Layne took a check reading on the case. The child, Edgar reported, was developing normally and would continue to do so. The condition which had caused the illness was corrected. No further treatments were necessary.

After three months Mrs. Dietrich told Layne that her daughter was normal in all respects and was rapidly covering the educational ground that separated her from other children of her age. There had been no recurrence of the attacks.

Edgar was pleased and relieved, but he warned Layne not to publicize the case and continued to keep the meetings at Bowling Green a secret. He still had a single goal: marriage to Gertrude, with a natural, normal life thereafter in Bowling Green.

What he needed to realize this ambition was money. He was saving part of his salary, but he dreamed of making a big sum, so that he could buy a house and have it all furnished for his bride. During the winter he came close to getting just what he wanted.

He was placed on the entertainment committee at the Y.M.C.A., and along with an art teacher of the public schools, a man named F. O. Putnam, planned parties and dances for the members. For one of these affairs Putnam suggested that they devise a new card game. Edgar, who listened every evening at the dinner table to discussions of the wheat market in Chicago, worked out something he called "Pit," or "Board of Trade." The cards represented quantities of grain, and the idea was to corner the wheat market.

It was so popular at the entertainment for which it had been invented that special decks of cards were printed for "Y" members. Edgar sent a sample to a game company. He received a cordial letter, thanking him for the idea. Soon Pit games flooded the country. Edgar received a dozen decks of the cards, with the company's compliments.

He protested. He went to a lawyer. The company pointed out that it owned the copyright, and reminded him that he could be prosecuted if he attempted to print and sell the cards himself.

"You should have had a reading on it," Layne told him. "It would have warned you to copyright the game before sending it to the company."

"A lawyer would have told me the same thing, if I had had sense enough to ask him," Edgar said.

"Listen," Layne said, "I want to tell you what you've just done."

It was Sunday afternoon. Edgar had awakened from his sleep. Layne pointed to the notebook in which he had put down the suggestions for his patients which Edgar had given while asleep.

"One of these patients was in New York. His name is P. A. Andrews. According to his stationery he's managing director of the Mechanicsburg Railroad. He heard about you from Dr. Quackenboss. You see, I've been sending reports to the doctor."

He paused, waiting for Edgar to be impressed.

"What did I say about him?" Edgar asked.

"You gave a fine diagnosis, although I don't know whether it fits the case. You outlined treatments, too.

"What I'm driving at is that this man wants to pay you. He expects that you'll charge for your services. That's natural. You should. In no time at all you can make more money than you ever would have got from a card game."

Edgar shook his head.

"That's out," he said. "I'll have to solve it some other way!"

"What are you going to do?" Layne asked.

Edgar gazed out the window. It was spring. The birds were chattering in the trees on Fountain Square. The leaves were coming out. The odor of quickened earth drifted in to him.

"I'm going to get married anyhow," he said.

Layne stared absently at his notebook.

"Did you ever hear of clary water?" he said.

"No."

"You gave it for Mr. Andrews. It's probably some patented tonic. When are you getting married?"

"In June."

They were silent then. Across the street a mockingbird was building a nest in a tree in Mrs. McCluskey's yard.

8

They were married on Wednesday, June 17, 1903, at the Hill. Dr. Beazley and Bob Holland accompanied Edgar from Bowling Green, to give him moral support. With Hugh and Lynn, Gertrude's brothers, they formed a committee of four to serve as best man. The squire, with his wife and four daughters, arrived with Harry Smith, minister of the Christian Church in Hopkinsville, who was to perform the ceremony. Carrie Salter, Stella, Aunt Kate, and Mrs. Evans all crowded into the bride's room to help her dress. Will and Hiram, assisted by Porter and Raymond, were hosts to the men. It was a lovely spring afternoon. They all gathered in the living room.

"I was afraid we were never going to make it," Edgar whispered to Gertrude.

"I always knew we would, someday," she said.

It was six years, three months, and three days since they had become engaged.

After the ceremony the committee serving as best man bundled them into a buggy and escorted them, in a second carriage, to Guthrie, one of the villages near Hopkinsville. There the party had dinner; afterward Gertrude and Edgar took the train to Bowling Green.

He had rented a room for them at Mrs. McCluskey's, just across the street from Mrs. Hollins's place. They were to take their meals with Mrs. Hollins. The McCluskey house was a large frame building; Gertrude walked up to it with her eyes fixed on the circular staircase that was visible through the open front door. She felt that it was a good omen. Her grandfather had come to Hopkinsville to build a circular staircase; he had stayed there and raised a family.

Their room looked toward the square. Gertrude leaned out

the window, inhaling the fresh odor that drifted to her from the trees and the gardens that had come to life around the fountain.

"You were right, Edgar," she said. "This is the place for us."

Next day she walked through the neighboring streets, fed the birds in the square, and wrote to her mother that, "I didn't believe there was such a lovely place in Kentucky."

On Sunday when she and Edgar crossed the street to Mrs. Hollins's for dinner she saw a familiar figure in the reception room.

"Edgar, what's Layne doing over here?" she asked.

Edgar explained, but he realized that his reasons sounded lame. Gertrude was ruffled.

"He could at least have stayed away today," she said. "This is the first Sunday of our married life."

At the dinner table she was cool to Layne. Judge Roup, an occasional boarder who rode a circuit as magistrate and was also a newspaperman, noticed it. He was curious about Layne, having seen him at the table on many Sundays.

"Mr. Layne," he said casually, "they tell me you're a doctor."

John Blackburn looked up; James Blackburn looked up; Beazley looked up. Edgar became very busy with his mashed potatoes.

"Yes," Layne said.

"Tell me," Roup went on, "how is it that you favor Bowling Green with a visit almost every Sunday?"

"I come to see Edgar," Layne said.

"Is he sick?" Roup asked. "We have several fine doctors here—" he nodded toward the Blackburn boys and Beazley— "can't they help?"

Edgar looked at his plate. Gertrude stared straight at Layne.

"Well," Layne said, "Edgar doesn't like to talk about it, but I come here to ask him about my patients."

Everyone looked at Edgar.

"Ask him about your patients?" Roup said. "Is Edgar a doctor? What's he been keeping from us?"

"He is gifted with a very unusual power," Layne said. "He has the ability to hypnotize himself, and while in that state he is clairvoyant. He can see other people and diagnose their ailments. He cured himself of aphonia after being unable to speak above a whisper for a year. He cured me of an illness that had bothered me for years. He has helped many others.

"If you wish, I will let you see a demonstration this afternoon. I am sure you will say it is the most unusual thing you have ever seen."

Nobody spoke. The meal was finished in a hurry. Roup finally managed to say, "I'd like to see it." Gertrude fled across the street and went to her room in tears.

They went upstairs to Beazley's room, and while Edgar waited for his dinner to settle—though he was sure this was one meal he would never digest—Layne told the story of his experiments, including the Dietrich case. The boys asked lots of questions, particularly John Blackburn, the physician.

Finally Edgar put himself to sleep. When he awakened his friends looked at him with speculation and wonder. John Blackburn spoke to Layne.

"Dr. Layne," he said, "the first person you asked about was given certain medicines to take. Are you going to give those medicines?"

"I am," Layne said.

"The second patient was advised to take electrical vibrations. Are you going to give them?"

"Yes," Layne said.

"The third person," said Blackburn, "was told to have osteopathic adjustments. Are you going to give those?"

"Yes," Layne said.

Blackburn smiled blandly.

"Dr. Layne," he asked, "what medical school did you attend?"

Layne blushed.

"I haven't been to any school—yet," he said. "I've studied a lot, by myself, but most of what I know has come from Edgar during the past two years, while he's been asleep."

"You have been treating patients?"

"Yes."

"You have an office?"

"Yes, in Hopkinsville."

"Your patients always improve or get well from these treatments?"

"Invariably, if they do as they are told."

"Tell me this. Why does Edgar mix up his treatments so? There are many schools of medicine—allopathic, homeopathic, naturopathic, osteopathic. Edgar seems to use them all. That doesn't make sense."

"I think it does. Some people need one form of treatment, some need another. No one school has all the remedies."

They talked on and on, until Layne had to leave to catch his train. Then they questioned Edgar. When he returned to Mrs. McCluskey's he was tired and bewildered. Gertrude had got over her own feelings. She put her arms around him.

"I'm glad it's out, and they know," she said. "You can't hide a thing like that. Just promise me that you won't let it take you away from me or from the things you want to do."

"I won't," he promised. "Someday I would like to know just what it is, and what I am supposed to do with it. I felt like such a fool in front of those boys—Jim and John and Hugh, all doctors with degrees and offices. And me telling people how to take osteopathic treatments and dictating prescriptions while I'm asleep! It's fantastic!"

She kissed him.

"Don't worry about it," she said. "Just don't use it for an evil purpose, and I'm sure it won't do you any harm."

But she wasn't sure. Neither was he.

"My mother says"—he was talking to convince both of them—"that if it's a thing of God, it will do only good. If it's a thing of the devil, it won't succeed."

"The devil has many disguises," Gertrude said. "I hope we recognize him when he comes."

The next evening there was an article in the Bowling Green *Times-Journal,* by Judge Roup, telling of the previous day's experiment. The Nashville papers copied the story. Edgar prepared to be peered at, questioned, and pointed out, as he had been in Hopkinsville during the time that Hart worked on him.

"I reckon I'm in for it," he said to Gertrude.

She laughed.

"You should see the ladies look at me!" she said.

Layne made two more visits to Bowling Green. Then, at the

request of the medical authorities of the state, he closed his office and discontinued practice.

"We can't have a man like that treating people," John Blackburn explained to Edgar. "He hasn't the knowledge or training. Even if there is something in what you're doing, a qualified doctor ought to be administering it.

"Or," he added, "a flock of them. You don't seem to have any prejudices."

Layne wrote Edgar that he was leaving immediately for Franklin, Kentucky, to enter the Southern School of Osteopathy and prepare himself to be a collaborator with the readings. A week later Edgar began to lose his voice again.

He appealed to John Blackburn. He felt indebted to him for handling the situation with Layne so tactfully that no unfavorable publicity resulted and no charges were brought. To be relieved of the fear of arrest or disgrace, which had been with him almost constantly while Layne was practicing, was a blessing. But he had to get his voice back.

Blackburn was not so reluctant as he had supposed. He was curious to experiment, but worried lest he be unable to bring Edgar out of it.

"Just tell me to wake up," Edgar said, "and in about a minute it will happen."

He wrote out the suggestion to be given for regaining his voice. Then he went to sleep. They were alone in Blackburn's office.

When he awakened, Blackburn was standing by the door, pale and trembling.

"Let's get out of here," he said.

Edgar went with him down the stairway and out into the street. They walked rapidly toward the square.

"You did it," Blackburn said. "I watched the blood go up into your chest and throat. Then I saw it come back again. As soon as you went to sleep you talked normally. Your voice is all right now. And you woke up when I told you to. I thought all that stuff with Layne might be hooey, but this is no fake. I saw it happen. What's it all about?"

"I wish I knew," Edgar said unhappily. "That's what worries me. I don't know what it's all about."

A few days later a letter arrived from Mr. Andrews, the New York man for whom clary water had been prescribed. He had been unable to find it, although he had inquired at all the leading drug houses. He was advertising for it in the medical journals, but in the meantime, why couldn't Edgar go to sleep and tell him where it could be found or of what ingredients it was composed? Edgar showed the letter to Blackburn.

"I don't seem to know what I'm talking about," he said. "This is what I've been afraid of all along. Layne always said he could find anything I prescribed, but here's proof against me."

"Let's try the experiment and see what we get," Blackburn said.

He was over his fear, and more curious than before. Whatever was wrong with Edgar could be discovered, he thought, and explained. It was probably a nerve distortion of some sort and would make an interesting case. He and Beazley had discussed the matter with some of their colleagues: Dr. J. E. Stone, Dr. Fred Reardon, Dr. Fred Cartwright, and Dr. George Meredith. They were thinking of forming a committee to investigate the phenomenon, providing Edgar would cooperate.

Some of the doctors were present when Blackburn conducted the check reading for Mr. Andrews. When Edgar awakened Blackburn had the formula for clary water written down.

"Sounds like a powerful tonic," he said. "Garden sage water is the base. That's what clary is—garden sage. Then ambergris, dissolved in grain alcohol. Then some gin and some cinnamon."

Edgar shook his head. "Lord, what a dose!" he said.

"It won't hurt him," Blackburn said.

The other doctors nodded. They were interested.

"Well send this to Mr. Andrews, and get his report on its effect," Blackburn said. "I'll mix some up, too. If it's really a good tonic— if you can go to sleep and toss off things like that, then we want to find out all we can about it. We'll investigate it thoroughly, and let you know whether you belong in a circus or an institution, eh, boys?"

They laughed, and Edgar laughed with them. Whatever happened now, he was being looked after by the right kind of people. They would not allow him to harm others through the readings, and they would not allow the thing, whatever it was, to harm him. They would find out what it was and what should be done with it.

*   *   *

He visited Layne several times at the Southern School of Osteopathy. He liked the man, and now that the fear of doing something wrong had passed, he enjoyed talking with him. Layne was interested when he heard that the doctors were going to conduct an investigation. He suggested an experiment of his own.

"We have cases from the clinic which we have to diagnose," he said. "The professors know what is wrong with these persons. They check on our knowledge by asking us what we think. Why couldn't we take readings on some of those cases, and see how your diagnosis checks with that of the professors?"

Edgar was willing. He arranged to come to the school on a weekend when Gertrude was in Hopkinsville, visiting at the Hill. Layne made preparations. He even confided in some of his fellow students and invited them to attend.

The idea backfired. Layne had been accorded a year's credit at the school because of his knowledge of anatomy, medicine, and osteopathy, although he had no regular credits for these subjects. The students resented the concession, and when they found out about Edgar they decided to frame Layne and expose him to Dr. Bowling, the head of the school.

To carry out their plans they enlisted the aid of one of their instructors, a medical doctor named Percy Woodall. A group attended the reading on Saturday, ascertained that the same classroom would be used for the Sunday experiment, and then with Dr. Woodall's help, lured Dr. Bowling into an adjoining classroom.

Dr. Bowling was blind, the result of an accident suffered during his student days, but he dissected corpses skillfully, lectured on anatomy, and made osteopathic diagnoses by running the tips of his fingers over the spine. He was generally around the school on Sunday, helping the students in their laboratory work and answering questions. The group of conspirators, led by Dr. Woodall, encountered him in the hall and began asking about a certain case. Dr. Woodall asked him to go into the lecture room to expand on the subject. Then one of the students opened the door leading to the room where Edgar was giving the reading. He had just begun and was speaking in a clear, loud voice. Layne sat beside him. He did not notice when the door behind him opened.

Dr. Bowling, irritated by the interrupting voice, stopped to listen to it.

"Who is that in the next room lecturing on anatomy?" he asked.

The students said they didn't know.

"I want to hear him," Dr. Bowling said. "Take me in there, Dr. Woodall."

They led him in and placed him beside Layne, who turned white at the sight of him. He could not stop Edgar, he knew. The reading, a diagnosis of one of the school's clinic cases, continued.

Dr. Bowling waited until Edgar said, "Ready for questions." Then he asked one. There was no answer.

"Why doesn't he answer me?" the doctor said. "Who is this man?"

Layne repeated the question. Edgar answered it.

"Who is the other man?" Dr. Bowling asked. "Why doesn't he answer me instead of him?"

Miserably Layne made the suggestion that Edgar wake up. Then he tried to explain things. Dr. Bowling listened. When Edgar was awake, he questioned him about his education and medical training.

"What Mr. Layne says is right," Edgar said. "I've never been to medical school. I never got further than grammar school."

"Ridiculous!" Dr. Bowling said. "That was a perfect diagnosis. I know the patient. Furthermore, your anatomy is flawless. Tell me about this business."

The students who had engineered the frame-up disappeared. Dr. Woodall and Dr. Bowling heard the story to its end. Getting up to go, Dr. Bowling reached for Edgar's hand and shook it.

"Come and see us again," he said. "This is very interesting.

What a marvelous brain yours would be to dissect!"

Edgar decided not to visit Layne again.

*   *   *

He was busy with a new idea. Working in a bookstore, he had discovered, was less interesting than taking pictures. Moreover, he didn't like being separated from Gertrude all day, especially when she had no home to keep and found time heavy on her hands. If he opened a photographic studio of his own she could be with him all day and help him a great deal. Already he had a prospective partner: Frank J. Potter, a distant cousin of Lucian Potter, who owned the bookstore. Frank was assistant county clerk, a tall, blond, handsome young man. He was anxious to learn photography and get away from marriage licenses and birth certificates.

"You two know everyone in town between you," John Blackburn said. "Why don't you buy out Harry Cook's studio over on College Street? I'd even let you take my picture."

"A beard like that should only be painted," Frank said.

They were standing in front of the bookstore, soaking up the September sunlight. The mailman came by and handed Edgar a letter.

It was from Mr. Andrews in New York. He had received a letter from a man in Paris, France. The man had read Mr. Andrews's advertisement for clary water in a medical journal and was writing to say that he knew it was unavailable, because his father had been its manufacturer. It had not been made or sold now for many years. However, the son had the formula, and would gladly give it to Mr. Andrews so that he could make the tonic himself. A copy of the prescription was enclosed.

It was identical with the one given by Edgar in his reading. Mr. Andrews was taking the mixture and feeling better.

Edgar read the letter to Blackburn. The doctor stroked his black beard.

"Reckon we'd better begin those experiments," he said.

9

"Well, Blackburn, you'll have to be Cayce's Jesus tonight. He's dead!"

John Blackburn stood in the doorway of the studio dressing room, taking in the scene before him. On a sofa, in a position similar to the one he usually assumed while giving a reading, lay Edgar. He seemed lifeless. Blood had clotted on his lips.

Around him stood half a dozen doctors. Two of them, Stone and Reardon, were members of the investigating group. It was one of the others who had spoken.

Blackburn approached the sofa and looked down at the body.

"What happened?" he asked.

A doctor named McCraken answered him.

"He was like this when I got here. Tom Barnes and Frank Porter came and got me. They said he slumped over and passed out while he was sitting by the stove."

Barnes and Porter, two boys who worked in the studio, spoke up from the edge of the group.

"He was working all day over at the furniture factory," Barnes said. "He was taking pictures for the factory catalogue."

"It was cold over there," Porter said. "There was no heat. When he got here about six o'clock he was nearly frozen."

"He went into the darkroom for a while," Barnes said, "but it was cold there, too, so he came out and sat by the stove. Pretty soon he just slid off the chair and fell on the floor."

"We carried him to the sofa and went to get a doctor," Porter said. "After Dr. McCraken couldn't wake him up we got the rest of you."

"What did you do?" Blackburn said to McCraken.

"I tried to pour whisky down his throat but his jaws were locked. I pried them open. That's where the blood came from.

A couple of the lower front teeth broke. I put a damp cloth in his mouth and gave him an injection of morphine. I couldn't detect any pulse."

One of the other doctors spoke up.

"I gave him an injection of strychnine."

Another said, "I gave him some more morphine."

They had put hot bricks, wrapped in towels, against his body and placed hot stove lids against the soles of his feet. Still there had been no sign of life.

Stone and Reardon said that all this had been done before they arrived. They were of the opinion that Edgar had fallen by accident into the kind of sleep he assumed when giving a reading. They thought nothing should have been done until Blackburn arrived, on the chance that he might be able to break the trance by suggestion.

"The stuff that's in him would kill him even if he had been all right to start with," one of the doctors said. "What are you going to do, Blackburn?"

Blackburn sat down by the sofa and began to talk to Edgar. He suggested that his pulse increase, that his blood circulate normally, that he wake up. Over and over he repeated the admonitions. Nothing happened.

One by one the other doctors left.

"He's done for," one of them said. "If I ever saw a dead man, he's it!"

"Worked himself to death," another said. "Ever since he and Frank Potter bought this place he's been at it day and night. Imagine, working all New Year's Day taking pictures in a cold, deserted factory!"

"How about the other stuff?" his colleague said. "Blackburn and the boys have been putting him through all sorts of stunts for over a year. You can't tell me that sort of thing isn't deleterious."

The other nodded.

"Nice fellow," he said. "Very good photographer, from what I hear. Wonder what it was that affected his mind like that? They say he knew all sorts of things when he was asleep."

"I don't know, but whatever it was, it's killed him. Reckon he wasn't a fake, anyhow."

Back in the studio Blackburn continued talking. After half an hour, when all but Stone and Reardon of the others had gone, one of Edgar's muscles twitched. His pulse became detectable; his breathing became noticeable. With a deep groan, he woke up.

Pain racked his body. His mouth was full of blood; some of his teeth were gone. The soles of his feet were blistered. His arms were so sore from the hypodermic injections that he could scarcely move them. Blackburn told him what had happened and asked him what to do.

"I don't know," he answered. "Let me go back to sleep and see if you can talk it out of me."

He put himself to sleep and Blackburn began to talk again. He suggested that normal conditions return to all parts of the body, that healing of the sore spots be speeded and pain be removed, and that whatever poisons were already in the system be thrown off. He had noticed that where the hypodermics had been administered the flesh of the arms was discolored and swollen; the doses had not yet been absorbed. He tried injecting a needle and withdrawing the plunger. Most of the stuff came out.

Now an hour passed. The pulse again receded; there was no sign of life. Stone and Reardon left.

"He's done for," they said to Blackburn.

Another hour passed. A muscle twitched. Again the pulse became detectable; breathing became noticeable. Again Edgar woke up.

"I feel better," he said. "I think I'm all right."

Most of the pain had gone, but he was sore from head to foot. His feet were so swollen he could not tie the laces of his shoes. Blackburn bundled him up and drove him home in his buggy.

"Fine way to start the year 1906," Blackburn said. "What happened to you?"

Edgar said he didn't know.

"I was tired and cold, and I hadn't stopped to eat much. I was sitting by the stove, getting warm, and that's all I remember."

"I wonder," Blackburn said, "if that crazy mind of yours didn't put you to sleep because you needed rest? It looks after other people's health when we ask it to. Why shouldn't it look after yours?"

"If it's going to do tricks like that I wish it would tell me, so I can go to bed and not have all the doctors in town trying to wake me up," Edgar said.

"Is Gertrude back from Hopkinsville yet?" Blackburn asked.

"No," Edgar said. "She decided to stay for New Year's and I'm glad of it. She'd have lost ten years of her life if she'd seen this thing tonight. What will she say when she finds my teeth missing?"

"We'll tell her you got them knocked out in a saloon fight," Blackburn said reassuringly. "I'd better stay with you tonight. I don't want anything else to happen to you after what you've been through."

They let themselves in and went to bed. In the morning Edgar was awakened by the sound of the front doorbell. A messenger boy handed him a large floral piece. The card, edged in black, began, "With deepest sympathy . . . "

*   *   *

The Blackburn brothers, Beazley, and Reardon were all members of a local organization known as the E.Q.B. Literary Club. Casually, without formal organization for any particular scientific purpose, they began to observe Edgar's readings, intending to record their evidence in the club's files. They were well aware of the attitude of their profession toward shenanigans of that sort, but they were familiar with such American books as Thomson J. Hudson's *The Law of Psychic Phenomena* and knew something about the studies of clairvoyance and somnambulism that had been going on in Europe for more than a century.

In the eighteenth century, before the discoveries of Mesmer and de Puysegur, a pioneer named Maxwell said, "There is no disease which is not curable by a spirit of life without help of a physician . . . The universal remedy is nothing but the spirit of life increased in a suitable subject." Mesmer found a means of stimulating this natural healing force and called the process "magnetism." In 1784 de Puysegur, attempting to magnetize Victor, the shepherd boy, discovered hypnotism: Victor, falling into a deep trance, began to speak and diagnosed the ailment of the person next to him. During the next generation persons with similar sensitiveness were found in France, Germany, and England. They were studied carefully; the best men of science gave them their attention and wrote books about them. Somnambulism became fashionable. People went by preference to a somnambulist rather than to a physician, and the results apparently were as efficacious as they were amazing. The somnambulists seemed infallible in diagnosis, and the remedies they suggested were simple and, according to the evidence, helpful.

It is not surprising, of course, that people in that time preferred a clairvoyant to a doctor. The medical profession was in a state of dark ignorance. Montaigne, the French essayist, when threatened with a physician, begged that he be allowed to recover his strength, that he might better resist the attack. Somnambulists, on the other hand, seldom prescribed anything violent, and frequently stated that the trouble was psychological and could be corrected by suggestion.

The material on somnambulism that was gathered and printed during the first half of the nineteenth century would seem to be overwhelming proof of the reality of the phenomenon. Karl du Prel, discussing the subject in *The Philosophy of Mysticism,* quoted a score of authors and predicted that one of them, Dr. Justinus Kerner, would be "among the most read in the next century." Dr. Kerner wrote about Frau Hauffe, the "Seeress of Prevorst," a somnambulist so sensitive that "upon approaching a patient, and even before contact, but still more after it, she at once experienced the same feeling and in the like place as the patient, and to the great astonishment of the latter, could exactly describe all his sufferings, without his having given her any previous verbal information."

Many somnambulists experienced this transference of the patient's symptoms to themselves. They were termed "sensitive." Others, particularly those who went into deep trance, on awakening neither knew what they had said nor felt any ill effects. These were called "intuitive." The sensitive type suffered constantly, picking up the pains of those about them, and were in danger of temporary blindness, melancholia, and almost anything else that the person examined was enduring. The intuitive somnambulist, on the other hand, had a rather easy time of it. He went to sleep, woke up, and his work was done. Many experiments were conducted to prove that in this state of trance the entire mechanism of normal physical life retreated beyond reach. A somnambulist would be given something to eat, such as an apple. He would then be put into a trance, and while in that condition be given a different food to eat—perhaps a piece of pastry. He would eat the pastry, relish it, and describe the taste; yet on awakening the only taste in his mouth would be that of the apple. Once a woman somnambulist was kept in a trance for six months, during which time her place of habitation was changed. She accustomed herself to the new house and lived in it, cooking and cleaning and entertaining. Yet when she was awakened finally the place was strange to her and she could not find her way around from room to room.

As the books on somnambulism rolled off the presses, orthodox medicine rallied to the opposition. Mesmer was condemned as a fraud, and the diverse phenomena discovered by other investigators were damned along with him. The hope for a new system of diagnosing physical ills—a system already inherent in man and magically sure—began to fade. Here is du Prel's report of one of the "investigations":

"When in the year 1831 the professional Commission, which had been engaged in its investigation since its appointment several years before, caused its Report, confirming all the substantial phenomena attributed to somnambulism, to be read in the Medical Academy of Paris, the deep silence of the assembly betrayed the disturbance of their minds. Then, when as usual it was proposed that this report should be printed, an Academician, Castel, rose and protested against the printing of it, *because if the facts reported were true, half of our physiological science would be destroyed.*"

Seventy-five years later somnambulism was all but forgotten; orthodox medicine was on the verge of a great era. Thus when the Blackburn brothers and their colleagues took up the study of the intuitive somnambulist Edgar Cayce, they approached him with the same skepticism which had prevailed in their profession a century before. They tried him with the same tests, and they got the same results.

He was asked to give a reading for the mother of a local dentist. She lived in a nearby town; the name and the address were read to him after he had gone to sleep. He diagnosed her ailment and outlined a system of treatment. He then was asked to describe the room in which the woman lay. He told what color the walls were painted, what pictures were on them, where the windows were located, and where the bed was situated. He located the origin of the steel in the bed springs, mentioned where the cotton in the mattress had been grown, and listed the cities in which the various sections of the bed had been manufactured. The doctors checked the information as far as they could. The description of the room was correct in every detail. They were, however, unable to trace the steel, the cotton, and the wood of the bed.

A Tennessee woman who was unable to get relief for her illness volunteered as a patient. She had, he said, a laceration of the stomach. Edgar told her to disregard the doctors. Each morning she was to take a lemon, roll it, cut it in half, and eat one of the halves. She was then to walk as far as she could, rest, walk home, sprinkle salt on the other half of the lemon, eat it, then immediately drink at least two glasses of water. The doctors thought it was a joke. The woman decided to follow the suggestion. In a few weeks she reported that she was feeling fine, could walk several miles, and found her food agreeing with her.

There were other readings, but they had an irritating habit of turning out in the same way—correct. A Bowling Green man wrote to an acquaintance in New York, describing Edgar's powers. The man said the whole thing was a fraud. As an experiment a reading was taken on him one morning. Edgar was told to find him in New York and to trace his progress through the streets as he approached his office. Edgar trailed him to a cigar store, then to his office, read part of his mail, and reported on a portion of a telephone conversation. The text of the reading was immediately telegraphed to the man. He wired back, "You are exactly right. I am coming to Bowling Green." He did come and tried to induce Edgar to go back with him to New York. They would, he said, make a million dollars. Edgar refused.

In the autumn of 1906 the E.Q.B. Literary Club chose hypnotism for the subject of one of its monthly dinner meetings. By way of demonstration, Edgar was invited to give a reading. Most of the local doctors were to be at the dinner, and many physicians from surrounding localities. In order to be ready for the reading, Edgar ate early, at home. Blackburn called for him. Gertrude, nervous and frightened, demanded a promise of Blackburn.

"Promise me you won't try any tricks with him while he is asleep," she said. "I don't want any pins stuck in him or any monkey business like that. I want him brought back in as good condition as he is going."

"I'll take care of him," Blackburn promised.

At the meeting Edgar went to sleep on a couch that was brought in and placed before the dais. He was given the name and address of a college student who was ill in a dormitory just outside the city. The boy was a patient of one of the doctors present.

"Yes, we have the body," he said. "He is recovering from an attack of typhoid fever. The pulse is 96, the temperature 101.4."

The doctor in charge of the patient said the diagnosis was correct. A committee of three was dispatched to check on the temperature and pulse. While they were gone an argument arose as to what state of consciousness or unconsciousness Edgar was in.

Some said hypnosis, some said trance, some said a dream state. The doctors who were witnessing their first reading wanted to find out. Over Blackburn's violent protests one of them stuck a needle in Edgar's arms, hands, and feet. There was no response. Another left the room, returned with a hatpin, and before Blackburn could stop him, thrust it entirely through Edgar's cheeks. Still there was no response.

"He's hardened to all of that," one of the other doctors said.

This one opened a penknife and ran the blade under one of Edgar's fingers. Slowly the nail was lifted away from the flesh. There was no indication of pain; no blood flowed. The knife was withdrawn.

Suddenly Edgar woke up. Immediately he felt pain. The doctors began to apologize. Just a few scientific tests, they said. No harm was meant. Edgar lost his temper. He turned on Blackburn and the other doctors.

"I'm through," he said. "I've let you do anything you wanted to do with me. I've given you my time and never asked that you even be polite enough to think me sincere.

"I thought you wanted to find out the truth. But you don't. Nothing will convince you. Nothing will convince any of you.

"No matter how many miracles you see you will never believe anything that will interfere with your smugness. You take it for granted that every man in the world is crooked except yourselves. And you will accept no proof of anyone's honesty.

"I'll never try to prove anything to any one of you again.

"I'll never give another reading unless it's for someone who needs help and believes I can give it to him!"

He walked out.

*　*　*

The nail of Edgar's finger never grew normally again. All that winter it festered and was sore, reminding him of the knife that had tried to find his secret by probing his flesh. There would be no more of that now; the E.Q.B. Literary Club's investigating committee had ceased to function. But the inquisitors of his conscience remained, and their questions hurt him more than anything that had been done on the night of the dinner.

Was this strange gift a virtue or a vice? Basically it had only one frightening aspect: it could not be explained—it could not be understood. Should it be used, or should it not be used? Would it be a blight to his children, or would it end, as it had begun, with himself, a strange and errant strand of fate, reaching out to strangle his peace and happiness?

Edgar had fled from the scientists, but he could not flee from himself. It was never a comfortable feeling to know that a force beyond the knowledge of man was coursing through him, waiting to be tapped, like an underground stream that roars beneath a quiet country field. But beyond this there was a larger disturbance, a cloud that formed often into a storm of fear, driving all other thoughts to cover. Now he faced it at every turn. What if he should pass on to a son or a daughter this wild ability of the mind?

Gertrude had the same fear, but her love for the exterior Edgar, the friendly, wide-awake young man to whom she had given her heart, was so great that she defied whatever lay within him to intrude on the sanctity of their love. She had in those months a proud, uplifted look, and her eyes dared any but the friends of heaven to walk with her while she waited for the spring.

10

In November of 1906 the Cayce Studio on College Street held an art exhibit. A collection of paintings, carbon prints, and water colors valued at $40,000 was taken on consignment from one Franz Von Hanfstangl, an art dealer, of New York. The show was well attended, and so many carbon prints and water colors were sold that the remainder was kept for the Christmas season when the show closed and the paintings were returned to New York. Business was so good that Edgar was sure he would be able by spring to start building the house he and Gertrude were planning.

On December 23rd the College Street Studio was destroyed by fire. None of the pictures was saved. Edgar, reading over his insurance policies, discovered that none of them covered goods on consignment. Von Hanfstangl's lists showed that the value of the merchandise which had not been returned to him was $8,000. Edgar was broke; the studio was in debt.

Business went on in the State Street Studio and was better than ever. Edgar worked every day and almost every night, taking only Sunday mornings off to teach his Sunday school class. His only vacation came on the afternoon of March 16, 1907. He stayed at home after lunch that day, pacing up and down the living room of the little cottage on Park Avenue where he and Gertrude now lived, smoking innumerable cigarettes. Now and then Mrs. Evans, who was visiting them, came out of the bedroom to tell him something. Once the nurse, Daisy Dean, emerged and stared at him coldly. Finally Blackburn came out, smiling.

"Did you hear him?" he said. "He let out a pretty good squawk."

Edgar gulped. "It's a boy?" he asked. He felt foolish.

"'A son' is the technical phrase," Blackburn said. "Healthy as a wildcat, and Gertrude is fine."

Mrs. Evans opened the bedroom door and called to them. "Nine-and-a-half pounds," she said.

Edgar sat down.

"I didn't mean any harm," he said weakly. "I didn't know it was like this—so much pain and suffering for Gertrude. Why was I let off so easily?"

Blackburn restrained a smile. "You've suffered," he said. "And from now on you can worry. There's another mouth to feed."

"I'd like a dozen, but not this way," Edgar said.

"Let's take a reading and find out how to get them some other way," Blackburn suggested.

He went back into the bedroom. Mrs. Evans came out with the baby.

"Isn't he beautiful?" she said.

"Yes," Edgar said, but he didn't think so. Privately he asked Blackburn if all babies looked like skinned rabbits.

Blackburn nodded glumly. "Even Cleopatra was like that," he said, "when she was born. He'll grow out of it."

They named him Hugh Lynn, after Gertrude's two brothers. Mrs. Evans stayed to look after him until Gertrude was recovered. She declared him to be an angel.

All that spring and summer the angel cried. He didn't even stop when the second fire came, in September. It wrecked the State Street Studio, but this time there were no goods on consignment, and the insurance adjustors were inclined to be generous.

"You've had hard luck, Cayce," one of them said. "Just tell us the amount and we won't bother checking it. You'll get the money."

Edgar put carpenters to work immediately, and in two weeks was open for business again. Then his partner got frightened and threw the firm into bankruptcy. Frank Potter, the original partner, had sold his interest to Edgar and had been replaced by Lynn, Gertrude's brother, and Joe Adcock. It was Adcock who initiated bankruptcy, though none of the creditors was worried. The studio was closed for seven minutes while the formalities were staged. Then it opened again. There were more customers than ever.

Because she had been named as Edgar's chief creditor in the bankruptcy proceedings, Carrie Salter was called to Bowling Green. She came with her husband, Dr. Thomas Burr House, of Springfield, Tennessee.

"Edgar, can you imagine me marrying not one doctor, but two?" she said. "He's not only a medical doctor, but an osteopath."

Dr. House was a genial, medium-sized man with handlebar mustaches and brown eyes that twinkled and betrayed him when he tried to tease someone. He liked Bowling Green. It would be a nice place to spend the winter, he thought, before opening an office in Hopkinsville in the spring.

"You're supposed to run the studio," he told Carrie. "We can't leave."

"I'll stay with Gertrude so Lizzie can go home," Carrie said. "You run the studio. I don't know anything about it. Edgar knows what he's doing anyhow."

"I'll help him," Dr. House said.

Thereafter he passed the days in the studio, smoking cigars, watching Edgar take pictures, and talking to the doctors who, out of long habit, stopped in to visit with Edgar and each other. He paid no attention to the business, nor to the talk he heard about the readings. "Very interesting" was all he ever said. He was intent on a vacation, and he was determined that nothing was going to interrupt it.

Edgar forgot everything but work. He wanted to pay off his debts and be a free man again. He also wanted to leave Bowling Green. The two fires and the bitter experience with the doctors had spoiled his love for the place. He wanted to get away and make a fresh start. Gertrude agreed with him.

By early spring things were in pretty good shape. Dr. House and Carrie returned to Hopkinsville, and Gertrude and Hugh Lynn went with them for a visit to the Hill. Edgar gave up the cottage and moved into the studio.

The folks left at the end of March. One evening late in May Dr. House called on the telephone from Hopkinsville.

"Carrie's sick," he said, "and she wants you to come over here and give a reading for her. I've had Dr. Haggard up from

Nashville and he wants to operate, but she won't do a thing without getting your consent. You'd better come over. She's pretty badly off."

Edgar took the night train. All the way to Hopkinsville he prayed. Carrie's faith in him had always made him feel warm and good. She had insisted that the readings were correct in their diagnoses, and that the power was a gift from God. She had trusted him in other things, too. She had given him money when he needed it, and now, with the money in jeopardy because of the fires, she was putting her life in his hands. Was her faith justified?

How could he possibly know what was wrong with her? How would Dr. House feel, watching an untrained man go to sleep and diagnose his wife's condition, while he, a trained physician, stood by, helpless to interfere?

The next morning, facing the couple in the living room at the Hill, he felt even worse. Carrie was obviously quite sick, and in pain. But her faith was unwavering.

"A reading will tell what's wrong with me and what to do for it," she insisted. "Get it as soon as you can, Edgar. Dr. House will take down what you say." In the presence of other people she never called her husband anything but Dr. House.

Edgar went into one of the bedrooms and put himself to sleep, first instructing Dr. House about the suggestions, especially the one for waking him up. That, he had discovered, was the only important point about the phenomenon. Anyone could "conduct" a reading, so long as the proper suggestion for waking was given, and the conductor was careful not to move away from the sleeping body while the trance persisted.

When he awakened, Dr. House looked glum.

"Haggard thinks she has a tumor of the abdomen," he said. "I've had all the local doctors in. They agree with the diagnosis.

"You say there is no tumor. You say she is pregnant, and the trouble is a locked bowel.

"What you suggest for the locked bowel sounds reasonable— warm oil enemas and some other things."

He shook his head.

"But I don't see how she can be pregnant. She's not supposed to be able to have children."

Edgar felt miserable. He had hoped that he would agree with the doctors. It would have made things so much easier. W. H. Haggard was one of the leading specialists in Nashville.

"I'm going to try these things," Dr. House said. "We'll see what happens."

Edgar stayed that day and night at the Hill. Next morning Dr. House came from Carrie's bedroom and shook his hand.

"You were right about the locked bowel," he said. "She's better now. But I don't see how it can be a pregnancy."

Edgar returned to Bowling Green. The following November Thomas Burr House, Jr., was born, a seven months' baby. He was so small and fragile that he was carried around on a pillow. No one but Carrie believed he would survive the winter. He was sick most of the time and inclined to convulsions. One day in March he had so many that Carrie asked Dr. House to call Edgar.

This time when he arrived from Bowling Green there were two local doctors present besides Dr. House. One of them pointed at Edgar and said, "If you're going to fool with that faker, I'm through." He left. The other physician, Dr. J. B. Jackson, who had long been the Cayce family doctor, remained.

Carrie was sitting in a low rocker in the living room, by the front window. In her lap lay the baby, convulsing regularly every twenty minutes. Edgar turned away and went into the bedroom across the hall. Dr. House and Dr. Jackson followed him. He lay on the bed and went to sleep. When he woke, Dr. House was sitting beside him; Dr. Jackson had gone back into the living room. The door was open. Edgar could hear him talking to Carrie.

"Now, Mrs. House, you can't do what that man tells you to," he was saying. "What he tells you to give your child is poison."

Edgar walked in and stood by the fireplace. Carrie kept rocking, staring down at the baby. Dr. House came in and sat beside her.

Carrie spoke to Jackson.

"You're one of the doctors who told me I had to have an operation, aren't you?" she said. "I didn't have one. Now my baby's dying, and you can't help him. But you don't want me to do what Edgar says. Well, I'm going to do it."

Dr. House spoke to her coaxingly.

"What he prescribes is an overdose of belladonna," he said. "You know yourself how poisonous that is. Of course, he gives an antidote. But how do we know it will work?"

"The only thing we know is that the baby's going to die if we don't do something," Carrie said. "This is our only chance. Measure out the dose, Dr. House. I'll give it to him myself."

Dr. House went to his room and came back with the belladonna. Carrie administered it. In a few minutes the baby relaxed, stretched, and went to sleep.

"Get the antidote ready," Carrie said.

Jackson turned to Edgar.

"You gave something else," he said. "A peach-tree poultice. I don't know how to make it, or what good it will do, but you prescribed it. Do you know what it is?"

"I'll fix it," Edgar said.

He was glad to get out of the house. He wanted something to do. Standing there, watching the baby as it lay in Carrie's arms, waiting for it to live or die, was more than he could bear.

What could a peach-tree poultice be? It couldn't be made of leaves, for every limb in the orchard was bare. He shinned up one of the peach trees and picked off the youngest, tenderest branches. They would make a good brew, if that was what was meant. He took them over to the kitchen, a building separate from the house, and put them in a pot, pouring hot water from the kettle over them.

Mrs. Evans came from the house to help him. When the brew was strong enough they dipped towels in it, rinsed them, and carried them into the house. Hours that seemed endless to Edgar dragged by. Then, as he brought a fresh batch of towels into the living room, Carrie looked up at him and said:

"He's all right. I knew if anyone could save him, you could, Edgar."

He went outside and stood in the cold night, taking deep breaths. Dr. House joined him.

"There's no use in being a mule," the doctor said. "You saved Carrie, and now you've saved the boy with this trance business of yours. It still sounds like foolishness, but it's pretty accurate foolishness. I'm afraid I'll have to believe in it myself."

"I hope you're right," Edgar said. "After tonight, I'm beginning to believe in it, too."

Standing under the winter sky, watching the stars and knowing he had done a good thing, he felt that he understood himself for the first time. He had saved a human being, a child, from suffering—perhaps from death, by the use of a power that had been given to him by God. It was his greatest dream come true. Wasn't his life meant to be lived that way?

Back in Bowling Green his burst of faith passed. Every day he saw his doctor friends. Their quiet cocksureness, their facile handling of medical and scientific terms, their occasional suggestions that he let bygones be bygones and continue the "interesting experiments" bogged him in a melancholia that deepened as he realized that the goal he now had set for himself was the lowest of his life: he merely wanted to be free of debt.

In August, 1909, the last bill was paid and receipted. After seven years of labor he was stone broke.

He went to Hopkinsville and stayed at the Hill with Gertrude, Hugh Lynn, Dr. and Mrs. House, little Tommy, and the rest of the family. To keep himself busy and to cover the humiliation he felt at being out of a job and without funds, he offered to move the kitchen over to the house and join it to the main building. It was a prodigious task, involving all sorts of impromptu engineering feats. During one of them, while the kitchen was moving on its rollers, Aunt Kate, who was helping him, said quietly to Edgar:

"You'd better stop the blasted thing if you can. My finger's caught underneath it."

There was no way of stopping the movement or even checking it. The kitchen rolled on, leaving the finger a battered mess.

The job was finished without further mishap. When it was done, Edgar packed up and went off to look for work.

*   *   *

He returned for Christmas, though it was necessary to give up the job he had found in Gadsden, Alabama, to do so.

"I couldn't stay away any longer," he told Gertrude. "I'll get another job. Photographers are scarce in Alabama. I've already been offered a job in Anniston, with Russell Brothers. I'm going to work around the state until I find the right town, and then open a studio of my own."

"We'll start all over again," Gertrude said. "We can't *always* have such bad luck."

During the holidays the squire took him to meet Dr. Wesley H. Ketchum, a homeopath who had opened an office in Hopkinsville. Homeopaths at the time were numerous and popular. They were called "spoon up and spoon down" doctors, owing to their custom of giving medicine in small and frequent doses, usually a teaspoonful at a time. Some people called their medicines "stomach water," but the homeopaths, who mixed their own prescriptions, had a large following.

Ketchum, a keen-faced, pince-nezed young man in his early thirties, greeted Edgar cordially. He had heard of the readings. He had talked with some of Layne's old patients. He wanted to see a reading. Edgar said he no longer gave them for exhibition purposes.

"How can I get one?" Ketchum asked.

"If you come with a written request from a person who really needs help," Edgar said, "I'll give one. That's the only condition."

"Wait here," Ketchum said.

They were in his office. He went out of the office and across the street to the Latham Hotel. In a few minutes he came back, waving a paper.

"I have it," he said. "This person needs help very much."

"Is it genuine?" Edgar asked.

"On my honor," Ketchum said.

"Then I'll give it," Edgar said.

"When?" Ketchum asked.

"Right here, now," Edgar said. He took off his tie, loosened his collar, cuffs, and shoelaces, and lay down on the examination table. The squire said he would give the suggestion. Ketchum handed him the paper. Edgar went to sleep.

When he woke up, Ketchum was standing in the middle of

the room, his thumbs hooked in his vest, teetering back and forth on his heels, smiling to himself.

"Well, that beats anything I've ever seen," he said. "You know, that would fool anybody but a fellow like me."

He teetered some more.

"Yes, sir, if you'll tie up with me we'll make a barrel of money."

He laughed. "You were talking about me," he said.

"You say I think I've got appendicitis. Man, I *know* I've got it! I've been examined by six of the best doctors in the state. I'm going to be operated on next Wednesday.

"You say I fell over a box and hurt myself. You tell me to go to an osteopath, and he'll fix me up.

"My boy, you're a fake, but if you'll tie up with me we'll go all over the country and fool everybody. Yes, sir, you're smooth. You'd fool anybody but me."

Edgar was boiling with rage. He tried to control himself when he spoke.

"If it's a fake," he said, "it's not my fake. I don't know anything about it.

"But maybe you can tell me how I happened to pick on appendicitis. If I'm a fake why didn't I say you had stomach trouble, or sore feet, or a bad heart?

"If I'm a fake, I dare you to prove it. And if you do, I'll never give another reading as long as I live!"

He strode out of the office. The squire followed him.

When they had gone, Ketchum called to his secretary. She had been sitting behind the half-opened door to the inner room, taking down Edgar's words in shorthand.

"Type out those notes as soon as you can," Ketchum said. "I think I have this fellow where the hair is short."

When the transcript of the reading was ready, he put it in his pocket and went up the street to the office of Dr. James E. Oldham, the local osteopath.

"Oldham," he said, "I'm Ketchum, the new homeopath. The regular doctors don't like me any better than they like you. I thought we ought to get together. Maybe we could be friends."

Oldham acknowledged the introduction and shook hands.

"How about looking me over?" Ketchum said. "I'm not feeling too well."

"Glad to," Oldham said. "Just strip to the waist and get on the table."

While he was disrobing, Ketchum continued the conversation.

"Do you know this fellow Cayce, who gives readings?" he asked.

"Oh, yes," Oldham said.

"What do you think of him?" Ketchum said.

"He's smart," Oldham said. "He catches on quickly. He usually shows a pretty good smattering of medicine."

"I suppose people tell him things," Ketchum said.

"Yes," Oldham said. "I treated him when he couldn't talk. He learned all he knows from me."

"He recommended patients to you in his readings, didn't he," Ketchum said, "when he was working with Layne?"

"Yes," Oldham said, "but I diagnosed the cases myself."

"Suppose he took a patient away from you? He did that, didn't he?"

"Yes," Oldham said.

"Did the patient die?"

"Not that I know of."

Ketchum got on the treatment table. In one hand he held the folded copy of the reading.

"Well," he said, "I think he's a fake, too. To tell you the truth I have a reading that he gave on me, this afternoon. I think I've got him trapped. Now you go ahead and examine me and tell me what you find."

He lay on his face and Oldham examined his spine, pressing on various vertebrae.

"Have you had a pain in your right side?" Oldham asked.

"Yes," Ketchum said.

"I'll bet you think you've got appendicitis," Oldham said.

"Good God! That's exactly what Cayce said!" Ketchum unfolded the reading and stared at it, his head hanging over the end of the table.

"There's a lesion here," Oldham said, pressing on two vertebrae. "Probably caused by a fall or strain."

"What would you do for it?" Ketchum asked.

"It's not hard to fix," Oldham said. "I'll get my wife in here and have her hold your feet while I give your back a twist."

"That's what Cayce says," Ketchum answered from the end of the table. "He even says your wife should hold my feet."

That night Edgar and Leslie went back to Ketchum's office, at his request. He was holding on to his side with his right hand when they entered. With his left he waved them to a seat.

"You're not a fake," he said to Edgar. "I've just been a damned fool."

He related his experience with Oldham.

"I was fooling this afternoon about teaming up with me," he said, "but I mean it now. We can do a great deal of good for a lot of people and make a fortune for ourselves. We can find new cures for diseases. We can revolutionize medicine. What do you say?"

"Nothing doing," Edgar said. He was still mad. "I'm glad you discovered your mistake," he said. "You've found out I'm not a fake, like all the other doctors who've investigated me. Now if you fellows could convince me that you-all are not fakes, maybe I'd join up with you!"

11

It was a quiet Sunday night in Montgomery, Alabama, late in October, 1910. A photographer of the H. P. Tressler staff, returning from a week's trip into the country, entered the studio building and trudged upstairs, lugging his equipment. He was a slim, tired-looking young man, with long legs and arms and a round, boyish face that made him seem younger than his thirty-three years.

A light was burning in the reception room of the studio. A man was curled up in one of the easy chairs, dozing. He leaped to his feet when the photographer walked in.

"Are you Edgar Cayce?" he asked.

The photographer nodded. "Yes," he said.

"We've been looking all over for you," the man said. "You're famous."

He pulled a fistful of clippings from his pocket.

"New York *Times,* St. Louis *Post-Dispatch,* Denver *Post,* Kansas City *Star* . . . "

He handed the clippings to Edgar. The first one was a page from the New York *Times* of Sunday, October 9th. From it stared two pictures that were familiar—they hung on the walls of the Cayce living room in Hopkinsville. One was of Edgar, the other of the squire. Between them on the newspaper page was a picture of Ketchum. A streamer headline said: ILLITERATE MAN BECOMES A DOCTOR WHEN HYPNOTIZED—STRANGE POWER SHOWN BY EDGAR CAYCE PUZZLES PHYSICIANS.

Edgar sank into a chair and began to read:

The medical fraternity of the country is taking a lively interest in the strange power said to be possessed by Edgar Cayce of

Hopkinsville, Ky., to diagnose difficult diseases while in a semiconscious state, though he has not the slightest knowledge of medicine when not in that condition.

During a visit to California last summer Dr. W. H. Ketchum, who was attending a meeting of the National Society of Homeopathic Physicians, had occasion to mention the young man's case and was invited to discuss it at a banquet attended by about thirty-five of the doctors of the Greek letter fraternity given at Pasadena.

Dr. Ketchum made a speech of considerable length . . . He created such widespread interest . . . that one of the leading Boston medical men who heard his speech invited Dr. Ketchum to prepare a paper as a part of the programme of the September meetings of the American Society of Clinical Research. Dr. Ketchum sent the paper, but did not go to Boston . . .

The man coughed to attract Edgar's attention.

"I'm a reporter," he said. "I wanted to ask you about this. What's it all about? Is it true?"

"I don't know," Edgar said.

He smiled helplessly.

"I'm the man," he said, "but I don't know anything about this report. I know Ketchum. I've given some readings for him, when I've been at home for visits. But I had no idea he was going to make a report about it. I've been out in the country for a week. I haven't heard from my wife in that time."

"That's what I want to get," the reporter said. "The personal stuff. How do you happen to be here in Montgomery, working for Tressler? He wasn't sure it was the same man, when the stories began to break, but he knew you were from Hopkinsville, and when he saw the picture of you he was sure. But he said you came to him from Russell Brothers, and that you had been working for them over in Anniston and Jacksonville."

Edgar explained. "I used to have a studio in Bowling Green, Kentucky. It was burned out. So I left my family in Hopkinsville while I came down here to work, until I could save enough money to open another place of my own. I left Russell Brothers last July Fourth and came over here."

"Well, your troubles are over," the reporter said. "Looks as if you can forget photography now. Say, how does it feel to be famous?"

Edgar looked at the clippings.

"Would you call it fame," he asked, "or notoriety?"

"That's up to you, I'd say," the reporter said. "It depends on what you do with it. People are continually popping up as nine-day wonders. Some stay on top, some are never heard of again."

Edgar nodded. "It depends on what I do with it," he said, "and what others do with it. That's the trouble. I never know what's going on when I'm asleep. I have to be sure the people I work with are honest and have the same ideas about it as I have."

"What is it, anyhow?" the reporter asked. "How does it feel?"

"I can't describe it," Edgar said, "or explain it. It's just something that's in my mind, like knowing how to take a picture, or like writing a letter, or even like getting up out of a chair. You think you'll get up out of a chair, and you do, and all the things that happen to bring it about are mysterious—but they're mysterious because you do it so easily that you don't think about them. Maybe that's not just the way it is, but when I lie down and want to go into this sleep, I do. And when I lie down and want to go into the other kind of sleep—the kind we all know, that rests us—I do. That's all I know."

"Sure," the reporter said. "Well, I want to catch the paper with this, so I'll run along. Congratulations on your fame or notoriety, whichever it is."

When he had gone, Edgar looked again at the clippings, reading them over and over, trying to figure out what had happened.

"In all, young Cayce has given more than 1,000 readings . . . "

Probably he had, but not for Ketchum. Some of these reported were Layne's cases—there was a description of the Dietrich experience, for instance. For Ketchum he had given only two sets of readings. He had succumbed twice to the doctor's offer of transportation to and from Hopkinsville in return for his services. During the visits he had gone to Ketchum's office each day, given readings, asked no questions, and requested only the assurance that the cases were all people in need of help.

Apparently Ketchum, on a visit to California, had told some tall tales and, when asked to elaborate them in a scientific paper, had rounded up all the available evidence in Hopkinsville. It made a good story.

What interested Edgar most was the explanation of the phenomenon, which he was supposed to have given in a reading:

Our subject, while under auto-hypnosis, on one occasion, explained as follows:

When asked to give the source of his knowledge, he being at this time in the subconscious state, he stated: "Edgar Cayce's mind is amenable to suggestion, the same as all other subconscious minds, but in addition thereto it has the power to interpret to the objective mind of others what it acquires from the subconscious mind of other individuals of the same kind. The subconscious mind forgets nothing. The conscious mind receives the impression from without and transfers all thought to the subconscious, where it remains even though the conscious be destroyed." He described himself as a third person, saying further that his subconscious mind is in direct communication with all other subconscious minds, and is capable of interpreting through his objective mind and imparting impressions received to other objective minds, gathering in this way all the knowledge possessed by millions of other subconscious minds.

So that was it. Well, it didn't mean much, because it didn't tell *why* he could do what others could not. Apparently his mind was not different from others' except that it could work backward. If all people were like him, they could all be hypnotized and would then be able to send back through the conscious what their subconscious minds knew.

Apparently God did not intend it that way. He made man to walk through the world in darkness except for what he learned by experience and what he believed by faith.

Why, then, was he different? The vision of the lady was the answer, if he could accept it. Sometimes he could; he accepted it on that March night when he stood in the cold still air and knew that Carrie's baby had been saved. Sometimes he couldn't accept it: when he washed his hands and saw that they were the rough tools of a workman; when he shaved in the morning and saw that his face wore the countenance of a simple, uneducated man who was wishful, stubborn, sentimental, even foolish at times; when he sat at night reading his Bible and knew that he was a country boy with far less magic in all of his being than was contained in the stem of a May flower.

President James Hyslop of the American Psychic Society has made suggestions in regard to the development of the subject's powers. Other psychologists in Europe and America are seeking information, and Dr. Ketchum's plan is to have a committee of scientists of the highest standing come to Hopkinsville and investigate in most rigid manner and make a report as to the truth of what is claimed but not understood.

Edgar went to his desk and got his mail. What was up? Were the scientists about to descend on him? Gertrude's letter didn't enlighten him. All she knew was what she had seen in the newspapers. She wanted to know what he was going to do. His mother's letter gave part of the story.

"Dr. Ketchum didn't give your name in his original report," she wrote, "but the newspapermen came to town in droves and found everything out. They stole the pictures off the living room walls, and I didn't even know it until I saw them in the newspapers. It's been terribly confusing. The house has been full of people all of the time. I hope that it will be for the best. Your father is very proud."

There was a letter from Ketchum, too. He offered no explanation of what he had done. Instead he urged Edgar to come back to Hopkinsville and make a business of giving readings. A company would be formed: Ketchum, the squire, and Mr. Albert D. Noe, owner of the Latham Hotel in Hopkinsville, were already in partnership on the deal. If Edgar would cooperate, he would be made a full partner. All they wanted to know was what terms he would accept for his services. They would agree to anything reasonable, and so far as Ketchum was concerned there was no such word as unreasonable. "You can have what you want," he wrote.

Edgar snapped off the light. For the rest of the night he sat in the dark studio, staring through the skylight windows at the stars. His hour had come: he had to make up his mind about himself and his strange power.

It should, he knew, be an easy decision. He wanted to believe that God had given him a gift to be used to help humanity. But he was like Moses. He could not believe it had happened to him.

One thing was certain: it was a talent, not a trick, not a maladjustment, not an ailment. He was a well man; he had been well for years, except for the trouble with his voice.

It was not something that demanded an unnatural condition of his body. He did not need to get himself into a mood by burning incense, listening to music, or muttering incantations. He did not need darkness. He did not find it necessary to abstain from certain foods. He smoked whenever he wanted to smoke.

It did not require religious ecstasy, prayers, or even a period of quiet and meditation beforehand. All that was necessary was that he be in normal health and that his stomach have finished with its digestion of the last meal.

It did not tire him. He usually awakened feeling refreshed. He always felt hungry, but a cracker and a glass of milk satisfied this feeling. He could not do it more than twice a day without feeling a sense of weariness and depletion, but it was not reasonable to expect so complicated a procedure to be executed more often.

So it was, apparently, something that was natural to him—something like an ability to write, or paint, or sing. It was an expression of himself. He wanted to help people, just as comedians wanted to make people laugh. This was the way which had been given to him for the satisfaction of his desire. He had only to use it for that intended purpose.

Obviously it was not meant that he help only a select few, such as the members of his family or those who heard about it from persons who had been helped, like the Dietrichs. It was a gift of God, destined for everyone.

But a gift of God could be controlled by the devil. Every talent could choose one of two masters, and in his case the choice was not entirely his own. When he used his talent, he was asleep.

Who would watch, to see that it was not misused? How would he know whether his mind was up to good or evil?

Blackburn had always contended that his sleep mind contained his conscience and could not be led astray. He pointed to the collapse on New Year's Eve as an example of the guardianship of the sleep mind over the body. On the other hand, Edgar had himself said, in a reading, "Edgar Cayce's mind is amenable to suggestion, the same as all other subconscious minds." Those other subconscious minds, when in a state of hypnosis, would do whatever they were told to do. So would his mind, apparently, for did it not seek out people and diagnose their ailments? Suppose it was told to do something else—give information that would be valuable for unscrupulous purposes? Would it do it?

His only safeguard would be himself. If he remained incorruptible in his own life, and prayed for guidance and help while giving readings, surely God would not let him be duped.

That was the best he could do—and it was his duty to do it, for all those who needed help. And for Cousin Ike.

The memory of Cousin Ike had always haunted him. Years before, when he was working with Layne, Ike had come to them for help. He had been to many doctors; they had not helped him. He was in bad shape. A reading was given, Layne began treating him, and he improved. He moved into town and stayed with the squire in the house on West Seventh Street, so he could be near Layne's office. Then Layne was ordered to cease practice. Ike got worse. He sent for Edgar, who had come to Hopkinsville for the weekend.

He was very ill that day. His wife and daughters were with him. He waved them out.

"Let me talk to Old Man alone," he said.

He asked Edgar to sit beside him. Then he took his hand and said:

"How do you do this stuff, Old Man? How do you tell people what is wrong with them? How does Layne know how to treat people as you tell him to?"

Edgar told him he didn't know. He repeated his experiences, except for the vision of the lady.

"Listen to me," Ike said. "I've known your mother and father since they were little children. I was present when they were married. I've known you since the day you were born. I saw you every day of your life until a few years ago. I know you are unusual in some ways—your knowledge of the Bible, for one thing. But this other thing—do you think it is some trick you've learned under Layne's guidance?"

Edgar shook his head. "I don't know," he said.

"I'm a dying man," Ike said. "They say a dying man has wisdom in his words. I don't know, but I want to tell you to consider this thing you have, find out what it is, and act accordingly. Is it a gift of God? I think it must be.

"I have been ill for years. I've been to hospitals all over the country. They kept me in them for weeks at a time, then let me go and told me they didn't know what my trouble was. Then you, a boy I've known all my life, laid down, went to sleep, and told me what was wrong with me. What's more, you told a man who doesn't know anything about doctoring what to do to bring me relief, and when he did it I got relief—more than I ever got from all the other treatments I took.

"Now they've stopped Layne from practicing and I'm getting worse fast. I'm going to die.

"But you, Old Man, you've got to keep going with this thing. Don't let anybody stop you from helping people with it. You may never understand it, but if it comes from God and you are faithful to the trust He put in you when He gave it to you, it won't bring you to harm."

He released Edgar's hand.

"I must rest now," he said. "Send me Pearl."

Edgar went out of the room and sent Pearl, one of the daughters, to take care of her father.

He never saw Ike again. Without Layne's treatments he failed rapidly. What was really wrong with him no one ever knew. The reading had said he suffered from a growth on the side of the peritoneum—a long thread which could have been removed by operation in the early stages, but was now too far advanced. Surgery would mean death. Layne had given him magnetic treatments and massage.

So Ike died. His time had run out anyhow, but it could have been lengthened and made more comfortable had the treatments been continued. There were others who could be helped in the same way. There were younger people. There were children.

He had been staring through the skylight windows at the stars. Now the stars were fading. Dawn was near. Things in the studio became visible in outline. On the desk before him he saw his Bible.

In a few minutes he would be able to read it by the morning light. He would let it guide him.

He opened it, put his finger in the middle of the left-hand page and waited for the words to become visible. When they did, he read them:

PSALM 46

God is our refuge and our strength, a very present help in trouble.

Therefore will we not fear, though the earth be removed, and though the mountains be carried into the midst of the sea;

Though the waters thereof roar and be troubled, though the mountains shake with the swelling thereof. Selah.

There is a river, the streams whereof shall make glad the city of God . . .

He stopped reading and began a letter to Ketchum.

"On certain conditions," he wrote, "I will accept your offer. It is to be understood that my father will act as conductor of all readings, and that a stenographic account of all that is said be taken down, and at least two copies of it made, one for the patient and one for our files. No readings are to be given except for sick people who make the request themselves.

"Furthermore, it must be understood that I am not to consider this as a profession or a means of livelihood. The company which has been formed is to completely equip for me a photographic studio, which is to be mine to conduct, as a means of my livelihood. The company is to equip another office for the readings, which I will give twice a day. Not less than five hundred dollars is to be spent on the equipment of the photographic studio, for the materials are to be all of the best . . . ”

When the letter arrived in Hopkinsville, Ketchum was amused. He showed it to the squire and Mr. Noe, the genial hotel man who was their partner.

"He doesn't know what he's got," Ketchum said.

They wired Edgar to come to Hopkinsville at once. When he arrived, they showed him the mail: nearly ten thousand letters. Some of them contained money; there was more than $2,000 in cash.

"What shall we do with it?" Ketchum asked.

"Send it back," Edgar said. "We don't want any money until the goods are delivered."

They set about drawing up a contract. First there was a special reading, at which the city, county, and circuit judges were present, along with several lawyers. They were asked to give an opinion on the legality of selling information from such a source. They said they knew of no law prohibiting it. The state medical authorities were asked for an opinion. They replied that nothing could prevent such a practice unless a law were enacted against it, and because of the peculiar nature of the operation such a law would have to name Edgar specifically, and since this in itself was unconstitutional, it appeared that nothing whatever could be done to hinder the enterprise.

The terms of the contract were those set by Edgar, plus the provision, offered by Noe and Ketchum, that he receive fifty per cent of the gross receipts. He was to divide this with the squire. Noe and Ketchum were to receive the other fifty per cent, and pay the rent and all expenses from it.

"How much will it cost to get the photographic equipment you want?" Noe asked Edgar.

"About five hundred dollars," he said.

Noe handed him five hundred-dollar bills.

"Get what you want," he said.

Edgar stared at the money. He had never seen a hundred-dollar bill before.

The furniture for the office was dazzling. It included a special couch, handmade, standing high from the floor, so that the person who gave the suggestion had to stand in order to talk to

Edgar Cayce's sons, Edgar Evans (l.) and Hugh Lynn Cayce. Virginia Beach, Va., around 1939.

Top Right: David E. Kahn with Edgar Cayce in Virginia Beach, Va., September, 1940.

Edgar and Annie Cayce, 1939.

Hugh Lynn Cayce (standing) with Thomas Sugrue at the dedication of the A.R.E. offices and vault at Arctic Crescent, Virginia Beach, Va., September, 1940.

A family portrait taken in front of the "old headquarters": (l. to r.) Hugh Lynn, Gertrude, Edgar Evans, and Edgar Cayce. Arctic Crescent, Virginia Beach, Va., around 1940.

At the Kahn home in Scarsdale, New York, on Thanksgiving Day, November 25, 1937: (clockwise from left) Lucille Kahn, Gertrude Cayce, Edgar Cayce, Mary Sugrue, David E. Kahn, S. David Kahn, Hugh Lynn Cayce, Gladys Davis, Thomas Sugrue.

Left: Edgar Cayce with his sisters in 1939: (seated l. to r.) Ola Crume and Annie Cayce; (l. to r. standing) Mary McPherson, Edgar Cayce, and Sarah Hesson.

Right: Edgar, Gertrude, and Gladys Davis at the dedication of the vault on Arctic Crescent, September, 1940.

Above: The Norfolk Search for God Study Group #1, taken by Edgar Cayce. Gladys Davis can be seen, standing second from left, Leslie B. Cayce at center back, and Hugh Lynn Cayce, standing fourth from right. April, 1932.

Left: Edgar Cayce fishing at the St. Lawrence River in 1937.

Far Left: An Edgar Cayce press release photograph used from 1932 to 1938.

Right: Gladys Davis, Leslie B. Cayce, Edgar Cayce. and Gertrude Cayce (l. to r.) at Lake Drive cottage, Virginia Beach, in 1932.

Front porch of the Cayce Hospital, 1929.

Second floor ward of the Cayce Hospital, 1929.

A.C. Preston, the first manager of the A.R.E., around 1930.

Dr. Thomas B. House at his desk at the Cayce Hospital, 1929.

Above: Morton H. Blumenthal, New York, around 1928.

Above Right: Edwin David Blumenthal, New York, 1928.

Right: A portrait of David E. Kahn taken in New York in 1928, presented to Edgar Cayce with the caption, "To My Best and Closest Friend 'Edgar Cayce.'"

Edgar Cayce with his son, Edgar Evans. Miami, Florida, January, 1927.

Top Right: Edgar Cayce and Linden Shroyer on a picnic at Overlook Park, Dayton, Ohio, 1924.

Edgar Cayce lived in the upstairs of this home at 2411 East 5th Street, Dayton, Ohio, from November, 1923, to April, 1924.

Home of Edgar Cayce and family at 35th Street, Virginia Beach, Va., when they moved there in September, 1925.

Above: Edgar Cayce's father Leslie B. "The Squire" Cayce. Selma, Alabama, 1922.

Top Right: Wesley Harrington Ketchum, 1922.

Gladys and Mildred Davis. Selma, Alabama. Summer, 1922. (Taken at Cayce Studio.)

Glady Davis. Selma, Alabama. Early summer, 1923. (Photo by Leslie B. Cayce at the Cayce Art Co. Studio.)

A portrait of Edgar, Hugh Lynn, and infant Edgar Evans. Taken in Selma, Alabama, around 1920.

Hugh Lynn Cayce (left) and Thomas B. House, Jr., around 1921.

Edgar Cayce at oil well site, Comyn, Texas, around 1921.

The Edgar Cayce family, Selma, Alabama, around 1921: (l. to r.) Edgar Evans, Gertrude, Edgar, and Hugh Lynn.

Edgar Cayce as photographed by Wilfred Sechrist in Virginia Beach, around 1943.

Edgar and Gertrude Cayce, probably taken during the 1944 A.R.E. Congress.

Edgar Cayce and Gladys Davis, June, 1944.

Thomas Sugrue at the entrance to the Clearwater Yacht Club in 1944.

The Cayce home and garden, 1941. Arctic Crescent, Virginia Beach, Va.

Left: Edgar Cayce, 1941. This is the only original portrait in the Cayce family.

Left: Edgar Cayce seated upon the famous "couch" in the library on Arctic Crescent, Virginia Beach, Va., in June, 1941.

Right: Edgar Cayce and family, around 1942: (front row, l. to r.) Sally Cayce, Edgar Evans Cayce, and Kathryn Cayce; (back row, l. to r.) Hugh Lynn Cayce, Gertrude Cayce, and Edgar Cayce.

Above: Edgar Cayce's Sunday school class. Selma, Alabama, 1913. Edgar Cayce is seated in the center of the second row.

Left: Edgar Cayce's mother Mrs. Carrie E. Cayce. Selma, Alabama, around 1913.

Below Left: Edgar and Gertrude Cayce. Selma, Alabama, around 1917.

Gertrude and Edgar Cayce in Selma, Alabama, around 1915.

Left: A family portrait taken around 1907 in Hopkinsville, Kentucky: (seated l. to r.) Edgar Cayce's parents Leslie B. "The Squire" Cayce and Carrie Elizabeth Cayce; (standing l. to r.) young Hugh Lynn being held by his father Edgar Cayce, Gertrude, and Edgar's sister Annie.

Above: Portrait of the newlyweds, Gertrude Evans and Edgar Cayce. Hopkinsville, Kentucky, 1903.

Below: Edgar Cayce at age 29. Montgomery, Alabama, 1909.

Above: Hugh Lynn Cayce. Selma, Alabama, 1913. (Taken by Edgar Cayce.)

The Cayce Hospital around 1929.

Living room of the Cayce Hospital, 1929.

Violet ray sun porch of the Cayce Hospital, 1929.

Library and lecture room of the Cayce Hospital, 1929.

The Cayce Hospital, Virginia Beach, Va., 1928.

Edgar and Gertrude gave these cameos to each other as Christmas gifts in 1900, during their third year of courtship. Hopkinsville, Kentucky.

Above: A wedding portrait of Edgar and Gertrude Evans Cayce. Hopkinsville, Kentucky, 1903.

Right: Edgar Cayce and his father, Leslie B. "The Squire" Cayce. Probably taken in Hopkinsville, Kentucky, around 1902.

Edgar Cayce's grandparents, Sarah and Thomas Jefferson Cayce, taken around 1865.

Edgar Cayce at age 15. Hopkinsville, Kentucky, 1895.

Edgar Cayce at age 19, taken during his photographic apprenticeship around 1899. Hopkinsville, Kentucky.

Edgar. He couldn't see the sense of it: it looked dramatic, but it only succeeded in keeping the squire, who did the suggesting, on his feet during the whole of the reading. A stenographer sat at a table nearby.

The stationery also tended toward the dramatic. The letterhead contained a picture of "Edgar Cayce, Jr., Psychic Diagnostician." The "Jr." was a bit of folk etymology. The uncle for whom Edgar was named now lived in Hopkinsville. To distinguish between the two the townspeople referred to one as Edgar and one as Edgar, Jr., though everyone was aware that they were uncle and nephew. The printer, when he got the order for the stationery, put the "Jr." on without a second thought.

The job of sending the money back was laborious. Edgar wrote most of the letters himself, offering to make appointments and, if the readings were satisfactory, take payment. There was no set price for a reading, and this annoyed him. Noe and Ketchum seemed to think it better to proceed on the plan used by all physicians: a final bill to include all services. There might be more than one reading; there might be medical supervision by Ketchum.

Edgar made a habit of reading the stenographic transcript of each reading. He wanted to find out what was coming out of him while he was asleep. The stuff amazed him: it read like a scientific fairy tale, a witch doctor's dream, or some mumbo-jumbo plucked out of an encyclopedia.

"We find in this body a degenerate condition of the white matter in the nerve tissues . . . a lack of connection between the sympathetic and cerebrospinal nervous systems . . . a lesion at the seventh dorsal . . . "

After each session he went back to the photographic studio in a state of complete confusion. He had thought that a study of the transcripts might help his conscious mind to understand what it was that his subconscious mind did. If he understood a little medicine, the thing might not seem so strange and improbable to him. He might learn to believe in it implicitly, from a faith within himself, instead of spasmodically, as a reflection of other people's belief. But the words blurred before his eyes. The language was too technical. He was worse off than before.

One of the first out-of-town visitors to the new office was a man from Nortonville, Kentucky, a town about thirty-five miles north of Hopkinsville. He introduced himself as Frank E. Mohr.

"I bought a coal mine recently from a man in Nortonville named Elgin," he told Edgar. "When I was discussing price and terms I asked him if there were another vein in the mine. He said he didn't know because the place hadn't been surveyed or examined by engineers.

"I asked him how he knew where to dig. He said he came over here and got a man named Layne to ask a fellow named Cayce about it, while Cayce was asleep. He said that Cayce told him to dig in Nortonville where the L. & N. and I.C. railroads cross. That's where the mine is located. Are you the fellow who did it?"

Edgar shook his head.

"I don't know anything about it," he said. He explained his relationship with Layne.

"I never knew he took readings for any but sick people," he said.

"Well, never mind," Mohr said. "I've had my own engineers go over the mine. You aren't necessary for a thing like that. But if you can help sick people, I have a little niece over in Williamson, West Virginia, who had an attack of infantile paralysis. She can't walk yet, and I'd like to see what can be done to speed her recovery. Want to try it?"

Edgar gave the reading and Mohr became so interested that he offered to buy the contract from Ketchum, Noe, and the squire. When his niece in West Virginia reported that she was progressing, he began to build a hospital in Nortonville, so determined was he to put the readings on a scientific basis. Patients were having trouble getting the treatments outlined by Edgar carried out. They found that where the attention of a medical doctor was prescribed, the doctor almost always refused to have anything to do with the case. Osteopaths were usually willing to give treatments, but only after making their own diagnosis. They treated as the reading suggested so long as it agreed with their own ideas.

In Hopkinsville it was possible to get cooperation among the various doctors, but most of the patients were not in Hopkinsville, or even near it. Mohr thought that a hospital would solve the problem—at least for those who could afford to come to it. There the readings could be carried out exactly, and the cases could be followed until the readings discharged them.

While dickering with Ketchum, Noe, and the squire, Mohr went ahead with his plans. By January, 1911, the cellar and foundation of a small hospital building were completed. Then Mohr was badly hurt in a mine accident. Edgar went to Nortonville and gave readings for him, but it was a case for surgery and rest, and Mohr eventually had to go back to his home in Ohio. It took him a long time to recover, and he lost his holdings in Nortonville. The hospital was not completed, the contract stayed in Hopkinsville. When he left Nortonville, Mohr took with him a reading which said that his injuries might sometime cause blindness. In case this occurred, treatment for it was outlined.

Edgar was beginning to realize, as the days went by and the readings piled up, that Mohr was right. To get the treatments carried out properly it was necessary that cooperation exist between the different schools of medicine, or a place be established where practitioners of differing medical theories could be employed to carry out the suggestions. There was Ketchum, for instance. He was a homeopath. There was Dr. House. He was a medical doctor who had also studied osteopathy. There was Layne, who had completed his education and was now an osteopath, practicing in Georgia. These men all believed in the readings. If they could be brought together at a hospital, what might not be done?

But there were other necessities: people who knew about treatment by electricity, people who knew massage, people who knew psychiatry, people who knew scientific diet, people who specialized in the nervous system, people who specialized in female disorders. As Edgar looked over the diagnoses and treatments that came out of him day by day he decided that only a medical Jack-of-all-trades would do; and he would have to be master of them all.

Late in February, Roswell Field, brother of Eugene Field, came to Hopkinsville to do a series of stories about Edgar for Hearst's

Chicago *Examiner*. Edgar was photographed holding Hugh Lynn on his lap, and lying on the reading table with the squire standing by him and a stenographer seated at a table. The pictures, along with Field's stories, were sent to all the Hearst newspapers.

Field described Edgar as he found him in the company office, killing time "in the most approved Kentucky fashion.

"His appearance was neither conspicuously encouraging nor disappointing. His photograph, which is an admirable one, bears out the impression of a tall, slender young man, with good, honest eyes, sufficiently wide apart, a high forehead, and just the ordinary features.

"He admitted that he is thirty-three years of age, though he does not look over twenty-five . . . "

Field listened to the yarns which were already becoming legends in Hopkinsville and sat in on several readings. As a result of his stories, Edgar was invited to visit Chicago as a guest of the Hearst papers. He went, early in March, along with Noe and the squire, and stayed for ten days, meeting people, giving readings, and answering the most preposterous questions he had ever heard. Everyone considered him a freak, and the bellboys charged people five dollars to slip them into the crowded living room of the bridal suite where they could watch the marvel of the age as he talked, smoked, and told tales.

A few days after returning to Hopkinsville, he again became a father. Gertrude bore her second son, Milton Porter, on March 28th. Edgar was happier than he had ever been before.

But the baby became ill. He developed whooping cough, and this was succeeded by colitis. Gertrude did not ask for a reading, nor did it occur to Edgar that anything was seriously wrong until the doctors suddenly gave up hope. Then a reading was taken. It was too late; acid had permeated the system. The baby died.

Edgar was stunned. The reading hadn't been taken in time, obviously. He and Gertrude had depended on doctors. In their smug way they had relied on the medical profession, while every day Edgar was going to sleep, diagnosing, and prescribing for other people. It had never occurred to him to question whether, in an emergency involving himself, or his child, or Gertrude, he would turn to a reading for help. He had worried about whether to offer his powers to other people and had decided that he should, because so many had been helped by them and so many believed in them. But he had not really answered the question—even during that long night in the studio at Montgomery—of whether he believed in the readings himself. He was a prophet without honor in his own heart.

He would have quit had he not been under contract and had he not begun to be deeply affected by the stream of letters of thanks which poured into the office. Other people had faith in him; they seemed sure of his powers; they had been helped by the treatments suggested in their readings. They thanked him profusely. Some said they remembered him in their prayers. Was it possible for a man to mean so much to others and so little to himself?

If only Gertrude believed. If she had faith, he would have faith, too. But she looked at it from the viewpoint of a woman in love. She had not liked Layne. She did not like Ketchum. She feared what the readings might do to Edgar or what he might be tempted to do by reason of them. She said nothing, but she was like a parent with a beautiful daughter, who fears for her child's virtue because it has become so desirable.

After the baby died, her health declined. Dr. Jackson told her she had pleurisy, but it hung on through the spring and into the summer. Each night Edgar came home she seemed a little weaker. She was unable to do any housework; she seemed to care little for anything except the company of Hugh Lynn.

Each day, reading through the transcripts of the readings he had given, Edgar thought of her and felt guilty.

"Yes, we have the body . . . it has become impoverished, or thin, from conditions existing in the circulation, produced by lack of nutriment in the blood to supply the rebuilding forces in the body . . . until we have a seat of trouble in the left side, at the lower extremity of the lung itself . . . "

If he could do that for others, why not for Gertrude? If she would only ask!

July came, and August. One hot morning Dr. Jackson called him into his office.

"Edgar," he said, "I've known you and Gertrude all your lives. I know you want me to be frank with you about her illness."

"Yes, sir," Edgar said. He sat down weakly.

"She's in bad shape. I've called you in because there's nothing more I can do. She has tuberculosis. Her brother died of it; you know that.

"I've had the other doctors look her over. Beazley's been there along with the others. We've talked it over. We disagree on what it's coming from, but we agree on what she has.

"So far as we can see there is no hope. I don't know how long she will live; perhaps another week.

"You've been doing things for other people. If there's anything in that monkey business, now is the time to try it. It's your only hope. We've done all we can. You'd better get a reading."

Edgar got up and walked out into the street. Somehow he got to the office and telephoned to the Hill. He told Carrie and Mrs. Evans that Dr. Jackson wanted to see them. He met them and waited while they went into Jackson's office. They came out weeping. Jackson was with them.

"How soon can you get a reading?" he said.

"Right away," Edgar said.

"Wait a few minutes," Jackson said. "There are some men I want to be there. We'll need them if there is anything that can be done."

A tuberculosis specialist from Louisville was in town. Jackson brought him to the office, along with Dr. A. Seargeant, a local specialist in the same field. He asked Louis Elgin, the druggist, to come in. Ketchum was there. The squire was the conductor. Dr. Kasey, the Methodist preacher, and Harry Smith, who had married Edgar and Gertrude, heard what was going on and came in.

When Edgar woke up, the doctors were pacing up and down the room, shaking their heads and muttering. The specialist from Louisville started talking as soon as he saw that Edgar was awake.

"Your anatomy is fine, fine," he said. "Your diagnosis is excellent. But your *materia medica* is rotten.

"The things you suggest are what we make medicines with. We don't use them as they are. They won't make a compound.

Heroin, you say, mixed to make a liquid, given in a capsule, and manufacture only three at a time, because after three days the compound will disintegrate. That's just weird!"

"These drugs are principles," Seargeant said. "We don't use them as they are . . . The diet is the same as the one used at Battle Creek."

"It's the one used generally for all tuberculosis now," the specialist from Louisville said.

"It's tuberculosis all right," Jackson said. "But even if all these things work, it still won't help. It's too late."

"I'd like to get a whiff of that keg," the specialist from Louisville said.

He smiled at Edgar.

"You said to put apple brandy in a charred keg and let her inhale the fumes."

"It can't do any harm," Jackson said, "though I never heard of it before."

They argued and discussed, pacing the floor, while Edgar sat, miserable and silent, watching them.

"Did I say she could get well?" he whispered to the squire.

His father nodded. He was waiting for the doctors to leave.

When they and the ministers had gone, leaving the squire, Ketchum, Elgin, and Edgar, there was no prescription for the compound containing heroin. The doctors had refused to write it.

"Will you?" Elgin said to Ketchum.

Ketchum hesitated.

"If you won't," Elgin went on, "I'm going to make it up anyhow. I may go to jail, but if Edgar wants it and his wife needs it, I'll prepare it."

"Then I'll write it," Ketchum said. His confidence in Edgar returned; he had been temporarily awed by the manner of his distinguished colleagues.

Jackson told Gertrude he wanted her to do what the reading suggested. She was too weak to resist or care. She could barely raise her head from the pillow. After the first capsule she ceased to have hemorrhages. After the second day her fever disappeared. The fumes of the apple brandy helped the congestion in her lungs. Very slowly she gained strength, falling time and again into relapse.

They took frequent check readings on her. Edgar watched them anxiously for indications that the tuberculosis was checked. By September the reading reported: "The condition in the body now is quite different from what we have had before . . . from the head, pains along through the body from the second, fifth and sixth dorsals, and from the first and second lumbar . . . tie-ups here, or floating lesions, or lateral lesions, in the muscular and nerve forces which supply the lower end of the lung and the diaphragm . . . in conjunction with the sympathetic nerve of the solar plexus, coming in conjunction with the solar plexus at the end of the stomach . . . we have had, as we had before in the system, a tie-up through the digestive tract . . . a state of impact through the large colon most all the time . . . the faecal matter lying in the body producing irritation through the whole digestive system, leaving the body in a state of collapse, as we have at present . . . allowed this congestion to form in the lung from the air breathed in . . . and bacilli . . . until we have a congestion in the lung . . . choked, or clogged, leaving the air to pass through the right, and upper part of the left . . .

" . . . it has been somewhat relieved by the application of forces to the exterior . . . and to the blood from the circulation . . . but the condition of the lung, of choking . . . is still in the system because of the faecal matter in the intestine . . . through the circulation of the hepatics there has been produced the temperatures we have in the body . . . a chilling or congestion of the circulation produces the temperature . . . from the condition in the lung . . . that is, the air, not coming in perfect contact with circulation (lack of reoxidization of the blood) produced the condition . . . still, we have some bacilli here in the lung set up in these forces."

On November 21st there was a "good deal of difference in the condition in the body now and what we had before. We have some parts better and others not so well. We have some inflammation in the throat and larynx . . . more than we had before . . . less congestion in the lung, though we still have some . . . the eliminating power of the liver is not as good . . . the blood is weaker, thinner, for the lack of hemoglobin in it . . . the troubles we have through the pelvis are aggravated by the condition we find in the parts themselves . . .

" . . . the congestion is lower in the lung than we have had before . . . a good deal of soreness on the left side of the throat . . . produced by the conditions in the lung and liver . . .

" . . . we have not stirred up the liver enough to produce the secretions to eliminate and carry off the particles through the dross and through the intestinal tract . . . along the spine manipulation has relieved the muscular forces and conditions through the lungs and cells themselves . . . or the cover of the lungs, the pleura . . .

" . . . the condition, of course, has been aggravated through taking cold . . . congestion in the chest and head . . . aggravated condition, of course, of the catarrh that existed before in the head . . . "

Edgar was up all that night, with the doctors. The language of the reading was calm and matter-of-fact, but there was no mistaking the seriousness of the situation. Gertrude had taken cold; she was gradually choking and coughing herself to death. The next morning another reading was taken.

"We haven't much change in the body . . . some better through the condition of the throat; not quite so much inflammation . . . more inflammation, though, through the intestinal tract; that is, below the stomach . . . we have a disturbance through the stomach . . . some congestion through the lung . . . a great deal in the bronchials and head, and in the nasal ducts . . . good deal of soreness in the throat and across the diaphragm from coughing . . . cough produced by lack of blood to remove those particles from the body through the proper channels . . . impoverishment of the blood makes it easy to take cold . . . "

That morning Gertrude could not raise her hand or lift her head from the pillow to take a drink of water. They gave her the little "goose," the glass with a tube at its end. She smiled wanly at her mother, who was nursing her.

The readings were followed carefully, but it was slow, uphill work. When they could keep her from taking cold, she improved. By the first of January she was much better.

"The inflammation we had in the lower part of the lung here, close to the diaphragm, and the abrasion we had on the diaphragm and pleura below . . . are removed and absorbed into the system itself . . . "

That night Edgar sat by her bedside, reading to her. She put out her hand and took hold of his. He looked at her. She was smiling.

"The readings saved me, Edgar," she said. "Thank you."

He looked at the book again, but the page blurred. He sat in silence staring at it, still holding her hand.

"Thank you," she said again.

12

The shutter clicked again.

"That's all, Mrs. Doolittle," he said. "I think we'll get some nice prints from these. I'll have the proofs in a few days."

"You can let Jim know," she said. "You'll be seeing him, I expect."

He helped her with her coat and escorted her from the studio to the stairway, with Daniel leading the way.

"Good-bye, Daniel," he said gravely.

The boy shook hands with him and turned to help his mother down the stairs. Edgar went into the other office.

The squire and Ketchum had gone. The stenographer was working on the transcript of the morning reading.

"They've gone to the hotel for lunch," she told him. "They took the young man with them. I promised to have this ready for them when they return."

He looked at his watch. It was after twelve, but he wasn't hungry. Through the window he could see Mrs. Doolittle and Daniel crossing the street. It had begun to snow again, very lightly. The 12:15 train, bearing Dr. Münsterberg, was pulling out of the station.

The snow turned into a near blizzard, and next morning Edgar stayed at home, shoveling paths and building a snowman for Hugh Lynn. That night he got out a copy of "Snowbound" and read it to Gertrude and Hugh Lynn. Gertrude was much better, and the next morning, at Hugh Lynn's insistence, they built a snowman for her, outside her window. They put a hat on it and called it "The Professor."

It was another two days before the town dug itself out of the storm. The squire, while walking to the office, had slipped and fallen, breaking his kneecap. He was put to bed, and a reading was given for him. Ketchum conducted the reading, and the subsequent ones taken at the office for regular patients.

Frequently he dispensed with the stenographer at the time of the reading, took notes, and then dictated his own version of what had been said. Looking over one of these reports Edgar had a hunch. He had been feeling badly after the readings; his head often ached. He wrote a letter to the patient, a woman, saying that he hoped her reading was proving of benefit. She replied that she had not received a reading. She had applied for one, but no appointment had been made, and nothing so far had been sent to her.

Edgar faced Ketchum with the letter. Ketchum tried to explain.

"We need money," he said. "We always have enough to get along on, of course, but we want to get ahead so we can build a hospital. We're handicapped now because so many of our patients can't get the treatments carried out properly.

"All the rich people we've tried give us only promises. The scientists look wise and shake their hands and go away. Look at Münsterberg. There's money at Harvard that has been set aside to study such things as this. But did he offer to do it? We haven't heard a word from him. Not even a note of thanks.

"I expected a committee of doctors to come here and test you. I hoped that the medical profession would back us. But the doctors didn't come. They were afraid, probably, that they'd have to admit something they don't want to admit.

"So we've been going along, getting five, ten, twenty dollars . . . sometimes more, and a lot of times less, for readings. If we let you have your way, you'd give them all away. You never turn anyone down.

"We'll never get anyplace that way. We can stay here the rest of our lives, giving readings that are not followed out properly, sending them to people on whom we can't check up . . . what will we ever prove or accomplish?"

"So?" Edgar said.

"So we haven't taken some of the readings you think we have. I wrote those reports for you, so you wouldn't worry.

"We've been taking other readings. We've been gambling a

little . . . just finding out, you know . . . getting a few tips . . . "

Edgar put the letter down on the desk, picked up his hat and coat, and left.

At home he found Gertrude sitting up, feeling better.

"I've quit Ketchum and Noe," he said.

"I'm glad," she said, "very glad."

"Do you think you're well enough so that I can go to Alabama and get a job with Tressler? I'll send you check readings as often as you need them."

Gertrude smiled.

"I know I'm going to be all right now," she said. "You go ahead. I'm glad this business is all over."

He packed and came to kiss her good-bye. His face was like a thundercloud.

"Don't worry about it," she said. "I'll join you soon."

He bought a ticket for Montgomery and caught the St. Louis-New Orleans flyer.

13

The man ran out into Broad Street carrying the screaming child in his arms. He raced to the corner and turned down Dallas Avenue, going as fast as he could.

Doors and windows popped open. It was a cool, gloomy January day in Selma, Alabama, and most people in the business district were indoors. The child's piercing, agonized cries brought them out. When the man reached the office of Dr. Eugene Callaway, the eye specialist, the doctor was out in the street. He led the man inside, turning to shout to two other doctors who had come out of their offices across the street.

"Come on over!" he called.

When they got there, the man was explaining what had happened, shouting to Dr. Callaway above the pitiful shrieking of the child.

"It's flash powder! I found him on the floor of the workroom. He must have made a big pile of it and put a match to it! It exploded in his face!"

They tried to examine the boy, but it was difficult to hold him still. Finally they got a dressing on his eyes, and some bandages. The man picked him up and carried him back up the avenue. People who had gathered in the street watched sympathetically.

"It's Edgar Cayce, the photographer, and his little boy Hugh Lynn," they whispered to newcomers. "The boy burned his eyes with flash powder."

Back in the studio that looked down over Broad Street Gertrude was waiting. She led the way to her room, and Edgar laid his burden on the bed. In a little while the doctors came in, one by one. A conference was held in the reception room. None had any hope for the child's sight.

A week passed. Hugh Lynn was worse. One of the doctors

said that an eye would have to be removed if his life was to be
saved. The others agreed. They asked Edgar to tell the boy. He
went into the bedroom, with the doctors following timidly behind,
looking as if they were attending a funeral.

"The doctors say they will have to take one of your eyes out,
Hugh Lynn," Edgar said.

Hugh Lynn's head was swathed in bandages. He could see nothing,
but he knew the doctors were there. He spoke to them directly.

"If you had a little boy, you wouldn't take his eye out, would
you?" he asked.

"I wouldn't take any little boy's eye out if I could help it," one
of the doctors said. "We're only trying to do what is best for you."

"My daddy knows what is best for me," Hugh Lynn said. "When
my daddy goes to sleep, he's the best doctor in the world."

He groped for his father's hand.

"Please, Daddy, will you go to sleep and see if you can help
me?" he asked.

Edgar looked at Dr. Callaway. Dr. Callaway nodded his head.
"Go ahead," he said. "We can't offer much. We'll listen and do
what we can afterward."

An hour later the reading was taken. Word of it had got abroad.
There were more than thirty people in the big reception room. Many
of them were members of the Christian Church, which the Cayces
attended. One of them suggested that they pray. While Edgar
went to sleep they recited, in subdued voices, the Lord's Prayer.

The suggestion was given. Edgar began to speak. He could
see the body. Sight was not gone. The solution used by the doctors
was helpful, but to it should be added tannic acid. Dressings
should be changed frequently and applied constantly for fifteen
days, during which the body was to be kept in a darkened room.
After that the eyes would be well.

When Edgar awoke the doctors told him that tannic acid was
too strong for use on the eyes. However, they were sure that
sight was gone, so their objections were technical. They agreed
to make the new solution and apply it. The operation could be
postponed temporarily.

As soon as the fresh bandages were put on his eyes Hugh
Lynn said:

"That must be daddy's medicine. It doesn't hurt."

The studio emptied slowly. Edgar did not move. He sat on the edge of the couch, staring out the window at the sluggish, swirling waters of the Alabama River, as they came into view at the end of Broad Street.

In a little while Gertrude came out of the bedroom and sat down beside him.

"He's asleep now," she said.

Together they watched the life of Broad Street as it moved below them. Selma was a quiet, happy place. They liked its atmosphere, its people, its broad, tree-lined streets. They had been happy there.

It was 1914, two years since Edgar had come to the busy city of 20,000 that marked the head of all-year navigation on the Alabama River. Selma had been the arsenal of the Confederacy. It was now an important freight center and the seat of Dallas County. Through its streets ebbed and flowed the purchasing power of a rich agricultural district. Its business streets were lined with wholesale warehouses; at its docks river steamers were constantly being loaded and unloaded.

Edgar was an agent of the H. P. Tressler Company when he arrived. He opened a branch studio for the company, but after a year bought it for himself. In the spring of 1913 Dr. Jackson declared Gertrude well, and in the autumn she came south. She liked Selma as much as Edgar did, and they decided to make it their home. Edgar had already joined the Christian Church and was teaching a Sunday school class. On the roster of the church it was the Seven Class, and soon it became famous, for young people from all the other churches joined it. The class published a weekly paper called the Sevenette, which everyone in town took to reading.

The story of the readings did not follow them from Hopkinsville. Gertrude conducted the check readings that were regularly sent to friends and relatives in Hopkinsville. Before Gertrude came, her brother Lynn, who was working in Anniston for the Louisville and Nashville Railroad, came to Selma on weekends and conducted.

The doctors who looked after them in Selma—Dr. Callaway,

the eye specialist, and Dr. S. Gay, a former army surgeon—learned about it eventually and listened in at times. They expressed no opinion one way or the other.

What would they say now, if the reading were right?

Edgar and Gertrude got up from the couch. They had been stricken by the same thought. What if the reading were wrong?

"I'd better see about dinner," Gertrude said.

The days dragged by. On the sixteenth morning after the reading, a white mass sloughed off with the bandages. Two brown eyes looked up at two anxious faces.

"I can see," Hugh Lynn said.

They gave him dark glasses and made him stay inside for another week. He was forbidden to go into the workroom.

It was not a great hardship. There was plenty of room elsewhere for play. The studio occupied the entire second and third floors of 21½ Broad Street. On the second floor was a giant reception room with showcases, tables, easy chairs, and a big desk. Next to it were the workroom and the stockroom. A back stairway led up to the family entrance of the living quarters. There was a small bedroom for Hugh Lynn, a large one for his parents, a dining room and a kitchen. The main stairway led to the big room with the skylight, where the pictures were taken. The darkroom was behind this, and then came a dressing room. Another dressing room was in the main hallway. It was an ideal setup for playing Cowboy and Indian.

Down at the bottom of the main stairs, above the street entrance, was a large clock. When wound, it ran for eight days. Edgar put photographs on all the numerals, and let the clock run down. When it stopped, the persons whose photographs were nearest the two hands won prizes. Everyone wanted to be eligible, so everyone had his picture taken.

When he was finally allowed to return to school and to play out of doors in the afternoons, Hugh Lynn returned to his greatest love—the river. He liked to sit and watch the steamers dock; he would count the bales of cotton that came until the numbers got too big for him to handle. In summer, when the water was shallow, he roamed along the banks and played on the sand bars. In spring, when the floods came, he went with his father to make pictures from the bridge of the high water. The lowlands across the river were flooded then, and on his way to school, passing the big red-brick houses of the old families of Selma, he saw the magnolia trees in bloom and smelled the sweet bud shrubs.

In summer he went with his mother to Hopkinsville, to visit at the Hill, and his father spent the hot months canning fruits and vegetables. He liked to do that better than anything except making pictures, and there were always plenty of good things to eat in the winter.

At the Hill he played with his cousins, Tommy House and Gray Salter. He liked them, but he was always glad to get back to Selma to see his father and to enjoy the autumn, when the older boys played football and there were lots of people coming to the studio to have their pictures made.

*   *   *

A few weeks after Hugh Lynn's recovery Edgar developed symptoms of appendicitis. Dr. Gay treated him, but said there was no reason for operating. An X ray showed that the condition demanding surgery was not present. The symptoms remained, however, and on March 8th a reading was taken. It advised an appendectomy within twenty-four hours; the case, it said, was strangular.

"Will you operate?" Edgar asked Gay.

"That's my business," Gay said. "If you have the money, I'll operate."

He was a friendly man, with a round stomach, a l ean face, sparse gray hair, and glasses that magnified his eyes and made them seem to twinkle.

"We'll do it this afternoon," he said.

The operation was performed successfully. The diagnosis of the reading was found to be correct.

The convalescents, Hugh Lynn and Edgar, enjoyed the spring. Hugh Lynn had developed into a checker shark, and under Edgar's management engaged the cigar store champions along Broad Street. He won all his matches.

Edgar did the cheering and coaching, and succeeded in losing his voice. He got one of his friends to conduct a reading; Gertrude was in Anniston for the day. The conductor, in giving the suggestion, said the body of Edgar Cayce would be found "at 22½ Broad Street," which was the address of the building across the street.

"We do not find the body here," Edgar said.

"The body is there," the conductor said, staring at Edgar.

"We do not find it," Edgar said.

"Describe the room," the conductor said.

Edgar did so. The room described resembled the studio not at all. The conductor reached to the desk, looked at a piece of Edgar's stationery, and saw his mistake. When the description of the room at 22½ was completed, he suggested that the body be sought at 21½.

"Yes, we have the body now," Edgar said. "This we have had before. Now as we find . . . "

When he awakened, the conductor told him what had happened and showed him the description of the room at 22½, which he had taken down. The second floor had been specified. They could see its window from where they stood. They went downstairs, crossed the street, and entered 22½. Upstairs, in a room answering in every detail to the description Edgar had given, a bookkeeper was working. His appearance, even to the color of his suit, had been described without error.

Ordinarily readings were few and far between. Most of them were for friends or friends of friends, and there was seldom any remuneration: none was ever asked. Edgar and Gertrude preferred it that way. They worked for their living, as did all honest people. In addition they helped friends who were in trouble, as did all good Christians. In this way of life they found happiness.

They asked nothing more. Edgar was completely wrapped up in his Sunday school class and his Christian Endeavour work. His group in Christian Endeavour had the largest number of "junior experts" ever credited to a single class in the history of the movement. He was proud of that, and of the constant growth of the Seven Class. He also enjoyed the letters he received from members of his old class in Hopkinsville. Many of them were serving as missionaries, and they described their activities for him. Often they asked for readings—for themselves, their friends, or their charges. The first readings for people in foreign countries were given at the request of these former pupils. Edgar was pleased to find that he could locate an address in Mexico or England as easily as one in the United States. Once he was asked to locate "Signora Adelaide Albanese Ruggiero, Piazza del Campo alle Falde Pellegrino, Villino Albanese, Palermo, Cicilia . . . house is northeast and east . . . she sleeps on the ground floor."

It took no longer to find her than had she been in the room. Soon Edgar was saying, "We have in this body conditions well fitted to demonstrate the power of mind over matter, for the principal strength in this body is derived from the actual flexes and reflexes from the brain itself . . . the condition has been brought about first by that condition that has existed in the body for a long time, especially in the pelvis and along the excretory organism in this region . . . the nerves and reflexes of the kidneys . . . "

Eventually all his friends in Selma heard about the readings, and many tried them for themselves and members of their families. One of these cases was the talk of the town for a while.

A sister of one of Edgar's Sunday school pupils went out of her mind suddenly. The reading said she was only temporarily upset, owing to an impacted wisdom tooth which had not come through. It suggested certain sedatives and advised that a dental surgeon take out the tooth. The girl was taken to Tuscaloosa, where her jaw was X-rayed in the presence of her aunt, who was a nurse. A physician was also present. The impacted tooth showed in the X ray and was removed. After eight days the patient's mind returned to normal.

Most of the people for whom check readings were regularly given had troubles of long standing; their illnesses were complicated, and their readings outlined many treatments. There was always diet, and there were usually medicines, plus massage or some other means of stimulating areas where circulation was poor. Often osteopathic adjustments were advised; sometimes patients were instructed to take medicines or adjustments in cycles, on certain days of the week, or at stated intervals.

Whether they followed these instructions Edgar never knew. They wrote to tell him that they were feeling better, that they had found one of the aids mentioned to be very efficacious, that they were planning to start all of the treatments soon. It was obvious that some of them needed supervision; others needed cooperation. Few were carrying out the readings to the letter and getting the results which were possible. Nothing was being proved, and almost no one was being cured. It made Edgar think of Ketchum, who had been right in his ideas, if not in his methods; it made him think of Frank Mohr and the hospital he had begun at Nortonville.

But all that was behind him. He was living the life he wanted to live at last. Dragging up old dreams would only spoil his happiness. Yet someone was always dragging him up.

Once it was Dr. Gay. In the spring of 1915 Gertrude complained of symptoms of appendicitis, and Dr. Gay prepared to operate. The day before she was to go to the hospital a reading was taken. It said surgery was unnecessary and suggested that the capsules which Gay had prescribed be reinforced with one-sixtieth of a grain of another drug and that they be continued as a medicine. Since the case was not yet serious Gay tried the suggestion. After a week the symptoms disappeared.

"You're doing this on purpose," Gay said good-naturedly. "I think that subconscious of yours likes to play jokes."

He sat down and took off his glasses.

"Seriously," he said, "I think a lot about this thing. I knew very well that you didn't have appendicitis last year, and I knew very well last week that your wife did. Even the X ray agreed with me about your case. Yet I was wrong both times, and you were able to tell me so by going to sleep.

"Your appendix undoubtedly had to be taken out, or you would have died. When I gave your wife the medicine you suggested, she got well.

"The boy's eyes are all right. They might have been anyhow, but we wouldn't have put tannic acid in the solution, and we might have taken one of the eyes out.

"Do you know what it is, or how it works?"

Edgar repeated the explanation he was supposed to have given while asleep, as reported by Ketchum. Gay smiled.

"It's a law in action all right," he said, "but in reverse, or sideways. Something's gone wrong somewhere, and this stuff runs out of you like water through a hole in a dam. We've all had the sensation of feeling that knowledge was around us all the while, if we knew how to get it. This seems to be one of the ways."

He sighed.

"I wish I were a little younger. I'd like to go into this and follow it through. But I don't know whether I have the stuff to tackle it, at my age."

He put his glasses back on.

"But somebody should, and I hope somebody does, someday. It's worth studying."

*   *   *

He was continually getting requests for readings from people who had met the Dietrichs. One of these came in the fall of 1914, from a lumber merchant in Lexington, Kentucky, named W. L. DeLaney. DeLaney wanted Edgar to come to Lexington and give a reading for Mrs. DeLaney, who had been ill for many years. He wanted Edgar to bring a physician with him, if possible, to take down the suggestions and inaugurate the treatments.

Edgar wired Blackburn and stopped in Bowling Green to pick him up. Blackburn was willing to go but had to give up the trip at the last minute because of an emergency operation. Edgar went on to Lexington alone.

The DeLaneys lived in Hampton Court, a dead-end street. Mrs. DeLaney, a patient, pleasant woman, suffered from what was vaguely described as swelling arthritis. Her joints and flesh were enlarged; she was paralyzed so badly that for three years she had not been able to feed herself, and for five years she had been unable to comb her own hair. She lay on a stretcher; she could not bear to be touched by sheets.

Mr. DeLaney, who was quiet and small, conducted the reading, taking down only the prescriptions and suggestions for treatment. A physician was present. When Edgar woke up, he asked what had been given.

"Everything," Mr. DeLaney said. "Everything, including the kitchen sink. You have something for every square inch of her body, I think. If we do all this, something has GOT to happen."

Six months later Edgar returned and gave a check reading. Mrs. DeLaney called him in and proudly combed her hair for him. She was slowly getting well. Later a strange rash broke out all over her body. A check reading, taken in Selma, said an ingredient had been left out of the medicines—black sulphur. The lack of this had caused the rash.

After another six months—in the autumn of 1915—Edgar again returned. Mrs. DeLaney now could walk a little; she fed herself and had almost normal movement throughout the upper part of her body. The rash was gone.

During that visit Edgar was introduced to a neighboring family, the Kahns. They were Reformed Jews. Solomon, the father, ran a grocery business and all his children helped him. There were eight of them: David, Julian, DeVera, Raymond, Yetra, Hazel, Leon, and Joe. Fanny, the mother, was a tall handsome woman with the face of an Arab. She had been talking with Mr. and Mrs. DeLaney, and she wanted to get a reading for Leon, who was not well. Edgar sat up half the night with the family grouped about him, telling tales and answering questions. David, the eldest boy, was especially inquisitive. He was eighteen and had been studying at the state university in Lexington.

The reading for Leon outlined treatments. When Edgar called to say good-bye, Fanny gathered her husband and children together and spoke to them.

"We have seen a wonderful thing," she said. "I want you children to promise me that you will never forget this man.

"David, you are the eldest. I want you to promise that you will devote a portion of your life to seeing that the work of this man is made known to the world. The world needs it."

"I promise," David said.

Riding home on the train, Edgar puzzled over the scene. Back in Hopkinsville several readings had been taken on the manner of conducting the business and making it known to the public. One of these had said that the work would succeed when there was a Jew in it. They knew no Jews; Edgar had never known one. But ever since then he had been on the lookout for a likable one, wondering who the fellow would be. The eager young face of David Kahn had impressed him. Was he the touchstone?

Selma was a sweet narcosis for such thoughts. It reduced them to daydreams and embroidered them with all sorts of pleasant fancies: a reading would be given for a mysterious person who only sent his name and address. The person would turn out to be a philanthropist, anxious to find a worthy cause for his money. He would build a great hospital in Selma, and there, after a great many cures had been effected, doctors would come from all over the world to study the treatments and get readings on diseases in which they were specialists. Sometimes the thought would strike Edgar that he ought to go out and look for the philanthropist, but he rationalized such ideas away with the facts before him: he had a wife, a child, and a business; he could not go off and leave them. Perhaps a man who was free of such responsibilities, like young David Kahn, might go out and find the philanthropist.

Meanwhile he was doing what work he could in the field before him. He gave readings for those who asked for them; he worked in all the activities of his church; he was a good neighbor; he was a sincere Christian, though imperfect like all others. He would live thus until the way to greater service was shown to him.

When the war came in 1917 it took many of his young friends to France, including David Kahn. Watching the members of his Sunday school class leave for training camp he realized he was forty—getting old. He also realized how much he depended on these young friends. Slowly, in his thoughts and daydreams, he had been turning to them for the hope of realizing his dreams. He had never told them about these dreams; he would be ashamed to do that. But he nourished them with the youth he gathered about him.

They wrote to him from the trenches and told him how much the training he had given them in the Bible and Christian action was helping them in their hours of crisis. One of them told this story:

Driving an ammunition truck up to the front one night through an enemy artillery attack, he found himself getting more and more frightened. To bolster his courage he began to sing, as loudly as he could, the favorite hymn of the Seven Class, "I Love to Tell the Story."

His singing punctuated the detonations. Suddenly the tune was taken up on all sides of him. He was not alone. Soldiers were moving up with him on both sides. They adopted the hymn as a marching song, and when the attack ceased and the air was quiet, it roared out into the night. The ammunition truck drove through to its destination.

The war ended, and the country became filled with a restless energy that looked for new ways in which to expend itself. Soldiers began arriving home, looking for jobs. Some wanted to return to their old occupations; others, stimulated and made dissatisfied by their uprooting, wanted to seek greener fields. Might not this be a good time, before they all settled themselves again, to get something started for the readings? A hospital, perhaps?

He himself was more of a family man than ever. On February 9, 1918, Gertrude had given birth to another son, Edgar Evans Cayce. It would have to be someone else who started things. Yet the itch to see something under way had got hold of him. The old wounds had healed.

The itch apparently got hold of his subconscious, too. One day in March, 1919, when he had not given a reading for several weeks, he went to sleep to give one diagnosis, and eight more tumbled out of him voluntarily. Seven of these were check-ups, and the requests for them were in the mail. The eighth diagnosis was for a new patient. The request for this reading also was in the mail. The patient was one of his female cousins in Hopkinsville, who was pregnant. The reading said that the child would be born and would survive, but that conditions indicated a very hard time for the mother, with a possibility that the birth would be fatal for her. Extreme caution was urged. The child, a girl, was born in due time. The mother died.

Finally David Kahn returned from France. He wired Edgar

from the transport, asking him to be his guest in Lexington. When Edgar got there, David was enthroned as the family hero. He had become a captain and looked very handsome in his uniform. He was full of plans for the future, both for himself and for Edgar. His mother urged them on. She had complete faith in the readings. Another child, Eleanor, had been born to her, but Leon had died, because the treatments were not carried out: no doctor would administer them.

"I do not want that to happen to others," she said.

"What do we need to get this work in shape so the people can get the benefits of it?" David asked Edgar. "Whatever it is, it will take money. That's what I've been thinking about. We've got to raise some money."

"A hospital," Edgar said.

He knew exactly what he wanted; he knew exactly what to say.

"A hospital where we can give the kind of treatments the readings outline," he said. "If we had a place that would follow the diet, give the right electrical and osteopathic treatments—and give them at the right time—and give the medicines, too, then we'd have something. If we had enough money, we could run it free."

"There's money everywhere," David said. "How about the oil fields that are opening up in Texas? I'm going out there and look things over. It should be easy. There isn't any person who wouldn't give money to a cause like this. I have a friend in Atlanta . . . "

"We could keep copies of all the readings and have people correlate the things in them and experiment with the medicines and treatments," Edgar went on. "We could take special readings on certain diseases . . . "

"I told my friends in the army about this, and they were all interested," David said. "They are in all parts of the country. We could go to different cities and present it to the people in them . . . "

They talked all night, each about a different thing, but in perfect accord. They left Lexington together, heading for Atlanta. David—he was now Dave to Edgar—exuded energy, enthusiasm, and optimism. They would make millions; they would build a hospital; they would run it free. They would make a scientific fact of psychic phenomena; they would produce medicines and medical truths that would benefit the whole world.

From Atlanta they went to Birmingham; from Birmingham they went to Selma, where Edgar packed the rest of his clothes while Dave explained their plans to Gertrude. She was dazed.

"Who is going to run the studio?" she asked.

"Dad's coming down from Hopkinsville to be the manager," Edgar said. "I'll get a photographer to work for him."

"Where are you going?"

"To Texas."

Hugh Lynn looked admiringly at his father.

"Are you going to be a cowboy?" he asked.

His father patted him on the shoulder.

"No, we're going to find oil, and make a lot of money, and build a hospital where sick people can come and get well."

"How much money are you going to make?"

"Oh, about a million dollars."

Hugh Lynn smiled.

"Can I have a pony then?" he asked.

14

When Hugh Lynn stepped off the train in Texas, his feet sank in mud up to his ankles. His brown and white sport shoes were ruined.

"Hey!" his father called. "That's no way to dress in cowboy country. Where are your boots?"

"Where's your gun?" Dave Kahn called. "Reach for it!"

They had come to meet him and drive him to the well at Comyn. They wore leather boots that laced to the knee, rough clothes that were stained with mud, and ten-gallon hats. He hardly knew his father in such an outfit. Edgar had gained weight and looked strong and healthy.

"Your mother says you're to look after us," Dave said. "How can you do that without a gun? Our enemies are pretty powerful here. They've got the biggest cattle-rustling gang in the country. They all carry two guns."

Hugh Lynn didn't answer. He was staring at the cow ponies tied to the hitching post at the station. Across the street he could see men who were dressed like cowboys, except that they didn't have chaps and weren't carrying guns.

"Come along," his father said, "I want to hear all about home. How is mother? How is the baby?"

They bundled him into a big Marmon car and roared off down the mud track that seemed to be the road. Hugh Lynn was bounced back and forth between his father and Dave, while he tried to shout answers to his father's questions above the noise of the exhaust, which apparently had no muffler.

Comyn turned out to be a crossroads rather than a town. The well was in a field, and it wasn't the sort of well Hugh Lynn was used to seeing. It was a massive wooden derrick, sixty feet high, which lifted and dropped a pipe into a hole far too small for any respectable well. Near it was a small engine which made a terrible sound. It needed a muffler worse than the Marmon.

All the ground was muddy. Water was pumped into the hole to lubricate the pipe and the bit at its end, and it was supposed to drain off into a homemade pond; but most of it wandered around through the black dirt, turning it into a sticky mire.

"When it comes in," Edgar shouted above the din of the steam engine, "it'll spout oil higher than the derrick!"

Hugh Lynn wondered what was keeping it from coming in. It was now the summer of 1921. Why did it take the readings so long to find oil, when other people were hitting it without any such help? That was what his mother had sent him to find out. He was only fourteen, and she had been reluctant to let him go, but her worry about what had already happened to Edgar finally overcame her worry about what might happen to Hugh Lynn. Both were sure that Edgar was being used to give readings, without his knowledge, on things other than the oil well. They suspected that the well that was constantly about to come in, but somehow never did, was a blind to keep him there, giving readings on wells that were being drilled elsewhere.

This, so far as Hugh Lynn could discover, was not true. Everyone was concentrating on bringing in the well at Comyn, and most of the time Edgar and Dave were driving around the country getting leases on the surrounding land, so that when oil was finally struck, they would have command of the whole region.

When not touring in search of leases they stayed in a group of double-roofed shacks about fifty yards from the well. These were the property of the Ringles, a terrifying family of gigantic men who worked on the well and had an interest in the company. Old Man Ringle, the father, was the biggest and most frightening of them; the smallest was Cecil, his nephew, who was married and occupied one of the shacks with his wife. Edgar and Dave and Hugh Lynn lodged with Cecil, while the two Ringle sons stayed with their father.

After his arrival Hugh Lynn was present at all the readings. All of them were on the Comyn well, and they were accurate so far as predicting the stratum that would next be encountered in the drilling. It was on the strength of these predictions that the company's funds were being spent on leases.

One thing about the readings struck Hugh Lynn as curious. He wrote to his mother about it.

"I'm afraid to copy it down during the reading," he wrote, "and they don't pay any attention to it. But each time the reading says that unless all the people are 'in accord' about the purpose for which the money is to be used, nothing will ever come of it. I have been wondering if it could mean that the well won't come in. How could it keep the well from coming in if it is being drilled in the right place? If the well keeps going down, won't it strike oil no matter what the men think?"

He got his answer in a few days. There was trouble at the well. Someone dropped a tool down the hole, and operations had to be suspended while it was fished out. Old Man Ringle was mad, and he posted himself or one of his sons at the well every night to keep an eye on things. Nevertheless, another accident occurred. The bit that was digging out the hole far down in the earth ceased functioning. It was broken, and its parts had to be fished up.

Now everyone stayed at the well, watching the pipe, or casing, rise and fall, to the tortured breathing of the small engine. Hugh Lynn looked apprehensively at the Ringles, who had taken to carrying guns in their belts. He was particularly impressed with the way they handled the six-foot monkey wrenches that were used to fit the casing together. They held them as if they were nail scissors.

The other men on the job were his friends, particularly Dad Roust, an old driller who told wonderful tales, and Joshua, a strong young man who had been a cowboy and told stories of the plains that made William S. Hart seem tame.

"It's all changed now, though," he would say. "A man can go for months without getting into a shootin' scrape. It's more excitin' in this country, around the wells."

Now and then Joshua would stare off into space and sigh.

"Son," he would say, "the only thing I don't like about this job is the lonesomeness. Sometimes it just gets me down."

His sighs would become deeper.

"You see, son," he would say, "I'm powerful fond of women."

Old Man Ringle's suspicions finally centered on Dave Kahn. A third accident occurred—this time a wedge was found in the hole. Ringle thought Dave was attempting to hold up the drilling so that the local men would be frozen out when the leases expired, and Dave and some others—no one knew who they were—could come in and snap them up.

Dave offered to submit the whole thing to a reading. It was taken at night, after supper, in Cecil's house. Hugh Lynn trembled when he saw Old Man Ringle and his two sons walk in. All three were carrying guns. A neutral member of the company was chosen to conduct the reading. Dave sat by, showing no fear. The conductor asked whether Mr. Kahn was causing trouble at the well and carrying on activities detrimental to the interests of the company.

"This, we find," Edgar said, "is untrue. The interruptions are coming from outside sources. Now, as we have given before, unless those here associated are united in their purpose and ideals, and are agreed that such moneys as may be obtained from this enterprise are used for those intentions which have been stated, which is for the good of all, and the help of their fellow man, then as we find, there will be frustrations . . . "

Hugh Lynn wrote about it to his mother:

"The men all say they will build Dad as many hospitals as he wants when the well comes in, but I suppose what the readings mean is that they will have to give a lot more to charity than they plan to give. I think they all expect to make millions and then give a few thousand to the hospital.

"Dad doesn't think so. He says the men are rough, but they are all right underneath. He's been getting readings on the hospital, and he is quite excited about it. He says the readings have picked out a place for it. The place is Virginia Beach, Virginia. He says that a long time ago a reading said the same thing, but one of Uncle Lynn's friends on the railroad went there to see it when his train took him to Norfolk, and it was just a fishing village. Dad says that is what is needed, a nice quiet place near the sea. I hope it turns out that way, because I'd like to see the real ocean and swim in it.

"I'm leaving here the Saturday before Labor Day, so I'll be

home in time for school. Dad is going to get me some long pants. He's feeling fine and wishes he could come home, but he says he has to wait now until the well comes in . . . "

*   *   *

In the summer of 1922 Gertrude returned to the Hill for her annual visit, taking Hugh Lynn and Edgar Evans with her. Hugh Lynn shook hands gravely with his cousins, Tommy House and Gray Salter. Gray was Will Salter's youngest son. His mother had died when he was born, and Aunt Kate was raising him. He was older than Tommy, but younger than Hugh Lynn.

"Sorry I couldn't come last summer," Hugh Lynn said casually. "I had to go out to Texas and see about the well."

"What's going on out there?" Tommy asked. "Edgar is still there. When's the well coming in?"

"Oh, there's been trouble," Hugh Lynn said airily. "We have enemies, you know. We all have to carry guns out there."

"Can you smoke?" Gray said. "We can smoke."

"No," Hugh Lynn said. "It's not good for you. It stunts your growth. But I can outshoot you with a .22."

"Oh," Tommy said, "you're just afraid to smoke. Anybody can shoot a .22."

"I'll bet a cornsilk cigarette would knock you out," Gray said.

"I'll tell you about Texas," Hugh Lynn said. "I know a whole bunch of cowboys. I was in the house where Zane Grey wrote *The Border Legion.*"

They wandered off to the orchard, where Gray and Tommy had a package of cigarettes hidden.

Gertrude told her suspicions to Dr. House. Something was wrong with the goings-on in Texas, she knew. Another year had passed, and nothing had happened but delays. Drilling had been suspended on the well again and again. Feuds had broken out between members of the company. They seemed always to be only a few feet away from oil, but they could not get at it.

"I'll go out and see," Dr. House said.

He was anxious for a vacation. He was now assistant superintendent of Western State Hospital, near the Hill, and his

practicing osteopathy, having taken it up while teaching anatomy to the students at Franklin. He remembered Edgar and reminded him of the reading given while the blind Dr. Bowling was present.

"You're still a marvel at anatomy," he said, "but I don't know about the treatment you suggest. I'll tell you just what I told the woman herself—she's losing her hearing, you know.

"I told her I had never done what you suggest. You tell me to go up under the palate and perform finger surgery in the region of the Eustachian tube. I'm going to do it, but I don't know what will happen. I'll keep you informed."

The lady herself reported, six weeks later, that her hearing was normal.

Early in March the city officials decided to ask Edgar for a license, a situation which involved the embarrassing necessity for explaining what it was he was doing. About the same time enthusiastic friends reported that they had pledged, among local people, the sum of $60,000 for a hospital. A reading was taken to settle the question of where, in Birmingham and its environs, the building should be erected. Again it suggested Virginia Beach, as it had before, in Selma and Texas. The Birmingham committee disbanded. Edgar, morose but determined, packed his bags and started traveling again.

He went to Texas, but things were worse there than when he had left. He went to New York, Pittsburgh, Chicago, Kansas City, Dayton, and finally back to Selma. He was determined, suddenly, to carry the thing on by himself. If others could not do it for him, then he would do it himself. He wrote to Gertrude, who had stayed the winter at the Hill, that he was coming home for good. She returned to Selma to meet him.

Hugh Lynn was sad at leaving the Hill. He and Tommy and Gray were good companions. They had dug the trench for the water main that brought modern plumbing to the house, and with but a single accident: Gray put his pickax in Tommy's skull one afternoon. To celebrate the advent of running water they burned the outhouse down. It was distinctly not the season for outhouse burning, and everyone in the neighborhood spent a horrible day.

Tommy and Gray taught Hugh Lynn to smoke, but he didn't

like it. One day Aunt Kate caught Gray smoking. He fled to the cherry tree and refused to come down. Aunt Kate brought a switch, a chair, and the evening paper to the foot of the tree and settled down to wait.

"How long are you going to stay there?" Gray asked.

"As long as my heart beats," Aunt Kate said grimly.

"Kate the skate," Gray said.

Eventually he came down and took his licking. Later he showed his welts to Tommy and Hugh Lynn.

"You two are afraid to get licked," he said.

"I am not," Tommy said.

"Neither am I," Hugh Lynn said.

"Nobody ever licks you," Gray said.

"We're not afraid," Tommy said.

"No," Hugh Lynn said. "We can take as much as you."

"Bet you can't," Gray said.

"Bet we can," Tommy said.

To settle it they let Gray give them a licking. He whipped them to a frazzle. They didn't cry.

"Now do you believe us?" they asked when he was finished.

"Sure," he said. "Put 'er there! You're real he-men!"

The night before Hugh Lynn was to leave they went out to the bottom land for a final smoke together. Tommy spat reflectively when his cigarette was lighted.

"Why couldn't Edgar make a lot of money and build that hospital?" he asked Hugh Lynn. "The readings know everything, don't they?"

Hugh Lynn tried to explain.

"God won't let people make money unless they deserve to," he said.

Gray sneered.

"The whole world is full of crooks," he said.

"But they didn't make their money through the readings," Hugh Lynn said. "If God gave Dad this power He meant it to be used for good, and those fellows who've been taking him around here and there must be just promoters and maybe they were planning when they got the money to run off and leave Dad and not put up the hospital."

"Why wouldn't the readings know that?" Tommy asked. "They ought to know that."

"Maybe they do," Hugh Lynn said, "but Dad's asleep and doesn't know what he says. Maybe he says that and they don't tell him."

"Why, those crooks!" Gray said. "I'll bet if I was there I'd put a bullet right through a fellow's eyes if he tried to pull a thing like that on Edgar!"

"We ought to go with him," Tommy said. "Then everything would be all right. Then Edgar could tell us where to dig for buried treasure and we'd dig it up and build the hospital. We could do it!"

"Sure!" Gray said.

"Sure," Hugh Lynn said.

But he wasn't sure; he wasn't at all sure. Why hadn't the hospital been built at Birmingham, when the money was raised? Why did the readings keep saying Virginia Beach, which was over on the Atlantic Ocean, away from everybody and everything? Why couldn't his father just cut away from all those people and take readings for himself, and ask how he could get the money to build the hospital? Why couldn't the readings tell what rich man to go to for help? Why didn't they name the ones in the company in Texas who were crooked? Why didn't they tell where money could be found, just as Tommy suggested, so they could dig it up by themselves?

It looked as if something was wrong. Could it be that the wrong was with his father? Had he changed? Was he crazy for money, too? If that was so, the readings would naturally go haywire, and after a while they might not be any good even for telling sick people what was wrong with them.

"Let's have another cigarette," Tommy said.

"Sure!" Gray said.

"Sure," Hugh Lynn said.

He sucked eagerly at the smoke.

"You're learning," Gray admitted.

Tommy said, "You'll be able to inhale soon!"

15

Selma was glad to see the Cayces back. Edgar was especially welcomed; he had been absent four years, and no one in that time had been able adequately to carry on the work he had begun with the young people of the Christian Church. He took it up again, and soon the Seven Class and his Christian Endeavour group were functioning as before. Most of the old members returned, bringing with them younger sisters and brothers.

His friends found Edgar an older man in every way. His appearance had not greatly changed, except for some gray in his hair, but his manner was different; he was more reserved, more hesitant about expressing himself on questions that involved broad principles of human conduct, more inclined to be tolerant of human weaknesses. He did not seem cynical or disillusioned, but he apparently expected less of his fellow man and was inclined to judge him more softly. Yet he seemed determined to get more out of himself.

During the seven quiet years in Selma between 1912 and 1919, he had built up a sureness of himself; he had piled up within his mind an integrity that he believed would not break down. He had fought out his battles with the force he thought of as the devil, and he had come to feel that he was safe from it. This was the conviction that made him feel he must do something with the strange power, or talent, which he possessed. He had become afraid that unless he found a way to give it to the world he would himself be lost.

So he had tried. For four years he had given everyone he met an opportunity to participate in the venture. He had tried with all the powers of both his conscious and his subconscious mind to find ways of making enough money to build and endow a hospital. All these efforts had failed. He had discovered that his individual victory over the devil was one that had no effect upon other men. It had to be repeated in each of them; and because this had not taken place, the plans he had tried to carry out with them had failed. He had been certain before he left that no one could make of him, consciously or unconsciously, a tool for evil. That had been proved true. But he had been unable to gather about him the men necessary to make him a tool for good. There were honest men; there were brilliant men; there were good men. But there seemed to be no wise men.

He believed that they existed somewhere, and that he would eventually meet them. Meanwhile it was better to go on by himself, making preparations. "They also serve," he remembered from Milton, "who only stand and wait."

The workroom of the studio was converted into an office for the business of the readings. Stationery was printed, and Edgar sent an announcement to everyone on his mailing list. He also advertised for a stenographer and tried each applicant by having her attempt to take down a reading.

Most of them did poorly, for Edgar spoke in technical language, often with long, involved sentence structures, and a plethora of conjunctions, prepositions, and relative pronouns. Punctuation was a difficult matter; sometimes he seemed to be trying out different ways of expressing a thought and would wander around in the middle of an involved syntax until the best grammarian could do no more than roughly separate the phrases by dashes, parentheses, and colons. More than a dozen girls were tried before one turned up who wrote accurate, readable versions of all that was said. She was the older sister of one of the Junior Christian Endeavour experts, a pretty blonde named Gladys Davis. She was hired as Edgar's secretary.

Now it was October. Hugh Lynn was a junior in high school. Edgar Evans, who called himself Ecken because as a baby he couldn't pronounce his real name, was in kindergarten. Peace and security settled over the family again.

One day a man named Arthur Lammers walked into the studio. He was a wealthy printer from Dayton, Ohio; a short, powerful man with broad shoulders, brown hair, and blue, searching eyes.

Edgar had met him casually while on a trip to Dayton. He had received one of the announcements and had come to get some readings.

They were not to be for sick people. He was quite well himself, and so were the members of his family. He had other interests: philosophy, metaphysics, esoteric astrology, psychic phenomena. He asked questions Edgar did not understand—what were the mechanics of the subconscious, what was the difference between spirit and soul, what were the reasons for personality and talent? He mentioned such things as the cabala, the mystery religions of Egypt and Greece, the medieval alchemists, the mystics of Tibet, yoga, Madame Blavatsky and theosophy, the Great White Brotherhood, the Etheric World. Edgar was dazed.

"You ought to find out about these things," Lammers said. "If there is any way of finding it out, it's through you. The world is full of notions about its own beginning, its meaning, and its end. There are hundreds of philosophic and thousands of theological systems. Which are right and which are wrong? Which is the closest to the truth? What is the real nature of the soul and what is the purpose of this experience on earth? Where do we go from here? What for? Where did we come from? What were we doing before we came here? Haven't you asked any of those questions?"

"No," Edgar said.

He couldn't think of another word to say. He didn't dare tell the truth: that he had always considered such an idea sacrilegious, because God was revealed in the Bible, and to suppose that he could answer the mysteries of the universe would be an open invitation for Satan to speak through him.

That was what he had felt. Now, as he heard Lammers speak, he knew the feeling had passed. He had not been aware of its passing, but it was gone. As Lammers tossed questions he felt something spring up within himself, something which said, "This is the way to get the answer."

"I can only stay here a few days," Lammers went on, "but if you will come to Dayton as my guest I'll take a series of readings on these subjects and see what we get.

"Philosophy and metaphysics have been my hobbies, but they

only lead me to confusion, because there is no definite authority on the details. They all agree on the one God, the need of morality, the efficacy of prayer, the brotherhood of the spirit, but beyond that it is a sea of guesses. If these readings of yours are accurate, it means your subconscious mind can be reached, and if these occult and mystic theories are correct, that subconscious mind ought to be aware of its own identity and ought to be able to tell us as much of ourselves and the world as we want to know—or at least as much as we can understand."

Edgar could feel his own thoughts being expressed in Lammers's words. He had returned to Selma convinced of his mission. It had taken him forty-six years to reach the decision. Now he wanted to know why he had a mission and how it was to be fulfilled.

"Why not finish up your work here in the next few days," Lammers said, "and come up to Dayton with me for a few weeks? You'll be a wiser and richer man when you return, I'm sure."

"I'll go," Edgar said. "I'll finish up the appointments for readings I have, tomorrow and the next day. They're all local people."

"Good," Lammers said. "I want to start at the bottom with this thing. The most enduring and popular belief about the universe of which we are skeptical is astrology. First we'll ask the readings for a horoscope and see what happens."

"They're fakes, aren't they?" Edgar said. He was sure, now, that he wanted to find out about everything by way of the readings. It was just the assurance he needed. It would join together, at least in *his* mind, the two great conflicting forces of his life, the Bible and the readings. Out of the truth of one had come the power of the other. He was certain of that. It would be a comfort to have it proved.

Gertrude was dubious as she saw him pack his bags, but she liked Lammers, and the subject of the readings to be taken interested her.

"Write me all about what they say," she said when Edgar kissed her good-bye.

In Dayton he registered at the Phillips Hotel, an old, homey place with big rooms and lots of red plush on the furnishings.

In the morning Lammers brought his secretary, Linden Shroyer, and a stenographer to the readings. Shroyer, a small, thin man with black hair, eyes, and mustache, seemed ill at ease.

"What's he going to do?" he kept asking Lammers.

Edgar laughed.

"What I'm going to do shouldn't bother you," he said. "It's what I'm going to say that has me worried."

"I'm going to ask him for my horoscope," Lammers explained.

Lammers conducted the reading. When Edgar woke up, he spoke to him gravely.

"There is something wrong with our notion of astrology, apparently," he said. "It doesn't affect us as we think it does."

Edgar smiled. He was relieved.

"We leave out a factor that is very important," Lammers went on.

"What's that?" Edgar said.

"Reincarnation."

Edgar stared. Shroyer smiled at him. Lammers began to laugh.

"You thought astrology was a fake," he said, "and now you hand out a story that's a dozen times more fantastic than the rule of the stars. You say I've lived before on this earth. You say this is my third appearance in this 'sphere,' and that I still have some of the inclinations from my last life, when I was a monk."

Mechanically Edgar put on his tie, fastened his cuff links, and tied his shoelaces.

"Is that the stuff they believe in India?" he asked. "Is that reincarnation?"

Lammers nodded.

"You say," he went on, "that the solar system is a cycle of experiences for the soul. It has eight dimensions, corresponding to the planets; they represent focal points for the dimensions, or environments in which the dimensions can express and materialize themselves—although materialization of each dimension is different. This is the third dimension, and it is a sort of laboratory for the whole system, because only here is free will completely dominant. On the other planes, or dimensions, some measure of control is kept over the soul to see that it learns the proper lessons.

"The control is usually by the soul itself, if it has evolved sufficiently, because once the body of this dimension has been left and the consciousness of this life has been absorbed into the subconscious, the veil between the two is lifted.

"The subconscious, you see, is the record of all the lives of the soul, in this system and in other systems, out among the stars. It's the record we think of as being kept by the Recording Angel. It's the story of what we do with our spirit—the portion of God that is given to us for life, with the gift of individuality, or separate existence from God. Our problem is to perfect our individuality, and then we return to God. Our spirit and soul, or individuality, are joined to Him."

Edgar shook his head.

"I said all that?" he asked in a low tone.

Lammers nodded. Shroyer smiled. He was friendly now. He seemed to realize that Edgar was suffering.

"So you see," Lammers said, "our astrological influences from the planets or dimensions we have inhabited will be good or bad, weak or strong, according to the experiences we have had there and how we handled our problems.

"For example, we react to the earth according to the manner in which we have handled the problems of earth in our other lives—brotherly love, material possessions, sex, food and drink. Sometimes we are working on an earth problem to the exclusion of any influence from the stars or planets at all.

"The stars represent soul patterns, not experiences. The twelve signs of the zodiac are twelve patterns from which the soul chooses when coming into the earth plane. They are like races—patterns of temperament, personality, etc."

Edgar interrupted him.

"I couldn't have said all that in one reading," he said.

He looked toward the stenographer for confirmation. She was sitting with a bemused, dreamy smile on her face.

"No," Lammers said; "but you confirmed it. You see, I've been studying metaphysics for years, and I was able by a few questions, and by the facts you gave, to check what is right and what is wrong with a whole lot of the stuff I've been reading.

"The important thing is that the basic system which runs through all the mystery religions, whether they come from Tibet or the pyramids of Egypt, is backed up by you. It's actually the right system."

Edgar sucked slowly at his cigarette. Lammers was excited. He was like a man who has hunted treasure for years, following old maps and charts, and finally found it.

"It's Hermetic, it's Pythagorean, it's Jewish, it's Christian!" he said. "The Egyptians put it in the pyramids, on the Emerald Tablet of Hermes, and on the Bembine Table of Isis. Pythagoras put it in numbers, and in the theorem that the square of the hypotenuse of a right triangle is equal to the sum of the squares of the other two sides. Jesus put it in the Sermon on the Mount and in the remainder of the fifth chapter of St. Matthew."

"I never heard of any of those things except the Sermon on the Mount and the rest of the fifth of Matthew," Edgar said.

"The fifth chapter of Matthew is the constitution of Christianity," Lammers said. "The Sermon on the Mount is its Declaration of Independence.

"Jesus said He came to fulfill the law, not to abolish it. The Mosaic law had to do with external acts. It did not consider internal morality except as it was reflected in physical acts.

"Of course, the law of internal morality existed all this time. But it was the property of the priests, the initiates. That would be true today, too, were it not for the fact that the priests seem to have lost the key. They don't understand their symbology much better than does the average parishioner. There seems to have been too much simplification.

"The mission of Christ was to reveal this inner morality to all people, and then to give them an example, in Himself, of the fulfillment of that pattern. He is the way, He is the truth, He is the life. Sometime, somewhere, here or on some other planet, or out among the stars where worlds are as common as grains of sand on a beach, each of us must reach the perfection of Christ. Then we can return to God, and be one with Him—perfect, as Christ Himself said—as is our Father in heaven."

Edgar was running his hands through his hair. Shroyer was staring out the window. The stenographer sat entranced, still smiling.

"A body is only an objectification of the soul pattern," Lammers went on. "That's why each one is different in build, in physiognomy, in basic health. It is a reflection of the individuality of the soul, which gives it life. The record of this particular experience, the conscious mind—that's the personality. It's like a day in the course of a life, compared to the actual history of the soul."

He spoke to the stenographer.

"Read back the last few paragraphs of the reading," he asked.

She picked up her notebook and translated the shorthand characters:

> In this we see the plan of development of those individuals set upon this plane, meaning the ability (as would be manifested from the physical) to enter again into the presence of the Creator and become a full part of that creation.
>
> Insofar as this entity is concerned, this is the third appearance on this plane, and before this one, as the monk. We see glimpses in the life of the entity now as were shown in the monk, in his mode of living.
>
> The body is only the vehicle ever of that spirit and soul that waft through all times and ever remain the same.

"You see?" Lammers said. "It opens up the door. It's like finding the secret chamber of the Great Pyramid. It's the Philosopher's Stone. It's Sesame!

"Come on, let's get some lunch, so you'll be ready to give another one this afternoon!"

During the meal Lammers continued his explanations. He spoke of the medieval Rosicrucians, the oracles of Nostradamus, the Enneads of Plotinus, the mysteries of Eleusis, Bacchus, Mithras, and Osiris. He told them of the "lost keys" of Freemasonry, the Hindu samadhi, Saracen mathematics, tarot cards, the precession of the equinoxes and its connection with the worship of the bull and the ram, the meaning of the scarab, and the Tetragrammaton of the Jews.

"Every 2,160 years a different sign of the zodiac is in the position dominating earth," he said. "It goes backward, and is therefore called a precession. During the heyday of Egypt the sign of Taurus, the Bull, was in the commanding position. So the people worshiped the bull. But Taurus ruled only by reflection, as it were. It was the overt sign. The sun, actually in Scorpio, was shining *across* into Taurus. So Scorpio, the real sign, the spiritual guide of the earth, appeared on the foreheads and staffs of the priests of the time."

Edgar shook his head.

"I haven't the slightest idea what you're talking about," he confessed. "What interests me is this: You say that I agree with all this stuff in my reading. Does that imply that my subconscious mind understands it, or was I just being a stooge for your suggestions?"

Lammers laughed.

"You not only understand it," he said, "you explained several things that heretofore had no explanations, so far as I know."

Edgar nodded. "Good," he said. "Now answer me this:

"Is all this stuff which you've been telling about, and with which my subconscious mind apparently agrees, in conformity with the best ethics of religion and society? Is it really Christian, or is it pagan?"

"One at a time," Lammers said. "First, it not only agrees with the best ethics of religion and society, it is the source of them. It is the ancient wisdom which inspired them and gave them to the world with a simple explanation which most men could understand. Christ—or God, who sent Him—believed the people were ready for a higher conception of their living code, so He gave it to them.

"He spoke to the people in parables. The symbology was simple. But the morality He taught was a higher one than they had been following. It was the next step in the revelation of truth."

Edgar started to ask a question, then stopped. He paled noticeably. Lammers took his arm and smiled reassuringly.

"I know what you're thinking," he said. "You wonder if I'm going to say this is the next step in revealing truth.

"Don't worry. I wouldn't be that audacious, and this particular truth has been in existence and known to a minority of the people ever since man began inhabiting the earth. He brought it with him, and such phenomena as clairvoyance have always been available for aid in checking the mistakes that occur from generation to generation as the wisdom is handed down in writing and by word of mouth. Both are treacherous in the hands of amateurs.

"No, it has all been put down many times before, and taught to initiates over and over again. What I have not been able to find out is just how much of it Christ taught to the more intelligent of His disciples—or to all of them, for that matter, because its understanding requires native ability rather than training—and how much He left unsaid. Obviously He knew it all.

"I've often suspected it's all in the latter part of the Gospel of St. John, in the chapters covering the discourses at the Last Supper. At any rate, after the church ceased to be an extension, or sect, of Jewry and began to rise in power in the Roman Empire, its leaders made a decision to change it from an idealistic philosophy appealing to intellectuals, to a broad, practical religion for the common man. From that time on it made great strides, but over the course of the centuries the original metaphysical structure has been either lost or permanently submerged."

Edgar still was worried.

"If the leaders of the church thought it was best to keep these things secret, why should we expose them?" he asked.

Lammers did not answer immediately. His brow pressed vertical wrinkles into place above his nose. His round face was solemn.

"I don't know whether it is meant to be exposed now or whether it was meant to be exposed nineteen hundred years ago," he finally said. "It seems always to have been available for those who sought it. Maybe that's the answer.

"First we'll get it, from the readings. Then we'll find out what to do with it."

They returned to the room to prepare for the afternoon reading. The stenographer was already there. She had typed the morning reading. Edgar, looking it over, could not find all the things Lammers had mentioned, but there was enough to indicate the broad outlines of a theory and to prove that his subconscious mind was as much at home with Lammers's metaphysical vocabulary as it was with the language of anatomy and medicine.

When he woke from the reading, Lammers was nodding his head.

"Just as I thought," he said. "Just as I thought, only better and simpler.

"Now, it's like this. The conscious mind is the record of this life. Just as an emotion is the experience of a single moment, so the conscious mind is the record of a single life. This conscious mind is located in the pituitary gland. That, at least, is its focal point—the gland has a purely physical function also.

"The thoughts go from the conscious to the imaginative, or introspective, mind, which is seated in the pineal gland. There the thoughts are compared with all that has gone before that is in any way related to them, and when this is done, the thoughts— properly conditioned and judged—pass on to the subconscious, or soul mind, which is seated, with its spirit, just above the heart. There the thoughts are kept as a record, and as they are constructive they quicken the spirit and lower the barrier between the soul and the pure essence of life. As they are destructive they are rejected, but kept as a record, and as they are repeated they build up the barrier between the soul and the spirit and dim the radiance of the life essence that shines through the subconscious to the imaginative, and by refraction, or hunch, intuition, and yearning, into the conscious."

Edgar looked at Shroyer. The quiet, dark little man could contain himself no longer. He began to laugh. Edgar joined him. Lammers, after a moment, began to chuckle.

When they had settled down, Lammers looked at Edgar and said:

"It sounds medieval, or worse, but it's not. Modern science throws a lot of sense into what used to be thought of as nonsense. For a long time we were taught that only the tangible existed. Now we know that the most important forces in our lives are invisible—electricity, for instance, and the waves that make wireless possible."

"Thought has always been invisible," Shroyer put in.

"And pretty much discouraged," Lammers said. "It isn't supposed to be good for the average man. Gets him into trouble.

"But look here—" he turned to Edgar—"you've got to give

your time to this thing, man. You're as out of place in a photographer's studio as Joseph was in Pharaoh's prison. Bring your family up to Dayton and let me back this thing the way it should be backed. No oil wells, no lectures—just readings of this type, for enlightenment, and physical readings for those who need them. We ought to build up an organization which will take care of the sick, whether they be ill in body, mind, or spirit. Then you'll really be doing something."

"That's what I'd like," Edgar said. "It's always been my dream. But I've never been able to reconcile it with the fact that in my conscious mind, as you put it, I'm uneducated.

"Shucks!" he added. "It's worse than that. I'm ignorant!"

"I was about to explain that," Lammers said, "but my language threw you off. I was getting too technical.

"Remember what I said about the subconscious mind being the storehouse of all our experiences and thoughts, for all our lives, here and elsewhere? Well, to the degree that these experiences and thoughts have been in the right direction, a man is civilized, cultured, humane, and so forth: his past record shines through his conscious mind and present body, making the pattern of the body and the character of the person.

"Nothing is forgotten or lost by the subconscious. Therefore, if you in one or more of your past lives, or in your studies in other dimensions and other worlds, learned this wisdom which comes through you, it is not at all to be wondered at that you still possess it. The fact that your subconscious mind is articulate—this clairvoyance—that is the strange thing. But once the subconscious is reached, it's not surprising that it is full of wisdom. That is, providing first of all that you are allied with the forces of good. That's where the inevitability of morality comes in. As a man thinketh in his heart, so is he, Jesus said. You couldn't use this force for evil purposes without one of two things happening—the power would be lost to you or the information would cease to be right. In one case your soul would remain uncorrupted, by retreating within itself. In the other case it would be corrupted, by partaking of your conscious venality."

Edgar made no comment. He was smoking quietly, staring at the floor.

"Tomorrow," Lammers went on, "we'll take a reading on you, and ask why you were given the power and for what purpose it is to be used. After that you can make your decision."

"I'd like to get the reading," Edgar said, "but I think I'd better make my decision before we do that."

He crushed his cigarette in the ash tray.

"This is something I should decide by myself, without help from the readings," he said. "I'd always suspect them of leading me into it, if they said I should devote myself to this work exclusively, and I decided to do it because of that.

"The power was given to me without explanation. I've tried to discover what to do with it; it's been hit and miss, trial and error. It was never considered from this angle—it was just an odd trait that was useful in medicine. That's because no one ever got hold of it who thought people were anything more than what we've always been taught—souls born into the earth, to live a while, die, and be judged. Under that system it wouldn't be accounted for by anything but an answer to my childhood prayers and my reading of the Bible.

"That's what I always thought, and against this I put the idea that the devil might be tempting me to do his work by operating through me when I was conceited enough to think God had given me special power.

"But I've watched it for years, and I've studied myself as best I can; I've prayed, and I've waited to see what would come of it. I've been convinced for quite a while that it's a good power or force. It hasn't ever done evil, and it won't let me do it. A few times when people were taking readings which shouldn't have been taken, without my knowledge, I suspected it because I began to feel badly after each reading. I know now that when I've given my best and someone has been helped I wake up feeling refreshed."

He took another cigarette and accepted a light from Shroyer.

"But what you've been telling me today, and what the readings have been saying, is foreign to all I've believed and been taught, and all I have taught others, all my life. If ever the devil was going to play a trick on me, this would be it."

Lammers laughed and stood up.

"I know how you feel," he said. "I remember how upset I was the first time I ran across the idea of reincarnation. It turned me wrong side out for a while. Then I began applying it to what I knew and what was obvious about people, and the first thing I knew I was making the observation that psychology and psychoanalysis had to be invented to provide the explanations of life which are inherent in the doctrine of reincarnation."

Shroyer stood up and went to get his overcoat.

"Why can't we remember our former lives?" he asked.

"Because we'd never learn anything if we did," Lammers said. "We'd carry over all our prejudices, weaknesses, strengths, likes and dislikes, and have them in active, rather than suppressed form. They would make a mess of free will on this plane. What we have been, builds our character and intellect and makes us charming or hateful; then, with free will as the active agent, we go forth with this equipment in a world that is like a succession of laboratory tests."

He put on his topcoat and went to shake hands with Edgar.

"We'll leave you now," he said. "You have a lot to think over. Don't rush yourself. If you like, wait until the reading tomorrow, then decide. Or wait longer. It's the most important decision of your life; and it's going to be the most important decision in a lot of other lives, too."

They left, taking the stenographer with them. Edgar remained seated on the couch, smoking cigarettes, lighting one off the other. When it grew dark, he went into the street and walked. When he was tired, he returned to the hotel and read the New Testament.

He knew the Gospels well. In none of them was there a condemnation of astrology or of reincarnation. There was, in fact, no mention of reincarnation whatsoever. But there was no comfort in this. If reincarnation were a truth, why had not Jesus mentioned it?

What He did mention—what was mentioned throughout the Bible—was the false prophet.

Old ghosts rose up in the room, haunting him.

He read on.

Why was reincarnation not mentioned anywhere in the Bible?

It was different with astrology. People had believed in the stars in Biblical times. And there might, by simple reasoning, be something in it. Everyone knew the influence of the sun on the earth, and the sun was a star. It certainly made a pattern, so far as life on earth was concerned—it shaped everything, or at least nourished everything—and the shape had to be such as to allow the sun to give life to it. Why could not the other stars, the signs of the zodiac, for instance, influence people in subtler ways: by making them bullish, or lionish, or airy, or gay, or introspective? And if the planets were old dwelling places of the soul, why would they not influence people when they came to a point of prominence in the sky just as a man who had once lived in Hopkinsville would be influenced by reading of it, or meeting someone from the town, or by seeing photographs of it?

It might be. Take the moon, for instance. Its influence was obvious on such things as the tides and the female cycle. Any farmer could tell you that a fence rail laid on the wane of the moon will sink into the ground, just as bacon from a hog killed on the wane of the moon will shrivel in the pan and be worthless. The fence rail has to be laid when the moon is on the increase, and the hog has to be killed at the same period.

These things were observable because the moon was so close. The other planets were farther away, and the stars were far beyond them. But their light came to the earth, and might it not influence in some way the heart, or the brain, or the emotions?

Lammers had said it was all a pattern. The body was an objectification of the soul, responding to it as a swimmer responds to the sea—sometimes fighting against it, sometimes going willingly with its current, sometimes carried helplessly in its tide. And this life was but one of many—perhaps of thousands, spent here and on the other planets of the system, and out in far-flung worlds that stretched to the horizons of the cosmos.

What drivel—running around on the planets and among the stars!

What would his friends in Selma say to that? What would his Sunday school pupils say? What would Gertrude and Hugh Lynn say?

Drivel, nonsense, quackery, fraud, hocus-pocus, monkey business—

That's what the doctors had said about the medical diagnoses of the readings.

They were experts in their field. He was an expert in the field of the Bible. What was his opinion of the things he had heard that day?

Drivel? Nonsense? Quackery? Fraud? Hocus-pocus? Monkey business?

*   *   *

He walked through the night until he came to the river that wound its way through the city. The water shimmered in the bright radiance of the autumn sky. To watch it better he went halfway across the bridge. There, leaning against the concrete ledge, he could alternately look upward at the sky and downward at the moving stream.

The water of the spirit: on earth water was the symbol of the spirit. In the heavens the stars represented His glory. Between them was man, transfixed, pulled in both directions, and in the end usually falling back to earth.

There was a man named Saul, who was a great believer in things as they were. He persecuted the innovations of a new religious sect. Then he was smitten, on the road to Damascus, and heard the voice of God. He changed his ways, his thoughts, his life, his name. Almost singlehanded, he raised the new sect to a world religion.

There was Augustine, who studied the philosophy of the pagans and believed in it until he was forty. Then he changed his ideas and convictions and wrote the philosophy of the church which Paul had established.

Looking back at them now, it was easy to see the wisdom of their decisions, difficult to understand the darkness in which they had walked for so long. That was because Christianity had triumphed and been proved right. Suppose it had lost and been proved wrong? Where would the memory of Augustine and Paul be now?

It would be buried. Instead, the memory of the men who continued to believe in paganism was buried; Paul and Augustine had been right. History remembered them, as it remembered all men who helped humanity and civilization to march forward a little.

Who were these men? Every one of them was a person who started by disbelieving in things as they were and discovering something new. All were scoffed at in the beginning. Most of them were not appreciated until after their death. None died rich. Few were happy. They had been beheaded, broken on the rack, scourged, fed to lions, burned at the stake. Their Master had been crucified.

What was His way of life? Love your brothers, love your enemies, love God. Return evil with good; turn the other cheek; be humble. Thirst after righteousness; pray for the world; forgive your debtors and those who seek to harm you.

Once a young man asked how he might serve Him more completely, having fulfilled all the obligations of prayer and sacrifice and righteousness. The answer was to go and sell what he had, give it to the poor, and follow in His footsteps with the disciples. The young man turned away and was sad, for he had great possessions.

There is no other mention of that young man in the Gospels. Did he fail to fulfill the last test? He must have, for he was not numbered among the disciples. He was the one who was chosen and did not respond. What else was that order, but a call to join the little band of followers?

The call came to every man who sought it. Whoever asked for an opportunity to serve was given it. Many faltered. The opportunity wasn't what they had expected. It demanded too much personal sacrifice. They fell back. They failed.

They were forgotten, nameless souls, hundreds of thousands of millions of them, swirling through eternity like the drops of water making up the river below.

He, the man on the bridge, was such a person. He had asked for service; he had been given an opportunity; he was faltering; he was falling back; he was failing.

For he had many possessions: a beloved wife, two sons, a

mother and father and sisters, many devoted friends. These he would have to give up to follow a rebellious path.

Or would he? Might not they be won over? Might not they follow him? If they believed in readings for the body, could they not accept readings for the soul?

Would they not be forced to admit, as he was forced to admit—standing there above the Dayton River, looking at the stars—that what the readings had said that day, what Lammers had said that day, was logical: inescapably, unavoidably, irrevocably logical?

They might.

They might not.

"Got a match, buddy?"

He turned to answer the man, surprised that he could see him so well. The stars had been fading, the sky brightening without his realizing it.

"Sure." He fished a package from the pocket of his overcoat.

"Thanks. Gettin' cold these mornings, eh?"

The man was a worker of some sort, on his way to the job. He wore rough clothes. Under his arm he carried a bundle wrapped in newspaper; his lunch, probably.

His face was seamed, though it was young. In the wrinkles the dirt had not been washed away; the rest of the skin was clean. He had already been to a speakeasy. The odor of alcohol cut cleanly into the air.

"Yes, I reckon it gets mighty cold up in this country."

"Yeah." He struck the match, cupped his hands, and sucked at the cigarette.

"Shot o' booze feels good on a mornin' like this. Well, thanks, buddy."

He returned the matches and continued on his way, his hands in his trouser pockets, smoke streaming out behind him, legs hurrying.

"Feed my sheep . . . "

The river was changing. Light crept out to it from its banks.

"Come to me all ye who are heavy laden . . .

"Love me. Keep my commandments . . .

"In my Father's house are many mansions . . . I go to prepare a place for you . . . that where I am, there ye may be also.

"Feed my sheep . . .

"If the world hate you, ye know that it hated me before it hated you . . .

"Feed my sheep . . . "

Now the river belonged to the world again. The shimmer was gone from its surface. It was muddy, torpid, tired. He walked over the bridge and away from it, back to the hotel.

In his room he sat at the desk and wrote a letter to Gertrude. " . . . So much has happened in the last few days that I cannot begin to tell you about it. The important thing is that I am remaining here to organize the work of the readings with Mr. Lammers. He will back it. I want you and the boys to join me as soon as you can, along with Miss Davis, if she will come. I'd like to have her take the readings, and it will be a good job for her. First of all you had better dispose of the studio, or get it rented. You see, we won't be in the photographic business any more. That won't be necessary . . . "

When it was finished he sent for coffee and breakfast. Waiting for it, sitting by the window, he remembered another October morning when he had seen the sun rise. He picked up his Bible and turned to the Psalms. There it was, the 46th:

God is our refuge and our strength, a very present help in trouble.

Therefore will we not fear, though the earth be removed, and though the mountains be carried into the midst of the sea;

Though the waters thereof roar and be troubled, though the mountains shake with the swelling thereof. Selah.

There is a river, the streams whereof shall make glad the city of God . . .

16

As the train approached Dayton, Hugh Lynn looked more and more apprehensively at the barren fields he was passing. They were powdered with snow; their trees were bare; the wind lashed their thin patches of dead grass.

He wiggled his feet nervously. There were holes in his shoes. He had no rubbers or galoshes. His overcoat was light, unlined. The temperature in Selma when he left was sixty. Here it must be forty below zero.

There was more than the weather to be apprehensive about. A month before, his mother, his brother, and Miss Davis had come north to join his father. They were to live in Dayton, where the readings were to be backed by Mr. Lammers, who was rich.

That was all he knew. Letters had told him of an apartment on Fifth Street, of meeting interesting people, of readings that revealed "most unusual" information. But they had seldom contained any money. In Selma, where he had remained with family friends in order to finish the school term, he had become embarrassed for pocket money, and for such things as socks, ties, and a new pair of shoes. Finally, a few days before Christmas, the money for his transportation to Dayton arrived—just enough to get him there. What was the matter? What had happened to the rich Mr. Lammers?

They met him at the station and bustled him off to a streetcar. He was aware of a line of taxicabs, but his father carefully avoided these, asking questions the while and joking about friends in Selma. His mother squeezed his arm, pointed out public buildings, and told him he looked fat. Finally they got home.

It was an upstairs apartment, in a not too fashionable section. Miss Davis was wearing the same dress he had seen on her in the studio in Selma.

He let them talk themselves out. Then he asked, point-blank, what the matter was. Where was Lammers with all his money?

His father explained. Lammers had got into financial difficulties. He was enmeshed in lawsuits that kept him in Cincinnati and required his presence in court every day. All his money was tied up. He was in danger of losing his home in Dayton. He had been unable to contribute to the work since early in November.

"Let's go back to Selma," Hugh Lynn said. He was cold. The wind whistling against the windowpanes frightened him.

Edgar shook his head.

"I have lots of things to talk to you about," he said. "They are the things that make it impossible for me to go back. I've got to stick to this work now, no matter what happens. This setback is just a test. And whatever happens to Lammers, he has done a lot for me. He opened my eyes to many things. He has been a great help."

"Dinner's ready!" Gertrude called. She put an arm around Hugh Lynn and walked him to the dining room.

"You must be hungry," she said.

"Where did the money come from to get me here?" Hugh Lynn asked.

He had taken a quick look at the meal on the table. It was scanty.

"Oh, that was an old twenty-dollar gold piece I had lying around," his mother said. "I had no other use for it."

Hugh Lynn asked the blessing. They ate silently for a while. Then Edgar, Gertrude and Miss Davis began to talk, guardedly, about the "new developments" in the readings. Hugh Lynn listened, saying nothing.

When they finished eating, they told him about the new type of reading—it was called a Life Reading—and about reincarnation.

"You never told me anything about that in Sunday school," Hugh Lynn said. "Is it true? Do you believe it? Is it in the Bible?"

He asked questions quickly, to cover the feeling of bitterness and shame that was sweeping over him. It was bad enough that his father was psychic; the boys continually asked him, "What's the matter with your dad? What's that stuff he does?" But now it was worse. They weren't even to be Christians any more. They were to be heathens. And not even rich heathens; just poor heathens, living with Yankees.

"I don't know whether I believe it or not," Edgar said. "The readings say it's true. A lot of people believe it. It sounds logical.

"We asked a lot of questions. We asked why reincarnation isn't in Christianity.

"The answer was that it used to be in Christianity in the early days. There was a sect of Christians called the Gnostics. The readings say they kept the line unbroken between the old religions and the new one.

"You see—" Edgar was trying to convince himself as well as Hugh Lynn—"Christ was predicted by the old religion. The people who built the great pyramid in Egypt predicted Him."

"I never heard that," Hugh Lynn said.

"We found some books about it," Edgar explained. "There's a movement in England called British Israel, that's founded on the pyramid prophecies.

"Anyhow, you know that Christ didn't intend to found a new religion. He meant to reform the Jewish religion, which was one of the old religions worshiping the one God.

"Now, just like the other old religions—they are called 'mystery' religions—the Jewish faith had a secret doctrine. It was called 'cabala.' The students who learned it were called 'initiates,' and these were the high priests. They learned the esoteric part of the religion, and the people were given the exoteric version: they were given the same fundamental philosophy and the same moral code, but with a simple explanation."

"Is that the way it is today?" Hugh Lynn asked. "Do the heads of the church believe in reincarnation?"

"No," Edgar said. "The readings say that when the leaders of the early church decided to propagate the faith to all people, indiscriminately, they decided to drop the doctrine of reincarnation. It was difficult to explain, for one thing, and it was difficult to swallow, for another. It made life more complex. It made virtue even more necessary. A man had to be pretty brave to face the fact that one life of suffering was only a step toward heaven.

"On the other hand, people who didn't examine the theory

could easily say, 'Oh, well, we have other lives to live. We won't be sent to hell after this one. So let's enjoy it.'

"So they fought the Gnostics and won the battle. What they did was right, I suppose, because without a simplification of the faith it wouldn't have spread. It would have remained a small sect, for intellectuals and students of metaphysics."

"Is that what we're supposed to be?" Hugh Lynn asked.

"Students of metaphysics, maybe," his father said, "though I don't know anything about it. I never heard of it until two months ago.

"But the readings say that no sect, or schism, should ever be allowed to form around this work. They say we are merely to present what we have, to those who seek it. Truth will prove itself, in time.

"And the first thing to do—the most important—is to make it work in our own lives. We can't teach truth to others when we do not possess it ourselves.

"That's the way we are supposed to do it. First we are to bring it to ourselves, then to other individuals, then to groups, then to the classes and masses. But it must always be presented as something which is the natural property of all."

"I don't understand reincarnation," Hugh Lynn said.

"Neither do I," Edgar said, "but then, there are a lot of things we believe but don't understand. I believe what Einstein says about relativity, but I don't understand it. I believe in atoms, but I don't understand them. Do you?"

"No, but some people do. Scientists do."

"Some people understand reincarnation. The Hindus believe in it. They understand it."

Hugh Lynn was silent.

"I believe Jesus taught it, too," Edgar said.

He got up and went for his Bible.

"Listen to this," he said. "It's from John, the third chapter, where He is talking with Nicodemus. He tells Nicodemus that unless a man be born again he cannot see the kingdom of heaven. Now, in the fifth chapter of Matthew, you remember, Jesus says that unless a man be perfect he cannot enter the kingdom.

"Well, what man, when he dies, is perfect? Once in a while a man dies who is good enough to go to heaven, but not often. So, isn't it logical that we have to be born again, and keep trying?

"Then, when Nicodemus asks Him how these things may be, He says, 'Art thou a master of Israel, and knowest not these things?' Nicodemus was a member of the Sanhedrin. He was one of the initiates of the cabala, then, and should have known about reincarnation."

"Why wasn't Christ more specific?" Hugh Lynn said. "Why didn't He instruct the disciples to teach it?"

"He taught the common people," Edgar said. "He said that He came not to change the law, but to fulfill it. The world was at a point where it could—and should—realize that virtue is more mental than physical, and love is not a matter of receiving, or bartering, but of giving. It's all in the fifth chapter of Matthew.

"Now, if you will examine that, you will find that it fits exactly into the theory of reincarnation—the idea that only the mind is real, and that thought builds the soul more than deeds. Deeds are only the expressions of thought, anyhow.

"So Jesus gave them the law which results from a belief in reincarnation. The theory itself was too complex for the people, so He let the emphasis go to Himself, as an example of the perfect life.

"There is no doubt about what He taught. Only a perfect soul may enter heaven. Only Jesus was perfect.

"But Christianity gradually allowed people to think of Jesus as an unattainable ideal. Nobody nowadays thinks it necessary to be like Jesus in order to get to heaven."

"Yet He said so Himself."

"It isn't the church's fault that people aren't good Christians," Hugh Lynn said.

Edgar was turning the pages of the Bible.

"This is the ninth chapter of John, where He heals the man blind from birth. Remember, the man was born blind. 'And his disciples asked him, saying, Master, who did sin, this man, or his parents, that he was born blind?'

"Well, since he was born blind, how could his own sin have caused his blindness, unless it was committed in another life?

Doesn't that indicate that the disciples were familiar with reincarnation and the law of karma?

"And here's another one, in the seventeenth chapter of Matthew. It is after the Transfiguration, and Jesus tells the disciples not to reveal what they have seen, 'until the Son of man be risen again from the dead.

"'And his disciples asked him, saying, Why then say the scribes that Elias must first come?

"'And Jesus answered and said unto them, Elias truly shall first come, and restore all things.

"'But I say unto you, That Elias is come already, and they knew him not, but have done unto him whatsover they listed. Likewise shall also the Son of man suffer of them.

"'Then the disciples understood that he spake unto them of John the Baptist.'

"Now, how did they understand that He was speaking of John the Baptist, unless they understood that John the Baptist was the incarnation of Elias?"

"All that's farfetched," Hugh Lynn said. "Anybody can prove anything by the Bible. You said that yourself."

"All right; listen to this one. This is from Revelation, thirteenth chapter, tenth verse. 'He that leadeth into captivity shall go into captivity: he that killeth with the sword must be killed with the sword. Here is the patience and the faith of the saints.'

"Certainly every man who killed another with a sword wasn't killed by a sword himself—not in the same life. And what is the patience and faith of the saints but an understanding that surpasses man's understanding and leaves justice to God's law?"

Gertrude and Miss Davis had finished the dishes. They sat down at the table and joined the discussion.

"I want to know why if I was very beautiful and exotic once, I'm not that way now," Gertrude said.

"You are," Edgar said gallantly.

"I'm not," Gertrude said. "Men don't follow me in the street and send me orchids, do they?"

"You didn't use it in the right way when you had it," Edgar said. "Now you've got to do without it. Whatever virtue you possess and misuse, you lose. That's the way I understand it. So

I'm poor and you don't get orchids."

Hugh Lynn leaned forward, interested.

"Who were you?" he said.

They told him, then showed him their readings and the other Life Readings which had been taken. An average one began by saying, "We find the spirit and soul took possession and completed this entity, as we have it at present, late in the evening—11:29. We find the soul and spirit took its flight—from that of Venus' forces, with those of Jupiter, Mercury, Neptune being the ones in assistance to the conditions bringing the forces to this present plane's development, with afflictions in Mars and in that of Septimus."

After an explanation of the astrological urges, some of the incarnations were described.

"It is to be understood that only that which may be helpful is given. It is also to be understood that only those former appearances in the earth's plane which are now affecting the entity are given."

The incarnations stretched back a long way, but there was a similarity observable: all seemed concerned with the same basic problems of soul development. In this they were related, however diverse were the lives in other respects: place, time, occupation, social status, etc. It was the task of working out these basic problems that concerned the present personality. All that had been done about them previously, one way or the other, was active in the personality. The rest of the individuality was passive.

"What I like about the Life Readings is that they tell you what to do," Miss Davis said. "Most people don't know whether they are doing the right thing. They like their work but they don't know whether it's the job they should be doing.

"The Life Readings tell what the abilities are and what the person should be doing."

"Why don't people know those things about themselves?" Hugh Lynn asked.

"They do," Edgar said, "but they are afraid to follow their inner feelings. They take a job because it's a job, and then for economic reasons they are afraid to leave it and try what they really want to do. Other people talk them out of it, sometimes.

The free will has to face all those obstacles. If the person knew what he was to do and just did it, without opposition or doubt, it would be a cut-and-dried affair. Life would be easy."

"Have you found out how you got your psychic power?" Hugh Lynn said.

They showed him the explanation, as given in Edgar's Life Reading. Two things were responsible for it. He had once attained a great height in soul development, only to slip downward through a series of lives until he had reached an almost opposite position of instability. The present life was a chance to atone for some of his mistakes. It was a crucial life: he had purposely been given a great temptation, balanced by an equal opportunity for good.

During one of his appearances he had been wounded in a battle and left on the field for dead. He lived for several days, conscious and in extreme agony. Being unable to move or help himself in any way, he had only his mind as a weapon against pain. Just before he died he succeeded in elevating his mind beyond reach of his body and its suffering. Since no achievement, good or bad, is ever lost, the ability to subdue the body and its feelings became part of the pattern of his individuality. It was now being employed to present the test to the personality of Edgar Cayce. Used for good, it would raise him back to a portion of the spiritual estate he once possessed. Used for selfish, material purposes, it would sink him to the lower levels of humanity.

"Have you got a Life Reading on me?" Hugh Lynn was interested, but he hated to show it. It sounded plausible, but it couldn't be right. And it put him beyond all legitimacy. The church wouldn't have anything to do with such stuff and neither would the public. Just the nuts—that was all they would have coming to them, that was all he would have to associate with.

Up to now he had been able to say that his father was a photographer. The other stuff was just a hobby—"experiment." Now when people asked him what his father did, he would have to say, "He's a psychic medium." And he would have to say it to Yankees.

They showed him his Life Reading. They had got it a few days before, as a sort of Christmas present.

"I don't understand it," he said when he had read it. "If I were these people, I don't recognize myself. They weren't like me."

"They weren't like you," Edgar said. "But you're not the same person now that you were a few days ago in Selma; you're not the same person you were a few hours ago on the train. You're not the same person you were when you sat down here to dinner a little while ago.

"Every time a thought goes through your head it changes your whole being. Some thoughts change you only a little; some thoughts change you a great deal. But all of them change you.

"Your conscious mind compares every new experience and every new thought with all the experiences and thoughts of a related nature which you have had in this life.

"Your subconscious mind—the soul mind—compares every new experience and thought with every related experience and thought you have had in all your lives. And beyond that the superconscious mind—the awareness of your spirit—compares every new experience and thought with truth—the law itself.

"But what you are going to experience and think is affected by what you have already experienced and thought.

"For instance: you experience something. Your conscious mind makes its comparison and judgment; your subconscious mind makes its comparison and judgment; your superconscious mind makes its comparison and judgment. As a result of these comparisons and judgments you, as a whole, adopt an attitude, an opinion, a feeling, about the experience.

"It may take a little time. For a few days the judgment of your conscious mind will be uppermost. Then after what you call 'reflection,' a more reasonable, long-range opinion is adopted. And finally, after a period of 'understanding,' a wise, detached, universal opinion prevails.

"But that's not the end, either. All your future experiences and thoughts which are related to this experience influence your attitude toward it, your opinion.

"So, while your past is continually influencing you, you are continually influencing your past. Your past, your present, and your future all change from day to day, from minute to minute, from thought to thought."

"Do you think this reading fits me?" Hugh Lynn said.

"As far as you have gone, I'd say it does. You're only sixteen. This is a full-length portrait. Some of the characteristics attributed to you are those of a mature person. We'll have to wait and see.

"I know that mine fits me!" he added.

"It certainly does," Gertrude said.

The discussion lasted until past midnight. Next day it was resumed. Thereafter, at meals and in the evenings, reincarnation and Life Readings were the subjects of conversation.

Hugh Lynn remained skeptical. To him it all smacked of occultism, and occultism was something he associated with shady fortunetellers, women who believed in theosophy, and Hindus wearing turbans and bending over crystal balls.

Yet the reasonableness of the theory pounded away at him and he found that, skeptical as he was, the thing was changing his life. When he saw an ill-tempered boy, or an awkward boy, or a crippled boy, he immediately thought of karma. His attitude toward the boy was shaped by the thought that the boy was paying for something, and should therefore be helped and cheered. Quite suddenly he found himself understanding and wanting to help the unfortunate and handicapped.

Through a friend of Lammers's, a scholarship had been secured for him at Moraine Park, a fashionable private high school. Progressive education had been installed at Moraine Park, and there was a grammar school section which his brother Ecken, now nearly six, attended.

This was the only part of Lammers's plans which he was able to carry out. The boys had the best schooling available, but that was as far as the well-being of the family went. Money was scarce, and there was never any certainty about where the next sum would come from. The chicken for Christmas dinner was scrawny; there were no adequate clothes for the bitter weather; the rent for the office room at the Phillips Hotel was unpaid for months.

The man who helped most was Thomas B. Brown, an inventor who was troubled with a tendency to deafness. By following the advice of the readings he was able to improve his hearing, and thereafter bought much of Edgar's time for readings on the problems he encountered in his laboratory.

Another man who helped was Madison Byron Wyrick, then plant superintendent of Western Union in Chicago. Wyrick had diabetic tendencies and was helped by following a diet outlined in the readings. In this diet, as in every one ever outlined for a diabetic, the reading stressed Jerusalem artichokes, a natural source of insulin.

Other men were interested, and tentative plans were made to form an association and erect a hospital. One group, with co-operation promised from several doctors, wanted to build in Chicago. Another group chose a rural site about a hundred miles from Dayton.

The readings vetoed both suggestions. Virginia Beach, the information said, was the place to build. It gave reasons: Edgar Cayce should live near large bodies of water. It was best for his health and for his psychic abilities. It was also best for psychic work of any kind to be carried on near water. It was best that people, coming for readings, travel over water to get them. It would put them in the right vibration and help them to cooperate in the "experiment." The attitude of the person asking for the reading was of great importance.

Moreover, Virginia Beach was overnight from New York, Philadelphia, Baltimore, and Washington. Many people would find it possible to make the trip, yet it would sufficiently remove them from their occupations and distractions.

Also, the area of Tidewater Virginia was to be of increasing importance in the future, financially and commercially. It was the ideal spot for such plans as were being formed around the work; they could best be accomplished there.

The insistence on Virginia Beach threw a damper on the general idea of a psychic society. The groups gradually broke up and only individuals, with their own problems and approaches, were left.

One of these was Morton Harry Blumenthal, a short, quiet, amiable young Jew. He was a stockbroker in New York, in partnership with his brother Edwin. Through Dave Kahn—who had gone to New York on the advice of readings and entered the furniture business—he heard of Edgar and came to Dayton to get a physical reading. He was troubled with a running ear. Following a series of treatments, the ear improved. He got a Life Reading, and several supplementary readings on the appearances which were listed for him. A boyhood interest in philosophy was reawakened. He began to get readings on all kinds of metaphysical and theological questions.

Meanwhile his brokerage business prospered. He and his brother were then in their middle thirties. They had come originally from Altoona, Pennsylvania, where their father ran a tobacco store. Morton had studied for a while at the University of Pittsburgh. In New York the boys had worked hard, finally achieving their ambition—a seat on the exchange. Edwin, a canny trader, worked on the floor. Morton remained in the office of the company. On a generally rising market they were slowly getting rich.

When Morton heard that the readings insisted on Virginia Beach as a location for any hospital or permanent organization founded on the readings, he was enthusiastic. He believed in following the readings exactly, and Virginia Beach would be convenient for him.

"You must go there," he told Edgar. "I'll provide the money."

Edgar wondered what calamity would overtake Morton's finances, now that he had decided to back the readings. Everyone who had undertaken the task had gone broke. Was Morton the right one? Was he the Jew the readings had foretold? He agreed to the change. It couldn't be much worse than Dayton, and if Morton's promises collapsed, they would at least be stranded in the spot chosen by the readings.

First there was a trip to New York for a set of readings on the proposed organization, and to meet friends of Morton's and Dave's who had heard of Edgar and wanted to meet him and see him demonstrate.

Gertrude was now conducting all readings, and the results were better and more uniform. She had decided that so long as the fortunes of the family were with the readings, she ought to do as much as she could to make them successful. Moreover, there was the matter of Edgar's health. The conductor was the link between the medium and his normal state of existence. One as close and as sympathetic as a wife would make a better connecting rod. The readings agreed with this theory, and suggested that for Life Readings the medium change the position of his body. He had always reclined with his head to the south, in a straight north-south line. By lying with his head to the north, the information said, he would avoid the dizzy spells experienced sometimes after a Life Reading. "Matter of polarity" was the explanation given.

The readings were consulted for details of the organization and people to run it. In these matters the information was dogmatic to the point of monotony. Over and over again it insisted that no device of law or plan of control could do the slightest good unless there was the proper spirit among the members of the organization and its leaders. "Let those serve who wish to serve; let those be chosen who choose to offer themselves." There had to be an ideal, and it had to be lived as well as believed. Since such an organization was to be founded on the idea of service, its members would have to be servers. Since its purpose was to enlighten, its members would have to be enlightened.

"That's what it has always said," Edgar explained to Morton, "and that's why all the attempts to do something with it have failed. The people involved have wanted to get something out of it for themselves."

Morton nodded. "I understand," he said. "It won't be that way this time. When can you move to the beach? I've secured a house for you there. If you like it, I'll buy it for you."

"Buy it?"

"Yes, it's on Thirty-fifth Street. The number is 115. You'd better write it down; and you'd better hurry if you want to get there for any of the season. August is nearly over."

Edgar didn't hear the last part. He went to find Gertrude. She sat down suddenly when he told her the news.

"A house of our own that's bought and paid for?" she said. "It's too much."

"Let's hurry and go down there," Hugh Lynn said, "before it's too late to swim."

"It won't be so cold there in the winter," Miss Davis—who had become Gladys to the family—said.

17

They stepped off the bus into a howling northeast storm that had whipped the sea to a white fury and transformed the road on which they stood into a trough of brown mud. Slowly they trudged up Thirty-fifth Street, raising their faces into the rain to look for their new home.

It stood on a sand hill, on the south side of the street, staring at empty lots and, beyond them, where the coast turned inward, at the ocean. There was no walk leading to it, no driveway. The lights had been blown out by the storm. Edgar made a tour of inspection and reported that there was no furnace. It was a summer residence, with a fireplace for chilly nights.

The storm lasted three days. When it ended, they went out to examine Virginia Beach. It was a forlorn sight. Down by the ocean the old boardwalk, ravaged by storms, had been entirely dismantled; its wreckage strewed the sand. A new, concrete sea wall was to be erected, but construction had not begun. Most of the hotels were closed; all the shops but those at Seventeenth Street, the center of town, were shut up. Practically all the houses were boarded up. It was September; the season was over.

The homes of the permanent residents were widely scattered, each one tucked away in a cluster of silent summer homes. There were no neighbors within three blocks of Thirty-fifth Street. The only grocery store was at Seventeenth Street. There was a delivery once a day, maybe.

After they were settled, they spent their evenings by the fireplace holding impromptu debates. The subject was always the same: "Why did the readings send us to Virginia Beach?"

The beach for fifty years had been a fashionable summer resort for Virginians and North Carolinians. It had grown slowly, changed little, until the 1920s. Now it was experiencing a boom created by the motorcar. Automobiles made it accessible as a weekend retreat for a large section of the Virginia and North Carolina population, and it became a target for tourists. It was also practical as a suburban area for Norfolk residents, some of whom were building year-round homes. A gigantic hotel, the Cavalier, was about to be built, and with it as a nucleus the local Chamber of Commerce planned to make a bid for the New York trade. The Cavalier laid out two golf courses, set up a riding academy, and fostered an exclusive dancing and supper club.

All this was just beginning. They could see the foundations of the Cavalier being erected; they walked along the ocean and watched construction of the sea wall; they read in the Virginia Beach *News*—a weekly—of sales of land and permits for building. But they knew no one, they had no neighbors, and time was heavy on their hands. The ocean was their best friend.

One day Gertrude, wandering through the dunes across the street, came upon a heap of bricks, apparently discarded. Joyfully the whole family set to work, carted the bricks to the house, and built a walk. The delivery boy for the grocery store reported the event to his employer, and there was quite a bit of talk around town about "the enterprising Yankees on Thirty-fifth Street who are building their own walk."

Most of the readings were for Morton. He got them on every subject and on every aspect of the subjects. He sent long letters describing his reactions to the answers given his questions and asked questions on these reactions. His enthusiasm freshened daily. He took courses in philosophy at night, and the problems raised by his studies were presented to the readings. His thoughts, his dreams, his feelings, his hunches, his plans, all were presented for analysis. He telephoned once, sometimes twice, a day. He came to the beach whenever he could.

Morton worked hard to build his philosophy into a complete system. The complexity of the problems he sought to solve was his chief difficulty. Sometimes the questions were answered, but he did not understand the answers. Sometimes he was told that the answer was beyond human comprehension. Often he was told that unless he incorporated the truths he was discovering into his personality and lived them, they would do him more harm than good.

Once when he was told that Arcturus is the next stop for souls leaving the solar system and that this star represents the point of choice for the soul's next adventure, he asked what was the state of the soul's evolution when it was able to reach Arcturus.

"This may not be given," was the answer.

He began to write a book to be called Heaven on Earth. It began:

"The soul of man cries out for peace! The spirit protests, raising each experience to emotional heights, from which sensuous ecstasy we must inevitably fall into the opposite depths of disillusionment and disappointment. Excitement, but not real or lasting happiness, results from a so-called thrill. A sensation may not be drawn out to become permanent, or, in other words, happiness is not to be found by living the present moment as though it would last eternally."

*   *   *

It was a bleak winter. There was nothing to do but give readings for Morton, huddle around the fireplace, or walk along the beach and through the dunes. Hugh Lynn attended a business school in Norfolk and was gone all day. Ecken went to the local public school.

Spring came early, and Edgar got to work. He laid out a garden and built a chicken house. He planted a lawn, and made flower boxes for the porch. Morton had paid promptly for each of his readings, and there was money in the bank. The family bought a Ford and a furnace. Hugh Lynn was told he could go to college in the fall. He thumbed through stacks of catalogues, and then had a reading and asked where he should go.

He was told to enter Washington and Lee University, at Lexington, Virginia, because there he would meet many boys with whom he had been associated in his past lives, and he would have an opportunity to make practical tests of reincarnation. He was still skeptical of the theory.

"I'll go up there and either prove it or disprove it," he said.

Summer, they found, was heavenly at the beach. The houses

that had been empty all winter filled with people; all along Atlantic Avenue, from the Cavalier to beyond Seventeenth Street, shops and hotels opened. The population swelled from three hundred to thirty thousand. Hugh Lynn saw so many pretty girls that he stopped being afraid of them.

He left for college in mid-September.

On October 20th, Edgar received a wire from his sister Annie in Hopkinsville. His mother, who had been ailing for a long time, was much worse. Would he give a check reading for her?

When he woke from the reading, Gertrude and Gladys were crying. "You must go home at once, Edgar; she can't live," Gertrude said.

He arrived in Hopkinsville on the morning of the 22nd. His mother met him at the door. She was pale and obviously weak, but smiling.

"I'm so glad you came," she said. "I need you."

During the morning the squire drew him aside and suggested that he give another reading. While she was resting, it was taken, but the result was the same: "The soul is about to take flight; do not grieve."

That evening she felt worse; she went to bed and did not get up again. She died on the evening of the 26th. Edgar was sitting by her. She was conscious and aware to the last, talking to him, smiling at him.

"Son, you've kept your old mother alive a long time," she said, "but I'm going now . . .

"We've been good friends. You've been a good son . . .

"Stay close to your father and your sisters. They look to you for guidance. God has given you something He hasn't given to everyone . . .

"Be faithful to the trust . . .

"Never forget to pray. Never give a reading when you can't take Jesus with you . . .

"It's hard to go, but your prayers have been answered, down there at the beach. I know you will stay there and succeed . . .

"Someone is waiting for me . . . "

* * *

On May 6, 1927, The Association of National Investigators was incorporated in the state of Virginia. Its motto was: "That We May Make Manifest Our Love for God and Man." Its purpose was: "To engage in general psychic research, and to provide for the practical application of any knowledge obtainable through the medium of psychic phenomena.

"Although founded upon the psychic work of Mr. Edgar Cayce, and although the immediate basis of its formation was to further foster and encourage the physical, mental, and spiritual aid that thousands have and are receiving from Mr. Cayce's endeavors in the psychic—the primary purpose—is education: the education of the individual, that he may attain a closer relationship to the higher powers of his own mind, that he may for and by himself achieve greater development of mind, as well as greater material benefit, for his physical being in the material environment. The achievement of our purpose will enable the human race to use for its own good, in every department of its life, physical and spiritual, an introspective method of obtaining knowledge, that individuals may so develop their intuitional forces as to become able to be guided by a higher dimensional viewpoint, the viewpoint that such intuitional development brings self-realization of possessing. This is the all-embracing aim and deeper purpose, the whole ideal, of this Association."

Edgar didn't quite understand all this (it was Morton's prose) but he got the general idea, and the idea was that a hospital was to be built and the readings scientifically studied.

Morton was president. His brother Edwin, Dave Kahn, Wyrick and Brown, Hugh Lynn, and a Virginia Beach real estate operator, F. A. Van Patten, were the vice-presidents. Edgar was secretary and treasurer, Gladys was assistant secretary. There was a board of governors, consisting of Dave, Edwin, and a Chicago businessman, Franklin F. Bradley. The board of trustees contained the officers and governors, plus Gertrude and the wives of Dave and Morton.

The bylaws provided that any person requesting a reading had first to become a member of the Association, agreeing that he was participating in an experiment in psychic research. This protected Edgar and the Association from any legal prosecution. It had never happened, but with the anticipated publicity it was a possibility.

Members were to have access to the facilities of the Association: its hospital, library, records, research data, etc. All readings were to be considered the property of the person for whom they were secured, but copies were to be kept by the Association and extracts could be made by students, providing the identity of the owner was withheld. Owners could give permission for the examination and study of their readings or could request that friends be allowed to see them.

The Life Readings were to be especially guarded, as they were considered more personal and revealing than physical diagnoses.

"Nobody is interested in your kidneys," Edgar observed, "but everyone is interested in your past lives."

He was becoming acutely aware that, if it were true that the early church had dropped reincarnation as a dangerous and impractical thesis, the decision had been a wise one. People almost invariably got the wrong idea about their Life Readings.

If a man were told that he had once, as another personality, been rich and powerful, he was inclined to be content with his present mediocrity and regard his past as an inheritance he had just come into. If a woman were told that she had once been glamorous and irresistible, she was inclined to relax smugly, overlooking her present obesity and lack of charm.

Edgar found it difficult to point out to these people that such records were evidence that the soul was on the downgrade. The Life Reading was a balance sheet, and if an asset once possessed was missing, it was something to be alarmed about. Most souls possessed greater virtue in their earlier lives than at present anyhow, but this virtue was through grace: it was the virtue of innocence. The path of the soul was downward until free will made the turn upward. So there was no reason whatsoever to feel proud of a good or intelligent life ten or fifteen thousand years ago. Only when such goodness and intelligence were attained again, this time by the use of free will, would a measure of satisfaction be permissible.

There was a tendency also to regard the soul as a permanent personality. People would say, "I was So-and-so. In my last appearance I was in England." When Edgar tried to combat this notion by saying that each personality of a soul was a separate experience, in no way related to other experiences of the soul except by common inclusion in a large enterprise, he found the going heavy, especially with the ladies.

"But you said so yourself," one of them would say. "You said I was a slave girl and was freed by my master because he loved me!"

"From what you say about me I imagine I was a sort of courtesan," another lady—usually an old maid—would say.

Edgar sympathized deeply with the early church Fathers who had set upon the Gnostics. He would leave the ladies and go out to feed his chickens.

The house was never lonely any more. The squire had come to live with his son, and that summer, 1927, Tommy House came to visit Hugh Lynn. In the fall Tommy stayed to attend the local high school. Morton came to the beach frequently, and Dave Kahn, now married and the president of a furniture company, dropped in frequently. Morton was buying land for the hospital and university. He was determined to get things started. Riding to wealth on a bull market, he could see no reason for delay.

One afternoon early in 1928 a short, stocky man with a great many gold keys on his watch chain drove up to the house. He introduced himself as Dr. William Moseley Brown, head of the psychology department at Washington and Lee.

"Hugh Lynn is one of my students," he said. "I made a statement that I could expose any medium. He told me to come down here and expose his father."

He smiled. Edgar smiled. They shook hands, and Dr. Brown settled down to ask questions. He examined readings, listened to several, and finally, running his fingers through his thinning hair, admitted that he was stumped. "I can't expose it," he said. "Still, it's not the sort of thing you can do nothing about. I can't ignore it. I'll have to believe in it."

He joined the Association, had a reading for himself, and got others for members of his family. Edgar wagged his head in wonder.

"The millennium has come," he said.

18

It was a young spring day, with the tide running high and the wind from the south, when they broke ground for the hospital. The site was a high dune at 105th Street, halfway between the Cavalier and Cape Henry. Standing on it, looking toward the sea, Edgar felt fulfilled. Looking at Morton, he felt frightened.

Here was all he had ever dreamed or desired; yet it rested for security on the whim of a single man. What went through Morton's head, what thoughts stirred his mind and heart, governed what would happen to the hospital and the readings. He wished it were not so. There had been others: Ketchum and Noe, Frank Mohr, Dave and the Texas people, his friends in Birmingham, and Lammers. All these had tried, and failed. Was this slight, frail Jew, who stood so placid, smoking a cigar as he watched the workmen, to succeed?

He hoped so. For, once the hospital was operating, others would come, and an endowment fund that would make it independent of Morton could be raised. That would be the best way. Then Morton could devote himself to the university, which was becoming more and more his main interest.

While the building was going on, he and Gertrude came to watch it every day. Often he picked up a hammer or a saw and went to work. The carpenters watched him oddly the first time, until they saw he was no amateur.

"Guess you've done a little carpentering before, eh?" one of them asked.

"I was raised on a farm," Edgar said. "We did our own work."

The carpenter nodded. The others smiled at him. One of them offered him a chew of tobacco.

During the summer Hugh Lynn and Tommy House worked

as laborers on the building. Tommy had finished high school and was trying to select a college. Hugh Lynn urged him to enter Washington and Lee.

"Finest school in the South," he argued. "George Washington endowed it; General Lee was its president. It's a school for gentlemen. Best-dressed school in the South. It has tradition. Everybody speaks to everyone else. Everybody is dressed up. No sweaters or sweat shirts."

"I don't like to dress up," Tommy said.

"The professors are really fine fellows," Hugh Lynn went on. "We have a young English professor who invites us to his home every Sunday afternoon to read plays and drink tea."

"Oh, really?" Tommy said.

"Don't you want to be a gentleman?" Hugh Lynn asked.

"Why don't they have coeds at Washington and Lee?" Tommy said.

Hugh Lynn was disgusted. "That girl of yours!" he said.

Toward the end of the summer Tommy changed his mind.

"I think I'll go up there with you," he said.

"I knew I'd argue you into it," Hugh Lynn said proudly.

"My girl's going to Teachers College at Farmville," Tommy said. "I can see her weekends if I go to Washington and Lee."

Dr. House and Carrie were now at the beach. Dr. House had resigned his post in Hopkinsville and was ready to take charge of the hospital. Carrie was to be its matron.

"When I was in Hopkinsville all my patients were nuts," Dr. House said wistfully. "Now I'm the one who's considered crazy. I've been waiting twenty years for this, Edgar."

In September the boys left for school. Construction proceeded rapidly. By November the building was finished and ready for occupancy. The cost was in the neighborhood of $200,000. Morton had asked for the best of materials. He got them.

It was a thirty-bed hospital, but it was a good deal more than a hospital. It was designed to be a home for the patients, especially those who were unable to get around. Temporarily it was also to be a center for the Association's other activities. There was a lecture hall and library, a vault for housing the readings, and offices for research workers. The living room was spacious, richly furnished, and fronted on a view of the ocean. A porch, screened in summer, glassed-in in winter, ran around three sides. In the rear was a twelve-car garage, servants' quarters, and a tennis court. In front, terraces stepped down three hundred yards to the ocean boulevard. Every inch of this space was covered with sod, so there might be a lawn—the largest lawn, the only lawn—between the Cavalier and Cape Henry. The bill for the sodding and grading was $10,000.

Dedication ceremonies were held on November 11th, Armistice Day. Hugh Lynn and Tommy came down from Washington and Lee, as did Dr. Brown, who made the principal address. Morton, Dave, Edwin, and their wives arrived from New York, Brown from Dayton, and Bradley from Chicago. Before the visitors arrived, Edgar wandered through the corridors, now and then walking into a room and standing there, lost in dreams.

Again and again he said to Gertrude, "It's just what I wanted. I hope it succeeds."

The crowd filled the living room and overflowed to the library and lecture hall. Morton, smiling and happy, turned the building over to the Association. Edgar, hardly knowing what he said, his eyes fixed on the ocean that shimmered in the background, accepted it.

"When your prayers are answered, you find out that prayers are about the only things that words are good for, so there's nothing to say, except to give thanks . . . then it's time to start praying again . . . that we will succeed in what we are trying to do here. After all, though it seems we have reached a goal, this is only the beginning. We have been given a trust. It is ours to execute well or poorly . . . I will do my best, for every one of you and everyone who enters this hospital . . . "

When he had finished, Morton introduced Dr. Brown. Sitting behind him, listening to him talk, Edgar realized that Dr. Brown had almost as many college degrees as he himself had years of schooling. It gave him a weird feeling of unreality, and the autumn sunset, coming early and throwing shadows over the room and the faces of the people, almost convinced him that it was a dream. He looked at Gertrude, Carrie, Dr. House, Hugh Lynn, Tommy, and little Ecken, who was hunched on a chair in a corner. They looked unreal, too. Would they all wake up and find themselves at the Hill, arguing with Aunt Kate about politics?

Dr. Brown's voice droned on:

"This is a great occasion, and a happy one. I congratulate the founders of this movement—and they are here among us—for the vision which they have conceived of the possibilities of this new line of study and investigation. I honor those who have contributed of their time and means to bring about the realization, at least to some extent, of a dream of years. I believe that this experimental laboratory, which has as its chief object the utilization of any knowledge, any discovery, any invention, which will make life fuller and richer for human beings, will become renowned as a center of truth and wisdom and, to use the expression of Emerson, the world will make a beaten path to its front door.

"Religion and science, philosophy and psychology, the truths discovered by the ancients as well as by the moderns, will be equally welcome here. Nothing is banned except trickery, sham, falsehood. All truth will be used so far as it may be applicable to the betterment of human life, no matter who was its discoverer or in what country or age it was found. An ambitious project, you say. Ah, yes, but unless we can bring together under one roof, as it were, and into one laboratory, religious, scientific, philosophic, and every other kind of truth, we shall not have that integration of human knowledge which is the *sine qua non* of all human progress. Here, then, we have a pioneer institution in the field of human endeavor. As human life itself is a most complex process involving all kinds of experience, so we find here a kind of laboratory in which human life will go forward, but under observable and controlled conditions, so far as possible. This is not merely a physical or a psychological or even a theological laboratory, as such. Much more than that, it is a center in which the rather unusual attempt is made to bring every kind of truth together as needed in the solution of the particular problem under investigation. Always, however, the motif is the betterment of human life and all other endeavors are to be subsidiary to this chief aim. So far as I am aware, such an undertaking has never been attempted before in this country, and probably in the entire world. Here will be your expert in medicine, another expert in psychology, another in theology, another in chemistry, another in psychiatry, and so on as many as may be needed and can be provided with the funds in hand. There are in this country today thousands of specialized laboratories, each of which limits itself to one particular field of investigation. But never before has there been a concerted and successful effort to bring together in one single laboratory every kind of discovery possible which will give the patient, or the subject, relief from his trouble, be it physical, mental, or spiritual. Surely this is a pioneer enterprise and more; it is even daring in its scope. And it has every possibility and probability of success!

"Who can compass the possibilities of such an organization and such a center? Only time can tell the story adequately. It may be that the results of the work done here in this place will mark the beginning of a new era for the cause of humanity. Others will undoubtedly come to observe the methods used and the effects achieved. The advances in the entire realm of human endeavor over the past twenty-five years lead me to believe that we have but scratched the surface of what will be known and achieved within the next century. The radio, the airplane, the automobile, television, and all the advances which are being made in this 'era of electricity' are but an image of many still greater things to come. Who can say what we shall soon find out as to mental telepathy, the characteristics of the subconscious mind, the influence of mind on body, and a thousand and one similar things? Indeed, I have come literally to believe that all things are possible to him that believeth. The millennium will be upon us ere we are aware of it!

"The day of miracles is not past but has only begun. And I recall that, on one occasion, the Master Himself said: 'The works that I do shall ye do also, and greater things than these shall ye do, because I go unto my Father.' 'Greater things than these,' you will notice; that is, greater things even than the miracles which His humble followers had seen Him perform as He walked up and down in the little country of Palestine and by the shores of the Lake of Galilee. And we have witnessed in our own day the actual fulfillment of these words. 'The blind see, the lame walk, the lepers are cleansed, the deaf hear, the dead are raised, to the poor the gospel is preached.' Are not all these things true today just as they were nineteen hundred years ago? Yea, verily, and more also.

"And this building and this spot are here and now dedicated to the bringing to pass of these 'greater things.'"

He stopped. The crowd applauded. Edgar found that his hands were clapping, that he was smiling and nodding at Morton, who was saying something to him. It was not a dream. It was real.

The first patient was admitted next day. He was an old friend of Edgar's, an engineer engaged in the construction of coke furnaces. In trying to finish a job within the allotted time he had overworked himself, caught cold, and neglected it. He had a chronic sinus irritation and his blood showed diabetic tendencies. His reading suggested baths, packs, osteopathy, medicine, and diet. The treatments were carried out; in two weeks a check reading discharged him as suffciently well to go back to work, providing he continued some of the treatments at home.

To Edgar there was a peculiar joy in seeing all the treatments suggested by a reading carried out, with cooperation between the people administering them and an attempt to harmonize their effects on the patient.

Over the years certain ideas about health, the causes of disease, and cures, had been repeated over and over again in readings. There was a compound that was given for every person suffering from pyorrhea; there was an inhalant suggested for one of the three types of hay fever; there was a salve for hemorrhoids; there were castor oil packs for appendicitis and intestinal complications; there were grape poultices for intestinal fevers; there was the suggestion to some people that they eat a few almonds a day to thwart a tendency toward cancer; there was the suggestion to others that they massage peanut oil into their skin to head off arthritis; there was a dose which time and again had proved efficacious in breaking up a common cold.

At the hospital these and other remedies could be checked and rechecked until their value was beyond doubt. Then they could be turned over to the medical profession and the public. There were skin lotions, intestinal antiseptics, treatments for stimulating the growth of hair, diets helpful to certain conditions, and mechanical appliances.

Two general types of appliance had for many years been prescribed in readings. One, the radioactive, was connected so that the electrical current of the body passed through the appliance, which acted as a transformer, sending the current back at a regular rate of impulse. In cases where the circulation was impaired, this meant a speeding up; where the circulation was too rapid, it meant a slowing down. This device was often specified in circulatory conditions, and for nervous disorders.

The other type, the wet cell, operated on the theory that a very low electrical charge set up in an ordinary wet solution of acid, metal, and copper sulphate can be discharged through solutions of gold chloride, camphor, iodine, etc., and the vibratory impulse can be carried to the body, causing it to extract more of the particular property in the solution from its digested foods. In commenting on the theory behind this, a reading said:

"The human body is made up of electronic vibrations, with each atom and element of the body, each organ and organism, having its electronic unit of vibration necessary for the sustenance of, and equilibrium in, that particular organism. Each unit, then, being a cell or a unit of life in itself has its capacity of reproducing itself by the first law as is known of reproduction-division. When a force in any organ, or element of the body, becomes deficient in its ability to reproduce that equilibrium necessary for the sustenance of the physical existence and its reproduction, that portion becomes deficient in electronic energy. This may come by injury or by disease, received from external forces. It may come from internal forces through lack of eliminations produced in the system, or by the lack of other agencies to meet its requirements in the body."

These appliances, now properly built and maintained, were in the hospital, along with cabinets where sweat baths could be had while the fumes of needed elements enveloped the body, entering it through the opened pores.

There was all the regular equipment of a hospital, of course, and the orthodox physiotherapy laboratory: sinusoidal machines, ultraviolet and infrared lamps, baths, cabinets, rubbing tables.

Dr. House, being both a medical doctor and an osteopath, supervised the allopathic treatments and administered the mechanical adjustments. Mrs. House saw to it that each patient's diet was kept; she had charge of the kitchen and dining room. The nurses, in addition to their ordinary duties, learned to give the rubs prescribed for certain patients and took others to the beach—weather permitting—for sand packs. Hot sand was packed around a body wet with sea water. The readings said the sand at Virginia Beach had a large gold content and was highly radioactive.

When summer came the boys were put to work. Hugh Lynn and Tommy took over the job of acquainting newcomers and visitors with the history and theory of the readings. Gray, who liked to build things, took over the manufacture of the radioactive appliances and the maintenance of the electrical machines.

"I don't see any use in going to college, Edgar," he said; "I can learn more here about the things that interest me than any school can teach me."

"Good," Edgar said. "You can build yourself a workshop out back."

Work was begun on several medicines which, though the procedure was clearly outlined in readings, were difficult to produce. Two of these were carbon ash and animated ash. In each case the ash had to be that of the wood of a bamboo tree, burned with the flame of a carbon lamp, and treated in a vacuum. These were to be taken internally, for such things as tuberculosis.

The readings had always been democratic in the selection of medicines as they were in the selection of treatments. No drug manufacturer was shown the slightest favor. Smith's preparation for one ailment might be preferred, while his product for another trouble was snubbed in favor of that of his rival, Jones. Often the readings suggested uses for the drugs which were not listed by the manufacturer. In one instance they helped the chemist perfect his formula, and then put it to a use which had not entered the inventor's head.

The chemist was a distinguished and learned Hindu, Dr. Sunker A. Bisey, who had won his doctorate in chemistry at Oxford

University in England. He had been concerned for years with the problem of producing iodine in a form that could be taken internally in doses large enough to have an appreciable effect on diseases caused by its lack in the body.

He had himself been psychic since birth, and was in the habit of taking his problems to bed with him and sleeping on them. When he heard of Edgar and came to him with the problem of "atomic iodine," the formula was almost perfected. The readings offered suggestions, and whether it was these or Dr. Bisey's dreams or his continued laboratory experiments, the product was eventually marketed successfully as Atomidine. Promptly the readings began to prescribe it for infantile paralysis, particularly as a preventive for this disease in times of epidemic. Dr. Bisey hadn't thought of such a use: the readings gave the cause of infantile paralysis as a filterable virus which can enter the body through the mucous membranes (being carried in the air), or even by way of the sensitive skin under the arms, or in drinking water.

The explanation of infantile paralysis was only one of the things which Edgar felt hopeless about, so far as the world was concerned. Even with a hospital, how could such a thing be proved? How could anyone prove the statement that the appendix and tonsils should not be removed, because they act as focal points for poisons, gathering and sending them out through the proper channels? Only when overloaded to the point of breaking down should they be removed, the readings said, and such a breaking down meant that some part of the body was overproducing waste material.

What about the implication of a cycle in the metabolism of each body? The readings gave medicines in cycles: ten days, then a three-day rest, for example. Or, "For this body it is best to take the prescription on Tuesdays and Thursdays."

"Maybe science will discover those things someday," Mrs. House would say as they sat on the hospital porch after dinner.

"Keep the records," Dr. House would say. "Keep everything. Someday they'll catch up with us."

"If they do, and the records are here, that will at least prove that psychic phenomena aren't frauds," Edgar would say.

Gertrude would shake her head.

"I don't know how you can explain those things to people," she would say. "How would you go about telling someone a thing like this: The readings say that when an ultraviolet ray treatment is given, the ozone created is as beneficial, or more so, than the rays from the lamp, because the ozone kills bacteria. The patient should stay in the room where the treatment was given and breathe in the ozone."

Edgar would look at the boys.

"Maybe the younger generation will prove it for us," he would say.

"I'll build the things," Gray would say.

"I'll sell them," Tommy would say.

"I'll explain them," Hugh Lynn would say, "if I can ever learn to understand them."

About this time Mrs. House would drop her sewing, turn her piercing brown eyes on the group, and say:

"Edgar, shouldn't the people themselves do something? If you have to stuff truth down a man's throat it's not going to do him any good. He at least ought to want it."

"More cases, more cases," Dr. House would say. "That'll prove it to them."

More cases were coming in every day, and they were providing all the variety needed to illustrate the latitude of the readings.

There was apparently no elaborate medical system, or theory, to be got from the cures. Glandular conditions were the basic causes for many disturbances; childhood bumps and bruises often caused lesions that brought on obscure ailments; karmic conditions predisposed a body to a certain trouble or gave it a weakness. Once diagnosed, an affliction was attacked at its source. No cure could come except through the natural channel: assimilation of needed properties through the digestive system, from food taken into the body. An affliction or disturbance upset the natural equilibrium of this process; certain necessary properties for the maintenance of the body were not extracted from the digested food (in cases of malnutrition the necessary ingredients were not in the food). The proper equilibrium of the assimilating system had to be restored. All treatments were aimed at this accomplishment.

That, if anything, was the medical philosophy of the readings. It made no difference about the treatments—all schools and types were useful in one way or another—so long as health was procured for the patient. There was a difference between the aim of the readings and the aim of the average doctor. The doctor aimed at curing a specific ailment. The readings aimed at producing a healthy body, which would itself get rid of the ailment. In one case the evidence of the ailment was removed. In the other case its cause was eliminated.

In cases of chronic disturbance the readings outlined systems of treatment far more complex and detailed than a doctor would devise; and the treatments lasted longer (sometimes for years) than the average physician would consider necessary for recovery from the same ailment.

A typical example was the check reading for a patient suffering from arthritis and destruction of nerve tissue. The patient had lost the use of his legs and was affected in the elbows, neck, and lower back.

> As has been heretofore indicated, the nerve ends have been destroyed throughout the locomotory activities of the lumbar and sacral, or the nerves of the sciatic portions of the limbs themselves—the outer nerves, or the superficial circulation; and atrophy is indicated.
>
> Now, the rubs and those influences which have been applied, as well as the low electrical forces, have been to stimulate these areas from which impulses arise for the completing of the circulation, sufficient to bring recuperative forces to these areas.
>
> At the same time properties have been indicated to be taken with the assimilating forces of the system, and to prevent a spread of the atrophy, or to prevent the nerve forces becoming so inactive as to produce static conditions; and this to a great extent has been accomplished.
>
> Now the conditions, as we find, are at a turning point. Either the body from the waist up will continue to develop towards

a greater normalcy, and the lower extremities become more atrophied, or static in their reactions . . . and thus leaving the body incapacitated for locomotion; or the pathological, the physiological and the psychological conditions or activities will be so stimulated as to allow a greater tendency . . . gradually, but continually . . . towards the abilities of the assimilating forces of the body to not only resuscitate but to revivify, reanimate, the nerve forces through the areas indicated—to such an extent as to become more and more active, with a greater and a better resuscitation.

Then—it is necessary that there be cooperation in regard to the applications, the persistency and consistency as related to all influences and forces towards this one direction.

Little has been done that is of a curative nature. Little may be done, in the present, that is of any great curative value.

However, the impulses may be stimulated so as to allow the natural, living cellular force of the body to recuperate itself! so that the natural sources, or nature's sources, or the psychological reactions may be such as to enable nature to produce in the body-physical a physiological reaction; and thus bring a pathological condition to the portions of the body now under distress.

Now, as to the activity of those things that may be administered in the present:

The continued use of the aspirin with the soda-mint is as yet very well, and it may be necessary that this be taken in a regular order. *But,* if it is practical or possible for the body, do not set hours for this to be administered! For this only tends to lessen pain; and the activity of this by mouth (which is the only way to take it) is such that it still leaves drosses, being an active force which prevents the full elimination of poisons that are the result of tissue being enlivened. For, dead cellular forces are being released in the blood stream for elimination, from the flesh as well as muscle and bone portions even—from the activity of those properties within the blood stream, as the effluvium—as fast as there is the ability of the cell to reproduce itself.

And these properties are only as sedatives, or palliatives

for the moment, and not curatives; only adding to the drosses for elimination.

Then, let's not produce a greater burden than the system is capable of adjusting itself to; so that at the same time we may bring resuscitating, revivifying forces to the body.

The mechanical osteopathic adjustments:

While these are not curative, neither palliative, they are that means by which impulses may be stimulated from centers in the cerebrospinal nervous system; and the pelvis, sacral and ileac plexus, and *throughout* the lower portion, are the areas to be stressed, in such stimulation. There is not to be such activity as to break up and cause bruises, ever, but the bursa about ganglia heads and centers are to be greatly stressed— especially in the lumbar axis, the lower lumbar areas, through the sacral, even to the ends . . . especially . . . of the spinal plexus.

These have not been given as thoroughly, nor as consistently, as they may be done. Give more time to these. For, with greater activity there comes a greater strain, especially on the nerves and muscles about the head of the sacral bones, and the limbs, and especially at the branch of the sciatic center, or the last bones or joints or segments in the end of the spine. These must be gradually . . . *easily,* but *consistently* . . . relaxed.

And after such let the body rest for at least two or three hours, that there may be the greater flow of impulse from the improved circulation throughout the body.

So much, for the physiological and pathological effects.

The applications of the low electrical vibrations carrying the solutions that act upon the glandular forces of the body:

The Gold Solution—make the attachments to the last dorsal plexus, and to the lacteal duct and umbilical plexus; this to be given on every third day, you see. Watch the Gold Solution, that it does not deteriorate too fast, but is kept at near a normal strength.

The Atomidine, now—attach the copper plate at the brachial center, and the one carrying the electrical charge more over the liver area; not the plexus, but on the right side about the distance from the center area of the body that the little finger of the hand would touch, with the hand turned diagonally across the body—not from the umbilical plexus, but more from the sternum plexus.

The Camphor Solution—this we would keep to the lower limbs, or to the bursa about the heel, and to the fore portion of the foot, *and* to the lacteal duct and umbilical plexus.

The strength of the charge should be almost three times, or two and a half times, above the *normal* solution ordinarily indicated. Leave off the doubling, or tripling, of the quantity of charcoal. Only use one-half pound of the charcoal in this solution.

Now, as to the activity of these:

The Gold Solution is nerve building, supplying a balance in the vibratory forces of the energies of the system to work with glandular reactions, as to stimulate the nerve building plasm in the white cellular force.

The Atomidine adds the vibrations to minimize the pain that is active in the movement of poisons through the channels of the superficial circulation, or perspiratory system; as well as to set up drainages in the circulatory system for the eliminating of drosses through the dross channels, as well as the general circulation.

The Camphor Solution is a healing property, as well as an active force for the better eliminations through the alimentary canal.

Keep up the rubs and the applications for the external portions. Now, we find that the Peanut Oil and the Olive Oil may be applied singly or in the same combinations that have been indicated; but keep these in different solutions, and use them at different periods.

Also we would now have the stimulations or vibrations occasionally from the Ultra-Violet, that should be given to the *back* portions of the body, but as far *from* the body as is possible with this particular type of light indicated here. In the beginning give this for not more than ten to eighteen minutes—never more than eighteen minutes—for the first fifteen to eighteen days, or for the first few applications . . .

which would be five to six days apart. For, the body easily irritates.

But if there is all the stimulation mechanically (osteopathically), all the stimulation dietetically, all the stimulation as may be given through the rubs, the body may be able to take more of this. But do not *burn,* nor irritate the body!

Occasionally . . . once a month, oftener as improvements are shown . . . give the Epsom Salts bath. While in such a bath, massage especially the soles of the feet, the knees, and the muscular forces under the limbs—both above and below the knees.

At least once each week apply the Epsom Salts saturated solution in packs for the knees. Following this massage the oils into them.

As to the activity of these:

The baths are to stimulate the superficial circulation, and the massaging while in them is to break up the static forces about the tendon and muscular forces; that the activity of the circulation from those properties given vibratorially may become more efficient. The local applications are to break up the cystic forces that are static in the cartilage about the end of the bones in the knee.

Then, as to the diet, and as to the ingredients to be taken otherwise internally:

Take three to four drops of the Wheat Oil about three times each week; not oftener, *but do not miss taking it at these periods!* Its active principle is upon the stimulated glandular system, for not only reproduction of the red blood supply but of the genital reaction in the system; for, as "germ" indicates, this is the activity in the system.

The *diet*—this must be, as the rest, *consistently, persistently,* followed!

Take more of the vegetable forces that are life-giving in their assimilation through the body; more carrots (raw), celery and lettuce. These, at least these three, should be combined to make the greater part of one meal each day; or they may be taken with *each* meal if it is the more preferable. They *must be taken,* if there will be better recuperative forces, or the supplying to the system of properties and energies that are to be the real *healing* forces!

For here alone (in the diet) will there be the coming of curative or healing powers. All the rest are for the *preparations* of the body for the *usage* of energies in food values, which may be had from those foods indicated to be supplied.

With the taking of the Wheat Oil in the manner indicated, supply vitamins B-1 . . . as well as A, B, and G . . . through the cereals. We do not mean dried cereals! These should be cooked cereals! The cracked Whole Wheat at one time, the Steel Cut Oats at another time, and wheat and barley at another time! These should be taken with cream or milk, and *not too much sugar!* Put barely sufficient for making same palatable!

Have plenty (and more than has been taken!) of oranges, lemons, limes, grapefruit and the like. These supply salts that should be had by the body. Preferably use the fresh fruits, though grapefruit juice is preferable to the green fruit, and is more vitamin-giving.

Fish, fowl, lamb. Occasionally . . . about once a week . . . give the body a good, stiff steak, *smothered in onions!* and mushrooms may be added if so desired.

Rye bread, or brown bread, is preferable.

The Wine—red wine *only,* or the light wines, as a stimulant.

Do these, and we may expect bettered conditions.

All these treatments were carried out; the patient continued to get well.

Day after day new patients appeared for readings, old ones had their condition checked and rechecked. The mail brought more and more requests; the calendar was crowded for weeks and months ahead. Notes on an average span of two weeks ran as follows:

Monday A.M.   Check Reading. Mrs. L. N. Advised continuance of former suggestions, adding more olive oil as food value for digestive system and to aid in eliminations; continue violet ray and manipulations; not a growth: merely a thickening of walls in tissue of cardiac portion of stomach. Body much improved from last reading.

Check.   Mrs. M. D. Z. Baby developing normally. Strains in cervical and dorsal from a fall; need correction by osteopath. Little more calcium needed, or vitamin D, for teeth. Get it through sunshine, diet, and limewater.

P.M.   Check. Miss B. M. She is concerned over eruption on her body. Prescribed drastic liver stir-up. First, castor oil packs; then olive oil, then P—— tablets; then Castoria; diet; further instructions later.

Check.   Mr. K J. Liver, kidneys, and glands affected. Recommended Atomidine, calcium; gargle of salt, soda, and cream of tartar. Special diet. Plenty of outdoors, but not fatigue in hot sunshine. Retardment of growth due to gland condition. Teeth need attention.

Check.   Mr. T. H. Many changes, some good and some bad. Poisons from nonelimination causing strain in neck, eyes and shoulders. Cathartic of equal parts salts and soda recommended; several rounds of ten days each, with a rest of several days in between. Use of appliance to be continued.

Tuesday A.M.   Check. Miss B. H. G. Emergency. Telephoned request from New York. Abscess of eye, which doctors say is produced by condition in system. Prescribed poultice of scraped old Irish potato, cleanse with boracic acid, then use poultice again. Follow this with doses of salts, soda, and cream of tartar; then castoria. Produced by grain of infectious dust in eye, which with rubbing and distribution through tear gland, produced inflammation. General condition very good. Special diet during period of cleansing system.

Tuesday P.M.   First Reading. Mr. M. W. Injury of long standing produces pressures that affect primarily the lacteals and assimilation. Suggested radioactive appliance for first thirty-six days of treatment. Further instructions to be given. Cure and length of time to produce it depend on consistence and persistence of applications.

Wednesday A.M.   Check. Mrs. E. G. Wants treatment for absorbing and eliminating warts on feet, and cure for blackheads and large pores. Prescribed soda, wet with spirits of camphor, applied each evening on warts. Hot towels on face and neck, followed by wash with C—— soaps, then cold cloths, then patting. Doses internally of Rochelle salts and olive oil. Misdirected eliminations causing trouble.

Check.   Mrs. E. H. Improved since last time; only goes back when worry prevents hopeful and helpful attitude. Growth being eliminated; only needs patience, persistence, and careful cleansing with antiseptics. Magnetic and other treatments to be continued.

P.M.   First Reading. Mrs. C. D. Plethora condition, may be removed by absorption without operation; will take longer, but will be more effective. Prescribed deep osteopathic manipulations, salt packs, tonic, diet, etc.

Thursday A.M.   First Reading. Mrs. O. M. Poisons from cold cause pressure; toxic conditions of long standing. Recommended high colonics, doses of salts each morning, vibrator along spine in evening, strict diet (without salt and meats), and both cause and effect will be removed.

P.M.   First Reading. Mr. J. H. Serious condition; character of sarcoma, from weakening of walls of veins and arteries. Not serious from malignant standpoint, but anaesthetic and gas taken produced strangulation and inability for coagulation in glands of throat, in muscle and tissue, etc. Oxygen only aid—through tank inhalations and animated ash with heavy ultraviolet rays to stimulate it. In seven days he will either respond or not.

Friday A.M.   First Reading. Mr. H. J. F. Poisons in system produced from pressure—adhesions, caused by old injury. Advised T—— compound; use of aconite, iodine, and laudanum on spine when attacks occur, followed by Epsom Salts packs. Appears to have convulsions; intense pain in back, jerking of limbs, etc. In three or four months should be all right.

P.M.   First Reading. Mrs. M. W. Blind tumor in left breast, produced by excess of alkali and potash, with irritation. Two methods for remedy, operation and absorption. Necessary to prepare for operation by cleansing the system, and better to operate unless longer method is to be strictly followed. Absorption method—Atomidine, animated ash with lights, local application of I—— and ash covered with hare fur. Special diet, free from meats, greases, or fats, consisting chiefly of leafy vegetables, fruits and nuts; no walnuts or pecans, but almonds are especially good. In three to five months condition should be dried up, if absorption method is followed carefully. If not, the sooner the operation is performed the better, but care should be taken beforehand that coagulation is equally balanced (through blood testing).

Saturday A.M.   First Reading. Mr. R. W. Z. Bordering on hay fever. If condition not corrected in time will produce effects hard to remove. Manipulations to prevent impingements in upper dorsal and cervical, producing irritation to soft tissue of head, face, throat, and nasal cavities. Inhalant prescribed for antiseptics, to relieve coughing, sneezing, throat irritation, etc.

P.M.   First Reading. Mr. E. C. McP. Anemia. Impairment of lymph ducts; scar tissue from throat operation of years ago. Very strict diet—said it would be hard for the body, but would be worth it. Exercise a.m. and p.m., gargle, etc. Explanation of why cereal and citrus fruit should not be eaten at the same meal. Smoking beneficial in moderation.

Monday A.M.   First Reading. Miss H. S. Suppression of years past causing misdirected nerves, glands, and circulation. Vibrator treatments each night; charcoal and pepsin after each meal for indigestion; B—— cosmetics best. Keep cheerful; don't worry over things you can't help. Expect to be well, strong, and as fat as you want to be.

P.M.   First Reading. Mr. T. L. Hernia; also nasal trouble. Advised Swedish massage and manipulation, telling exactly how it should be done. I—— spray, telling how it should be prepared; special diet, including especially vitamins D and E.

Tuesday A.M.   First Reading. Mr. B. L. M. High blood pressure, produced by poor eliminations, poisons in blood. Colonic irrigations. X ray will show dilation in colon. General manipulations between colonics. Sufficient food for weight, but no greases and fats until better condition is established. Nearly normal conditions can be achieved.

P.M.   First Reading. Mrs. A. G. M. Condition in lumbar, caused by childbirth. Manipulations, external and internal adjustments, will prevent much trouble later on.

Wednesday A.M.   First Reading. Mrs. E. L. Heart and dropsical condition. Entire recovery not promised, but treatment for this condition by homeopathic school will bring greatest relief. Portion of adrenalin, also bedbug juice—which is the homeopath's specific for such conditions. Advised finding a homeopathic physician.

P.M.   Check. Mrs. E. B. H. Body in better condition. Keep up treatments as outlined. Vegetables grown in vicinity are always better for body than those grown elsewhere and shipped in.

Check.   Miss B. S. Nervous shock to system from automobile accident. Advised hot baths, massages with cocoa butter; prescription for liver and eliminations generally; diet for building up body. Should be up and about in three weeks.

Check.   Mrs. M. W. Continue treatments as given, increasing amount of ash in I—— for massage; also increase light treatments. Beware of fats or greases in diet.

Check.   Mrs. S. H. Congestion from cold; also from condition of long standing in colon. Horehound prescription for expectorant, special diet, vibrator and violet ray treatments. No vegetable sweets, such as potatoes, sweet corn—they cause choking up.

Thursday A.M.   First Reading. Miss E. W. Hindered spleen, torpid liver, tipped stomach, bad digestion. Sinusoidal treatments, tonic, special diet.

P.M. Check. Mr. J. S. Accentuation of old disorders. Lacerations, acidity, disturbed circulation, torpid liver, unbalancing—tendency to fall, overflow of blood to upper portion. Glands produce too much fluid through capillary circulation; kidneys and hepatic circulation disturbed. These are results. Advised castor oil packs over lower stomach and liver area; alkaline diet; olive oil internally; lactated pepsin; mixture of olive oil, tincture of myrrh, and turpentine to be massaged into spine. Crude oil massage for scalp—for falling hair.

Check. Mrs. E. J. B. Suggestions not followed wholeheartedly, response not what it should be. Follow them closely, and add digestive stimuli (alternate doses of magnesia, bismuth, Castoria, enema) and mud baths—mud especially prepared for the purpose.

Friday A.M. First Reading. Miss G. J. Physical condition generally good. Some pressure in lumbar and sacral areas causing weakness in bursa of heels. Unless corrected will be aggravating later. Massage—by neuropath or masseuse—followed by rubs with lotion of oils, alcohol, witch hazel, rosewater, etc.; then violet ray for pressure in upper dorsal and cervical which produces strain and irritation to soft tissue in head, neck, throat, nasal cavities. Correction will prevent tendency to colds and irritation in throat and head.

P.M. First Reading. Miss M. J. Excessive functioning of glands in some portions, deficient functioning in others; hidden infection. Strict diet, free from salines, limes, or silicon; abundant amounts of iron, iodine, and phosphorus. Itemized diet, including certain fruit, nuts, and vegetables. Atomidine, salt packs, rubs with oil, etc. Further instructions later.

Saturday A.M. First Reading. Miss E. H. Incoordination; interesting from psychopathic angle. Prenatal cause, psychic forces being basis. Description of glands, psychic forces, etc. Wet cell appliance. Description of electrical life fluids on body, and vibrations. Keep high eliminations through sweats with salt baths, witch hazel, etc. Further suggestions as she progresses. In two or three years may be normal.

P.M.   First Reading. Mrs. C. L. Unbalancing of forces from poor eliminations, cold, congestion in antrums and bronchi, blood overcharged, unbalanced metabolism, temperature. Basic condition in cerebrospinal system, functioning through digestion. Use lights or B—— as counter-irritation to spine; turpentine, spirits of camphor, and tallow to throat, face and feet. Take liver prescription; also tonic of herbs, wild cherry bark, etc. Itemized diet.

Only a small portion of the readings were for patients in the hospital, though most of its beds were filled all of the time. Special days were set aside for checking on these patients. The remainder of the periods was used in an attempt to dent the pile of requests from people all over the country, who had read or heard of the hospital and had written for appointments.

"We're booked three months ahead, except for the periods I've left open for Morton," Gladys said one morning.

"Fill up those appointments of Morton's," Edgar said. "Philosophy can wait. Sick people can't. Some of these folks may die before they get their readings."

"I'll give Morton his on Sundays."

"You're not supposed to work on Sundays," Gertrude said.

"I'll have to."

"You can't. The readings say you mustn't overdo it. You need at least one day's rest a week. Besides, you teach Sunday school in the morning and lecture at thehospital in the afternoon. What time have you to give readings?"

Edgar went off to feed his chickens, grumbling.

"He'll do it," the squire said.

"I know it," Gertrude said wearily.

19

Sunday was a busy day at the hospital. In the morning patients were bundled off to the various churches; in the afternoon visitors were shown through the building and a crowd—usually in excess of a hundred persons—gathered for the lecture. Morton and Edgar spoke on alternate Sundays, and Morton conducted a philosophy class on the Saturday afternoons when he was at the beach. The class had a textbook, Ouspensky's *Tertium Organum,* and did outside reading in Bergson's *Creative Evolution* and *Mind Energy,* James's *Varieties of Religious Experience,* and Hudson's *Law of Psychic Phenomena.* The Sunday lectures were on such subjects as "The Value of Introspection," "My Idea of God," and "The Fourth-Dimensional Viewpoint." Edgar talked very much as he did in Sunday school. The Bible was his textbook.

The same people, largely, came to hear both men; both covered the same territory, took up the same subjects. Both, in essence, often said the same thing, but in quite different words. Speaking of man's relationship to God, Morton said:

"Bearing in mind the difference between the fourth-dimensional viewpoint of mind in the elemental state (i.e., the dematerialized subconscious state of the Creator's mind) and the oneness of life to the mind of such a being, and the three-dimensional viewpoint of mind in materialized form—in the case of man not only an animal subconscious changed to materialized form, but also a universally evolved subconscious kind of mind, by virtue of which addition a combination is effected that in materialized form becomes man—bearing in mind, we say, the difference between the fourth and higher dimensional subconscious viewpoint of mind of the elemental life essence in its universal totality, and the more limited three-dimensional view-

point of this same mind changed to add itself to a sectional
formation of mind; remembering the difference between the
Creator's mind with its infinite viewpoint and the mind of the
created with its finite viewpoint, yet the oneness of both kinds
of mind, we are prepared to form some intelligent concept of
God."

Edgar said:

"What is your relationship to your God? Remember that He
is the God of the living, not of the dead. Remember that in serving
Him you must serve your fellow man, that you must become a
channel through which God may work His divine will here on
earth. When burdens become hard to bear and you feel yourself
beginning to slip away from the path you know is right, draw
nearer to your God and He will draw nearer to you. As a child
will come and sit at the feet of its parents, seeking their guidance and advice, asking their help, just so we must approach
through prayer the God who is our Father and Creator."

The crowds at the lectures respected Morton, but they loved
Edgar. They were polite and attentive while Morton showed them
a chair and a table, and assured them that from the fourth-dimensional viewpoint there was no difference between the two;
but they relaxed and enjoyed themselves when Edgar spoke about
Moses, Joshua, David and Solomon, or told them about the time
he bet a man fifty dollars that trees talked and won the bet.

"He was to pick a time during the day, and every day for a
week at that hour he was to go and sit under a tree and listen.
He was to choose the tree and it was to be in a quiet spot.

"He chose five o'clock in the afternoon. Every day at that
time he went to a big tree in the woods nearby and sat under it.
Then for fifteen minutes he listened to the tree.

"On the fifth afternoon he came running out of the woods.
When he met me he said, 'You win the fifty dollars. I don't
know what that tree said to me, but it said something!'"

Edgar told the story to illustrate the truth that when any person
who is habitually an objective thinker begins to experiment with
subjective thinking, he sees and hears strange things and imag-
ines he is having psychic experiences.

"Actually he is only meeting the reality of himself," Edgar

explained. "It's just the opposite sort of thing when a man who has been too concerned with his inner thoughts goes out into the world and mixes with other people. In each case it is new to the person just experiencing it, but common to everyone else."

He was aware of a dangerous trend among the people who were now being attracted to the work. They came by dozens and scores and many were the kind who reason with their emotions and are ready to exclaim over any new psychic fad. Others were looking for an opportunity to dramatize their own dreams, hunches, and intuitive flashes. They were the sort of people who would turn the thing into a cult, if allowed, or make it ridiculous by their attitude toward it. Yeoman work was done on these people by Hugh Lynn and Tommy, who devoted their time in the summer to interviewing visitors and answering questions. To the best of their ability they foiled the crackpots and faddists, and presented a sane, sensible view of the work.

"They always look at me as if I were crazy," Tommy used to say, "but I keep after them until they change their minds. They finally agree with me, and then they think we're both crazy."

Morton was already looking for new fields to conquer. The hospital was a fulfillment for Edgar; Morton needed a university to hold his dreams. He began buying up land opposite the hospital, on the other side of the boulevard, between it and the ocean. Here he planned to establish Atlantic University.

It was to be a modest project at first, until a staff of teachers was gathered which could integrate the "new" philosophy with the old, orthodox system of education. He decided to erect two buildings as a nucleus. What he needed first, however, was a man to take charge of the undertaking.

In the autumn of 1929 Dr. Brown left his post at Washington and Lee to run for governor of Virginia on the Republican ticket. His defeat was a foregone conclusion unless he could take advantage of the split in the solid South caused by the candidacy on the national ticket in 1928 of Alfred E. Smith. During the campaign Dr. Brown made several speeches in Alexandria and other Virginia towns near Washington. Morton went to Washington, and at a luncheon in the Willard Hotel offered Dr. Brown the job of inaugurating Atlantic University in the event of his defeat in the election.

"I don't know," Dr. Brown said. "Starting a university is expensive."

"Would $50,000 take care of it the first year?" Morton said.

Dr. Brown hesitated.

"$100,000?" Morton said.

"Yes," Dr. Brown said. "I'm sure it could be started on less than that. Of course it depends on what you want—how extensive a curriculum, how experienced a faculty . . . "

"We want the best," Morton said.

They didn't discuss details, since it was necessary, for the sake of good manners, to pretend that Dr. Brown was to be the next governor of Virginia. They left with an understanding, however, and when Dr. Brown was soundly beaten at the polls a few weeks later both got busy. Morton authorized the laying of foundations for two buildings—one for classrooms, one for a dormitory—and Dr. Brown started rounding up a faculty.

Meanwhile, on October 12th, Dr. House died. He had been sick a long time, following a serious illness and years of overwork at the hospital in Hopkinsville. The readings had outlined treatments which kept him active, but offered no hope for anything but alleviation, since his entire system was affected. Late in the summer of 1929 they suggested a trip to Dayton, for treatments by Dr. Lyman A. Lydic, an osteopath who had become interested in the readings and worked with them while Edgar was in Dayton. The treatments were given, and Dr. House responded at first, but suddenly took a turn for the worse and died. He was buried in Hopkinsville, in the Salter family plot. Carrie did not return to the beach. Tommy left Washington and Lee and joined her in Hopkinsville.

The hospital experimented with several osteopaths during the fall. It was impossible at the moment to get a man with both a medical degree and osteopathic training. Ordinary medical doctors were out of the question; they either laughed at the readings or condemned them as quackery. It was an osteopath or nothing.

In January of 1930, Dr. Lydic was induced to abandon his practice and take charge of the hospital. Miss Annie Cayce, Edgar's only unmarried sister, took Carrie's place as housekeeper, and things were on an even keel again. At the beginning of March, Dr. Lydic's chart showed patients receiving treatment for congenital incoordination of mental and physical faculties, ulcers of the stomach, acute gastritis, general pruritis, mucous colitis, spastic paraplegia, tabes dorsalis, optic neuritis with partial blindness, shell shock with its typical manifestations, hysteria, acute osteomyelitis, and several types of gynecological trouble. All were responding in what Dr. Lydic described as "an encouraging manner."

His report was printed in the quarterly magazine of the Association, *The New Tomorrow.* In the same issue—dated April, 1930—the first yearbook of the Association was announced, and subscriptions were offered at one dollar each. In the "News and Views" section of the forty-page periodical it was reported that 210 check readings had been given during the first three months of the year and the calendar was filled until June 1st. It was also reported that President Morton H. Blumenthal, Mrs. Blumenthal, and their son, Morton, Jr., had returned from a six weeks' vacation in southern France. At the hospital the hydrotherapy room had been enlarged, the electrotherapy room had been removed to "more suitable quarters," and a recreation room had been opened in the basement. Headway was being made by the datastician on the job of setting up a system for cross-indexing the readings and extracting from them information on various subjects and specific ailments.

In the spring Dr. Brown moved to the beach, and plans for the university crystallized. It was to open in the fall, without waiting for the erection of buildings. An office was opened in Norfolk to handle inquiries and to register students. Dr. Brown, from the basement of the hospital, sent out catalogues and announced the purpose of the new institution:

"The founders of the university have in mind the establishment of an institution which will eventually be second to none among educational institutions in this country. We are well aware of the fact that it will require some years and a considerable financial outlay to attain to this ideal. At the same time, however, we have definitely determined upon this objective and we shall make every effort to realize it as rapidly as possible.

Naturally, we do not expect the institution ever to reach a stage of completion, but we do hope to make it a center of learning, culture, and research in which all branches of human knowledge and scientific research will sooner or later be represented. In a sense, we shall endeavor to make our own application of the statement of Ezra Cornell, the founder of Cornell University, who expressed his aim thus: 'I would found an institution where any person may obtain instruction in any study.' Similarly, we shall strive to coordinate within the scope of Atlantic University, so far as may be humanly possible, all the branches of knowledge and scientific endeavor which offer any contribution to what has been called 'the amenities of living' and to the worthwhileness of human life.

"We are well aware of the fact that there will be many difficulties in the way of accomplishing our objective. There will doubtless even be those who will openly declare that we are attempting to overshoot the mark. We only bespeak for our plan the open-mindedness which should characterize any enlightened individual, and such cooperation as each interested person feels inclined to give in a sympathetic endeavor to bring to pass the purposes which we have in mind. We do not intend to rival or supplant any existing institution of learning. We desire, on the other hand, to cooperate in every way possible with all existing institutions and agencies of educational and altruistic character, and we invite the same degree of cooperation from them."

The Association announced the university as a supplement to the hospital, "a parallel service for the mind and spirit." Actually there was to be no connection between the Association and the university. Dr. Brown's theory was that scholastic respectability should first be won, after which the subject of psychic phenomena could be taken up in a proper, respectable manner. The university, in fact, was to dwarf the Association and its hospital; it was to be a modern institution of higher learning with a faculty second to none and a complete and elaborate curriculum, especially in the arts.

This was not Morton's original intention. The Association needed a small school where philosophy, metaphysics, psychic phenomena, psychology, and occultism could be studied in an intelligent manner, with facilities for the proper research and laboratory experiments. No such program was in Dr. Brown's outline. He wanted a university like other universities, only a little better. Apparently he sold Morton on this idea, at least temporarily.

Edgar looked askance at the whole project. If a university were to grow from the work it should do so, he thought, as a logical outgrowth of the research program, not as an institution superimposed on the structure of the Association and dwarfing it. According to the plan of Dr. Brown, it was to be just another college, no different from the hundreds of colleges already existing in the country. The idea of a small group of students applying themselves to the study of the readings, and then gradually gathering around them students interested in metaphysics and philosophy, was lost in the grandiose scheme of a big-time school with a high-class faculty and a winning football team.

"What do you make of it?" Edgar asked Hugh Lynn.

"It's not what I expected," Hugh Lynn answered. He had been graduated from Washington and Lee in June and was to be the university's librarian.

Edgar shook his head. He was not so worried about the development of the university itself as he was concerned with its effect on the hospital. Already checks from New York were arriving late. Morton was making remarks about economy and the need for lowering the hospital's budget. Of course, there was a depression abroad—the whole country was in a slough of economic despond. But Morton had stoutly maintained that he was better off than he had been before the stock market crash of the preceding October.

"He can't be," the squire said bluntly. "Nobody else is. I look for trouble, Edgar; especially with the university costing him so much."

"I hope not," Edgar said fervently. "I hope not."

A new building was finished in the hospital grounds that summer, a home for the nurses. Across the boulevard, foundations were laid for the buildings of the university.

The school was to open on September 22nd, in two of the ocean-front hotels which closed after Labor Day. The Old Waverly served as the boys' dormitory; the girls were housed in the New Waverly. The buildings stood side by side at Twenty-second Street. Classes were to be held in office buildings all over the beach; assemblies were scheduled for the Presbyterian church. On the ground floor of the boys' dormitory Hugh Lynn was housed in a temporary library. As opening day approached there were two hundred students enrolled—a remarkable beginning.

Meanwhile members of the board of directors of the Association received notice of a meeting to be held on September 16th, in the Nurses' Home.

"This is it," the squire said. "Something is going to happen."

Edgar was glum. He set out for the meeting with Gertrude and Hugh Lynn.

"Maybe he's going to ditch the university and put all his interest in the hospital," Gertrude said. "I hear he's been having lots of trouble with Dr. Brown."

"Everybody's talking about it," Hugh Lynn said. "Nobody knows what happened, but they think Morton pledged $5,000 a month and Dr. Brown's faculty is going to cost about twice that."

"He has some good men," Gertrude said. "He didn't get them to leave the jobs they had without offering them more money."

Edgar reached for a cigarette to hide his nervousness.

"It's what we don't know that makes it certain we're in for trouble," he said. "Morton used to confide in us. He used to tell us all his plans and thoughts. He's been drifting away from us ever since this university began to take shape."

He held a match to the cigarette.

"If only the school could have waited a few years, until we had an endowment for the hospital," he said.

Morton and Edwin were waiting at the Nurses' Home. As always they were quiet, smiling, immaculately dressed. When the meeting was called to order Morton began to speak. He sketched the history of the hospital in terms of money—his money. When it was opened, it cost him $3,000 a month. Gradually this had been cut down by income from patients. During one month the income from patients had matched the overhead.

Now, however, the hospital owed nearly $10,000 for items of overhead. Obviously there had been waste and extravagance.

Though it was a place of healing, it ought to be run on a more businesslike basis.

Therefore, it was his suggestion that the Association turn the hospital back to him and his brother, with the understanding that the bills would be paid and everything kept running as usual. Would the board vote on this suggestion?

A vote was taken. The members, stunned by the proposal, automatically voted against it. It was defeated. Morton was irritated. He said something about withdrawing all funds and forcing the hospital to close. Edwin spoke about the "seriousness" of the situation and suggested another vote.

Edgar got up to speak.

He looked over the heads of Morton, Edwin, and the other members of the board, as if he were addressing someone who stood beyond them.

"I have every confidence in Mr. Blumenthal," he said. "He built the hospital; he has maintained it. He understands the work I do better than almost anyone else. I am sure he is desirous of continuing the efforts we have so well begun. It would mean very little to me to have the hospital without his cooperation and interest. I suggest the board accede to his request."

Another vote was taken. The proposal won. The meeting adjourned. All the members except Morton and Edwin went to Thirty-fifth Street to ask Edgar what had happened.

"I don't know," he told them. "Maybe Morton is right; maybe we've been inefficient in handling the money. If he thinks so, he has a right to handle it himself. It's his."

"He's in trouble," the squire said. "The depression is getting him."

Edgar didn't answer. He had been aware from the beginning that the hospital and Association were heavy structures to erect on the foundation of one man's whim. Morton had not possessed the money to endow the hospital; he had paid for it out of his winnings in the market, and as these went, so went everything he had built at the beach. The hospital, with its income from patients, might have got by with what help he could offer. The university was apparently the straw that broke the camel's back.

Unless the readings themselves were responsible: physical

readings had so crowded the calendar that Morton's requests
for philosophical guidance had been postponed time and again.
He had grown used to this help and seemed at a loss without it.
When even the Sunday periods were taken by emergency physical
readings, he was cut off from a source of mental food which
had become necessary to him. He had become fascinated by the
subconscious and was attempting to fathom its language by having
his dreams interpreted. He was also delving deeper and deeper
into the metaphysical structure of the universe. To be stopped
in all this must have irritated him.

One thing was certain. The readings had repeatedly told Morton
that knowledge of philosophical truths meant nothing in itself.
The truths had to become part of his life to mean anything. Morton
had ignored this. He had plunged into water that was over his
head, without learning to swim.

"For to know, and not to do, becomes sin," the readings had
said. "Hence in such an approach each should weigh well—
whether there are ulterior motives, or just wonderment, with
little thought or idea of what such information might put upon
him as an individual." Morton had learned a lot, and he had
done something about it in an external way; but there had apparently been little change within himself. When he couldn't
get what he wanted for himself from the readings, he wasn't
enthusiastic about helping others get what they needed.

"Maybe everything will be all right," Edgar said. "Maybe things
will swing upward on the market. Maybe the hospital can make
enough to meet its overhead."

But the depression deepened.

Atlantic University opened, and for the first semester Morton
met all the bills. Then he ceased his support. The hospital continued to run; the outstanding bills were paid, the staff was cut,
and the budget reduced. After January, Dr. Brown endeavored
to keep the university going by his own efforts. He cut all salaries in half, started a movement among Norfolk people to support the school as a local project, and solicited donations wherever
possible. Some of the professors were paid by Morton, because
they had letters from him which confirmed their contracts. For
a time it was rumored that Morton only wanted Dr. Brown's

resignation, after which he would reorganize the school along different lines, resuming his support.

"He's strapped," the squire kept saying. "That's what's the matter. He can't be the only one in Wall Street making money. He must be losing, too."

On February 26, 1931, a meeting of the board of trustees of the Association was held in New York in the offices of the Blumenthal Brothers, at 71 Broadway. Hugh Lynn and Edgar drove up from the beach to attend it. Morton moved that all activities of the Association cease. Hugh Lynn and Edgar didn't vote. The others present—Morton, Edwin, and T. B. Brown— voted yes. The motion was declared carried, though there wasn't a quorum.

Patients at the hospital had already been notified that they would have to leave. On February 28th the staff was paid off and the doors closed.

Morton had told Edgar he could remove any personal items from the building. The first thing he did was arrange to have the files of the readings taken from the basement. When these were safely on their way to Thirty-fifth Street he wandered through the rooms, looking from the windows of each at the sea. Finally he left, carrying with him three things: his mother's picture, Dr. House's picture, and an oil painting of himself which had been presented by the father of one of the patients.

As he walked along the porch to the steps he recalled the words attributed to Talleyrand: "It is worse than a crime—it is a blunder." He could not feel that way about the hospital. In two years it had demonstrated its worth; in the office was a list of patients asking for entrance. Those who received treatment had been helped or cured. The files bulged with affidavits and letters of thanks. A tragedy it might be: conceived in impracticality, executed in haste, abandoned in its hour of victory; but not a mistake.

Gertrude was waiting for him in the car.

"I should never have allowed it to open without being sure it would be kept open," he said when they were out of the driveway and on the boulevard. "If I had held out for that, we'd have won."

"We'll get it back," Gertrude said. "There are lots of people willing to put up money. We can raise a fund and buy it from Morton."

"I'm not so sure," Edgar said.

He was silent until they were nearly home. Then he said, "I've been tested, and I've failed."

It rained that night.

It had to rain. Edgar's tears were not enough to drain the misery in his soul. He needed help from heaven.

20

The meeting was held in the living room of the house on Thirty-fifth Street, on the afternoon of June 6, 1931. Sixty-one people attended, overflowing to the porch and up the stairs. Most of them were from Norfolk or Virginia Beach. None was wealthy, or even influential. Dave Kahn was present, and Dr. Brown, whose university had staggered to the end of its first year.

Edgar opened the meeting and explained its purpose.

"Last winter, when the hospital closed and the Association was dissolved," he said, "I sent a letter to everyone on my mailing list. Each of you received one. In it I asked a question: whether in your opinion another organization should be formed. If this work of mine is worthwhile, I asked you, tell me so. Tell me what, in your opinion, is its value. I don't want to fool myself or anyone else. If it has all been a mistake, I want to quit now, before any more damage is done.

"I received hundreds of replies. They all said the same thing. They urged me to continue the work, to form a new organization, to carry on the program that was begun and abandoned.

"A reading was taken, and the same question was asked. The reading said to leave it to those who had been helped or benefited; if they thought the work was worth continuing, they would continue it.

"That is why this meeting was called. That is why you are here. You have been helped or benefited by the work. You want to see it continue. You want to form a new organization."

He paused, as if there were nothing more to say. Then, slowly, he went on:

"All my life I've wondered what it is that comes through me. It could be of the devil; it could be of God; it could be just foolishness.

"If it were of the devil it would produce evil. To my knowledge it never has produced evil; I know that at times it has refused to do this.

"If it were of God it would produce good. I know that it has done some good; people have told me so. I have seen good come of it for members of my family. You people have seen good come of it, I'm sure, or you wouldn't be here.

"Is it just foolishness then? Would foolishness make a man well if he were sick? Would foolishness make a child walk straight if he were lame?

"I have many memories of the hospital. I saw two men come in on stretchers. I saw them both walk out. I saw a girl come in on crutches. I saw her walk out without them.

"But the thing I will always remember is a summer day when I sat on the porch of the hospital with some friends. A man came out to thank me for a reading I had given for his wife.

"He was a Mennonite. You've seen them around the beach. They are a religious group; they live down in the country; they dress in simple clothes and the men do not shave their beards.

"Well, this one turned to my friends and asked them if they all knew about me and my work. They said they did. Then he asked each one his religion, and each told him. There was an Episcopalian, a Methodist, a Baptist, a Presbyterian, and a Catholic.

"'And you all believe in this man?' he said.

"They said they did. He tapped me on the shoulder and said,

"'That is a great thing.'

"Some of you here today may feel the same way. I hope so. Because it is for that thing—that great thing—that we are considering forming a new Association.

"I can go on giving readings for those who ask for them. I will do that anyhow. I always will, no matter what happens.

"But if it is ever to be anything else; if it is ever to mean anything to groups and masses of people; if it is ever to add one bit—however small—to the goodness of the world or its wisdom; it is up to you and the others who believe in it.

"I'm ready to do my part, and I'll do it as well as I can."

He sat down. Dave got up and told of his sixteen years of experience with the readings.

"They have never let me down. So far as I know they have never let anyone down," he said. "It's the people themselves who have failed."

Others spoke, telling of their interest in the work, the results they had obtained from readings. Dr. Brown suggested a name for the new organization: The Association for Research and Enlightenment. The title was adopted, and officers were elected. The meeting adjourned and a free-for-all pep rally started. Everyone assured Edgar that it wouldn't be long before either the hospital was reopened or a new one built.

In July the new Association was incorporated, with the same specified purpose as its predecessor. In the same month Edgar legally returned to Morton the house on Thirty-fifth Street. Forced to move in midsummer, when places to rent were few and prices high, the family trekked to a lonely house between the Cavalier and Cape Henry, on the ocean front and in full view of the closed hospital. It was a sad safari. Edgar hired a truck and Hugh Lynn, Gray, and Tommy, who had come from Hopkinsville with his mother for a visit, did the moving. They took the chickens first and put up a yard for them. Lastly they brought the precious readings.

Atlantic University meanwhile was conducting a summer session in the high school building at Oceana, a few miles from the beach. Dr. Brown felt that if he could hold some of the students for the summer and keep his movement among the people of Norfolk, Portsmouth, and Princess Anne County active, the idea of getting behind the school as a local project would crystallize and the school could open in the fall.

The summer session was successful. The Atlantic University Association was founded by civic-minded people of the surrounding communities, and the school was able to open. Its football team had a full schedule, there was a school song, a school newspaper—*The Atlantic Log*—and a dramatic organization. But there was practically no money; the biggest asset was enthusiasm. The professors, unpaid, began to suffer for the necessities of life—food, clothing, rent, heat for their homes. They ran up embarrassing bills at the grocery stores; they were forced to accept charity from the residents of the beach. One day a fish market donated a truckload of mackerel, and the auditor of the university made personal deliveries to the wives of the faculty members. They were glad to get the fish.

Edgar discovered that the new Association was in much the same fix as Atlantic University. Its main asset was enthusiasm. People on the whole were friendly; they wanted to be helpful; but they had no money. Businessmen, harassed by the depression, were in no mood for philanthropy. They had but one question: "What can Cayce do to help me in my business?" When they were told that he gave help to the sick or those in spiritual need, they were not interested.

In October, Edgar, Gertrude, and Gladys went to New York to talk things over with their friends and see what could be done. They stayed at the Victoria Hotel, at Seventh Avenue and Fifty-first Street, and gave readings daily for members of the Association. In the evenings, meetings of strategy were held regarding the hospital. The consensus was that a new building, or a fund to purchase the old building, would have to wait.

"This is going to be a long depression," one of the men said gloomily. "It may last ten years."

Edgar shuddered inwardly. He was fifty-four. Would he be alive in ten years?

On November 7th the family was packed and ready to leave for the beach. Two women, residents of the hotel, had for a week been trying to get a reading. All the time had been occupied; Gladys had given them an application blank and told them to fill it out and send it to the Association's office at the beach. The woman who wanted the reading—the other was her companion—said she needed it badly.

Early in the afternoon the Association member who had the reading appointment canceled it. Gladys telephoned the ladies in the hotel and told them they might have the time, if they still wanted it. They came to the suite, the reading was given, and the Cayces were arrested for fortunetelling. The ladies were policewomen.

For Edgar it seemed the end of the world. The road on which he had started with Layne thirty-one years before had come to the destination he had been afraid from the beginning it might reach. He was headed for jail. With Gertrude and Gladys he blinked at the photographer's flash bulbs. The judge sealed the papers in the case and seized the plates of the photographs taken in court to prevent prejudgment by the newspapers. But as they stepped into the street, free on bail, the bulbs flashed again, and that night they saw themselves in the tabloids. Reporters haunted the lobby. They stayed in their rooms, listening to friends who tried to cheer them up. Outwardly, Edgar was calm. He even joked about the situation. Inwardly he was inconsolable.

From the beginning the case was thin. The policewomen had no warrant, they had not been solicited for the reading, and one of them had signed an application blank. She was thus a member of the Association when the reading was given. The blank had disappeared, and the reading itself had been confiscated; even so there was little evidence for the charge preferred. But these facts did nothing to alleviate the misery and worry which settled on the defendants.

Local members of the Association rallied to their support. Lawyers were hired, a postponement was obtained, and when the case finally came to trial in West Side Court on November 16th, an adequate defense had been prepared. Thomas J. Ryan, a brilliant young attorney, appeared to represent them.

The prosecution was prepared for a routine case. Apparently the evidence taken by the policewomen—especially the literature pertaining to the Association—had not even been perused. An assistant from the district attorney's office appeared to prosecute.

Magistrate Francis I. Erwin heard the testimony. The policewoman for whom the reading had been given said she had not signed an application blank, but she could not produce the blank on which Gladys had written her name and address. On cross-examination she admitted that in giving the suggestion Gertrude had said that the subject for the reading sought, not information, but "advice and counsel." Her companion, in answer to a question by the court, admitted that she had been absent from the room for a period of time, during which the missing blank might have been signed.

Gertrude and Gladys testified that the blank had been signed. A statement of the Association's incorporation, its purpose, and its bylaws, was put in evidence. Dave Kahn, as a trustee, testified to the fact that the Association was a philanthropic, nonprofit organization, which was formed to study the readings, and which employed Edgar to work for it. Edgar testified that all money received for readings was paid to the Association.

"You claim you are a psychic?" Magistrate Erwin asked.

"No, sir, I make no claims whatsoever," Edgar said. "May I tell my story?"

"Yes," the magistrate said. "I would like to hear it."

"For thirty-one years," Edgar said, "I have been called or told that I was psychic. It first began as a child. I didn't know what it was. When many people, who had asked me to do things for them, asked for advice and counsel, after it had gone for years, it was investigated by individuals."

"And then the company was formed?" the judge asked.

"This company was formed to study the work," Edgar said.

"And they pay you a salary?"

"They pay me a salary."

"Do you go into a trance?"

"I do not know. I am unconscious."

"You are unconscious?"

"Unconscious. It has been investigated by some scientists. Some call it hypnotic influence, some call it a trance."

There was cross-examination. Then Magistrate Erwin, who had been watching Edgar closely, said, "Step down.

"Put this on the record. After seeing the people's witnesses and the three defendants and their witness on the stand and observing their manner of testifying, and after reading the exhibits in the case, I find as a fact that Mr. Cayce and his codefendants were not pretending to tell fortunes, and that to hold these defendants guilty of a violation of Section 899 of the Code of Criminal Procedure, Subdivision 3, would be an interference with the belief, practice, or usage of an incorporated ecclesiastical governing body, or the duly licensed teachers thereof, and they are discharged."

Gertrude and Gladys wept. Edgar stumbled out of the courtroom listening to Dave say, "I told you they'd never find you guilty!"

That afternoon Hugh Lynn, who had come up from the beach, bundled them into a car and started for home. They drove through the dusk in silence. Gertrude spoke once.

"Edgar, what is an incorporated ecclesiastical governing body?" she asked.

"I don't know," Edgar said, "but it's wonderful."

*   *   *

Back at the beach the family held a council of war. Edgar felt hunted. He was bewildered, uncertain, wondering where the next blow would strike. He didn't understand Morton's attitude; he didn't believe it possible for a man to believe so deeply in a thing and abandon it so casually. He had been stunned by his arrest. Was it another test of his faith in himself or had he in some way offended God? Should he go on, in spite of all obstacles, or cease before he destroyed himself and those he loved? Somehow he felt that he must go on. But toward what goal, now that a new hospital was out of the question?

"I don't seem to understand anything," he said, "or anybody."

Hugh Lynn made a suggestion.

"Maybe there's something wrong with us," he said. "Suppose we stop expecting people to do things for us and start doing them for ourselves. The world doesn't owe us a living because we have a psychic medium in the family; we ought to work for what we get just as everyone else does.

"In the first place, we don't know anything about the thing we're trying to sell. We look at the information as if it were a faucet. Just turn the tap and whatever we want flows out. We were going to give the world our wisdom—the wisdom that came out of the faucet when we turned the tap. We figured that it was our wisdom because we had the faucet.

"We don't know anything about psychic phenomena. We have our own experiences, but we don't know what else has been done in the field.

"What do we know about the Life Readings? Do we know history well enough to check the periods mentioned for people and give them a bibliography—a list of books and articles—

with each reading? Certainly not!

"Do we know enough about philosophy, metaphysics, and comparative religion to check the readings on what is said in these fields?

"When a reading makes a statement and says it is a philosophical truth, do we know what philosophers believed the same thing, and what religions have it in their dogma?

"When a statement about anatomy, or about a disease, or about the use of a medicine or herb is made, do we know whether medical authorities believe the same thing, or condemn it, or know nothing of the matter?

"If a person asked us for everything the readings have said about appendicitis, or ulcers of the stomach, or migraine, or the common cold, or epilepsy, or marriage, or forgiveness of sin, or love, could we produce it? Certainly not. That work was barely begun when the hospital closed.

"I think it would be wise if we stopped looking for large donations, stopped dreaming of another hospital, and concentrated on developing a little stock-in-trade. Then, when the next chance comes, we'll be better prepared, and we won't muff it."

"I don't know how to do that sort of work—" Edgar began.

"You don't have to do it," Hugh Lynn said. "I'll do it. Atlantic University is finished. I'll take over the job of manager of the Association. We'll keep it small; we'll have a modest budget and a modest program.

"We'll work quietly, by ourselves, with the help of the local people who are interested. We'll start study groups. We'll take series of readings on various subjects. We'll build up a library on psychic phenomena.

"Then when people come and ask what we do, we can say something other than that we take two readings a day, send them to people who pay for them, and put copies in our files. That isn't much for an organization that goes around under the name of The Association for Research and Enlightenment."

"It's all yours," Edgar said. "You take it over. I'll just give the readings."

"And worry," Gertrude said.

"I won't worry." A wave of relief swept over him. Not only

was he glad to have a burden lifted from him; he was happy that Hugh Lynn had decided to give himself to the work. More than anything else that proved to Edgar that the thing was worthwhile. His son could not be wrong.

He walked out to the dunes, happy for the first time in many months. It meant so much more than anything in the world to have the people he loved believe in him. And their way was the best way. Not with ostentation, or show, or fanfare, to serve God; but with charity, humility, and grace.

Hugh Lynn was right. They had nothing to offer that would keep a person interested after his wound was healed or his problem solved. They had no knowledge of their own profession; they had never taken inventory of their stock-in-trade. They had better do that. It would keep them busy, so that they could forget the past, and it would give them a future toward which they might work. He returned to the house feeling peaceful, content.

The program was begun right away. By Christmas it was producing results. Hugh Lynn came home waving a book and smiling.

"I've discovered that you're a legitimate child," he said to Edgar. "This is a book on hypnotism. I was reading about Mesmer's experiments. Mesmer didn't actually hypnotize his subjects, you know. Hypnotism was discovered by a follower of Mesmer, the Marquis de Puysegur. He discovered it accidentally in 1784, when he was trying Mesmer's magnetizing procedure on a young shepherd named Victor.

"Victor went into a trance, a sleeping trance, and remained in it for some time. De Puysegur then found that the boy was apparently clairvoyant. He seemed able to diagnose the physical ailments of other people while in this trance! A whole fad was started, and people began to go to somnambulists instead of doctors. The writer of this book says it was a 'wholly erroneous belief' that the somnambulists could diagnose diseases, and the fad died out after the eighteen-twenties.

"But do you realize what that means? The first person ever hypnotized showed the same ability which you have!"

Edgar nodded, half pleased, half puzzled.

"What sort of fellow was he, this Victor?" he asked.

Hugh Lynn referred to the book. "Ordinarily," he said, "he was a dull fellow."

Edgar nodded again. "That would check with me," he said.

Hugh Lynn went on, explaining:

"Hypnotism hasn't advanced any since then. It is continually being investigated, damned, and exploited. Apparently the boys missed the boat over a hundred years ago; they abandoned the kind of things you do, and it's been lost ever since. But we'll show them! We've got records to prove that we're right and they're wrong!"

"Maybe," Edgar said. "Records don't mean much to these fellows if they don't want to believe what the records say."

He took the book and read the pages from which Hugh Lynn had been quoting.

"It says that after the eighteen-twenties the fad died out," he said. "Looks as if it might die out after the nineteen-twenties, too."

Hugh Lynn shook his head. "Not a chance," he said. "Say, I wonder where this Victor is now? If he's on earth he'd be useful. We could use him as your assistant."

His father smiled. He remembered when his son did not believe in reincarnation.

* * *

Christmas was a tragedy for Atlantic University. Students and professors, knowing the school could not go on, shook hands like soldiers who had come to the end of a lost cause. Dr. Brown, who had housed and fed some of the teachers and given all his personal assets to the school, admitted defeat. The university closed its doors.

Hugh Lynn, freed of his duties as librarian, decided to start a monthly bulletin, as a means of keeping in touch with the members of the Association. He bought a secondhand mimeograph machine and got to work. For material he briefed readings on subjects of general interest, summarized interesting cases, wrote reviews of books on psychic subjects, quoted health hints from readings, and reported news of psychic phenomena in other fields.

A study group was formed in Norfolk to meet once a week. It chose for its subject, "How to Develop Psychic Powers," but the first reading pointed out that psychic powers are attributes of the soul and in the normal development of an individuality blossom as a result of an ascending consciousness, moving toward the subconscious and superconscious—away from time and space. There was black magic, it said, but white magic was only virtue and wisdom, the two weapons of faith.

The reading pointed out that there was little to be gained by a series of dissertations on soul development, if nothing was done actively by the group. It suggested that an outline be given, and with this as a basis for discussion, the group create a set of lessons, each working on a certain aspect, and one or two doing the synthesizing and writing. The information would then criticize the work. A new lesson was not to be undertaken until the one in hand was completed to the satisfaction of the information.

The wisdom of the suggestion was apparent when the group attempted to write its first lesson on prayer. It took months and months of labor before the information accepted it. "Now," said the reading, "practice it." One of the lessons that followed—the one on spirit—took more than a year. The definition of patience which the group worked out reflected the things it was learning.

"Through patience we learn to know ourselves; we learn to measure and test our ideals, to use faith, to seek understanding through virtue. All spiritual attributes are embraced in patience. In patience possess ye your soul."

It was patience that Edgar fell back on during those days. The ocean-front house was drafty, expensive, and too close to the water in time of storm. In March the family moved to a secluded spot at the south end of the beach, on a small fresh-water lake that lay within two hundred yards of the sea. In April the house was sold and they were asked to leave. In May they took a house on the opposite shore of the lake, on the bend of road joining Arctic Avenue and Fourteenth Street. There were no houses on either side of it, the lake was at its back, and across the street was the Star of the Sea Catholic Church.

Edgar liked the place. It was central to town, yet secluded; the lake was stocked with fish, and there was plenty of room for a garden. With the help of friends he bought the place, on a long-term, small-payment plan. It was here, in June, 1932, that the first annual congress of the Association was held.

The congress was a result of the success of the bulletin. During the year Hugh Lynn had been able, by the enthusiastic response to his publication, to clear the mailing list of all but those who were genuinely interested in the work and in psychic phenomena. With some three hundred members as a basis, he decided to test the practicality of a forum on psychic subjects. He chose the latter part of June, when the beach was naturally an attractive spot, but the hotels were not filled and summer rates—those in existence from July 4th to Labor Day—were not in effect. He procured speakers on various subjects: symbology, auras, numerology, modern trends in metaphysics, etc. He arranged for a series of public readings by Edgar. The result was gratifying. Attendance was large, and all were intelligently interested in what went on.

The congress was fertile soil for the study group idea. Members went away with copies of the first lessons and organized clubs in their towns and cities to study them.

Hugh Lynn's program expanded during the second year. He published some case studies—detailed reports of illnesses, including excerpts from the readings, letters from the patients, and statements from those administering the treatments. He also published papers on reincarnation, sources of psychic phenomena, and historical periods as described in the Life Readings.

A record was kept of everything untoward which happened during the readings. Edgar's attitude was noted, his remarks immediately before and after the reading were taken down, and the attitude of the person getting the reading—so far as it could be ascertained—was noted.

The time of the readings had always been the same: 10:30 in the morning and 3:30 in the afternoon. The suggestions had long been standard. For a physical reading Gertrude said, as Edgar's eyes closed:

"Now the body is assuming its normal forces, and will be

able, and will give, such information as is desired of it at the present time. The body physically will be perfectly normal, and will give that information now.

"Now you have before you the body of——who is located at——. You will go over this body carefully, examine it thoroughly, and tell me the conditions you find at the present time; giving the cause of the existing conditions, also suggestions for help and relief for this body. You will speak distinctly, at a normal rate of speech. You will answer the questions I will ask."

If check readings were to be taken, she would say, "You will give more than one reading at this time." For a Life Reading she said:

"You will have before you [name and place of individual at birth], and you will give the relation of this entity and the Universe, and the Universal Forces, giving the conditions that are as personalities, latent and exhibited, in the present life. Also the former appearances in the earth's plane, giving time, place, and the name, and that in that life which built or retarded the development for the entity, giving the abilities of the present entity and that to which it may attain, and how.

"You will answer the questions which I will ask regarding this entity. You will speak distinctly, at a normal rate of speech."

When Edgar said, "We are through for the present," she said:

"Now the body will be so equalized as to overcome all those things that might hinder or prevent it from being and giving its best mental, spiritual and physical self.

"The body physical will create within the system those properties necessary to cause the eliminations to be so increased as to bring the best normal physical conditions for the body.

"The mental will so give that impression to the system as to build the best moral, mental and physical forces for this body.

"The circulation will be so equalized as to remove strain from all centers of the nerve system, as to allow the organs of the system to assimilate and secrete properly those conditions necessary for normal conditions of this body.

"The nerve supplies of the whole body will assume their normal forces; the vitality will be stored in them, through the application of the physical being, as well as of the spiritual elements in the physical forces of the body.

"Now, perfectly normal, and perfectly balanced, you will wake up."

This was the pattern, and there was seldom any change in it. Edgar loosened his collar, cuffs, shoes and belt, lay down, and in a few minutes was asleep. On waking he ordinarily felt well, but craved something to eat: not much, but a cracker, or glass of milk, to take away the empty feeling in his stomach.

Sometimes, in going over the name and address of the subject of the reading, he contributed side remarks: "Pretty place here"; "that's a tall tree"; "he's not here now, but he's on his way—we'll wait"; "just finished reading a letter, he's looking at the clock"; "this is the same address we just had—there are two Jordans here—which do we want?" "She's here, on the porch—almost an invalid." In Life Readings he always went back over the years to the birth year. In doing this he sometimes offered comment: "'29, '28, '27, '26—changes here, '25, '24, '23—accident, badly hurt, '22, '21 . . . "

These things were checked with the subjects of the readings (most of whom were not present) and eventually Hugh Lynn was able to present the data in a study entitled, "100 Cases of Clairvoyance."

Also noted were the attitudes of the others concerned—Gertrude and Gladys and the guests, if any—and the comparative clarity and excellence of the reading itself. From this it became obvious that the two most important factors for a good reading were a genuine desire to get help on the part of the subject and an equally genuine desire to give help on Edgar's part. Gertrude's ideal attitude was passive, sympathetic, and receptive.

A second study group of local people took a series of readings on the glands, from a philosophical and metaphysical standpoint. They discovered, among other things, the existence of a gland unknown to science—the lyden—located above the gonads, and the point of entrance of the life force into the body.

At least the information said so. That was the catch. The results of the research were worthless outside the Association. They had no credence with any but those who believed in the readings.

This cry Hugh Lynn heard from doctors, professors, psychologists, and scientists: "All your records are your own. They were not made under test conditions." Hugh Lynn realized that the records of most doctors, professors, psychologists and scientists were their own, but there was a difference. Psychic phenomena were suspect. Mediums were considered to be no more honest than jailbirds. They had to be watched.

A reading was taken to discover the best method of scientifically observing the phenomenon. The information said that if a student would come to the beach and watch the readings day by day, examine the mail, both incoming and outgoing, and check up with the patients and their physicians, the work would be proved.

"But only," it said, "to that one man. He cannot convince others. For, what is wrong with the world today? Man has forgotten his God. He remembers only himself.

"So, if you would prove anything, first so live that your own life is an example, a testimony, that God is the God of truth, and the law is One."

Hugh Lynn was perplexed. He wanted to approach the scientists, especially the psychologists, but it was obvious that they were going to be hard nuts to crack.

"Better leave them alone," Edgar advised. "The more I sit out on my pier and catch fish from the lake, the more I think we'd be just like those fish if we went to the scientists. We'd be grabbing at their bait—the chance to be considered respectable—and we'd be hooked. There's enough food for us in our home waters. We'd better stay in them."

One day Hugh Lynn came out to visit him on the pier. He was carrying a large book, battered and obviously very old.

"This may help us with the scientists," he said. "It's a book I've been trying to get for a long time. Someone told me about it. It's the story of a man who lived in this country and did exactly the thing you do, less than a hundred years ago."

Edgar put down his fishing pole and grabbed the book. He read its title: *"The Principles of Nature, Her Divine Revelations, and A Voice to Mankind.* By and Through Andrew Jackson Davis, The Poughkeepsie Seer and Clairvoyant. Published by S. S. Lyon, and Wm. Fishbough. New York: For Sale, Wholesale and Retail, by J. S. Redfield, Clinton Hall. 1847."

21

Andrew Jackson Davis was born in Bloominggrove, Orange County, New York, on August 11, 1826. His father was a shoemaker; his mother, who died when he was young, was "one of those gentle beings whose supreme delight it is to mingle in scenes of sickness and sorrow, and to administer to the relief of suffering humanity." The family was poor, and the parents were not inclined to consider education a necessity for their son; his formal schooling was limited to five months. He worked at various jobs from early boyhood, being employed for several summers as a cattle tender by a Mr. W. W. Woodworth of Hyde Park. At the time the family was living in Hyde Park.

In September of 1838 father and son—the mother was then dead—moved to Poughkeepsie, where Mr. Davis set up a shoemaking shop and was assisted by Andrew. In 1841 Andrew went to work for Mr. Ira Armstrong, who reported to William Fishbough, the transcriber of the Davis book, as follows:

> I had occasion for the services of a boy somewhat acquainted with the shoe trade, and employed him for a fortnight to assist me. During this time, I was so much pleased with his good sense and industry, that, upon his own solicitation and the wish of his father, I took him as an apprentice. His education barely amounted to a knowledge of reading, writing, and the rudiments of arithmetic. His reading was exceedingly limited, and confined to that of a light and juvenile description. During his two years of apprenticeship, he established a character for faithfulness and integrity not to be surpassed, and which is seldom equaled.

While Andrew was serving Mr. Armstrong, a lecturer on

mesmerism came to town. He demonstrated on various members of the audience, but failed to have any success with Andrew. After the lecturer, a Mr. Grimes, had left, several local men began experimenting with the phenomenon. One, a tailor named William Levingston, had some success. One day Andrew wandered into Levingston's shop, and the tailor, remembering the lecturer's failure, asked for permission to try his luck at magnetizing the boy. Andrew consented.

The experiment was quite as successful as that of de Puysegur with Victor, the shepherd boy. Andrew fell into a deep trance and showed remarkable powers of clairvoyance. The experiment was repeated, the boy became a center of interest in Poughkeepsie, and "Mr. Levingston's house was for months the common resort of the curious who were indiscriminately invited to come and witness the experiments." The boy was put to all sorts of tests, which he passed, but finally he said, while in a trance, that his powers were to be used to help the sick.

Thereafter Mr. Levingston took him about the countryside and built up a medical practice. Eventually the pair reached Danbury, Connecticut, and Bridgeport, in the same state. There they met Dr. S. S. Lyon, who "had previously been an unbeliever in clairvoyance, but the evidence of its truth, as presented in the case of young Davis, proved too powerful for him to resist; and under a deep conviction of its importance, he did not hesitate to render it his open encouragement, and to avail himself of the clairvoyant's advice in treatment of some difficult cases of disease then under his charge."

That was in February, 1845. During the following May, Davis and Levingston met, in Bridgeport, William Fishbough. About the first of the following August the clairvoyant, having previously announced that he was to begin a series of readings on the cosmos and the destiny of man, chose Dr. Lyon as the conductor and Mr. Fishbough as the scribe. The readings were given in New York, and there were one hundred and fifty-seven of them in all, given between November 28, 1845, and January 25, 1847, a period of fourteen months. In the same year the results were published by Dr. Lyon and Mr. Fishbough.

Thus went the story of Andrew Jackson Davis, as told in Mr.

Fishbough's introduction to *The Principles of Nature, Her Divine Revelations, and A Voice to Mankind*.

Edgar, reading the small type, with Hugh Lynn peering over his shoulder, had a queer feeling.

"This sounds so much like me it gives me the creeps," he said.

They looked at the steel engraving of Andrew which occupied the frontispiece and read Mr. Fishbough's description of his appearance.

"He is of ordinary stature, with a well-proportioned physical frame, possessing a bilious-sanguine temperament. His features are prominent, and his head is of the medium size, and very smoothly developed, especially in the frontal and coronal regions. The base of the brain is small, except in the region of the perceptives, which are prominent. The head is covered with a profusion of jet-black hair. The expression of his countenance is mild, placid, and indicative of a peculiar degree of frankness and benevolence; and from his eyes beam forth a peculiar radiance which we have never witnessed in any other person."

Edgar stared at the steel engraving again. Andrew was dressed in the style of the period, with a bow tie and a satin-lapeled jacket. "He's a nice-looking lad," he said. "Whatever became of him?"

"His career is remarkable," Hugh Lynn said. "He continued to give readings for thirty-five years after the appearance of this 782-page book. Then he decided to study medicine. When he was sixty years old he received his degree and began to practice."

Edgar was browsing through the book.

"How did he diagnose his patient's trouble after he became a doctor?" he asked.

"He made the usual inquiries," Hugh Lynn said, "but he got most of his information by placing the tips of his fingers against the palm of the patient's hand. Apparently the mechanism of his clairvoyance had changed. He no longer had to go to sleep to become sensitive."

"He touched the patient," Edgar said. "That is psychometry."

"He lived to be a very old man," Hugh Lynn said. "He was

eighty-four when he died. This was his first book, but he wrote many more. They are out of print and their author seems to have been forgotten except by students of psychic phenomena and a small group of enthusiasts. But I understand the group is growing. Perhaps Andrew is in for a revival."

Edgar went back to the steel engraving, staring at it.

"How did he do it?" he asked. "How often did he give his readings?"

"Twice a day," Hugh Lynn said. "He used a magnetizer: that is, his conductor made passes at him; and he lay on his side while talking. Otherwise there seems to have been no difference between his method and yours."

Edgar closed the book and ran his fingers over the worn, black cover. On the edge of the binding, in gold letters, was the legend, "Revelations & C. By A. J. Davis The Clairvoyant."

Almost a hundred years ago some men had hoped to change the world with Davis and this book. Now the book was a collector's item, and Davis, though he had lived long, written much, and healed many, was all but forgotten.

"Well, at least you are not alone," Hugh Lynn said. "You have Andrew and Victor the shepherd boy, and hundreds of others whose cases have been recorded. But Andrew is most important, for the scientists will have to pay attention when they find that another man did precisely what you are doing, right here in America."

Edgar shook his head.

"If you had this fellow and Victor the shepherd boy and me lined up in the same room," he said, "and we all gave readings on the same case and agreed, and a doctor whom the scientists trusted went with them to the bedside of the sick man, and made a diagnosis, and said we were right, do you know what would happen? The scientists would hang the doctor as a fraud and a fake and run us out of town."

He handed the book to Hugh Lynn and went back to his fishing.

"Let Andrew and Victor and me rest in peace," he said.

* * *

In the fall of 1935, Edgar Evans Cayce entered Duke University to take up the study of electrical engineering. Edgar and Hugh Lynn drove him to Durham, North Carolina, and while there went to see Dr. J. B. Rhine of the Department of Psychology, who was then conducting his famous experiments in telepathy. They found him a pleasant person; he seemed interested in their story.

The following March, Dr. Lucian H. Warner, acting as a special investigator for Duke, spent a week at the beach, listening to readings and getting a few himself. He was enthusiastic, and because of his report Dr. Rhine in April secured a reading for his small daughter. He reported that the diagnosis did not seem to fit her condition, and his interest cooled.

In June, Dr. Warner arranged for a series of readings to be given for Dr. Gardner Murphy of the Department of Psychology of Columbia University in New York. The subjects were to be examined in New York while readings were given on them at the beach. The names and addresses were to be sent to the beach by special delivery letter, leaving New York the day before the reading.

Two letters were sent; two readings were given. Meanwhile Dr. Warner was taken ill and the work was turned over to one of Dr. Murphy's assistants, who sent no letters and made no reports on the readings given.

"I told you so," Edgar said to Hugh Lynn.

Several of Dr. Warner's readings were on telepathy. He asked for a theory, and the information said it was a matter of soul development; that communication took place when two minds reached a state of consciousness above time and space. In such cases both perceived the same thing, with their subconscious minds—their individualities. One took it from his conscious mind; the other perceived it and transmitted it to his conscious mind.

Some were good receivers and poor senders, some were good senders and poor receivers. People attuned through love and understanding transmitted thoughts to one another without conscious knowledge of it.

Pathologically, the information explained, there were "eugenics" that produced in the blood plasm vibratory rates that made reception and sending possible.

"What would be the pulse rate, the heartbeat, the vibratory forces of the body-influence itself?

"Those in which the ratio of cycles about each of the red corpuscles is one to three. Those whose body-vibratory forces are $87\frac{7}{10}$. Those having a pulse rate ranging the normal of 72 to $78\frac{6}{10}$."

In December, 1935, the family had another brush with the law. They were visiting in Detroit, and Edgar gave a reading for one of his hosts' friends. The reading was for a little girl, but the girl's father had not been consulted in the matter. It was a violation of the Association's bylaws, in fact, but the desire to help the child overcame this obstacle. The reading was given to the father, who took it to a doctor. The doctor disagreed on the treatment outlined; the father then went to the police. The family was arrested for practicing medicine without a license.

The letter of the law had, in fact, been violated, but the law was reluctant in its prosecution. The charges against the other participants were dropped, Edgar was found guilty, and paroled in custody of himself. There was no sentence or fine.

The year 1935 was a lamentable one for the Cayces. In April, Gertrude's mother, Mrs. Evans, died. In November, Health Home Remedies was incorporated by some of the New York members of the Association. Its function was twofold: to make available to members the mechanical appliances suggested so often in readings, and to manufacture and attempt to market nationally some of the remedies which over a period of years the information had specified for certain troubles. An office was opened in Norfolk and Tommy House was made manager.

The remedies selected for experimentation were Ipsab, a specific for bleeding gums and pyorrhoea, and Tim, an ointment for hemorrhoids. Readings were taken to perfect commercial formulae for these, and Tommy took the products to doctors and dentists for testing. He built wet cell and radioactive appliances for people for whom they were prescribed by readings, and kept reports on the results.

It was uphill work, and trouble came from an unexpected source. People receiving first physical readings which suggested the use of one or more of the products of Health Home Remedies were inclined to suspect that it was all a racket—Health Home Remedies had all the appearance of a company set up to sell things recommended by the readings, at a profit to itself and the Association.

Tommy discovered that the dental and medical organizations were in no hurry to give their approval to Ipsab and Tim, despite the long list of successful cases he had compiled. The corporation's funds dwindled; it sank into inactivity. The office was abandoned; Health Home Remedies became a sore subject with Hugh Lynn, who found himself forced to become a carpenter and chemist, building appliances for those who had to have them.

The cellar of the Cayce house became a laboratory. Tommy, who was preparing to return to Hopkinsville, showed his cousin how to build the batteries.

"The ingredients in this wet cell appliance cost a little over $18," he said. "By the time you've shipped it, the cost is $19. If you get paid, the price is $20. You get a dollar, maybe, for your labor."

"No wonder the corporation went broke," Hugh Lynn said.

"Most people complain about the price," Tommy said. "They say it's too high. I explain that we only make a few appliances, as a convenience to members, and the ingredients are expensive when bought in small quantities."

"What do they say to that?" Hugh Lynn asked.

"They say the price is too high," Tommy said.

Hugh Lynn picked up a hammer.

"We're learning," he said.

"Learning what?" Tommy said.

"Not to make mistakes," Hugh Lynn said.

He swung the hammer and hit one of his fingers.

*   *   *

The years whirled on. Hugh Lynn's files bulged with case histories, parallel studies in psychic phenomena, and research readings given for the study groups. Still the scientists showed no interest. Those who came to discuss, to argue, to learn were those already convinced of clairvoyance, of reincarnation, of karma. Some of these were psychologists by profession; a few were psychiatrists; but they were careful to keep such private beliefs out of their professional theory and practice.

"The time isn't ready for people as a whole to believe such things," Hugh Lynn told his father one day. "But I'm convinced that it will arrive before too long. Our job is to be ready for it."

Edgar agreed. "When the time comes, they will approach us," he said. "But remember this. We don't want people marching in here and saying, 'All right. I'm ready. Prove this thing to me.' We want people who come in humility and with good manners and say, 'I'd like to know what this is all about. Will you teach me?' Our job is to have something ready for those people."

Gradually Hugh Lynn realized that the best evidence of the consistency of the readings lay in the records of families whose members for many years had used Edgar as a family doctor. Frank Mohr's family was one of these: his niece, her husband, and their child had all had readings. Dave Kahn's family was another. His mother was kept alive, active, and without pain for seventeen years after the readings—which prescribed her treatments all this time—had agreed with the doctors that she was suffering from an incurable disease. Dave's sisters and brothers, their children and his, all were treated by readings. When Dave's youngest son fell and thrust the blades of a pair of scissors into his eye, the readings outlined treatments that were accurately and successfully followed, so that the cataract which formed was absorbed.

Perhaps the best family record was that of the Houses—Carrie, Dr. House, and Tommy. Since the collapse of Health Home Remedies, Tommy had lived in Hopkinsville. He married a Virginia Beach girl, and a daughter, Caroline, was born to them in September, 1939. When Caroline was scarcely a year old she pulled a pan of boiling water from the stove and emptied it over herself. Tommy telephoned Edgar, and an emergency reading was given immediately. The treatments were followed and Caroline escaped without a scar and without damage to her eye, which at first seemed badly affected.

When she was almost two, Caroline began to stammer and had consistent trouble in digesting her food. A reading said she had been slightly injured in a fall: there was pressure in the area of the second, third, and fourth cervicals. Osteopathic treatments, massage, diet, and an eliminant were prescribed. On September 30, 1941, Tommy wrote to Edgar:

"Just a note to tell you that we received Caroline's reading and have started the treatments. Dr. B—— has had some trouble getting Caroline to be still long enough to give her a complete treatment, but nevertheless she is responding nicely thus far. Her stuttering is very much improved, but she is still bothered with a bronchial condition which causes considerable coughing. Her general condition has improved a lot."

Another valuable source of evidence was the daily mail.

An average day's mail, chosen at random from the files for September, 1941, produced letters from the following:

A young woman, in Washington, D.C., who was cured by the readings of lead poisoning caused by a depilatory (since removed from the market by the Bureau of Pure Foods and Drugs). She had been overworking, felt tired, and asked for a check reading.

A woman in Pittsburgh who became interested in the work because of her studies of symbology. She obtained a physical reading and was writing to check up on the connections for a mechanical appliance, to be certain she had made them correctly.

The mother of a girl in Dayton, Ohio, who was cured of a complicated attack of arthritis, the treatments lasting five years. The mother, taking treatments for a certain ailment, reported general progress, but the recurrence of a specific pain. She quoted a letter from her daughter, who, away on a vacation, was frightened by a snake and "jumped at least eight feet." She also asked for a reading for her own mother, a woman of eighty.

The wife of a naval officer who met Edgar while she was living in Norfolk, and who had had some readings. Now living in New London she wrote to say she had formed a study group there and wanted a physical reading for a friend.

A young lady in New Hampshire, who verified an appointment for a physical reading. She sent the name and address of the doctor who had agreed to cooperate in giving the treatments.

A man in Darien, Connecticut, whose daughter had received a check reading a few days before. He reported that she was out of pain and improving rapidly.

A man in Washington, D. C., who asked for a copy of the *Congress Bulletin*. His mother, for whom physical readings had been given, was feeling better.

A young woman in Boston, Massachusetts, whose Life Reading had caused her to change careers, to her happiness. She asked for a Life Reading for a younger brother, who "is all mixed up."

A man in Delaware, Ohio, who had been referred to Edgar by a certain doctor. He asked for a physical reading for his wife.

A couple in New York, who, on the verge of divorce, decided to give marriage another chance after a joint reading. They announced that a baby was on the way.

A woman in Roanoke, Virginia, who had received her first physical reading. She reported her pleasure at the diagnosis. She had been suffering for years; the reading promised relief.

A lady in Guilford, Connecticut, who asked for literature concerning the work.

A man in Youngstown, Ohio, who canceled an appointment for a physical reading and set a new date.

There was also a telegram from Dave Kahn, saying that he was in Washington on business and would be at the beach next day for a visit.

The daily mail was Edgar's particular delight. It was proof to him that "here a little, there a little, thought upon thought, line upon line, stone upon stone," his work did not fail and that, as a reading once told him, "Every sincere try is counted to you for righteousness." This, with the work of the Association, which makes it possible for those who are interested to participate in a spiritual labor, was the answer to his dreams: the city of healing had arisen, but it was built by hearts, not hands. He understood that.

*   *   *

The activities of the Association remained, in accordance with the plan adopted in 1931, unostentatious and unpublicized, even to the meetings of the congress. Members raised a building fund for an office, library and vault, and these were erected in 1940, but they were incorporated into a single unit which was added to the Cayce residence, and there was not even a sign to guide the visitor to them.

The new building was a monument to the sincerity of the study groups and the perseverance of the family in its effort to justify the readings. It was paid for by small contributions: nickels, dimes, and quarters, piling up over a long period of time. Some of the groups contributed their dues; other groups voted, as individuals, to give a percentage of their salaries and wages over a certain period of time. Edgar worked as a carpenter on the job; he hung the doors and windows, painted the exterior and interior, and laid the walk leading to the entrance.

In the library the local groups held their meetings. One of these, which gathered on Tuesday nights, studied the Bible, with Edgar as teacher. It began with six students and soon increased to thirty.

The Association had an average membership of between five and six hundred. There was a turnover of about half of these from year to year; the other half remained as a solid basis for the Association's research work: an audience for the case studies, pamphlets, bulletins, and the *Congress Bulletin*, a combined yearbook and record of the speeches and readings given at the annual meetings. There was a mailing list of several thousand people who were interested in anything that pertained to Edgar. They never forgot him, apparently. Hugh Lynn discovered that among the six hundred readings during a certain year, forty-three were for people whose first reading had been obtained five years previously, thirteen were for people whose first reading had been obtained ten years previously, six were for people whose first reading had been obtained fifteen years previously, and eight were for people whose first reading had been obtained twenty years previously.

One day late in the summer of 1941, Edgar received a telephone call from a man in New York. He did not recognize either the voice or the name.

"I'm the fellow in the bank in Dayton, who lent you a hundred dollars in 1924," the man said. "Remember me now?"

"Very well," Edgar said.

"I'm not after the money," the man said. "You paid that. But I'm in trouble, and I want a reading."

Members of the Association were drawn from all of the Protestant churches; from the Roman, Greek, Syrian, and Armenian Catholic churches; from the ranks of Theosophy, Christian Science, and Spiritualism; and from many of the Oriental religions. Acceptance of the readings, of course, implied acceptance of Christianity, since the dominant note of all philosophical and moral disquisitions by the readings is the Christ pattern as the ideal of mankind.

"If it makes you a better member of your church, then it's good; if it takes you away from your church, it's bad," Edgar told a new member of one of the study groups, who asked him whether a belief in the readings would affect her position as a member of one of the Protestant churches.

Hugh Lynn's program had not been entirely fulfilled. To complete his evidence he needed sponsored readings on specific diseases and conditions, taking them generally, without reference to a particular patient. The budget of the Association was so small that there was no margin for a series of readings on cancer, old age, heart ailments, asthma, etc. The readings were to be sold to maintain sufficient income; only by selling such a series to a sponsor could it be got. There were sponsors available, but in view of the hopelessness of the task of convincing doctors that a remedy suggested by the readings might be efficacious, they preferred to investigate such subjects as the life of Christ before His ministry, the symbology of the Book of Revelation, and the story of the world before history began.

In the field of philosophy and metaphysics there was need for an extensive system of cross-indexing and checking, to match what the readings said against what had been said by theologians, heretics, and teachers of religion and morals in all countries and at all times. The readings have been as democratic in this respect as in medicine: "Wherever the Law of One has been taught, there truth has lived."

It is a stern set of ethics that emerges from the readings. No lukewarm embracing of theological virtues will satisfy them. They insist on perfection as the goal, and every misstep must be retraced, every injury undone, every injustice rectified. The newer, lenient interpretations of Christianity are not tolerated. Marriage, for instance, is treated as the Roman Catholic Church treats it, though the readings give a different reason for this attitude from that of the church Fathers. "Work it out now," say the readings, "or you will have to meet it later." Only in extreme circumstances, similar to those under which the Catholic Church grants annulment, do the readings advise divorce. Then one of the parties is usually hopelessly at fault, while the other is bearing an unreasonable burden. Usually the reading will say, speaking of the one who is attempting to cooperate and hold things together, "This has been met by the entity; the debt is paid."

The art of living that has emerged from the readings has one great danger. It attracts only those who are ready to measure up to an ideal path of existence, but it offers these same people the temptation of a new religious organization, a new philosophical system. Against this the readings continually warn. The end toward which they should all work is not something new and select, but something old and universal: this is the sum and burden of their labor. In the words of a reading:

"The ideals and purposes of the Association for Research and Enlightenment, Inc., are not to function as another schism or ism. Keep away from that! For these warnings have been given again and again. Less and less of personality, more and more of God and Christ in dealings with the fellow man.

"To be sure, those phases of the activity of the Association in the material plane must take concrete evidence and present concrete evidence of its being grounded in mental and spiritual truth. But not that it is to build up any organization that is to be as a schism or a cult or ism, or to build up money or wealth or fame or position, or an office that is to function in opposition with any already organized group.

"How did thy Master work? In the church, in the synagogue, in the field, in the lakes, upon the sands and the mountains, in the temple! And did He defy those? Did He set up anything different? Did He condemn the law even of the Roman, or the Jews, or the Essenes, or the Sadducees, or any of the cults or isms of the day? All, He gave, are as ONE . . . under the law! And grudges, schisms, isms, cults, must become as naught; that thy Guide, the Way, the Master, yea even Christ . . . as manifested in Jesus of Nazareth . . . may be made known to thy fellow man!

"So, in thy considerations, seek ye to know more and more of how each organization has its counterpart bodily, mentally, spiritually, and guidance may be given thee.

"Ye have an organization then with a physical being, with a mental being, with a spiritual concept. And only that which is not merely idealistic but in keeping with God's, Christ's precepts, Jesus' anointings, may be that which may grow and become as a living thing in the experience, in the bodies, in the minds; yea to the very awareness of the souls of men whom such a group, such an organization would serve.

"In the bodily functioning, then, the activities are to have due and proper consideration, to be sure. But let each phase of the work present how not only mentally but spiritually there is a grounding in truth, as is set forth in the Christ Consciousness as exemplified by Jesus, as has been proclaimed by many of the saints of old.

"And then ye may be very sure that all of those influences from the spiritual realm are one. For whether it be as ye have seen at times, the Lord of the Way or the Christ Himself as Jesus, or others be sent as an aid, depends upon whether ye hold that ideal that is One with the Universal Truth for and to man."

22

Through the 1930s Edgar Cayce lived quietly. Each day there were a few visitors, but they were part of the pattern; without them he would have been lonely. Except for his journey to church each Sunday and an occasional visit to the movies or the barbershop, he stayed at home working in his garden, fishing, or manufacturing something in the shop he built for himself behind the garage.

Each day he got up early and watched the sun rise out of the ocean. By its light he read the Bible. Usually he got his own breakfast, because he preferred his own version of coffee—hot, black, and strong. When weather permitted he worked outside until the mail came. His garden was extensive and he had a green thumb; anything would grow for him, in profusion. As a fisherman he was average. There was no magic in his rod, but the little lake behind the house was so well stocked with fish that he always caught a few. In late summer he engaged in his hobby of canning and preserving. By September the cellar shelves were crowded with the products of his art, but by spring he had given most of them away; his hand was prodigal with those he loved. The families he held in highest esteem received an example of his ultimate skill, a jar of brandied peaches. The morning mail arrived about ten, and when it was read the first reading of the day was taken. Afterward he worked at his typewriter, answering letters. Lunch was at one. Usually it was a light meal. When it was finished he returned to the typewriter and stayed there until he was caught up with his correspondence. When the afternoon reading was finished he went out to fish, to work in the garden, or to spend a few hours at his carpenter's bench. Dinner was at six, and he ate heartily, finishing with a cup of the same hot, black, strong coffee with which he had begun the day. In the evening he read a newspaper, listened to the radio, and played double solitaire or Russian bank with Gertrude. At eleven they listened to the news bulletins; then they went to bed. When there were visitors he talked with them in the long living room that faced the ocean and ended against an old-fashioned fireplace. If they came with troubles, he listened and did his best to give them hope; if they were to have readings, he told them stories that gave them faith in the information they were about to receive. They did not come in great numbers, but there was a steady trickle: the crippled, the malformed, the defective, the hopelessly ill, the nervously sick. Often they returned when they were well, and those were the times when he was happiest; then he listened to their stories of what the readings could do.

A listener to all of these tales was Polly, an ancient parrot full of wickedness and noise, who served a long term in the Navy and was given to Edgar by a friend. Polly was unmannerly. Often she would punctuate someone's tall tale with "Tsk, tsk," or whistle a long sigh of relief when a particularly tedious yarn was ended. She was devoted to her master and never interrupted him.

Whistling was her accomplishment; she whistled at all sailors who passed and at most pretty girls, sometimes throwing in a leering "Helloooo!" at the latter. She imitated any whistling she heard; association with Hugh Lynn provided her with a large repertoire of popular songs, which she faithfully reproduced, off key and out of tune. Occasionally she was allowed to leave her cage on the porch and enjoy the freedom of the living room. Once, on an autumn day, she flew into the large armchair by the fireplace and went to sleep.

It was dusk, Edgar was upstairs, and no lights were turned on. Two men came to the door and asked to see Mr. Cayce. They had heard something about him and wanted to find out exactly what he did. Gertrude showed them into the living room. They sat at the far end, which was still illuminated by daylight. At the other end, in the shadows, Polly was aroused from her nap by the noise.

"What do you want?" she said sharply.

Edgar came down the stairs just as the men were going out the front door. He reassured them, turned on the lights, and put

Polly back in her cage.

His other pets were two canaries, whose cage was in his office, far from Polly. They often sang during the readings, but it seemed to please rather than disturb him. For a while there was a big rabbit in the back yard, the gift of a friend, but one day a lame boy came to get a reading, and when he left he carried the rabbit with him.

Each summer Carrie came for a visit and usually Tommy, his wife, and their daughter Caroline accompanied her. Edgar's sisters came, too, and friends in New York, Washington, Selma, and other places made a habit of spending their vacations at Virginia Beach. The Squire died on April 11, 1937, while on a visit to one of his daughters in Nashville, Tennessee. He was buried at Hopkinsville by the side of his wife. After the funeral Edgar went to the old farm for a visit and walked through the woods until he came to the bend in the creek at the willows. There he said a prayer for his mother and father.

In June, 1939, Edgar Evans was graduated from Duke. He accepted a position with the Virginia Electric Power Company in Norfolk and lived at home. During that summer the family was happier, more united, than ever before. The Association was growing steadily and gaining strength. Plans were drawn for a new wing for the house, to contain a library and a set of offices. Construction was begun in 1940 and completed in 1941. In September of that year the building was dedicated, and the first reading was given in Edgar's office, a sunlit room overlooking the lake.

Twenty-two years before, when President Woodrow Wilson was in Paris setting up the machinery for the League of Nations, a reading had said: "Christ will sit with the American delegation at Versailles. If the purpose for which its leader has gone there is accomplished, the world will experience a millennium. If it is not accomplished, there will be another and greater world war, which will make the one just ended seem small. It will begin about 1940, and the same forces will begin the trouble." It was not an extraordinary forecast; men with no psychic powers whatever made the same prediction and were accurate even about the year in which the conflict would begin. But now in

September, 1939, the battle had been joined. An increasing number of people came for readings or requested them by mail. Early in 1941 Edgar Evans entered the army as a private. Later he became an officer and eventually rose to the rank of captain. Virginia Beach became the site of two Army camps, and the Navy, strongly entrenched in Norfolk even in peacetime, mushroomed until its units were distributed throughout Princess Anne County. Hugh Lynn supervised Virginia Beach's program of recreation for soldiers until the United Service Organization was able to take over. He then joined the special services division of the army, and with General Patton's tanks followed the war to its end in Germany.

Both boys married, Hugh Lynn in 1941, Edgar Evans in 1942. By the end of 1943 Edgar had two grandsons. Hugh Lynn's son, Charles Thomas Cayce, was born in October, 1942. His cousin, Evans Cayce, appeared a year later. Both boys came to visit their grandfather every day while their fathers were overseas.

In March, 1943, the first edition of *There Is a River* appeared. The mail began to mount and the telephone rang incessantly. The office force had to be increased and the mailman finally was unable to carry the stacks of letters. Gertrude had to go to the post office and bring them back in the car. With Hugh Lynn gone Edgar had to take over the job of examining the letters and dictating answers to them. The pattern of his day changed drastically. He lengthened his sleeping periods every morning and afternoon, and gave from four to six readings a day instead of two.

His hobbies were forgotten, his garden neglected. The bass in the lake jumped flirtatiously, but he had no time for them. Immediately after breakfast he began dictating, and this continued until it was time for the reading. Frequently he remained asleep for two hours, until 12:30. Lunch was at one. The afternoon was devoted to the mail. After the second reading period the list of applications was examined and appointments were made. If there was time left before dinner it was used for dictating, and after dinner work continued until 9:30 or 10. From June, 1943, to June, 1944, 1,385 readings were given. By August, 1944, the strain was so great that Edgar collapsed. He rallied his strength to give a reading for himself. Its instructions were simple and to the point. He was to go away and rest. For how long? "Until he is well or dead." He went to the mountains of Virginia, to Roanoke. Gertrude went with him. For a time he seemed to improve. He wrote letters to friends; he was cheerful about the future and full of plans for the expansion of the Association after the war. In September he suffered a stroke.

He came home in November, riding through the autumn-stained countryside where his ancestors fought against Cornwallis. In the house on Arctic Crescent he lay in his bed, looking out on the lake and the ocean. At 7:15 o'clock on the evening of January 3, 1945, he passed away. A few hours before, rousing from a sleep, he said: "How much the world needs God today." He was buried in Hopkinsville, in the family plot.

Three months later Gertrude was laid beside him. She died on Easter Sunday at sunrise. Thus ended the love story which almost half a century before had begun on a summer night when the world was a flower-strewn field, and the future was young in their arms.

*   *   *

With the death of Edgar the work of the Association began in earnest. In the files at Virginia Beach are over 14,000 readings. No other psychic has left so long and so large a record of his powers. The research staff, extracting from them what is of interest to the sciences and professions, and what is helpful for people in general, continues the work of classifying and compiling the material in its various categories, and integrating and formulating the theory and metaphysic that underlie the structure of the phenomena. The results are disseminated through the Association publications, and the members, whose number continues to increase, are the recipients of the essence of the material that issued from the subconscious of Edgar Cayce in the long period between the 31st of March, 1901, and the 17th of September, 1944. All of this information makes clear the stature and the meaning of Edgar Cayce.

Philosophy

The system of metaphysical thought which emerges from the readings of Edgar Cayce is a Christianized version of the mystery religions of ancient Egypt, Chaldea, Persia, India, and Greece. It fits the figure of Christ into the tradition of one God for all people, and places Him in His proper place, at the apex of the philosophical structure; He is the capstone of the pyramid.

The complex symbology employed by the mystery religions has survived fragmentarily in Christianity, notably in church architecture and in the sacrifice of the Mass, with its sacramental cup. But the continuity of the tradition of the one God has been lost. Paganism is condemned alike by religious authorities, archaeologists, and historians as an idolatrous fancy devoted to the worship of false gods.

Such was not the understanding of early Christians. Certainly the Essenes, who prepared Mary, selected Joseph, and taught Jesus, were initiates of the mysteries. Jesus said He came to fulfill the law, and part of that law was the cabala, the secret doctrine of the Jews—their version of the mysteries. Such converts to Jesus' teachings as Nicodemus and Joseph of Arimathea were undoubtedly learned in the cabala. So, no doubt, was Paul.

The mysteries were concerned with man's problem of freeing his soul from the world. In the mystery symbologies the earth was always represented as the underworld, and the soul was lost in this underworld until freed from it by wisdom, faith, and understanding. Persephone, for instance, was abducted by Pluto, Lord of Hades. Persephone is the soul of man, whose true home is in the heavens.

The mystery religions were, then, a preparation for the coming of Jesus. He was the fruit of their efforts, and His message was a fuller revelation to the people at large of the mysteries themselves. In the scramble which Christianity made to establish itself as the dominant religion of the decaying Roman Empire, the mysteries were denied their proper place, since to grant that they had truth in them would justify their further existence.

"The early Christians used every means possible to conceal the pagan origin of their symbols, doctrines, and rituals," Manly Hall says.* "They either destroyed the sacred books of other peoples among whom they settled or made them inaccessible to students of comparative philosophy, apparently believing that in this way they could stamp out all record of the pre-Christian origin of their doctrines."

It is interesting to speculate on the fact that Edgar Cayce was raised in strict nineteenth-century Bible tradition, and suffered the greatest mental and emotional shock of his life when he discovered that in his psychic readings he declared the truth of the mysteries and acclaimed Jesus as their crowning glory.

Up to that time Mr. Cayce had never heard of the mystery religions. Yet his readings check with everything about them that is known to be authentic. Much that he has given is not found in surviving records. Whether it is new material or was known to initiates of the mysteries cannot be checked except by the readings themselves. They say that all initiates, from the beginning of time, have known the full truth.

To describe the system of the readings in full, with its comparisons and parallels with the mysteries, would require a book in itself. For readers of this volume the following outline, containing all the essential points and some of the details, has been prepared.

*   *   *

Man demands a beginning and a boundary, so in the beginning there was a sea of spirit, and it filled all space. It was static, content, aware of itself, a giant resting on the bosom of its thought, contemplating that which it was.

An Encyclopedic Outline of Masonic, Hermetic, Qabbalistic and Rosacrucian Symbolical Philosophy, by Manly P. Hall. The Philosophical Research Society Press, Los Angels, Calif., sixth edition, 1936.

Then it moved. It withdrew into itself, until all space was empty, and that which had filled it was shining from its center, a restless, seething mind. This was the individuality of the spirit; this was what it discovered itself to be when it awakened; this was God.

God desired to express Himself, and He desired companionship. Therefore, He projected from Himself the cosmos and souls. The cosmos was built with the tools which man calls music, arithmetic, and geometry: harmony, system, and balance. The building blocks were all of the same material, which man calls the life essence. It was a power sent out from God, a primary ray, as man thinks of it, which by changing the length of its wave and the rate of its vibration became a pattern of differing forms, substance, and movement. This created the law of diversity which supplied endless designs for the pattern. God played on this law of diversity as a person plays on a piano, producing melodies and arranging them in a symphony.

Each design carried within it, inherently, the plan of its evolution, which was to be accomplished by movement, growth, or, as man calls it, change. This corresponds to the sound of a note struck on a piano. The sounds of several notes unite to make a chord; chords in turn become phrases; phrases become melodies; melodies intermingle and move back and forth, across and between and around each other, to make a symphony. The music ends as it began, leaving emptiness, but between the beginning and the finish there has been glorious beauty and a great experience.

(The terms "light," "heat," and "electricity" with regard to the cosmos are of no use in this type of discussion, since they are effects observed sensorily, within the earth's atmosphere. The human senses do not operate outside the earth's atmosphere: the sun might be, to the surviving individuality, an idea, an influence, or an angel.)

Everything moved, changed, and assumed its design in various states of form and substance. Activity was begun and maintained by the law of attraction and repulsion: positive and negative, attracting each other and repelling themselves, maintained the form and action of all things.

All this was a part of God, an expression of His thought. Mind was the force which propelled and perpetuated it: mind did everything God imagined; everything that came into being was an aspect, a posture, of mind.

Souls were created for companionship with God. The pattern used was that of God Himself: spirit, mind, individuality; cause, action, effect. First there had been spirit; then there had been the action which withdrew spirit into itself; then there had been the resulting individuality of God.

In building the soul there was spirit, with its knowledge of identity with God; there was the active principle of mind; and there was the ability to experience the activity of mind separately from God.

Thus a new individual, issuing from and dependent upon God, but aware of an existence apart from Him, came into being. To the new individual there was given, necessarily, the power to choose and direct its own activity; without free will it would remain a part of the individuality of God. Mind, issuing as a force from God, would naturally fulfill His thoughts, unless directed otherwise. The power to do this—to direct otherwise the force of mind—is what man calls his free will. The record of this free will is the soul. The soul began with the first expression which free will made of its power, through the force of mind. The first thought which it generated of itself, the first diversion of mind force from its normal path, was the beginning of the soul.

The nucleus of the soul was in balance, positive and negative force in equal power, producing harmonious activity: the positive initiating, impregnating, thrusting forward; the negative receiving, nourishing, ejecting. The steps of this action were the stages of thought: perception, reflection, opinion.

Thus the soul consisted of two states of consciousness: that of the spirit, bearing a knowledge of its identity with God, and that of the new individual, bearing a knowledge of everything it experienced.

The plan for the soul was a cycle of experience, unlimited in scope and duration, in which the new individual would come to know creation in all its aspects, at the discretion of will. The cycle would be completed when the desire of will was no longer different from the thought of God. The consciousness of the new individual would then merge with its spiritual consciousness of identity with God, and the soul would return to its source as the companion it was intended to be.

In this state the soul would retain its consciousness of a separate individuality and would be aware that of its own free will it now acted as a part of God, not diverting mind force because it was in agreement with the action toward which this force was directed. Until this state was reached the soul would not be a companion in the true sense of the word.

(The idea that a return to God means a loss of individuality is paradoxical, since God is aware of everything that happens and must therefore be aware of the consciousness of each individual. Thus the return of the soul is the return of the image to that which imagined it, and the consciousness of an individual—its record, written in mind—could not be destroyed without destroying part of God Himself. When a soul returns to God it becomes aware of itself not only as a part of God, but as a part of every other soul, and everything.

(What is lost is the ego—the desire to do other than the will of God. When the soul returns to God the ego is voluntarily relinquished; this is the symbology of the crucifixion.)

The plan for the soul included experience of all creation, but it did not necessarily mean identification with and participation in all forms and substance. Nor did it mean interference in creation by souls. It did not mean that they were to spin their own little worlds, twisting and bending laws to make images of their dreams.

But these things could happen. The soul was the greatest thing that was made; it had free will. Once free will was given, God did nothing to curb it; however it acted, it had to act within Him; by whatever route, it had to return to Him.

(The fact that man's body is a speck of dust on a small planet leads to the illusion that man himself is a small creation. The measure of the soul is the limitless activity of mind and the grandeur of imagination.)

At first there was little difference between the consciousness of the new individual and its consciousness of identity with God.

Free will merely watched the flow of mind, somewhat as man watches his fancy disport in daydreams, marveling at its power and versatility. Then it began to exercise itself, imitating and paralleling what mind was doing. Gradually it acquired experience, becoming a complementary rather than an imitative force. It helped to extend, modify, and regulate creation. It grew, as did Jesus, in "wisdom and beauty."

Certain souls became bemused with their own power and began to experiment with it. They mingled with the dust of the stars and the winds of the spheres, feeling them, becoming part of them. One result of this was an unbalancing of the positive-negative force, by accentuating one or the other; to feel things demanded the negative force; to express through things, and direct and manage them, required the positive force. Another result was the gradual weakening of the link between the two states of consciousness—that of the spirit and that of the individual. The individual became more concerned with, and aware of, his own creations than God's. This was the fall in spirit or the revolt of the angels.

To move into a portion of creation and become part of it, a soul had to assume a new or third aspect of consciousness—a method of experiencing that portion of creation and translating it into the basic substance of mind by means of thought. Man refers to this aspect of awareness as his "conscious mind." It is the device by which he experiences earth: physical body, five senses, glandular and nervous systems. In other worlds, in other systems, the device differed. Only the range and variation of man's own thoughts can give an idea of the number of these other worlds and systems and the aspects of divine mind which they represent.

When a soul took on the consciousness of a portion of creation it separated itself temporarily from the consciousness of its own individuality and became even further removed from the consciousness of its spirit. Thus, instead of helping to direct the flow of creation and contributing to it, it found itself in the stream, drifting along with it. The farther it went from shore, the more it succumbed to the pull of the current and the more difficult was the task of getting back to land.

Each of the systems of stars and planets represented, in this manner, a temptation to the souls. Each had its plan and moved toward it through the activity of a constant stream of mind. When a soul leaped into this stream (by immersing itself in the system through which the stream was flowing), it had the force of the current to contend with, and its free will was hampered. It was very easy, under these circumstances, to drift with the current.

(Each system also represented an opportunity for development, advancement, and growth toward the ideal of complete companionship with God—the position of co-creator in the vast system of universal mind.)

The solar system attracted souls, and since each system is a single expression, with its planets as integral parts, the earth came into the path of souls.

(The planets of the solar system represent the dimensions of consciousness of the system—its consciousness as a whole. There are eight dimensions to the consciousness of the system. The earth is the third dimension.)

The earth was an expression of divine mind with its own laws, its own plan, its own evolution. Souls, longing to feel the beauty of the seas, the winds, the forest, the flowers, mixed with them and expressed themselves through them. They also mingled with the animals and made, in imitation of them, thought forms: they played at creating; they imitated God. But it was a playing, an imitating, that interfered with what had already been set in motion, and thus the stream of mind carrying out the plan for earth gradually drew souls into its current. They had to go along with it in the bodies they had themselves created.

They were strange bodies: mixtures of animals, a patchwork of ideas about what it would be pleasant to enjoy in flesh. Down through the ages fables of centaurs, Cyclops, etc., have persisted as a relic of this beginning of the soul's tenancy of earth.

Sex already existed in the animal kingdom, but the souls, in their thought forms, were androgynous. To experience sex they created thought forms for companions, isolating the negative force in a separate structure, retaining the positive within themselves. This objectification is what man calls Lilith, the first woman.

This entanglement of souls in what man calls matter was a probability from the beginning, but God did not know when it would happen until the souls, of their own choice, had caused it to happen.

(Of the souls which God created—and He created all souls in the beginning; none has been made since—only a comparative few have come into the experience of the solar system, though many have gone through or are going through a similar entanglement in other systems.)

A way of escape for the souls which were entangled in matter was prepared. A form was chosen to be a vehicle for the soul on earth, and the way was made for souls to enter earth and experience it as part of their cycle. Of the forms already existing on earth one of the anthropoid apes most nearly approached the necessary pattern. Souls descended on these apes—hovering above and about them rather than inhabiting them—and influenced them to move toward a different goal from the simple one they had been pursuing. They came down out of the trees, built fires, made tools, lived in communities, and began to communicate with each other. Swiftly, even as man measures time, they lost their animal look, shed bodily hair, and took on refinements of manner and habit.

All this was done by the souls, working through glands, until the body of the ape was an objectification—in the third dimension of the solar system—of the soul that hovered above it. Then the soul descended into the body and earth had a new inhabitant: man.

He appeared as a consciousness within an animal, a consciousness which was felt on the earth in five different places at the same time, as the five races. The white race appeared in the Caucasus, the Carpathians, and Persia. The yellow race appeared in what is now the Gobi Desert. The black race appeared in the Sudan and upper west Africa; the red race appeared in Atlantis; the brown race appeared in the Andes.

(The Pacific coast of South America was then the western coast of Lemuria. The Atlantic seaboard of the United States comprised the lowlands of Atlantis. Persia and the Caucasus were rich lands—the Garden of Eden. The poles of the earth as we know them today were tropical and semitropical. The Nile emptied into the Atlantic Ocean. The Sahara was fertile and inhabited. The Mississippi basin was part of the ocean.)

The problem was to overcome the attractions of earth to the extent that the soul would be as free in the body as out of it. Only when the body was no longer a hindrance to the free expression of the soul would the cycle of earth be finished.

(In a smaller field this was the drama of free will and creation. In a still smaller field each atom of the physical body, being a world in itself, is a drama of free will and creation. The soul puts life into each atom, and each atom is a reflection in flesh of the soul's pattern.)

There were males and females in these new, pure races, and both had complete souls. Eve replaced Lilith and became a complement to Adam—the ideal companion for the threefold life on earth: physical, mental, and spiritual. In Eve the positive pole was suppressed and the negative pole expressed; in Adam the negative pole was suppressed, the positive expressed.

(Which a soul would become—male or female—was a matter of choice, unless the soul was already entangled and unbalanced. Eventually the positive and negative forces would have to be brought into balance, so there was not, basically, more advantage in one than in the other. For souls in balance it was a device to be employed for the duration of the earth cycle, and whichever sex would best suit the problems to be attacked was chosen. It was a voluntary assumption of an attitude, not a fall into error, and once a sex was assumed it was generally retained through the cycle of earth lives, though it could be changed from life to life, if the change were considered advantageous. Awareness of sex was retained between lives but could only be expressed on earth.)

Man became aware, with the advent of his consciousness, that sex meant something more to him than to the animals. It was the door by which new souls entered the earth, a door unnecessary elsewhere in the system. It was the only means the trapped souls had of getting out of their predicament—by being reborn through the bodies of souls which had entered the earth through choice. These bodies were not entangled with animals or thought forms. They represented the ideal vehicle for the soul on earth.

Therefore sex was a creative power which could be used for good or evil. Used rightly, the race would be kept pure, the earth would be a paradise for souls in perfect bodies, the trapped souls could be freed of their cycle of rebirth in monstrous, half-animal forms and provided with perfect bodies.

(This is the story of Adam and Eve, the serpent, and the apple. The serpent, wisdom, offered the fruit of the tree of knowledge of good and evil. Eve, the negative, receptive force, took and fostered it. When Adam, the active force, partook of it, the peaceful animal life of man was ended.)

The plan for the earth cycle of souls was a series of incarnations, interlarded with periods of dwelling in other dimensions of consciousness in the system—the planets, until every thought and every action of the physical body, with its five senses and conscious mind, was in accord with the plan originally laid out for the soul. When the body was no longer a hindrance to the free expression of the soul—when the conscious mind had merged with the subconscious, and the atomic structure of the body could be controlled so that the soul was as free in it as out of it—the earth cycle was finished and the soul could go on to new adventures. This conquest of the physical body could not be attained until there was perfection in the other dimensions of consciousness in the system, for these made up, with the earth, the total expression of the sun and its satellites. Whichever state of consciousness the soul assumed became the focal point of activity. The other states of consciousness receded to the position of urges and influences.

The race of man was fostered by a soul which had completed its experience of creation and returned to God, becoming a companion to Him and a co-creator. This is the soul man knows as the Christ.

The Christ soul was interested in the plight of its brother souls trapped in earth, and after supervising the influx of the pure races, it took form itself, from time to time, to act as a leader for the people.

Though at first the souls but lightly inhabited bodies and remembered their identities, gradually, life after life, they descended into earthiness, into less mentality, less consciousness of the mind force. They remembered their true selves only in dreams, in stories and fables handed down from one generation to another. Religion came into being: a ritual of longing for lost memories. The arts were born: music, numbers, and geometry. These were brought to earth by the incoming souls; gradually their heavenly source was forgotten, and they had to be written down, learned, and taught to each new generation.

Finally man was left with a conscious mind definitely separated from his own individuality. (He now calls this individuality the subconscious mind; his awareness of earth is the conscious mind.) The subconscious mind influenced the conscious mind—gave it, in fact, its stature, breadth, and quality. It became the body under the suit of clothes. Only in sleep was it disrobed.

With his conscious mind man reasoned (for all mind, left to itself, will work out the plans of God). He built up theories for what he felt—but no longer knew—to be true. Philosophy and theology resulted. He began to look around him and discover, in the earth, secrets which he carried within himself but could no longer reach with his consciousness. The result was science.

The plan of man went into action. Downward he went from heavenly knowledge to mystical dreams, revealed religions, philosophy and theology, until the bottom was reached and he only believed what he could see and feel and prove in terms of his conscious mind. Then he began to fight his way upward, using the only tools he had left: suffering, patience, faith, and the power of mind.

Atlantis and Lemuria sank; civilizations rose and fell; man was here a little better, there a little worse. He descended to the depths of earth consciousness, then slowly began to climb back. In earthly seasons it was a long journey from the moment when the first soul, looking down through the trees, saw a violet and wanted to pluck it, to the instant when the last soul should leave its body forever.

The Christ soul helped man. As Enoch, as Melchizedek, it took on flesh, to teach and lead. (Since it was to be active it had to be male.) Enoch and Melchizedek were not born, did not die.

The Christ soul realized after these assumptions of flesh that it was necessary to set a pattern for man, to show him the way back to himself. It assumed this task and was born of woman, beginning voluntarily a new individuality, a new soul record; though behind this new individuality shone the pure Christ soul. But on this the veil dropped, and the Son of God began His pilgrimage. He was born as Joseph, again as Joshua, again as Jeshua—the scribe of Enoch who rewrote the Bible—and finally as Jesus. He, Jesus, triumphant over death and the body, became the way, laying down the ego of the will, accepting the crucifixion, returning to God. He is the pattern we are to follow.

(At present man is in a state of great spiritual darkness—the darkness which precedes dawn. He has carried his skepticism to the point where it is forcing him to conclusions he knows intuitively are wrong. At the same time he has carried his investigation of natural phenomena to the point where it is disproving all it seemed to prove in the beginning. Free will is finding that all roads lead finally to the same destination. Science, theology, and philosophy, having no desire to join forces, are approaching a point of merger. Skepticism faces destruction by its own hand.)

Man is at all times the total of what he has been and done, what he has fought and defended, what he has hated and loved. In the three-dimensional consciousness of earth every atom of his physical body is a reflection of his soul—a crystallization of his individuality. His emotional and nervous structures, his mental abilities, his aptitudes, his aversions and preferences, his fears, his follies, his ambitions, his character, are the sum of what he has done with his free will since it was given to him. So every personality—the earthly cloak of an individuality—is different from every other personality.

This has been true from the beginning. The first independent thought of each soul was a little different from the first independent thought of every other soul.

So people are different in their likes and dislikes, in their desires and dreams. The law of karma—cause and effect—likewise makes them different in their joys and sorrows, in their handicaps, their strengths, their weaknesses, their virtues and vices, their appreciation of beauty, and their comprehension of truth. Debts incurred in the flesh must be met in the flesh: natural law, not man or God, demands an eye for an eye, a tooth for a tooth.

The same law applies to groups of people as they act together. There is karma for families, for tribes, for races, for nations. When the souls who committed a war return to a nation, a war will be committed upon that nation. Only when defeat is endured by a nation with humility and understanding, only when victory is dispensed by a nation with justice and mercy, will the karma of battle be lifted from them.

Every person's life is shaped to some extent by karma: his own, that of his associates and loved ones, that of his nation and race, and that of the world itself. But these, singly or together, are not greater than free will. It is what the person does about these influences and urges, how he reacts to them, that makes a difference in his soul development. Because of karma some things are more probable than others, but so long as there is free will anything is possible.

Thus free will and predestination coexist in a person. His past experiences limit him in probability and incline him in certain directions, but free will can always draw the sword from the stone.

No soul takes on flesh without a general plan for the experience ahead. The personality expressed through the body is one of many which the individuality might have assumed. Its job is to work on one or several phases of the karma of the individuality. No task is undertaken which is too much for the personality to which it is assigned—or which chooses it. (Some souls choose their own entrances and set their own tasks; others, having made too many mistakes and become dangerously subject to earthly appetites, are sent back by law at a time and under circumstances best suited to help them.) The task is seldom perfectly fulfilled, and sometimes it is badly neglected.

Choice of incarnation is usually made at conception, when the channel for expression is opened by the parents. A pattern is made by the mingling of the soul patterns of the parents. This sets up certain conditions of karma. A soul whose own karma approximates these conditions will be attracted by the opportunity presented. Since the pattern will not be exactly his own, he must consider taking on some of the karma of the parents—relatively—in order to use the channel. This concerns environment, companionship with the parents, and certain marks of physiognomy.

Things other than pattern concern the soul in its selection of a body: coming situations in history, former associations with the parents, the incarnation, at about the same time, of souls it wishes to be with and with whom it has problems to work out. In some cases the parents are the whole cause of a soul's return—the child will be devoted to them and remain close to them until their death. In other cases the parents are used as a means to an end—the child will leave home early and be about its business.

The soul may occupy the body as early as six months before birth, or as late as a month after birth, though in the latter case it has been hovering over the body since birth, deciding whether or not to occupy it. Once the decision is made and the occupation completed, the veil drops between the new personality and the soul, and the earthly record of the child begins. (The fact that a baby is born dead does not mean that it was refused as a vehicle for a soul. Just the opposite is true: the channel is withdrawn from the soul; no occupation is possible.)

The body is formed in the womb according to the pattern made by the mingling of the life forces of the parents, each with its respective pattern. This is the metaphysical symbolism of the 47th problem of Euclid, the Pythagorean theorem: the square of the hypotenuse of a right triangle is equal to the sum of the squares of the other two sides. As soon as occupation by a soul takes place, the pattern of the soul begins to work its way through the body, and the child's personality begins.

The personality is a highlighted portion of the individuality, experiencing three-dimensional consciousness. The rest of the individuality remains in shadow, giving tone to the personality; urges, appreciation, tastes, avocations, and what is loosely termed "charm"—the background to which intuition responds.

The personality is shaped by three or four incarnations, the portions of the earthly experience on which the individuality wants to work. The emotions and talents of the person reflect these incarnations. The dreams, visions, meditations—the deep, closely guarded self-consciousness of the personality is the pattern of experience among the other states of consciousness of the solar system. The intellect is, roughly speaking, from the stars: it is the mind force of the soul, conditioned by its previous experience in creation outside the solar system, and dimmed or brightened by its recent experiences within the solar system.

Thus a personality is only an aspect of an individuality. A soul, deciding to experience earth again, might assume any of several personalities, each of which would express a portion of itself. As a soul approaches completion of the solar cycle, the personality becomes more many-sided, expressing greater portions of the individuality. This is because each incarnation has less adverse karma, requiring less attention. Finally the personality is a complete expression of the individuality, and the cycle is completed.

(As an individuality succumbs to earthiness, abandoning intellect for emotion and emotion for sensuality, it becomes more and more one-sided.)

The incarnations which influence the personality reflect their patterns in the person's life. Sometimes they intermingle: a child's parents may re-create the environment of one experience, while his playmates will re-create the environment of another. Sometimes the influences work in periods: home and childhood may re-create the conditions of one incarnation, school and college those of another, marriage those of a third, and a career those of a fourth. Usually the people and the problems of the incarnations have interlocking relationships, so that the pattern of the personality's experience is a rational development, and the problems are presented to him as he is prepared to meet them. Because the incarnations only reflect their problems (their blessings as well as their handicaps), usually the karma of more than one can be undertaken in a single life; if the life is successful, considerable progress is made toward freedom from flesh.

When a life is finished the personality vanishes. Its pattern is absorbed into the individuality. Its record is retained, but it becomes a part of the individuality, which at all times is the sum total of what it has been: all it has thought; all it has experienced; all it has eaten, drunk, and felt through the ages.

(Here is an example of how extremes may meet. Both the atheist and the Christian seem to be right. The atheist says the personality does not survive after death; the Christian says the soul is judged after death and returns to its Creator. Substituting personality for soul, both are expressing a truth. The personality is judged, returns to its creator—the individuality—and is absorbed, giving up its own independent existence.)

The general plan for perfecting the individuality in its experience of the solar system then proceeds. Another state or consciousness is assumed, as a trial or as a means of reinforcing the character of a future personality.

So the problems of individualities, the problems of groups, the problems of races and nations, are worked upon time and again until, by free will, they are solved, and the souls go on to other worlds, other systems, other universes. The readings say:

"Know that thyself, in its physical state, is a part of the plan of salvation, of righteousness, of truth, of the Creative Forces, or God, in the earth.

"Each person is a corpuscle in the body of that force called God.

"Each person is a manifestation of the Creative Forces in action in the earth. Each person finds himself with a body that seeks expression of itself, and a mind capable of becoming aware of what the body presents, what other men present, and what influences are acting upon the body and upon the mind itself.

"Each soul enters the material plane not by chance, but through the grace, the mercy, of a loving Father; that the soul may, through its own choice, work out those faults, those fancies, which prevent its communion and atonement with the Creative Forces.

"As to whether a soul is developed or retarded during a particular life depends on what the person holds as its ideal, and what it does in its mental and material relationships about that ideal.

"Life is a purposeful experience, and the place in which a person finds himself is one in which he may use his present abilities, faults, failures, virtues, in fulfilling the purpose for which the soul decided to manifest in the three-dimensional plane.

"Know in thyself that there are immutable laws, and the universe about thyself is directed by laws set in motion from the beginning.

"So, as ye condemn, so are ye condemned. As ye forgive, so may ye be forgiven. As ye do unto the least of thy brethren, so ye do it unto thy Maker. These are laws; these are truths; they are unfailing. And because He may often appear slow in meting out results does not alter or change the law. An error, a fault, a failure, must be met. Though the heavens, the earth, may pass away, His word will not pass away. His word is the way, the truth, the light. Each soul must pay to the last jot or tittle.

"How can ye do His bidding?

"Not in mighty deeds of valor, not in exaltation of thy knowledge or power; but in the gentleness of the things of the spirit: love, kindness, long-suffering, patience; these thy Elder Brother, the Christ, has shown thee . . . that thou, applying them in thy associations with thy fellow man day by day, here a little, there a little, may become one with Him as He has destined that thou shouldst be! Wilt thou separate thyself? For there is nothing in earth, in heaven, in hell, that may separate thee from the love of thy God, of thy brother, save thyself.

"Then, be up and doing; knowing that as thou hast met in life those things that would exalt thy personal self—these ye must lose in gentleness, in patience. For in patience ye become aware of your soul; your individuality lost in Him; your personality shining as that which is motivated by the individuality of thy Lord and Master. Thus does your destiny lie within yourself, and the destiny of the world.

"Hold fast to that faith exemplified in thy meditation, in thy counsels, in thy giving out to thy fellow man. For he that hides himself in the service of his fellow man through the gifts, through the promises as are in Him, hides many of the faults that have made him afraid through his experience in the earth. For it is not what one counts as knowledge that is important, nor what one would attain in material realms, but what one does about that which is known as constructive forces and influences in the experience of thyself and thy fellow man. For, as He has given, 'As ye do it unto others, ye do it unto Me.' He is the way, the life, the light. He is the Creator; He is the giver of all good and perfect gifts. Man may sow, man may act in material manifestations, in matter, of spiritual forces . . . yet the returns, the increase, must come from and through Him who is the gift of life. It is not a consideration of where or even how the seed of truth in Him is sown; for He gives the increase if it is sown in humbleness of spirit, in sincerity of purpose, with an eye-single that He may be glorified in and among thy fellow man. This is the way, this is the manner that He would have thee follow.

"Let thyself, then, become more and more a channel through which His manifestations in the earth may arise, through thy efforts, in the hearts, the minds, of thy fellow man. For mind—in man, to man—is the builder, ever. That, then, must be directed, given, lost in singleness of purpose, that there may come the greater awakening within the consciousness of thy fellow man that he is in the earth; that His words are as lights to men in dark places, to those that are weak, to those who stumble. For He will give thy efforts that necessary force, that necessary power, to quicken even those that are asleep in their own self-ishness, in their own self-indulgences, and bring to their awakening that which will make for glorious activities in the earth.

"Keep, then, the faith thou hast had in Him; for He is thy strength, He is thy bulwark; He is thy Elder Brother. In Him, ye may find that which will bring to thee, and others, joy, peace, happiness, and that which makes men not afraid. For He is peace; not as men count peace, not as men count happiness, but in that harmonious manner in which life, the expression of the Father in the earth, is one . . . even as He is one.

"Keep the faith."

Case Histories

The six case histories which follow illustrate the methodology of the psychic readings of Edgar Cayce in diagnosing and prescribing for physical ailments and disturbances. They do not, however, give an idea of the scope of the readings. That can be reckoned only by the measure of human misery itself. Every conceivable kind of trouble has been brought to the Cayce door since that Sunday afternoon nearly forty-three years ago when he first illustrated his powers of clairvoyance.

Generally speaking, Edgar Cayce's patients are his friends. People invariably like him, and once they have met him, they do not forget him. Sometimes it is difficult for the newcomer to dissociate the impersonal information of the reading from the warm, friendly character of the medium. This is the point which Mr. Cayce, in explaining himself, first brings up and continues to emphasize until the listener understands. "It isn't I; it isn't anything with which I have a conscious connection. But I can lead you to it. That is my function. The rest is up to you. Your attitude will govern the kind of information you get."

This participation of the patient in the experiment, by way of mental attitude, is a point which the readings themselves constantly stress. The person who desires help, and who seeks it humbly and prayerfully, as did the patient in the first of the case histories which follow, will invariably get a better reading than the cynic who wants to be shown, or the person who has lost hope and is willing to try anything as a last resort.

Consequently those who have gotten the best results from their readings are those who have realized the spiritual implications of the experiment in which they have participated. These, for the most part, have entered into the philosophical side of the work, and gained mentally and spiritually, as well as physi-

cally. Those who have gotten least from their readings are those who have treated the phenomenon as a freak or a fad, and have but haphazardly followed the instructions given them.

Some people allow the readings to take the place of a family doctor, getting checks for everything from a bilious headache to a head cold. Others use them for emergencies which get beyond the wisdom of their doctors. Still others, the chronically ill, employ them as a sustaining aid, so that they may remain alive and active as long as possible. One woman has been getting check-ups regularly for twelve years, during which time her malady has been kept under control and she has enjoyed an active physical and mental life.

The fundamental worth of a reading is, of course, the diagnosis it gives. If the phenomenon of clairvoyance is accepted as fact, the diagnosis is invariably correct. Armed with it alone, most people could get well, for the remedies for almost every trouble are known. The secondary worth of a reading is the basic, far-reaching nature of the treatment it outlines. It aims at eliminating the cause, not the effect, and it assumes for its goal a completely healthy body. For this reason it almost always gives instructions as to diet, eliminations, exercise, and rest. Consequently a great many patients, after they feel a little better, go back to their old habits of eating too much, working too hard, exercising too little, and never achieve the well-being which their readings point out as a possibility. These people waste their own and Mr. Cayce's time.

But on them, fortunately, Mr. Cayce does not have to depend. There are other cases, hundreds and hundreds of them, wherein the treatments have been faithfully followed, and the predicted results have been achieved. So that the reader may become acquainted with the step-by-step procedure in such cases, half a dozen typical examples have been selected from the files and are hereinafter set down.

*   *   *

I. EPILEPSY

The history of this case is best told through the correspondence. It is a typical example of the daily requests for help.

Sept. 25, 1939

Mr. Edgar Cayce
Virginia Beach, Va.
Dear Mr. Cayce:

Sometime ago, I read an article in the magazine "Health Culture," on the wonderful work you have been doing for the past twenty-five years, diagnosing diseases through the subconscious mind. The article was from the pen of Dr. Thos. Garrett, N.Y.

The article was like a ray of hope for me.

Briefly my case is this.

For the past twenty-five years, since my ordination to the priesthood in the Catholic Church, I have been engaged in the work of young missions.

About fifteen years ago, while at the altar, I suffered an attack that had all the appearances of epilepsy. There is no epilepsy to my knowledge in our family.

About every three to four years since that time, I have had (at the altar in all cases but one) a similar attack.

You can understand life under these circumstances is very trying, uncertainty of never knowing when an attack will come on makes life very trying. I feel like one caught in a trap. The attack is always preceded by a trembling of the hands and body, which I cannot control. Then follows a period of unconsciousness.

Knowing of the amazing gift which is yours, I am asking you to diagnose and cure my case.

Will you let me know what offering I can give you? I have very little money but will give what I can.

The article by Dr. Garrett has given me such hope. Will you kindly answer this letter at your earliest convenience? An early answer would be greatly appreciated by one who has been a constant sufferer from fear these past years.

Sincerely yours,

Sept. 27, 1939

Dear [name]—

I have yours of the 25th and sincerely hope that with His help I may be of a service to you. Thank you for writing me. I trust I may be of a service.

I would not have you pay me anything. I ask that you fill out the enclosed blank or give the information asked for on it, and if you wish to contribute anything say a Mass for my friend, a young Catholic who is in my home trying to regain his health. He was a schoolmate of my son. He is on the improve, slowly but surely, and is a lovely and competent young man.

I am sending you some data, Father. I hope you will enjoy reading it. I will appreciate any comment you may make.

Only two readings can be given each day. The time we have set for yours is the morning of the 6th of Oct., 10:30 to 11:30 EST. We ask that, if practical, you keep the hour in prayerful meditation. Please let me know if it is convenient for you to keep that hour.

Thanking you and sincerely hoping to be of a service, and asking that you remember me in your prayers, I am

Sincerely yours,

(Signed) EDGAR CAYCE

September 30, 1939

Dear Mr Cayce:

Your most welcome and cordial letter, together with the readings and case histories reached me this morning.

God has endowed you with an amazing power. I am seeking that power sincerely in the hope that by a permanent cure, I may be able to give my whole life to the work of helping humanity to a better knowledge of God. This has been my work through twenty-five years in the priesthood, young Catholic Missions, trying to lead people to God.

Let me thank you sincerely for your kindness in making me an Associate Member free of charge in the Association for Research and Enlightenment. Rest assured I will say Mass for your good friend. Rest assured also, Mr. Cayce, I will say Mass for you, and pray for you, to the end that God may give you, through your truly wonderful faculty, the power to restore me and others to good health and a better appreciation of life's purpose.

On the morning of October 6th, I will spend the hour from 10:30 to 11:30 EST. in prayerful meditation. This is the hour you have set aside for my reading.

May God bless you. You have my sincere prayers and belief in your great work.

Sincerely yours,

The reading was given on the morning of October 6, 1939. The major portion of this reading follows:

"Yes, we have the body here [name]—

"As we find, the general physical forces are very good in many respects; yet there are disturbances at times which prevent the normal reactions in the body.

"These, as will be seen, arise under conditions where strain is brought on the physical forces of the body—through the very necessity of the period of consecration.

"This is a physical condition that, as we find, may be removed or eliminated; and thus removing from the system the causes of these disturbances, also removing the necessity or cause for fear of any nature in relationship to same.

"In times back, there were periods when there was a depletion of the physical forces through the lack of supplying full nutriment to the system. This caused, in those areas about the lacteal and umbilical plexus, a form of lesion—a tautness.

"Not that it affects, as yet, the liver or the spleen, or even the gall duct's activity; though eventually, without its removal, it may cause disturbances through that area.

"But with the periods of activity in which there is the refraining from foods, this becomes a retroactive condition in the physical force of the body; thus producing a spasmodic reaction in the nerve forces about the area—causing a reaction through the sympathetic and cerebrospinal center, from the lower portion of the solar plexus center.

"Thus there is an inclination for the losing of control of the sensory forces; for it produces, from the reaction, a condition at the 1st cervical, or through the medulla oblongata—an un-balancing, as it were, of the reflexes to the sensory centers.

"This as we find also produces in the general elimination system the inclinations at times for the lack of proper or full eliminations.

"When there has been, and is, the better or perfect accord in this direction, there is not such a great stress upon this disturbance in the right portion of the upper abdomen—as has been indicated—about the umbilical and lacteal duct center. Here we would find, upon examination, a *cold* spot.

"In making applications for eradicating the causes, then:

"We would apply each evening, for two evenings, the heavy Castor Oil Packs; at least three thicknesses of heavy flannel, wrung out in Castor Oil, as hot as the body can stand same, and placed over the lower portion of the liver, gall duct and caecum area—this extending, of course, to the umbilical center. Let these remain for one hour at each application, keeping the Packs hot by wringing out of the hot Castor Oil two or three times during the application.

"After the two days of applying the Packs, we would begin then with the osteopathic adjustments—with particular reference to a subluxation as will be found indicated in the lower portion of the 9th dorsal center, or 9th, 10th and 11th. Coordinate such correction with the lumbar axis and the upper dorsal and cervical centers.

"There should not be required more than six adjustments to correct the condition.

"Two of the Castor Oil Packs should be sufficient, but if in the administration of the adjustments it is found that this has not relaxed nor removed the cold spot, then apply the Pack again.

"Then, be mindful that there are good eliminations, or a perfect or full evacuation of the alimentary canal each day.

"When necessary, use a vegetable compound as a laxative—such as——or that having a senna base.

"These done, in the manners indicated, will eradicate the causes of the disturbance, and produce throughout the physical forces of the body a better and a nearer normal reaction.

"Keep that attitude of consistent help, aid for others. This is in keeping with the purposes, the desires, the heart of the entity.

"We are through for the present."

October 9, 1939

Dear [name]—

I hope you find the information interesting and the suggestions as beneficial as so many hundreds have found them through the years. I do not know how to thank you for your letter. I can assure you that you have brought joy to the young man here, as well as to myself. We can only hope your experience with the information will be as helpful as our own has been.

I will appreciate hearing from you. Thanking you and trusting to have been of some service, I am

Sincerely,

EDGAR CAYCE

October 11, 1939

Dear Mr. Cayce:

Your reading and the suggestions for cure, also your personal letter came to me today. Thank God, and you through whom God is working, after all these years I have got, through your aid, at the root of the trouble and have had the remedies pointed out to me.

The osteopathic treatments can be secured here in———. I am just at a loss to know how to go about the application of the Castor Oil Packs. They should be applied by one who has a scientific knowledge of the areas mentioned in your reading. To go to a doctor here, who does not understand or who has no knowledge of your truly amazing power, would mean a refusal.

If you could suggest someone, who could apply those packs scientifically without the necessity of my going to a medical doctor, it would indeed solve my problem. I am so anxious to start the treatments at once.

I said Mass this morning for your good friend. I am saying Mass for you tomorrow that God may grant you many years of usefulness to mankind.

May I thank you again for your great kindness to me. I shall never forget you.

Sincerely,

October 14, 1939

Dear [name]—

Thank you for yours of the 11th. Let me tell you how appreciative my friend is for your saying Mass for him. I thank you also for your thoughtfulness of me.

Now don't think you have need to be disturbed about the Castor Oil Packs. You can apply them more scientifically than anyone else. This is what you do. First get a large piece of flannel, such as part of a blanket. Have it sufficiently large so that when folded three times it will cover the area from the lower portion of your right rib to the point of the hip on the same side and to the center of the abdomen and half round the right side to the spine. Heat sufficient oil so that you can wring the folded cloth out in it. When the oil gets very warm it is messy. Then, after wringing out the flannel in the oil, apply it directly to the body. Have other cloths and a piece of oilcloth to cover the flannel, so that it may not spoil the bed clothing. Apply it as warm as you can stand it. Then turn on your electric pad, and lie still for the time indicated. I am sure you can do this.

Where this treatment has been recommended it has been most effective and I am sure it will prove so for you. When you are ready to take the Oil Pack off, sponge the area covered by oil with a little warm soda water. This cleanses very nicely.

If I haven't been explicit enough, please don't hesitate to ask me about it.

You know I will be anxious to hear how you come along with the osteopath.

We can give the osteopath many references here in the states if he wishes them.

Thank you again. I hope that I have been of help in His name.

Sincerely,

December 18, 1939

Dear Mr. Cayce:

I am so happy to report to you that I have taken the treatments indicated in your reading for my case. Today I finished my sixth osteopathic treatment. The osteopath thinks several more adjustments are necessary to fully restore my body to complete normalcy.

My Christmas greetings to you are these. May God spare you many more years to carry on the good work. I am deeply grateful to you for your kindness. I am sure as I read (and I do often) your letter (my reading) that now I can go on in the full hope that there will be no reoccurrence of the attacks that have made each day an uncertain problem.

Since I began this letter, I have received your lovely Christmas greeting. Cod bless you with continued health and usefulness. Merry Christmas to you and your family and a happy New Year.

Sincerely,

December 20, 1939

Dear [name]—

Thank you for yours of the 18th. To feel that I may have been privileged to be the channel for some help or aid to you, is indeed a real Christmas to me, and I can only give humble thanks for this opportunity. I sincerely hope you took sufficient of the Oil Packs to break up the adhesions which were described as the basis of the trouble. With this accomplished, the adjustments from the osteopath will really be more helpful.

I am enclosing two pieces of work by my friend. He is still with us, and is looking forward to having his wife and baby with him tomorrow through Christmas Day. He is very happy about this, to be sure. Slowly but surely he is improving, and if it be His will he will continue until he is again in normal health. He is capable of making so many people happy through his work.

Thanking you for your prayers and blessings, and wishing that all that is good and true be yours, I am

Sincerely,

EDGAR CAYCE

On April 25, 1941, a request was made for a report on the case. The following letter was received with the case report.

April 28, 1941

Dear Mr. Cayce:

I am just in receipt of your letter. Let me state that I am sure my cure is permanent. To say I am grateful to you is only half stating my feelings. I pray for you daily that God may extend your life into many years to be of service to mankind.

I did not write chiefly for two reasons. First, I wished the element of time to prove my cure was permanent. Second, I was engaged in war work that precluded many times the possibility of correspondence.

It must be a source of great comfort to you to know you are doing so much good for humanity. Let me tell you, I will never forget your kindness to me. May God bless you always.

Sincerely,

INDIVIDUAL CASE REPORT:

Date of Reading October 6th, 1939.   Case No. 2019

PLEASE ANSWER THE FOLLOWING QUESTIONS CAREFULLY

(1) In your opinion did the analysis of the Reading cover the condition?

Ans.   Yes.

(2) Give symptoms of the condition described.

Ans.   Attacks over a period of nine years. These attacks looked like epilepsy. They occurred about twice a year for the period stated above.

(3) What was the physician's analysis of this condition?

Ans.   Attacks had all the appearances of epilepsy.

(4) Have the suggestions given in the reading been followed exactly as outlined?

Ans.   Yes.

(5) For how long?

Ans.   For the period stated in the reading.

(6) Describe the extent to which improvements have resulted.

Ans.   Complete cure, as far as I can judge, after the lapse of almost two years.

(7) Comment.
Ans.   I wish to state my deep gratitude to Mr. Cayce.
Date April 28, 1941.   Signed (name)

SUMMARY

This case is not presented with the idea of furnishing additional proof of the accuracy of the Physical Readings, for much of the information regarding the condition was given in the letter requesting the reading. Yet, detailed conditions described in the reading which were not given in the letters cannot be ignored— (1) bad eliminations, (2) a cold spot about the umbilical and lacteal duct center, (3) subluxations of the 9th, 10th and 11th dorsals.

The treatment outlined was simple and logical, evidently meeting this body's specific needs.

A bridge of mental attunement was set up through the seeking on the part of the priest, the offering of this help by Edgar Cayce, and the prayer and meditation at the time the reading was given.

II. INTESTINAL FEVER

This is the case study of a young woman eighteen years old, who had a critical attack of Intestinal Fever.

Before her first emergency reading was given on September 21, 1935, she had had two previous physical readings: one in 1927, and another in February, 1935.

The request for this emergency reading was made by telephone. The condition at the time the reading was given was afterwards described in a report submitted by Miss L. K. We quote from this report:

"I was taken with chills and a high fever. After taking the medicine given by the physician for what he termed malaria, the condition became worse, causing excessive vomiting. I could not retain anything, not even water. Then, I began to suffer with pains in my chest, abdomen, and right side. There was such a burning sensation in my stomach that it felt as if it were on fire, and this condition spread up into the chest.

"The physicians diagnosed the condition variously as malaria fever, malta fever, colitis, gastritis, and typhoid fever. One of the physicians stated it was appendicitis but after we received the readings, we knew from them that it was the inflammation that was causing the severe pain in the right side in the region of the appendix."

The telephone request indicated that this young woman was in a coma, and was not expected to live through the night. The seriousness of her condition was confirmed in the reading which follows:

FIRST READING

A.M. *Sept. 21, 1935.*

"Yes, we have the body here; this we have had before.

"Conditions are very serious in the physical forces of this body, and the causes are from temperature that arises from infectious forces.

"In the present we find the stomach is affected, or the duodenum . . . the infections from same to stomach. The greater distress is in the upper portion of jejunum, or in those cords that connect the intestines themselves through the lymph and emunctory circulation of same.

"These are infectious forces, and unless there is an allaying, peritonitis must come and the inflammations that arise from same . . . and disintegration.

"As we find in the present, we would apply over the abdominal area the grape poultice; the raw grapes crushed with hulls, in a thin cloth container and applied over the stomach and abdomen.

"We would massage gently the areas from which all these portions of the system obtain their impulses, with a combination of equal parts Olive Oil, Russian White Oil, Compound Tincture of Benzoin and Witch Hazel. Shake these well together, and let the massage extend particularly over the upper dorsal and cervical area . . . but extend gradually over the whole area, if the body responds at all.

"We would find that burned whiskey and then an eggnog made of same would be preferable for the diets in the present; this, of course, with small quantity given often, allowed to sip just a bit.

"These, as we find, would be the conditions as best.

"It would be well that the lower limbs, across the lower portion of the abdomen . . . that is, on the spine, not on the abdomen itself (sacral-lumbar), be massaged with grain alcohol, not rub alcohol but grain alcohol, to strengthen the body and yet allay temperature.

"These we would do for the immediate present.

"As conditions respond, or should they respond, it will be necessary . . . of course . . . that very small enemas be given at first. These will keep down the temperature and are the best to allay inflammation through the colon area; then the colonic may be given later. But do not give these too high at first; gradually increase. Use a warm soda solution in the first, followed with the Glyco-Thymoline in the solution . . . or the Alkalin Petrolagar (or alternated). These given every day or two will tend to make for better conditions.

"Ready for questions."

Q. "What should be done in regard to treatment being given by the doctors?"
A. "There's little being given except nursing, and sedatives . . . which are not allaying.

"The Oil Rubs, the Packs, as we find, are the better.

"Of course, the grape poultice is not to be heated. This should be changed about every hour, or as soon as the pack becomes heated by the body. Renew the crushed grapes, and keep up the packs for two or three, or four to five hours at the time. Then rest, and then give them again. Just crush the grapes in a cloth, or made so the pack extends over the whole of the abdomen and the stomach.

"The Oil Rubs should be given two to three times a day. Do not disturb the body, just turn gently on the side and massage just what the body will absorb. Shake the ingredients well together, because they'll separate.

"But these, as we find, are best for the conditions.

"It's very serious, and the peritonitis is that to be warned against.

"Hence very mild foods, and the stimulation more by absorption . . . which is, of course, the effect from the grain alcohol rubs and the burned whiskey with only the yolk of the egg and a little milk."

Q. "How often should the grain alcohol rubs be given?"
A. "Two to three times a day, as indicated, with the other oil rub. One is on the upper portion, the other is the lower.

"We are through for the present."

SECOND READING

P.M. *Sept. 21, 1935.*

"Yes, we have had the body here before.

"As we find, conditions are still very serious. While there are those reactions that apparently make for bloating or swelling, the reactions are not bad if there is the ability to get the reaction through the alimentary canal now.

"We would give immediately a Soda Solution Enema, with the Petrolagar enema following same. This we would repeat again in at least five or six hours, if there is the response.

"Compound or combine this for the nausea, which will work with the system:

Limewater	½ ounce
Cinnamon Water	½ ounce
10% solution Iodide of Potassium	15 minims
10% solution Bromide of Potassium	30 minims

Shake the solution together. Give a teaspoonful in two teaspoonfuls of water. Let it be sipped rather than attempt to be swallowed every two hours.

"We would keep the poultice and the rub. These are the best stimulants as we find for the body in the present.

"Ready for questions."

Q. "How much water should be used for the enema?"

A. "A quart of tepid water for the first, with a level tablespoonful of baking soda. A pint of tepid water for the last, with a tablespoonful of Petrolagar."

Q. "Should the grape poultice be kept up constantly now?"
A. "As indicated, keep it on for two to three hours; rest an hour, and then repeat again."

Q. "Would a transfusion be of any benefit?"
A. "We do not find it so in the present conditions."

Q. "Have the suggestions been followed in the correct manner?"
A. "Very good; best they can under the conditions."

Q. "Any particular kind of water the body should drink?"
A. "Just the plain water, boiled."

THIRD READING
Sept. 22, 1935.
   "Yes, we have the body here; this we have had before.
   "Conditions continue to be very serious. There is the necessity of removing those conditions through the alimentary canal. As we find, this is the only hope to relieve the pressure, as has been indicated . . . and carrying out same as has been indicated.
   "To be sure, there are weakening conditions, and the excruciating pains that come make for the rising of disturbing conditions.
   "But we would tend to be higher and higher with the enemas, and to make for the easing through the applications as given.
   "Ready for questions."

Q. "How often may the enemas be given?"
A. "They may be given, as we have indicated, every few hours, until there is the manner of allowing the gases to be eliminated . . . and the increasing forces that accumulate in the system from absorption to those conditions there to be prevented."

Q. "Should a colon tube be used, or an ordinary nozzle to a syringe?"
A. "A soft colon tube; one that does not allow too great a quantity of water or pressure from the end . . . let the pressure be more from the side than the end."

Q. "Is there any warning regarding giving the enemas?"
A. "The warnings have been given, as to how there should not be given too much water at once. Rather allow the reactions to take place in the system, if possible."

Q. "Should all other treatments be kept up?"
A. "As indicated, these are the only conditions that may suffice if there will be the response."

Q. "Any other helpful suggestions for the body, or advice to those attending same?"
A. "Be consistent and patient with those activities, and trust in that that it may respond in the body."

Q. "Has peritonitis set up yet?"
A. "The inflammation has increased; it has not broken as yet."

Q. "Has the body responded at all to the treatments?"
A. "If it hadn't, it would have passed long ago!"

Q. "Any advice regarding any stimulants?"
A. "The greater stimulants, as we have indicated, should be those things given; as we find, that may be absorbed at all.
    "Of course, the massaging . . . gently . . . of the area over the abdomen will be helpful; with that which would be absorbed to remove inflammation."

Q. "What should be used for the abdomen massage?"
A. "Oil; Olive Oil."

    "We are through for the present."

Fourth Reading

Sept. 23, 1935.

"Yes, we have the body here; this we have had before.

"Still conditions are very serious, but . . . as we find . . . there are greater chances for the recuperative forces with the body; for she has responded somewhat to those applications made.

"It is still necessary that the eliminations through the alimentary canal be continued, even though . . . if there is still the response . . . these will have the appearance of too great an activity, or for a time appear not under control. Still it will be well that there be used the enemas. Now we would change these just a little bit:

"With the soda solution add a little saline solution, that there may be a stimulation to the mucous membranes without same becoming too lax in the reaction. To the quart of water used, add a heaping teaspoonful of soda and a level teaspoonful of salt (table salt). And in the last water change from the Petrolagar to Glyco-Thymoline, a tablespoonful to the pint and a half of water. These should be given every four or five hours, until there is a thorough relaxation through the alimentary canal.

"Still use the grape poultices, but make these a little farther apart; and let these extend from the pit of the stomach to the lower portion of the abdomen, over the whole of the intestinal tract and stomach.

"It would be well to have right away a gentle massage osteopathically, stimulating especially the secondary cardiac plexus area; that there may be the emptying of the stomach itself from the stimulation. This should be given very gently. Coordinate the lumbar (4th lumbar) plexus with this, gently, that there may be the stimulation for the secondary activity of the kidneys and the lower portion of the abdominal area. This we would give about twice a day for the next two or three days.

"After the first manipulations have been given osteopathically, prepare an Alcaroid solution . . . a quarter teaspoonful to half a glass of water . . . and let this be sipped every few minutes; ten to fifteen minutes apart, until the whole quantity . . . or that left . . . can be retained by the body. This will change the reaction from the tendency for regurgitation and emit through the stomach itself. This will prevent these strains now, if there are the reactions from the manipulative forces. For the reaction will turn to the chyle activity.

"Then there may be a little stimulation given in the crushed grapes; that is, the juice only of crushed grapes. Not the same as used for the poultice, but the same character of grapes as used for the poultice. The colder this may be the better; just a little of this will be found to be retained . . . after there has been given the Alcaroid solution and it has been retained.

"Keep the oil rubs for the upper portion of the spine and the alcohol (grain alcohol) rubs for the lower spine; for these will be absorbed by the system.

"Keep the Olive Oil massage over the abdominal area during the rest periods from the grape poultice.

"These, as we find, are the best for the present.

"Ready for questions."

Q. "How long now should they wait between the poultices?"
A. "Hour and a half to two hours; that's between each one."

Q. "But they should be given for several hours straight along as indicated at first?"
A. "We have given, just given, that there is to be a rest period after each grape poultice! Let it stay on the body until it becomes hot, or very warm even to the outside. Then remove and wait an hour and a half to two hours before replacing with another; using the Olive Oil massage during the rest period from same. Let the poultice extend from the aesophagus end, or the cardiac end of the stomach to the lower portion . . . or to the caecum area and the ileum plexus area, across the whole of the abdomen and stomach and bowels."

Q. "Do the capsules the doctor inserts in the rectum, and the powder given, hinder or help?"
A. "They don't remain there long enough to do either! Don't refuse these, if they are necessary according to the doctor, but use the enemas as indicated . . . and if the time comes so that these are removed by the enemas, all right!

"The manipulative forces, now, are to stimulate the activity of the nerve forces and blood supply to the digestive area, and those portions where there is the inflammation. Not too severe. Twice a day these should be given for the next few days. Stimulate the cardiac and secondary cardiac plexus, coordinating such stimulation to the lumbar area.

"To be sure, the head and neck may be massaged for the general rest of the body; but these manipulations as indicated are to empty the stomach; not to make adjustments but to stimulate the plexus so that the activity of the gastric flow is downward and to prevent regurgitation.

"Twenty to thirty minutes after taking the manipulative forces, begin with the Alcaroid solution. Do not attempt to swallow too much. Do not be overanxious that the body is weak, or that it does not retain nourishment . . . if the oil rubs and the other things are provided.

"Then begin with the grape juice (from the crushed fresh grapes, not grape juice that has been allowed to stand). This may be strained; not seasoned with sugar or the like, but just the natural fresh juice. Gradually, later, there may be mixed orange juice with same, half and half; but use the grape juice first . . . from the fresh crushed grapes.

"These will be assimilated, and obtain from the absorption of the oil and the alcohol (grain alcohol) rubs the proper reaction.

"Do these.

"We are through for the present."

We do not often find such a comment as is contained in one of these early readings indicating the nearness of death.

The seriousness of this condition was confirmed not only by statements from members of the family, but by several physicians who were called in for consultation by the family doctor. This young woman was well known in a small community. The street in front of her home had been roped off for a block. In a local church, prayer services were being held for her. The doctors had commented to people in the town that L. K. could not possibly live for more than a day or so.

Other readings were secured on September 25th, September 28th, and October 4th. Suggestions in these readings were along the same general lines as those previously given, with additional information regarding the diet as the body grew stronger.

TREATMENT
The outstanding part of the treatment recommended in this case seems to have been a grape poultice. These poultices have been recommended most successfully in many other conditions of intestinal inflammation combined with the massages and enemas, and later the osteopathic stimulations. These seem to have been the means of saving this young woman's life. Crates of Concord grapes were rushed in from a nearby city to be used for this purpose.

SUMMARY
On June 15, 1937, we received the following report from L. K.:

"Under the care of six physicians I failed to respond to their treatment, and was gradually growing worse.

"I responded immediately to the treatments recommended in an emergency reading obtained from Edgar Cayce on September 21, 1935.

"I am now able to eat anything that is included in my diet, and in better physical condition than before my illness. I have not had any recurrence of malaria fever or gastritis."

Under date of October 3, 1937, we have a report from the osteopath, who was called in to give the massages which were recommended. This report states that in her opinion the reading described the condition of the patient accurately. She states that the results of the treatments recommended were splendid.

At the present time this young woman is in the best of health and has had no further complications of an intestinal nature.

III. ARTHRITIS

This individual case study of arthritis presents several interesting features: (1) the thoroughness of the analysis of the condition; (2) the inclusion in the readings of considerable general information on arthritis; (3) the detailed treatments suggested; (4) the complete recovery.

STATEMENT OF CONDITION

Under date of October 7, 1932, Mr. Edgar Cayce received a request for a reading from a young lady in Dayton, Ohio. In this letter no reference was made to the nature of the ailment. In a subsequent letter, before the first reading was given, the following information regarding the condition was given: "My trouble is in my joints. Doctors have told me it is arthritis; but can find no source of infection, no cause for it and, seemingly, know of very little help to offer me. I have considerable pain in all my joints, and am subject to severe night sweats." (Signed— M. J. McC.) This was the extent of the information furnished relative to the nature and extent of the disturbance.

In 1939, three years after completely recovering from this condition, M. J. McC. gave an oral account of her illness to Mr. Cayce and members of the Association staff. The suffering must have been intense, but the appalling factor was the utter hopelessness of the situation. The eighteen-year-old girl was gradually becoming an invalid, was slowly losing all power of movement in every joint in her body.

FIRST READING

"We have the body here, M. J. McC. Now, as we find, there are abnormal conditions in the physical functioning of this body. These conditions would prove very interesting and worthwhile in considering a condition that in many portions of the country, and in all portions to some extent, is gradually increasing and that proves unusually hard to cope with; for conditions are so often hidden that it is hard to find the source or the cause of that which the professions have called 'the point of infection.'

"Were the pathological conditions studied in the proper light, taking some that may be given here as the basis for investigations, this case would prove very helpful and beneficial in many other similar conditions. In this body the point of infection is hidden, yet may be located in the basic forces of the metabolism and katabolism of the system. It is the lack of elements necessary for the developing of that which makes for the regeneration, in the elemental forces of the living organism, of functions that provide the proper coordination and physical balance throughout the system.

"First, in the inception of this body, some nineteen years ago—not what may be termed properly (as in old considerations) prenatal conditions, but as of prenatal surroundings—there were those elements taken by the mother which affected the body. These made for first tendencies.

"Then, with the character of the surroundings of the body, the character of the water as assimilated, the general dispositions that made for the resuscitating forces in the assimilating system, in many portions of the body the glands have been deficient in some respects and overactive in others in supplying the elements necessary for the proper distribution of forces in the system.

"These are the points of infection, then, that make for tendencies in the structural portions of the body to become more active than other portions. This has not reached the point where the growth is turned into that position or manner where the elongation of bone itself begins, but rather the crystallization in the muscular forces and tendons. The substance is lacking that should supply to the joints of the extremities that oil or that plasm that makes possible normal functioning. Were this turned into one more infectious point, we would have rather the tendency of Elephantiasis Proboscidis in its inception. As it is in the present—from those glands of the lacteals in assimilation, from the activities from the spleen and those glands from the kidneys, the adrenal and those in the lyden, overactive at times, and those of the pancrean supplying to the blood stream those forces that are as the chrysalis of the infectious forces from the adrenals—all of this makes for the stoppage, rather than the drainage from extremities. This must eventually cause Sleeping Paralysis or Stony Paralysis, or bring on a condition that makes for a twisting and turning of the bones themselves, by the muscular forces becoming hardened in such conditions.

"Then, to meet the needs of such conditions, various stages

of this particular disorder necessarily indicate that different amounts of elements are lacking or are excessive in portions of the functioning body.

TREATMENT

"We would first be very mindful of the diet. Keep away from all forces that supply an overabundance of salines, limes, silicon, or the like, in the system. Supply an overabundant amount of those foods that carry iron, iodine and phosphorus in the system, for these will act against that already supplied to bum or destroy those tendencies of demarcation in the activities of the glands. We would outline something of this nature:

"In one meal each day we would supply principally citrus fruits, or nature's sugars, nature's laxatives in citrous fruits, figs, prunes, and berries. A great deal of those forces that may be found in the pieplant, or the like; salsify, gooseberries in any of their preparations—whether those that are preserved or otherwise, provided they are without any of the preservatives; currants and their derivatives (that is, properties that are made from them, you see, without preservatives). Beware of apples and bananas among the fruits. Beware of any that would carry more of those that would add silicon in the system. One meal each day would consist of foods from such as these.

"Then there should be one meal almost entirely of nuts, and the oils of nuts. The activities from these in the system are such as to produce a different character of fermentation with the gastric forces of the stomach and the duodenum itself. The type of the lactics that are formed in the assimilation must be entirely changed. The hydrochlorics that are formed in the system must be changed. The lacteals must be stimulated to throw off that which will gradually build in the pancreas, the spleen, the kidneys, the duodenum, more of those forces that will lessen the tendency for the accumulation of those conditions in extremities.

"The evening meal may be of well-balanced vegetables that are of the leafy nature, and that carry more of those properties as given. We will find much in turnips, eggplant (no cabbage of any nature, either cold or cooked), some characters of beans—

provided they are well dried and grown in a soil that is different from that carrying iron, see? These will aid. The meats should be preferably (when taken at all) of wild game, or take fish, or oysters, or sea foods. So much for the diet.

"Then we would take also, internally, those properties of Atomidine. This is iodine in a form which may be assimilated in the system. In the beginning, if this is taken in large quantities, it would tend to make for a greater stiffness. Then, we would begin with small quantities. Twice each day take three minims in water, morning and evening. Each day increase the amount one minim, until there is being taken at least ten minims twice a day; then stop for five days, then begin over again.

"At the end of the third period of taking the Atomidine, we would begin with Epsom Salts baths (not until the third period of taking the iodine). These would be taken once a week. Add five to eight pounds of the salts to sufficient water in the bath tub to cover the body up to the neck. This would be five to eight pounds to twenty or twenty-five gallons of water. The water should be just as hot as the body can well stand. As it cools add more hot water. The body should lie in this for at least twenty-five to thirty minutes.

"After coming from this bath, the body should be rinsed off in plain water, then rubbed down thoroughly. Massage thoroughly into the whole of the body (that is, all of the cerebrospinal, all of the shoulders, head, neck, ribs, arms, lower limbs, toes, feet, hands, fingers) a solution of equal parts of Olive Oil, tincture of myrrh, and Russian White Oil. Heat the Olive Oil first, then add the same amount of tincture of myrrh while the Olive Oil is hot, and while cooling stir in an equal amount of the Russian White Oil. This doesn't mean any of those that are of the paraffin base, but rather that which has been purified. This should be massaged in thoroughly, all that the body will absorb. Follow this (because it will make the body rather oily) with a general rub-off or sponge-off with rub alcohol. After such treatments, of course, the body should rest.

"When this has been taken for a period of three to five weeks, then we will give further instructions. Remember, the diet must be kept up; remember, the Atomidine must be kept up for this full period, and then further instructions will be given."

QUESTION

Q. "What causes severe night sweats, and what may be done to correct them?"

A. "We have given what may be done, and we have given the cause; for with these conditions that are caused by the glands' functioning, and the attempts of the system to reject these conditions, it would make sweat break out on anyone!"

"Do as we have outlined, and then when the period has passed as given, we will give further instructions."

COMMENT

A hasty reading of the preceding document may result in confusion owing to involved sentence structure and peculiar use of words. Naturally, our point of view must differ somewhat from that of the young woman who received this information. Her first consideration must have been, "What hope does this offer?" The reference to glandular conditions, improper assimilation, etc., may have been impressive; the warnings regarding serious complications certainly must have fitted in with the report from physicians; and the simplicity of the treatments probably impelled an effort to give the suggestions a trial. But we can well understand that faith in the reports from those who had followed similar readings, and desperate need, were the important factors which moved this young woman to give the information a thorough trial.

Back of this ready flow of technical terms there apparently lies a comprehensive understanding of this condition. This is no exposition of theory, but a definite application of general laws relative to arthritis to a particular case. The analysis includes not only present conditions, but future possibilities involved in the advancement of the trouble. The range of the perception seems unlimited.

REPORTS

These statements are taken from letters now in the Association files, written by the patient's mother. The first reading was given on October 21, 1932. Reports began on the first of the following month.

November 1, 1932—"It seems too soon to say or think that M. J. is better, but she seems to be. The pain in her knees is gone; they are still stiff. Her elbows are better (not so painful). There is color creeping into her face. She has been so white. She has had one spell of palpitation of the heart, and a night sweat last night (one night in 3, 4, or 5) as before it was every night."

November 18, 1932—"M. J. finished the second series of drops this morning. The pain and then the stiffness ceased in all joints, except the left elbow, with the first series. There could not have been such a marked change with the second series, but the left elbow has yielded and is practically as good as the other; there is some soreness in some of the joints upon pressure. The night sweats are better, but the last one (last Sunday night) was more profuse. They are further apart. This week (Wednesday night) she had an acute attack in her left thumb, the pain, as acute or more so, than ever it has been in any joint. Thursday it ceased, and by night a finger on the right hand hurt, but less severely."

December 3, 1932—"M. J. has finished her third series of Atomidine. She will take her first bath this coming Monday night . . . Her left thumb insisted on hurting her for three or four days this week but is some better today. The night sweats are remaining better. She had two during this series of drops. We believe they are of a different type as they are more profuse and more general (all over her from head to foot). Her heart palpitation seems better and her complexion is very good at present, clearing up in the past week."

December 17, 1932—"We saw no change after the first bath, except a hard night sweat. The second bath was this past Tuesday night. Wednesday she ached all over and had a headache. Pain in her left thumb is still persisting and Wednesday was more acute, hurting into her hand and arm. Her right knee felt queer, rather creepy; like when she first took this. Today (Saturday) the other knee hurt just a little. Friday evening she had several hard lumps in her fingers of the right hand, which got very sore. She has had them, at times, for the past seven or eight years, but they have been gone since just before she started your suggestions. Her face and neck broke out badly this week, even before the bath (per usual). This is accompanied each time, it seems, with acute gas pains. We think her shin bones are sharper and more prominent; her flesh seems flabby."

December 17, 1932—"We can feel a bump or lump along the right shin about two inches wide and three long; there are small lumps close against this shin bone at this spot. They are not sore. She starts with the Atomidine this morning and has the bath Tuesday night. We hope for favorable results next week . . . Besides taking iron and copper capsules, a white salicylate tablet and a strychnine tablet at bed time, she was taking diathermy treatments from an osteopath. We told him we wrote you. He asked what you were giving her, and we said iodide. He rather gasped, 'Iodide of Potassium?' There was a hushed 'Oh!' when we said, 'Atomidine.' "

December 28, 1932—"M. J.'s third bath was on last Tuesday (December 20) and since Thursday her pain is all gone. Her two thumbs are a little stiff. If you remember, the pain leaves first, then the stiffness. She has stood the holiday season very well. She has had a lot of extra work, trips to town for me, as I was not so good myself. She is tired, but no more than a well person would be. One more thing about the diet. We thought that 'no cabbage of any kind' included cauliflower, Chinese celery and Brussels sprouts, but I've changed my mind. I believe it was meant for kraut, slaw, etc., or cabbage proper. If we can add these to the diet it will help out a change of vegetables. I have trouble with this diet business . . . "

January 10, 1933—"M. J. is doing nicely (all the house work, cooking, and caring for me at present)!"

January 18, 1933—"M. J. has not been so well this week. She has pains in various joints. She has gotten better, but when she first gets up of a morning her thumb and knee will hurt for a while and sometimes in the afternoon or evening."

SECOND READING

The second reading, given on January 20, 1933, indicated a definite improvement in the whole system. The treatments previously outlined were to be continued. The following comment on the diet is of interest:

"Be mindful that the diet is kept in the manner that does not work crosswise with the elements that are being created in the system. As much sea foods as convenient will work with the balancing of the forces in system, for they create a character of element in the minutia, and supply, to the blood and nerve forces of the system, an assimilated character of force that works with the activities of the body. Also green vegetables; as, lettuce, celery, spinach, mustard greens, and the like. Also those foods that carry sufficient elements of gold and phosphorus are needed. These are found partially from sea foods and partially from vegetables—as in carrots, the oyster plant, and especially in those of that nature. These make for better forces with the system than those of the meats, that become more active with the other principles in the system that require more gastric forces in their digestion or assimilation.

"While the latter are necessary for the strength, for the vitality of the system, these may be kept in a consistent manner. Never any hog meat, very little of beef unless it is of the very lean (and the juices) but mutton and wild game—or the white meat of the fowl, or the like. These are very, very good for the body; provided, of course, they are not taken in excess for the system."

Very small quantities of Olive Oil were recommended to be taken two or three times each day for a week to ten days. This was to be followed by a rest period of a week or ten days and then repeated.

Suggestions were made to massage the bottoms of the feet, under the knees and the spine, below the kidneys, during the menstrual period with the following:

To four ounces of denatured alcohol or pure grain alcohol, add:

Russian White Oil .... 1 ounce
Oil of Cedar .... 1 ounce

Oil of Sassafras .... ½ ounce
Witch Hazel .... 1 ounce

"These will be strengthening, and have a tendency to draw the blood supply to these portions of the system, so that the eliminations will become more regular and the activities of the organs that are involved in the functioning during such periods will become coordinating and balanced with the rest of the system."

Warnings were given not to take drugs to relieve this condition.

The following questions and answers helped to clarify the conditions in the minds of those treating the body:

Q. "What is the cause of and remedy for scaly spots on face and neck?"

A. "Impure circulation, as we have given. When we apply these conditions from time to time, gradually the change will come in the circulation in such a way as to relieve these conditions. Not so much application is necessary from the external, but rather from the internal. To relieve the itching, or when the scalp or the cuticle become scaly, there may be the application of the violet ray over portions of the system. This would be very well, but—as we will find—these will be better relieved by the internal causes being treated, so that the external and internal—capillary and lymph—circulations become more normal."

Q. "Is the kernel at base of or below left ear causing these pains?"

A. "These come from the improper circulation, improper contribution of elements from various glands in the system—tending to accumulate or gather in portions of the system. Hence the applications that are turning these to the better coordination in the eliminating systems of the body."

Q. "Is there infection in the mastoid?"

A. "If we will follow the suggestions as given, we will remove these conditions. There is scarcely any organ in the system where there isn't some kind of infection, or some character of infection! For the natural condition of the system is to involve all forces in the body. We will eliminate these, if you will follow the suggestions that have been given."

FURTHER REPORTS

January 26, 1933—"For the past two weeks, M. J. has not been so good. She is having stiffness in her joints and soreness. Last night she had another night sweat, the first in a long time. The last two baths have left yellow stains on the tub and wash cloth . . . The lady at the library called M. J. and had a long chat, says she has more pep."

February 1, 1933—"M. J. is feeling better again. She has a little stiffness."

June 11, 1934—"We are so happy to answer your recent note inquiring about M. J.'s health. She was feeling better at the time, it seems. She has more strength and is feeling like a healthy person should . . . I would say that for the past two months she has had very little pain and has felt better generally."

Two months after the last report was received from the mother the Research Department of the Association requested Miss McC. to write a statement outlining her case and giving in brief the results obtained. A copy of this statement follows:

Dayton, Ohio
August 14, 1934

Dear Mr. Hugh Lynn Cayce:—

I am writing in answer to your request.

In July, of 1932, my right knee became affected with what we thought to be a very sore bruise or perhaps a strained ligament.

I had been having night sweats for some nights previous to this. I went to a doctor and he prescribed hot salt packs for the afflicted joint. This didn't help at all; in fact, I grew steadily worse.

During the month of August, I took diathermy treatments, as we heard that it ofttimes helped in similar cases to mine, but after quite a few treatments I had eight afflicted joints instead of the six I had when I started.

The pain was intense, so much so that at times I could hardly stand it. I couldn't sleep, could hardly walk and couldn't turn or twist my knees or ankles at all.

In September, I went to the best specialists that we could find here at home, and after being X-rayed completely and thoroughly examined, they said it was arthritis. This disease comes from some source of infection, but in my case they have never found that source.

The only thing that the doctors thought might help was for me to go to Arizona to live. The medicine I had been taking hadn't helped, and strychnine had been prescribed for my heart.

We were positively at the end of our rope, so my father decided to list our home for sale and send me to Arizona. In so doing we met the man who so graciously told us of Mr. Cayce.

We wrote to him that same day and a few days later he gave me a physical reading.

He told me where my trouble lay, what to do and take, and completely changed my diet. Mother and I started in to follow everything to the letter.

On the morning of the third day I awoke and could actually bend one knee! Our happiness knew no bounds, we were practically delirious with happiness.

Since then I have steadily improved and am now practically well. I seldom have even a touch of arthritis, but when I do, a dose of the medicine prescribed sets me on my feet again.

We will never be able to express our thanks to Mr. Cayce for curing me and saving me from so horrible a death, as the reading stated that I would gradually develop sleeping or stony paralysis.

(Signed) Miss M. J. McC.

SUMMARY

First, let us consider the personal side of this case.

This young woman had never seen Edgar Cayce when the

reading was given. Like so many who ask for readings, she sought it as a last resort. She followed the suggestions in every detail and obtained results.

Second, let us consider the case as it relates to the research work of the Association. The results obtained in following these readings would certainly indicate that such information may prove helpful in discovering the causes and suggesting aids for even the most serious types of arthritis.

Third, there is the possibility of securing information of a general nature on such ailments. To adequately carry forward research work of this character the cooperation of open-minded medical scientists must be secured. There is much to gain from such general studies, and nothing to lose.

IV. SCLERODERMA

In January, 1937, when D. E. H. returned from Vanderbilt Clinic, Nashville, Tennessee, to her home in a small Kentucky town, she was given up as a hopeless case.

From her waist to her knees her legs were like stone. The right arm was hard to the elbow. Her stomach and bowels were hard and her face was swollen and hard. The severe pain was constant. At times she could scarcely breathe, and rigors and sinking spells followed.

The telegram received on January 8, 1937, describes the condition in part:

GIVE ME PHYSICAL READING. IN BED EIGHT WEEKS. IS THERE ANY TROUBLE IN CHEST? WHAT CAUSES ACHING OVER ENTIRE BODY? WHAT IS HARDNESS THRU BUTTOCKS AND UPPER LEG? WHAT CAUSES TEMPERATURE AND SWEATING AND SHORTNESS OF BREATH? WHAT IS BURNING ALONG SPINE?

The first reading was given on January 14th and an outline of the suggested treatment was wired to the family. The suggestions were followed carefully with the assistance of a practical nurse, and later a doctor worked sympathetically in following the treatment.

Shortly after beginning the treatments recommended in the reading, some kind of injection was tried at the advice of a local physician. A relapse followed. The treatments which had in part been discontinued during the period of the injections, were taken up again and followed carefully through the year.

Progress was slow at first, but gradually the body responded, and this young woman was able finally to take up her normal activities.

EXTRACTS FROM READINGS

The following extracts from the twelve psychic readings given on this case have been selected with the view of presenting a picture of the gradual improvement. They also show the clarity of the analyses of the condition:

January 14, 1937—"As we find, it has been rather late in beginning with the disturbances that have arisen.

"These as we find are of a very subtle nature. Unless there can be some activities produced in which there is assistance to the vitality of the body, in resisting the inroads of a tubercle in the nature in which it is involving not only those areas through the respiratory system but even the structural portions of the body, from which the blood supply attains or gains its division of a supply of elements from which the red blood cells are builded, we find that the condition will rapidly continue to make inroads.

"Hence we find that which may be of an addition is to disseminate . . . such forces as will bring relief by heat and the elements that would carry those vibrations to not only the circulatory forces but through the muscular activities. Such measures must include elements which by the radical activity of their vibratory forces upon the physical body itself, may assist in the elimination of the conditions. At the same time these elements would supply to the system those forces to destroy or throw off the conditions by adding to the blood stream that which will give resistance in the hemoglobin and the effluvia of the blood."

TREATMENT

The following treatment was outlined: (a) sponge body with saturated solution of Bicarbonate of Soda; (b) heavy, hot Castor Oil Packs over abdominal area, lower lumbar, sacral, lower diaphragm and along spine; (c) half a teaspoonful of Ventriculin twice each day; (d) discontinue all starchy foods. Give small quantities of beef juice frequently; (e) give enemas at the temperature of body when necessary, rather than cathartics.

February 6, 1937—"As we would find, if there is the careful study of the conditions that exist . . . while not being fully understood by many . . . it will be seen that these are the indications and the disturbances as have been given: the effect of the tubercle activity to the superficial circulation, and with the properties in the system that make for the hardening through this portion of the system it works a hardship for the circulation and for the general condition of the body.

"And this may become constitutional, as the very nature of consumptive force . . . or the consumption of tissue by the disturbance . . . makes for this constitutional nature.

"Hence we would follow those suggestions as to external applications, as to massage, as to the diet, more closely . . . all of these; and we would find better conditions.

"The injections have caused disturbances to the heart's activity, to the coordination between the sympathetic and the cerebrospinal system. The sinking spells and the weakness are from the lack of assimilation of these conditions to the body.

"Either use one or the other."

TREATMENT

The following treatment was outlined: Wet Cell Appliance carrying alternate solutions of Atomidine, Chloride of Gold and Spirits of Camphor. Attachments for thirty minutes each day alternating over certain lumbar, dorsal and cervical areas and over the lacteal duct area.

February 24, 1937—"As we find, while the existing conditions appear somewhat disturbing . . . unless it breaks farther, through strain or through some other overactivity of the body, this is the system's attempting to adjust itself and eliminate those disturbances in the circulation that have caused the checking of the flow to the lymph circulation."

The following treatment was recommended: Glyco-Thymoline enema every other day. Diluted grain alcohol rub over limbs and shoulders. Begin use of Camphor solution with Appliance two days in succession.

March 5, 1937—"Now the conditions are much on the improve, by the vibrations that have been set up through the system by the low electrical forces and the rub. These should be kept.

"The plates of the Appliance should be kept a little cleaner. Not that the precautions haven't been taken, but so easily do the emanations from the body . . . with the little temperature and the poisons, and the very character of the condition . . . tend to clog that constant flow that should be had from the vibrations."

The following treatments were added: Inhale fumes two or three times each day from pure apple brandy in charred keg. Sip beef juice often. Use red wine with brown bread in afternoons.

NOTE: This reading was given voluntarily, while information was being sought for other individuals.

March 23, 1937—"While conditions as we find are far from being entirely satisfactory, there is much improvement shown in many ways . . . that should be most gratifying to the body, as well as to those so anxious about the conditions.

"As we find in the present, a disturbance arises mostly from lack of activity to make for the proper character and manner of eliminations.

"Hence those tendencies are existent for the hepatic circulation to gather the poisons that are being thrown off, and to tend to make for temperature that becomes aggravating to the circulation.

"Then, in those portions of the lymph circulation there is the hardening of the muscular forces in the activities . . . as through the shoulders and the neck, and as portions of the lower limbs and across the abdomen. These very influences then, of course, tend to make for a formation of gas.

"We would not change or alter so very much, then, the properties that have been indicated, in the blood building, blood purifying, the rubs and the vibratory forces for making for the better coordination with the low electrical forces."

Only the following treatments were added: High enemas about once each week, of soda and salt solutions. Small quantities of Olive Oil should be taken three or four times each day. Keep body in open air as much as possible.

April 26, 1937—"These are the conditions as we find them in the present, and . . . as has been indicated at other times, there is much improvement, yet much to be desired.

"In the blood stream and in the manner of its circulation in the superficial forces of the body, we still find there are the indications of the effect of those disturbing factors that are a portion of the cause of the disturbing condition, or the hardening and the withdrawal of proper circulation.

"These arise, to be sure, from an inherent condition from those things that have disturbed the body. This comes about by the lack of the ability of the glandular system to effect, through the assimilations, sufficient of the lecocytes to ward off or destroy this form or type of bacilli that has been and is still active. However, the causes are being reached, and the ability of building up in the blood supply is being gradually improved.

"Then as there is sufficient improvement for the body to become more active in the open and to keep the necessary balance through the diets and through the activities from those influences and forces as may be given, there will be more and more of a gain; and there should be an eliminating of the causes and a building back to normalcy for the body.

"As to just how long this will require, to be sure depends upon the responses of the system to a great extent to the applications and circumstances as it were for conditions as might cause or produce a detrimental condition in the experiences of the body."

The following additional suggestions were made: Keep up

all treatments. Use mineral oil and a liver regulator when needed. Salt air, pines and sand recommended as best environ as soon as body was able to travel. (This part of treatment was not followed.)

July 15, 1937—"While there is still much to be desired in the general physical forces of the body, as we find the conditions in the main continue on the improve.

"There is still the necessity of keeping much of those things suggested for the building of the body for the resistances in the system against the cellular forces that tend to break down in the superficial circulation, and to cause much of the inflammation and the activities in the muscular forces of the body . . . though, these, too, show improvements somewhat."

All treatments previously suggested were to be kept. A rub with a combination of Olive Oil and Tincture of Myrrh was to be given daily over knees, hips, abdomen and shoulders. A stricter alkaline diet was recommended.

October 8, 1937—"Now as we find, while there is still much to be desired, the body is on the improve.

"These are conditions as we find to be reckoned with in the present, and these the applications that are the better for the body in the present.

"The manipulations have been very good. These may be put a little further apart, but should be kept up as yet; say three in each two weeks for another six, or four to six weeks; then we would give the further instructions regarding these.

"There must be, as we find, care in the manner of the adjustments and manipulative measures. For, contrary to the ordinary conditions, we find in the upper dorsal, and even through the cervical areas, the inclinations for the segments to be far apart rather than close together. And this tends to make for leakages; or too easily does the body . . . or those portions of same . . . become influenced by the impulses that arise through those portions of the body from which there is not the tension. Hence this achy condition, or the hurting, or the feeling of a full flow.

"We find in the lumbar and through the sacral area a tendency of tightness. This makes for that inclination, now, from which there are the inclinations of a flushing; that is, in the circulation, to the lower portions of the body.

"Hence in the manipulations these would be not so much movements of the segments as to stimulate the muscular forces along the side of the spine and following the nerve ends . . . or the nerve branches from those portions to their extremities in the body."

All treatments were to be continued. One minim of Atomidine was to be taken each day in half a glass of water. The body was advised not to take the typhoid fever serum at this time.

January 17, 1938—"As we find, there has been the inclination for too severe a taxation to the body without taking those precautions to keep the body alkalized sufficiently. And the leaving off of sufficient of the corrections osteopathically to keep the conditions in the cerebrospinal system from leaking, as it were, in the circulation has caused the body to become disturbed with cold, congestion, and the effect of poisons in the system.

"We would rest from so much taxation. This does not mean go to bed, or not work or play. Keep in the open, active to be sure. Make those applications which will break up the congestion: by the manipulations osteopathically, and by the deep inhalations from the charred keg with brandy in it."

The solutions of Camphor and Gold Chloride were to be discontinued, but the Atomidine solution continued with the Appliance. The body was to begin with Halibut Oil with Viosterol. Osteopathic treatments were to be given once each week over the whole cerebrospinal system. Atomidine spray was to be used for throat and nose to prevent colds. General suggestions were made for keeping eliminations open. Warnings were given not to worry too much and not to overtax the nervous system.

SUMMARY

The reports on this case are contained in letters from the mother, nurse, doctor, and patient. They cover a period of a year. Each one shows a gradual improvement. Extracts follow:

January 26, 1937—(From mother) "We are so very anxious

over D.'s condition. She has not been so well since Sunday. She awakened with a weak spell Sunday morning, with another one at noon, and one at noon Monday . . . The hardness of the skin is very slightly less in the upper hips . . . "

March 5, 1937—(From mother) "D. has not been so well since I wired you last week. Her stomach is badly upset, she has severe pains in the lower abdomen and much gas. Her food will not digest and she aches badly over entire body, more however in the right shoulder and down all of back."

March 31, 1937—(From mother) "She is feeling fairly well, still aches badly and her skin is very sore. The stomach condition is some better. She is up for a few minutes each day now as you suggested, but is very weak."

June 8, 1937—(From patient) "I still ache awfully bad—of course it is worse in the back and across the shoulders, but the muscles over the entire body are affected. The right knee is sore at the place I bend it. The temperature started again after being free of it for about three weeks . . . "

June 22, 1937—(From patient) "You don't know how happy the last reading made me when you said to stay out of the oil packs. I was staying right with them but in the summer time they are not very funny. When I read that the aching will leave me and that I can go back to work and take up both the teaching and the choir, I did everything but shout . . . I want to go to work by September if I possibly can and I'm about to walk myself to death to get strong enough. I know that aching won't be gone by then because it sure is setting me wild now. When I get the Olive Oil rub, following the Appliance, my back between the shoulders and the neck burns and feels like needles are sticking in it . . . "

July 12, 1937—"I went to Mayo's Saturday two weeks ago. Nothing would do my family but that I go. We knew the hardness was much better but that aching still sticks with me. Sometimes it makes me so nervous that I feel I'll lose my mind. Don't you think for a minute that I had thought of not following the readings and my family have just as much confidence in them as I do. They just wanted me checked over on account of this aching. We couldn't tell just how much was hardness and how much was muscle. They said that just enough hardness was there with the symptoms for them to diagnose the trouble. They called it scleroderma. They said that there was fluid in the tissues and inflammation of the muscles. They found no focus of infection to cause the aching. All they told me to do was to take plenty of exercise and quit this high nervous tension I was under. They thought it came on from recurrent attacks of flu . . . I came straight home and got in the oil packs."

August 19, 1937—"I played on the organ for one-half hour yesterday and was I happy . . . "

September 6, 1937—"I think the choir practice on Friday night made my shoulders hurt a little more, at least that pulling sensation was a little worse . . . Last night though I got along better and wasn't so nervous. I was thrilled over going back but I knew the first time would be hard on me . . . I went over to Nashville last Saturday . . . "

Four years later D. H. recommended readings for two individuals afflicted with similar conditions. Extracts from their letters follow:

May 30, 1941—(From L. F. B.) "In April of 1938 I went to Vanderbilt Hospital to see if the doctors there could help me. They told me I had focal scleroderma and could do nothing to help me. Since then I have gradually grown worse. After seeing and talking to Miss D. H. last Sunday, I have renewed hope and wonder if you might help me, too. My skin is not hard and swollen like Miss H.'s was, but white spots have come over my body, especially on my arms and legs."

March 24, 1942—(From L. F. B.) "In the past six weeks much has happened. Of course, I'm certainly not well but I do believe

I'm lots better. If only something could be done about my knees. I feel real good sitting or lying down, but when I try to walk it's another story."

May 30, 1941—(From D. M. C.) "I heard of you through a former patient of yours, Miss D. H. And I want to see if you can do anything for me. She said you cured her. I have been examined by lots of doctors. They say I have scleroderma. It was found a year ago last September. I had an operation a year ago. They cut some nerves in my back, but it did not do any good. I want to get well if it is possible. Please let me hear from you."

February 5, 1942—(From D. M. C.) "Received my check reading and was very much pleased with it. I am feeling better, altho my arms and hands hurt me a lot. I was in hopes you would let me have some beef steak . . . I like it so well, but it is all right. I thank you for what you are doing for me."

V. GENERAL DEBILITATION

"When the application for the first reading was made Mrs. T. was supposed to be dying. A number of members of her family had been called to her bedside. The physician pronounced her condition to be one of general debilitation. She experienced violent pains in the head which the strongest opiates failed to relieve. She had had severe heart attacks, and her pulse was rapid and weak. At times she was delirious and at other times remained in an unconscious state for hours. She had no appetite and digestion and assimilation were poor. There were large lumps on the hips and buttocks, almost blue in color, which were very painful to touch. Her limbs were stiff and rigid. She had lost weight at an alarming rate during the last few weeks before the reading was given. Laxatives and purgatives had failed to act and the abdomen was distended and painful to touch. She had not been able to stand or walk for more than two years."

The above is a report secured from members of the family, describing conditions existing at the time the first reading was given.

The application for the reading came from the patient's son, who was living in Virginia Beach at the time. He had received a telegram telling him of his mother's critical condition and advising him to return home at once. He secured the first reading and took it home with him.

FIRST READING

"Now, as we find, those conditions that disturb the better physical forces of the body are rather of a complex nature. For, there are both causes and effects that must be considered in giving or bringing any relief for the body.

"Many of the disturbing conditions have been of long standing; hence have become of such a nature that the system has adjusted itself to the disorders.

"In bringing relief or resuscitating forces to the system, all of these conditions must be taken into consideration. For, many have reached the proportions where not only the physical body but the mental body is also affected.

"These, then, are the conditions as we find them with this body, J. H. T., we are speaking of:

"We find the blood supply very low in vitality, and while the circulation becomes disturbed—the ability in the circulation to carry on through a strong heart action has oft saved the body from disintegration. There needs to be assimilated in this portion, then, that which—with the strong heart's activity—will build resuscitating plasm through the circulatory system.

"The nerve system, as we find, has reached such a condition that at times it has become almost exhausted. Hence there are periods when there is not in any way near the normal reaction from administrated forces; or that reaction which might be expected to be the result from the administration of active principles into the system. Hence little medicine, as medicine, is effective; only palliatives, sedatives or hypnotics, and these at times lose their effectiveness in the system.

"What, then, are the causes in the physical functionings? Are the organs involved in their functioning, or have such inroads been made as to cause organic conditions? Or are the conditions of a general or a constitutional nature, with all of the organs working at variance one to another?

"All of these conditions exist and more; for, as seen, there has long been a disturbance in the sensory organism wherein the auditory forces have been affected. And in periods back there was such a plethora condition in the organs of the pelvis, in the activities of the assimilating system, as to necessitate the removal of portions of the organs themselves. Thus we have had an inroad into the effectual activity of the nerve forces in the action of organs, and in the creation of resuscitating forces in the system, until—working under the strain and stress of adhesions and lesions there has been little of a normal activity in digestion; surfeiting of the system, in relation to assimilations through the body.

"Hence a general debilitation has set in throughout the system, so that all of the organs are affected; not in the manner as of organic disturbances, other than in their abilities to create the proper functionings of their respective cycle of activity in the body. Hence the conditions in the present.

"Then, in meeting the conditions, as we find, the addition of certain forces that will work with the activities of the body may bring a much nearer normal force for the ability of the system to respond and become nearer in the way of distributing the necessary resuscitating forces throughout the system.

"One necessary factor, then, as we would find, would be in creating more oxygen, as released in the system, as to revivify the activity of the circulations (blood supply) in their relationship to the organs that function not only for the creating of necessary plasm for giving physical reaction in the body (in life forces) but that will aid in strengthening the resistances in the system.

"This, as we find, may be materially aided by the addition of small quantities of carbonated or carbon ash in the system. Give one-eighth grain each day, and—to produce or make a bettery activity of same—thirty minutes after the dose is given we would apply the plain violet ray vibrations over the portions of the body where assimilations would be created, for the activity of the ash to the blood supply. Hence, it would be applied over the upper dorsal and cervical area, or the cardiac and secondary cardiac area. Then it would be applied from the 9th and 10th dorsal area to the 3rd and 4th lumbar area.

"We would also find that it would be most beneficial, in supplying the necessary vitality, to add the active forces of low electrical vibrations that will carry into the system elements to create a better coordination in the nerve impulses to the system, that add to the sustaining forces in the activity of the glands themselves. These we would give in the wet cell battery formation, using those anodes that carry medical properties—through the low vibration—into the system; in three characters, that would be given in rotation day by day.

"One would carry the Chloride of Gold solution. In attaching the battery to the body for this particular activity, we would attach first the anode without the medicinal properties to the body at the 3rd and 4th dorsal segment or plexus of the system. The larger plate carrying the Gold solution would be attached to the plexus over the umbilical center, but more over the lacteal ducts or glands. The period of application would be for thirty minutes.

"The next day use a different connection but the same battery. The same plain or positive connection would be attached at the base of the brain, and the other carrying Spirits of Camphor—would be attached to the 4th lumbar plexus area. This would be applied for a period of thirty minutes also.

"The next day use a different solution . . . the first anode would be attached to the center entering into the stomach itself, or the cardiac center of the stomach, and the other plate or anode, carrying Atomidine in solution, would be attached at the 9th dorsal plexus—or that which distributes through the whole of the solar plexus area. Apply this for thirty minutes. Then begin over again.

"We would use a massage every other day, with a compound combined in this manner—or put together in the order given:

"To 2 ounces of cocoa butter (put in solution, and while still warm), add:

Russian White Oil .... 1 ounce
Sassafras Oil .... 1 ounce

Witch Hazel .... 1 ounce

This will only partially solidify, and should be stirred thoroughly each time before it is massaged into the spine. Especially massage it along those portions where the tired, achy feelings have come to the body from the bed—or over the portions in the lumbar and solar plexus area, and in the brachial area—and especially from the 4th and 5th cervical to the base of the brain.

"In the matter of the diet, keep much in the way and manner that has been outlined. When necessary, continue with the medicinal properties that rest, or keep the body quiet to make rest. See that the eliminations are kept as near normal as possible. And in thirty days from the beginning of these treatments we would give further instructions.

Q. "What part of present treatment should be continued or left off?"

A. "As just given, continue when necessary the ministration of properties that make for quietness to the body; of course, reducing as much as possible—as improvements begin—the bromides that affect the mental activities.

"For, the properties that we have given here, as indicated, are to make use of the physical resistances that still exist in the circulation—and to make response from all functioning organs and assimilation and distribution of that assimilated for recuperative forces in the body. These in low electrical form will aid.

"The addition of the ash is to relieve the pressure on the general system and revivify the blood supply; and the activity of the violet ray, given for fifteen to twenty minutes over those portions indicated, thirty minutes after the ash is taken, is only to make the effective activity of the ash of carbon in the system.

"The properties given through the battery formations are resuscitating forces to the organs and the glands of same, in the respective portions of the body, as they are applied through the low electrical form, to sustain and revivify the body.

"The massage of certain portions of the body, as given, is only to relax and make better coordination in the cerebrospinal, sympathetic and sensory systems. The mind will be much better.

"Let the body itself know the source from which these treatments are instructed, and what is to be accomplished by each."

OTHER READINGS

2nd Reading—September 15, 1933: Continued same treatments.

Report from friend of family on October 12, 1933: "She was pretty bad off . . . But now she has improved quite a bit. Tomorrow she may be worse again. The family want another reading."

3rd Reading—November 26, 1933: Adjustments necessary in upper dorsal and cervical areas. Advised cutting down on bromides. Stop use of Atomidine with appliance.

4th Reading—January 6, 1934: Neuropathic massages, corrections in lumbar, sacral and coccyx areas. Begin again with Atomidine solution.

5th Reading—February 15, 1934: Keep eliminations open; enemas and properties to be taken. Use Glyco-Thymoline in water for enemas. Special massage to be given daily over lumbar, sacral, sciatic nerve and lower limbs; ingredients: Olive Oil, Tincture of Myrrh, Russian White Oil, Rub Alcohol, Tincture of Benzoin, and Oil of Sassafras. Alkaline diet. Begin to try to walk.

6th Reading—March 11, 1934: (Emergency by wire as result of patient's having heart attack.) Setback due to overexertion. Keep body quiet. Stimulate superficial circulation and give small doses of Digital under doctor's directions. Continue other treatments.

7th Reading—July 17, 1934: More specific directions for corrections in lumbar and sacral areas.

REPORTS

Letter from patient—August 4, 1934: "Some day ere long I will write Mr. Cayce and personally tell him of my gratitude to him. Were it not for his readings or diagnosis and advice I would now be either in an insane asylum or Live Oak Cemetery.

"I am one thousand percent better (not one hundred percent), and am looking forward with hope of walking again ere many months have passed. As above stated I am greatly improved, yet I am far from being all right. It seems that about every five weeks I have an attack . . . Weeks pass before the effects wear away. The last one, which began June 10, was shorter and of less severity. That at least is encouraging. Dr.——— says that so long as there are poisons in my body these attacks will continue at intervals. Is that correct?

"Perhaps it is best to explain just how I am affected. Lightning-like flashes through the chest that end with stabbing pains in the heart. Also the left shoulder and arm pain very much. Nothing seems to relieve these paroxysms but hypodermics of morphine. At these times my bowels and intestines are in a bad way. The nerves or muscles in my neck and in other parts of my body are so tense that I cannot move myself, and what distresses me more than anything are my limbs. They become rigid and I cannot lift my feet even a fraction of an inch. Also the hips become angry and inflamed.

"After reading all this you will no doubt wonder in what way I have improved? Thank heavens that condition does not continue indefinitely. Most of the trouble gradually wears away until the next attack, and though not entirely free of pain I am fairly comfortable. At present I sit up an hour and a half each morning and again late in the afternoon. My limbs move slowly now and I can partly raise up in the chair by holding on to the arms. Each day I do a little more."

Letter from patient—April 3, 1935: "Strength is slowly returning and I walk a few steps each day that I am well enough to do so. I also sit up about three hours a day. Will I ever be able to sit up hours at a time? My lower back, hips and buttocks cause me much agony. At times I am comfortable and then again these places become red and swell in lumps, burn and throb like boils. The angina attacks are less severe and less frequent."

9th Reading— April 10, 1935: "As we find, conditions continue to be much on the improve. However, there is a great deal of improvement to be desired in some directions, especially in those tendencies for there to be periods when the reactions to the system call for or produce an unrecorded or an overactivity through the circulation or the palpitation of the heart, and these tendencies for the smothering spells. There is much to be desired also in the circulation through the lower limbs. But, as we find, there were periods when the nerve ends of the brush end of the cerebrospinal were so deadened, by cold that was applied, and by temperature, that the circulation was greatly disturbed. Thus in the superficial circulation there is produced at times, when there is not the proper elimination through the alimentary canal . . . or through cold or congestion, or through the excitement to the sympathetic nervous forces, those tendencies for the accumulation and for there to appear on the hips, in the groin, along portions of the lower limbs, nodules or accumulations that make for distresses to the body. We would give that there be this as a minor change in the applications of the active forces of the battery:

"On the wet cell battery change the connections, having these of a different type. The copper anode or plate would be attached to the 3rd dorsal plexus center, and the nickel anode (of the same size) would be attached one period to the left ankle and the next period to the right ankle . . . first to the left and then to the right ankle. The same attachment of the copper plate should be made to the dorsal area as indicated. The next day, in the application of same, we would make the attachments to the right wrist and the left ankle; then the next day to the left wrist and the right ankle. Then the next day back to the secondary or cardiac area, as indicated. Each application would be from thirty to sixty minutes. Not using now the medications as passing through same, but altering in the manner as indicated.

"We would alter the massage used as a stimulation with this alteration in the circulation, which will work together with the superficial activity as produced by something of a counterirritation to the lumbar and sacral and the groin and the upper portions of the sciatic nerve ends. This should be extended, though, along the lower limbs even to the toes; and about once or twice a week . . . along the cerebrospinal system . . . to the brachial center and out the under portion of the arms to the finger tips. Such a combination for massaging would be prepared in this manner:

"To 4 ounces of pure or virgin Olive Oil, as a basis for the properties, add . . . in the order named and in this proportion:

Oil of Cedar Wood	1 ounce
Oil of Wintergreen	1 ounce
Witch Hazell	1½ ounces
Kerosene	1 ounce
Compound Tincture Benzoin	½ ounce
Oil of Sassafras	1 dram

These, to be sure, will tend to separate; but before using shake well together. Pour a small quantity in an open container and massage into the cerebrospinal area, from the lower dorsal to those areas as indicated, all the body will absorb; then the rest of the portion of the body indicated. This we would do each day.

"We would continue with the neuropathic adjustments and neuropathic massage, but use oil rather than powder; that there may be the greater food value to the respiratory system. Not so as to clog same, for this should be cleansed thoroughly by the tepid baths regularly. For there must be the stimulation to the superficial circulation as the stimulation has been to the deeper or internal circulation.

"In the matter of the diet be mindful that there is a continuation of the adherence to an alkaline-reacting diet. In general beware, for this body, of these things: great quantities of starches. But if quantities of same are taken, as with spaghetti or potatoes or breads that carry same, do not take carbohydrates or sugars at the same time. Hence beware of pastries or tarts, though, any of these in moderation may be at times taken. Let the greater portion of food be those things that are nonacid producing for the system. Strengthening foods such as beef juices, or the extracts of liver, or the extracts from the caseins of the internal organs of beef or the like. These are very good in moderation for the strengthening of that tendency for the separation in the lymph circulation produced by this deadening in the nerve ends in these particular areas indicated. But these should be kept in moderation. No red meat, either beef or hog meat. No white breads. No apples raw; no bananas raw. Either of these may be taken cooked, provided they are cooked with not too great a quantity of sugar. The sweetening that would be used would be preferably honey or saccharin . . . that may make for a variation in its reaction in the assimilations through the lacteals of the system, that have had such an ordeal . . . as it were . . . in straining the vital forces from that assimilated."

Letter from patient, August 5, 1935: "First I will say that I am steadily improving, gaining in strength and weight. I am also making progress in walking. I walk from my bed to the front or back porch or across the hall, and sit up three to three and a half hours each day. Several times a week I am lifted into the car and enjoy a half hour's ride. I have had two heart attacks since June 15. However, since I am stronger, I recover more rapidly. The last attack was not so severe as the others."

Doctor's report, October 12, 1935: "The physical readings described the condition of this patient and the suggestions were in my opinion suitable for the condition. The patient has been relieved from headaches; improved in appetite; I note passing of inflammation of joints, gain in weight, control of angina; she learned to walk again, gained in strength, has better coordination of nerve."

Patient's report, October 12, 1935: "No pains in head. No heart attack for three months, the last ones less severe. Gained strength and weight. Appetite and digestion good. Lumps or nodules on hips and buttocks disappeared. Can now sit up four hours a day and walk without assistance from one room to another. Mental condition normal."

After this last report from her, J. H. T. lived seven more active years of usefulness with her family.

VI. EYE INJURY

Late in the afternoon of October 25, 1935, R. K., a five-year-old boy, stuck a pair of scissors in his right eye. His mother found him sitting on the bedroom floor of their New York City apartment, crying.

The child was immediately taken to a physician who examined the injury and stated that the cornea had been punctured. An injection for tetanus was given and an operation performed to sew up the puncture. This operation was performed in the Manhattan Eye, Ear and Throat Hospital by a well-known physician.

FIRST READING

On the day following the accident a reading was secured from Mr. Cayce.

"As we find, while great changes have come about in the body since last we had same here, the acute or specific conditions in the eye are being well cared for.

"From present indications, there should not be any bad results or effects, either to the vision or to the appearance of same.

"There's just the necessity, then, for precautions as to infectious forces from the natural accumulations of tissue . . . that may be said to be repair tissue in the system; and that there be no cold or congestion allowed to make for disturbing conditions in the body.

"Thus we should find that in just a few weeks there should be near normalcy in these directions.

"In the general physical forces, as we have indicated, there have been those tendencies for the lack of sufficient red blood cellular force; or a tendency towards anemia; yet these conditions have in a greater part been met . . . through those recent activities of the body in the open.

"We would, then, continue only those things that are indicated for keeping a nominal balance in the present; keeping the diets in that manner of body and blood building . . . as is indicated, and as has been outlined. Thus the body should grow, develop, in a normal, nominal manner."

Q. "What is the extent of the injury to the eye?"

A. "As indicated, from the manner in which it has been cared for, this should not extend to any injury that would be even noticeable . . . after a normal development. The injury was to the iris portion that has only been punctured in the first and second film. Hence, unless other conditions arise than are indicated in the present, it should not make for even any injury."

FURTHER DEVELOPMENTS

In the weeks immediately following the operation a white tissue covered the eye. The doctor advised another operation to remove this growth. On November 18, 1935, another reading was secured. Extracts from this reading follow:

"As we find, there need be only those precautions, those cares taken in the administration of the cleansing solutions for the eye yet; that there may be, with the absorptions from the general circulation, the removal of those tendencies for scar tissue to become permanent . . . or to produce upon the retinae a circulation that would produce greater elimations.

"And we would find that this may be best done not only with the wash, and the precautions and protections from the glass (which is being used, and is very good), but with manipulations osteopathically given; that may be had through the administrations of one in accord with those influences for the body itself.

"And we would find that in this manner the system would not only concur in reproducing those cellular forces necessary to overcome the injured portions, but there would be other conditions materially aided . . . through disturbances that have been existent in the system by the lack of the ministrations of cellular forces through the circulation.

"These osteopathic manipulations given once a week would be *most* helpful.

"Keep the diets that have been indicated for the body . . . "

Q. "The second doctor says the lens was punctured. Is it so?"

A. "We find, as given, this was not punctured, but was only injured by the activity of the effect of the injury upon the other portions as indicated . . . in the retina and in the cornea."

Q. "If not, why the cataract forming over the eye?"

A. "If there are the applications made as indicated, those accumulations would be gradually absorbed and not form a cataract.

"This is not a true cataract as yet. It is merely the secretions, or the attempts of the system in its activity to protect injured portions.

"Now, there is the necessity of absorption through drainages . . . or stimulated circulation to the centers from which the eyes or optic forces receive their stimuli; in the upper dorsal and through the cervical area . . . which would remove these conditions, if they are done consistently and persistently, and not leave injuries to the eye."

The doctors stated that these treatments would be a waste of time, but that no injury would result from delaying the operation.

The child was taken regularly to an osteopath who followed the suggestions carefully. Within a few weeks the tissue over the eye began to break up and dissolved piece by piece, until the eye was almost entirely clear.

On March 18, 1936, the following reading was secured:

"As we find, there is much to be desired outwardly, yet the general physical reactions that are taking place are very good. There are improvements in many directions.

"And there should be some precautions taken in adding to the enzymes of the body. As we find, given under the direction of a physician, Ventriculin with iron would provide much that would aid in the catabolism of the digestive and assimilating forces, and that would strengthen the blood supply for better reserve and better reaction through the physical forces of the body.

"In those conditions with the localized disturbance in the eye, we find that the manipulative measures have been most beneficial. We would continue with these once or twice a week, or once a week for one week and twice a week the next week; so that there are the drainages or accumulations continuing to be thrown off . . . and will be absorbed if there is kept the proper manner of circulation through the way in which the manipulative forces may not only aid in the drainage but in stimulating the circulation to the affected parts.

"When in strong light there should be used, to be sure, the glasses that would shade or protect the eye; or both eyes for that matter. Either the smoked or the rose glass would be preferable to brown or other shades . . . "

On May 29, 1936, a reading recommended that electrical treatments be given directly to the eye ball. Such treatments were given.

RESULTS

The child's mother reports the following results: the pupil has been restored to an almost even roundness; there is a slight, barely visible scar; the eye responds to light reflexes; with proper lens the eye may now be used for reading.

INDEX

A.R.E. PRESS

Edgar Cayce (1877–1945) founded the non-profit Association for Research and Enlightenment (A.R.E.) in 1931, to explore spirituality, holistic health, intuition, dream interpretation, psychic development, reincarnation, and ancient mysteries—all subjects that frequently came up in the more than 14,000 documented psychic readings given by Cayce.

Edgar Cayce's A.R.E. provides individuals from all walks of life and a variety of religious backgrounds with tools for personal transformation and healing at all levels—body, mind, and spirit.

A.R.E. Press has been publishing since 1931 as well, with the mission of furthering the work of A.R.E. by publishing books, DVDs, and CDs to support the organization's goal of helping people to change their lives for the better physically, mentally, and spiritually.

In 2009, A.R.E. Press launched its second imprint, 4th Dimension Press. While A.R.E. Press features topics directly related to the work of Edgar Cayce and often includes excerpts from the Cayce readings, 4th Dimension Press allows us to take our publishing efforts further with like-minded and expansive explorations into the mysteries and spirituality of our existence without direct reference to Cayce specific content.

A.R.E. Press/4th Dimension Press
215 67th Street
Virginia Beach, VA 23451

Learn more at EdgarCayce.org. Visit ARECatalog.com to browse and purchase additional titles.

ARE PRESS.COM

EDGAR CAYCE'S A.R.E.

Who Was Edgar Cayce?
Twentieth Century Psychic and Medical Clairvoyant

Edgar Cayce (pronounced Kay-Cee, 1877-1945) has been called the "sleeping prophet," the "father of holistic medicine," and the most-documented psychic of the 20th century. For more than 40 years of his adult life, Cayce gave psychic "readings" to thousands of seekers while in an unconscious state, diagnosing illnesses and revealing lives lived in the past and prophecies yet to come. But who, exactly, was Edgar Cayce?

Cayce was born on a farm in Hopkinsville, Kentucky, in 1877, and his psychic abilities began to appear as early as his childhood. He was able to see and talk to his late grandfather's spirit, and often played with "imaginary friends" whom he said were spirits on the other side. He also displayed an uncanny ability to memorize the pages of a book simply by sleeping on it. These gifts labeled the young

Cayce as strange, but all Cayce really wanted was to help others, especially children.

Later in life, Cayce would find that he had the ability to put himself into a sleep-like state by lying down on a couch, closing his eyes, and folding his hands over his stomach. In this state of relaxation and meditation, he was able to place his mind in contact with all time and space—the universal consciousness, also known as the super-conscious mind. From there, he could respond to questions as broad as, "What are the secrets of the universe?" and "What is my purpose in life?" to as specific as, "What can I do to help my arthritis?" and "How were the pyramids of Egypt built?" His responses to these questions came to be called "readings," and their insights offer practical help and advice to individuals even today.

The majority of Edgar Cayce's readings deal with holistic health and the treatment of illness. Yet, although best known for this material, the sleeping Cayce did not seem to be limited to concerns about the physical body. In fact, in their entirety, the readings discuss an astonishing 10,000 different topics. This vast array of subject matter can be narrowed down into a smaller group of topics that, when compiled together, deal with the following five categories: (1) Health-Related Information; (2) Philosophy and Reincarnation; (3) Dreams and Dream Interpretation; (4) ESP and Psychic Phenomena; and (5) Spiritual Growth, Meditation, and Prayer.

Learn more at EdgarCayce.org.

What Is A.R.E.?

Edgar Cayce founded the non-profit Association for Research and Enlightenment (A.R.E.) in 1931, to explore spirituality, holistic health, intuition, dream interpretation, psychic development, reincarnation, and ancient mysteries—all subjects that frequently came up in the more than 14,000 documented psychic readings given by Cayce.

The Mission of the A.R.E. is to help people transform their lives for the better, through research, education, and application of core concepts found in the Edgar Cayce readings and kindred materials that seek to manifest the love of God and all people and promote the purposefulness of life, the oneness of God, the spiritual nature of humankind, and the connection of body, mind, and spirit.

With an international headquarters in Virginia Beach, Va., a regional headquarters in Houston, regional representatives throughout the U.S., Edgar Cayce Centers in more than thirty countries, and individual members in more than seventy countries, the A.R.E. community is a global network of individuals.

A.R.E. conferences, international tours, camps for children and adults, regional activities, and study groups allow like-minded people to gather for educational and fellowship opportunities worldwide.

A.R.E. offers membership benefits and services that include a quarterly body-mind-spirit member magazine, *Venture Inward*, a member newsletter covering the major topics of the readings, and access to the entire set of readings in an exclusive online database.

Learn more at EdgarCayce.org.

EDGARCAYCE.ORG